The Imperial Executive
in America

Sir Edmund Andros, Knt.

Sir Edmund Andros (1637–1714).
Courtesy of the Virginia Historical Society, Richmond, Virginia

The Imperial Executive in America

Sir Edmund Andros, 1637–1714

Mary Lou Lustig

Madison • Teaneck
Fairleigh Dickinson University Press
London: Associated University Press

Associated University Presses
440 Forsgate Drive
Cranbury, NJ 08512

Associated University Presses
16 Barter Street
London WC1A 2AH, England

Associated University Presses
P.O. Box 338, Port Credit
Mississauga, Ontario
Canada L5G 4L8

The paper used in this publication meets the requirements of the American National Standard for Permanence of Paper for Printed Library Materials Z39.48-1984.

Library of Congress Cataloging-in-Publication Data

Lustig, Mary Lou.
    The imperial executive in America : Sir Edmund Andros, 1637–1714 / Mary Lou Lustig.
        p. cm.
    Includes bibliographical references and index.
    ISBN 0-8386-3936-4 (alk. paper)
    1. Andros, Edmund, Sir, 1637–1714.   2. Governors—New York (State)—Biography.   3. Governors—New England—Biography.   4. Governors—Virginia—Biography.   5. Colonial administrators—Great Britain—Biography.   6. Colonial administrators—United States—Biography.
7. New York (State)—History—Colonial period, ca. 1600–1775.   8. New England—History—Colonial period, ca. 1600–1775.   9. Virginia—History—Colonial period, ca. 1600–1775.   10. Great Britain—Colonies—North America—History.   I. Title.
    F122 .A53   2002
    974'.02'092—dc21
    [B]   2001054333

PRINTED IN THE UNITED STATES OF AMERICA

This book is dedicated to Ted: Husband and friend

A man is the whole encyclopaedia of facts. The creation of a thousand forests is in one acorn, and Egypt, Greece, Rome, Gaul, Britain, America, lie folded already in the first man. Epoch after epoch, camp, kingdom, empire, republic, democracy, are merely the application of his manifold spirit to the manifold world. . . . Civil and natural history, the history of art and of literature, must be explained from individual history, or must remain words.

—Ralph Waldo Emerson, "History"

There is no prince that ever governed without a nobility or an Army. If you will not have the one, you must have the other, or the monarchy cannot long support or keep itself from tumbling into a democratical republic.

—Earl of Shaftsbury

For if power without law may make laws, may alter the fundamental laws of the Kingdom, I do not know what subject he is in England, that can be sure of his life, or anything that he calls his own.

—Charles I

Contents

Acknowledgments

I AM INDEBTED TO THE SCHOLARS WHO PRECEDED ME IN THIS FIELD and the current scholars who willingly read the manuscript and made many suggestions as to how the work could be strengthened. Dr. David William Voorhees not only supplied me with numerous letters from his Leisler Paper Project but also read the manuscript with great care and attention, making many pertinent suggestions. Dr. Martha D. Shattuck read the manuscript in record time, making many helpful suggestions, which are all appreciated. I thank them both, as I do Stephen Saunders Webb, who initially sparked my interest in Sir Edmund Andros. Dr. Webb, in reading the manuscript, shared his extensive knowledge of late seventeenth-century Anglo-America and, in addition, sent me copies of his research notes on Andros's later career in Guernsey. Dr. Dennis J. Maika shared his knowledge of mercantile activity in seventeenth-century New York and contributed significantly to the New York chapters by calling several pertinent facts to my attention. I also appreciate the efforts of Jaap Jacobs, who searched archives in the Netherlands for Andros family records. I am certain that if such material existed, Dr. Jacobs would have found it.

I appreciate the support of successive chairpersons of the West Virginia University History Department, Ronald L. Lewis, Barbara J. Howe, and Robert Maxon, all of whom created an atmosphere in which research could flourish. I appreciate their efforts, as well as those of past and present deans of the College of Arts and Sciences, Gerald E. Lang and M. Duane Nellis. My thanks to the Radiological Consultants Association for a fellowship that made possible research in Great Britain. Portions of chapters 2 and 6 appeared in *de Halve Maen*, 69 (1996): 67–75, and is reprinted with the kind permission of the Holland Society. I am also indebted to my students, both graduate and undergraduate, who have willingly listened to me talk at length about Edmund Andros and, along the way, asked pertinent questions or made appropriate comments that led me to think and rethink my views toward my subject. There are too many of you to list, but please know that I appreciate your interest.

Many librarians at several institutions were helpful in completing this work, and I extend my thanks to all of them. Most particularly, I appreciate the willing and knowledgeable assistance given to me by the staff of the West Virginia University Library system. I literally could not have completed the manuscript without them. I also thank the staffs of other institutions, including the Public Record Office in Kew, the British Library, the Virginia Historical Society, Colonial Williamsburg, the Massachusetts Historical Society, and the New York State Library. I was particularly helped by interlibrary loans, and I appreciate the time and effort exerted by the staffs of all the libraries involved.

My greatest debt is, of course, to my family—parents, children, sons-in-law, and cousins—who have all supported me from beginning to end in this work, several of them even accompanying me to London when I did research there. A particular debt is owed my grandchildren: Kaitlin, Samantha, Daniel, Alex, Matthew, and Juliana. I appreciate their love and return it twofold. My last, and deepest debt is to my husband, Ted. For his constant support and encouragement over several decades, this book is dedicated to him.

All dates given are Old Style (Julian calendar) but with the year beginning on January 1 instead of March 25.

Abbreviations

Add. Mss.	Additional Manuscripts
Andros Papers	*The Andros Papers,* ed. Christoph and Christoph
Andros Tracts	*The Andros Tracts*, ed. W. H. Whitmore
BL	British Library
CSPC	*Calendar of State Papers Colonial*
Connecticut Collections	*Collections,* Connecticut Historical Society
CO	Colonial Office
DHNY	*Documentary History of the State of New York*
DRNJ	*Documents Relative to the Colonial History of the State of New Jersey*
DRNY	*Documents Relative to the Colonial History of New York*
Journal Virginia Council	*Executive Journals of the Council of Colonial Virginia*
Hutchinson, *History*	Thomas Hutchinson, *The History of the Colony and Province of Massachusetts-Bay*
Maryland Archives	*Archives of Maryland, Proceedings of the Council of Maryland*
PRO	Public Record Office, Kew Gardens
Public Records Connecticut	*Public Records of the Colony of Connecticut*
Randolph, *Papers*	*Edward Randolph, His Letters and Official Papers*
Rhode Island Records	*Records of the Colony of Rhode Island and Providence*
Virginia Church	*Papers Relating to the History of the Church in Virginia*
W&MQ	*William and Mary Quarterly*

The Imperial Executive
in America

Introduction: Other Worlds and Other Seas

The mind, that ocean where each kind
Does straight its own resemblance find;
Yet it creates, transcending these,
Far other worlds, and other seas.
                    —Andrew Marvell, "The Garden"[1]

ALTHOUGH EDMUND ANDROS WAS BORN AND DIED IN LONDON, HIS life experiences brought him in contact with "other worlds and other seas." As governor-general of New York, New England, and Virginia, Andros contributed to the shaping of both the first English empire and the future American nation. Andros's royalist roots, military training, and executive ability made him the ideal candidate to protect, defend, expand, and ensure the survival of England's presence in North America.

Several historians have commented on Andros's significant contributions. Viola Barnes, in her excellent survey of the Dominion of New England, referred to him as "a man of social position, personal integrity, military training, and administrative experience in colonial affairs."[2] Edith Carey offered a fair and perceptive summation of Andros's colonial career, noting that he was "one of the most distinguished soldiers and statesmen of which the Island [of Guernsey] can boast."[3] W. H. Whitmore, the editor of the *Andros Tracts*, pointed out Andros's many virtues and concluded that he "was an upright and honorable man, faithful to his employers, conscientious in his religious belief, an able soldier, possessed of great administrative abilities, a man worthy to be ranked among the leaders of his time."[4] Cadwallader Colden, an eighteenth century politician, called attention to Andros's "great moderation" while governor of New York. Colden characterized Andros's New England enemies as "bigoted" and marveled that Andros could "keep his temper among such a people."[5] More recently, Stephen Saunders Webb, commenting on Andros's accomplishments, noted that "in just the first two years of his epochal term in command of New York—[he] converted a market

15

town into a provincial metropolis, and established the physical and political presence of the imperial crown in mid-America."[6]

Other historians have downplayed Andros's many accomplishments, instead concentrating on the more negative side of his personality. Thomas Hutchinson, an eighteenth-century descendant of Puritans writing about his forefathers, compared him to Nero, noting that Andros "was known to be of an arbitrary disposition," and claiming that his correspondence reveals "much of the dictator."[7] John Gorham Palfrey, a nineteenth-century Puritan admirer, acknowledged that Andros was "a person of resolution and capacity," but one who held "arbitrary principles" that were alien to Puritan beliefs, coming to New England "prepared to be as oppressive as the King desired."[8] More recently, Jack P. Greene linked Andros with a group of colonial governors he termed "despotic, inefficient, or corrupt."[9] A recent reviewer of a book that puts Andros in a favorable light marveled that there was anything good to say about "the villainous Sir Edmund Andros."[10]

Andros was everything these historians claim, and more. An excellent administrator, an accomplished statesman, a brave soldier, a polished courtier, and a devoted servant to his employers, he could also be autocratic, arbitrary, and dictatorial. To modern eyes, perhaps his greatest flaws were an inability to compromise and a lack of tact, qualities that Andros would not have recognized as faults. Nor did his employers, a long string of Stuart monarchs, so recognize them. Andros did what he was expected to do. By advancing England's efforts in America, he helped to secure the empire.

Despite his pivotal role in Anglo-American history, to this date there is no published biography of Edmund Andros. The only full length study is an excellent, but necessarily dated, 1962 Ph.D. dissertation by Jeanne Gould Bloom.[11] While her work is admirable, Dr. Bloom rarely looks at the broader picture of Anglo-American history and thus ignores the impact of European events on the American provinces. Other historians have written extensively about Andros as governor of the Dominion of New England, with particular scrutiny of his participation in the American phase of the Glorious Revolution. Though concentration solely on this aspect of his career is inevitable and necessary, it gives at best a partial view of the man and his role in shaping the history of his time. Only a study of Andros's entire public career offers the possibility of understanding the forces that formed his actions, motivations, conduct, and the course of his governorships. A broader examination of Andros's career can lead to a deeper understanding of America in the late seventeenth century.

It is difficult for any biographer to assess the essence of Andros's personality. Though a man of wide acquaintances and many close friends, virtually none of his personal correspondence has survived. One looks in vain for letters that would reveal any of his innermost feelings. His official correspondence is sterile, only occasionally indicating strong emotions, such as his grief over his wife's death or his outrage when accused of appropriating money without authorization. In his official reports to the king and Board of Trade, Andros never complains he is over worked or over extended. His correspondence always conveys the impression that he is in control, even when he needed assistance. His reports were always succinct and to the point.

The only hints of Andros's humanity come from the assessments of other people, both friends and enemies. From these, we learn that he cared deeply for his first wife, that he was loyal to his friends, and that he liked to drink and carouse with those close to him. He also cared for his subordinates, once having the body of one of his officers, who died in "a private lodging," moved "to his own house hung 2 roomes in black: tooke extraordinary care for his decent interment."[12]

The absence of personal correspondence sets limits on any study of Andros's life. Only through indirect evidence does Andros's personality emerge slowly and reluctantly. Given this paucity of personal information, this work is not a biography in the traditional sense since there is so little that sheds light on his personal life or habits. This work falls in the category of career study, except that I try to relate Andros's actions to what I sense about his personality. As such, it is necessarily written from his perspective. It is far easier to assess Andros's career accomplishments than his personality. This is a revisionist study in that it attempts to shatter some misconceptions about Andros perpetrated by his contemporary colonial enemies or by Whig adversaries in England and accepted by generations of historians. In fact, he had a long record of accomplishments prior to his colonial governorships, enjoying a successful career as a soldier, courtier, and diplomat. Loyal to the Stuart monarchs, Andros served, in turn, Charles II, Charles's brother James, first as duke of York and then as James II, and then William III and Mary II, and Anne.

As a young man, he began his military career by serving in Denmark, Barbados, England, the Isle of Wight, and on Guernsey. During the Second and Third Anglo-Dutch Wars, as a soldier in the West Indies, England, and the continent, Andros gained invaluable administrative experience. As a courtier, he acquired polished manners and diplomatic skills. In the West Indies, he first recognized that Indians were more valuable as allies than as enemies. He also grasped the importance of an Atlantic economic community in which all segments were interdependent on the others. Above all, he learned that order had to be imposed from above.

Edmund Andros was a typical English aristocrat of the seventeenth century. Sharing the values and inborn prejudices of that class, he was a social snob who looked down on most provincials as his inferiors. Born to a royalist family, he despised the growing republican tendencies fostered by Calvinist thought. A believer in the divine right of kings, he could hold no other view than that the Puritans/Whigs, whether in England or New England, were wrong in their belief that the authority for government came from the people. That the world changed, and along with it the ground rules of politics, was something he could not anticipate.

Andros shared the imperial view of the Stuarts that provinces, being inferior, were to be exploited. Andros accepted, as did most imperial executives in England, that provincials should be permitted to make decent profits and be extended some rights. In exchange, the colonies were to be well governed, protected, and provided with a market for their goods. Such was Andros's intention in his first governorship, New York (1674–80), undoubtedly his most successful administration. As New York governor, Andros sought not only to protect but to expand the duke of York's domain by laying claim to half of Connecticut and attempting to establish the duke's privileges of government in neighboring New Jersey. He encouraged settlement on the west bank of the Delaware River, on land that would later form the states of Pennsylvania and Delaware, and kept that territory out of the grasp of Lord Baltimore's Maryland.

Andros's most significant achievement in New York was to avoid an Indian war like that which sparked rebellion in Virginia and a major conflict in New England. Andros believed all Indians should be treated with respect and consideration. As an imperial executive, Andros did not find it necessary to kill Indians who stood in the way of English settlement. Instead, Andros negotiated a lasting agreement with the Five Nations of the Iroquois. This pact, the 1677 Covenant Chain, eventually included New York, New England, and the Chesapeake. It ensured the survival in North America of both the Iroquois and the English. The Iroquois remained a formidable power until 1763, their commitment to the English ensuring that the English would ultimately triumph over the French. Much has been written about whether the Iroquois empire existed in fact or merely in fantasy.[13] Whether or not the Iroquois actually controlled the vast territory they claimed is unimportant. What is important is that both the French and the English believed the Iroquois did and acted accordingly throughout the provincial era.

Provincials often expelled Indians from territory they coveted, but Andros, particularly in New York where he was fairly sure of the allegiance of the Iroquois, did all he could to attract Indians to his province. If offered safety and treated with respect, he believed the Indians would become valuable allies. They would not only increase New York's population but would also help to protect the provinces from the encroaching French and their Indian allies. Andros's determination to treat Indians fairly brought him into conflict with those provincials, particularly frontier settlers, who favored tribal extermination.

Andros's entire approach to Indian relations was one worthy of emulation. He saw Indians not as enemies but as integral parts of England and its New World territory. His belief was that Indians could be incorporated into provincial society. To prevent Indian war, frontiersmen had to be controlled. If that proved impossible, Indians should be moved out of the path of white settlement, as Andros did in the aftermath of King Philip's War. By doing so, Andros perhaps unwittingly set the precedent for the wholesale Indian removal that began in the Jeffersonian era.[14] Andros's policy of winning Indians as allies was imperial policy. It was one that was used by the British with the 1763 Royal Proclamation and adopted by Henry Knox, first secretary of war of the United States. Knox and Washington sought to win Indian tribes as allies, much as Andros had. Only when this method failed because of the pressure of white settlement did Knox turn to a military solution, just as Andros did in Maine.[15]

Andros's contributions to the economic well being and political stability of New York were significant. On his 1674 arrival, New York was a thinly populated province with an economy still suffering from the after effects of the Third Anglo-Dutch War. Andros moved quickly to improve the economy, primarily by overseeing the construction of a mole or pier on the East River that facilitated trans-Atlantic and coastal commerce. He established quality standards for exported agricultural products, invigorated the profitable fur trade, and encouraged immigration through a liberal land policy. He ensured that Long Island would remain part of New York by thwarting Connecticut's attempts to assert authority there and countered with a claim to western Connecticut on behalf of the duke of York. While limiting the expansionist tendencies of Lord Baltimore in Maryland, Andros reasserted the duke's authority in both West and East New Jersey, and extended to the Delaware River settlements the benefits of government, improved trade, and security. William Penn, the founder of Pennsylvania, accurately assessed Andros's abilities when he commented that "he has no easy game to play yt comes after Sr Ed. Andros, for tho he was not without objection he certainly did great things more than both his predecessors."[16]

As governor of the Dominion of New England (1686–89), Andros drew criticism from New Englanders for his efforts to bring those colonies closer into the imperial orbit. Not only were Puritans reluctant to cede control of their own colonies, they resisted Andros's attempt to Anglicize them. The desire to regain position and influence by New England elites, both Puritan and non-Puritan alike, when coupled with the 1688 fall of James II in England, were underlying reasons for the 1689 overthrow of the Dominion government. The precipitating factor in instigating this rebellion was religion. Difference of belief pitted Protestant sects against each other, as well as Catholics against Protestants. If religion was not the direct cause of rebellion in all the provinces that staged their own versions of England's Glorious Revolution, then rebel leaders used it as a pretext. Complicating the issue was the fear and uncertainty among provincials raised by officials in England who sought to centralize government authority and interfere with government at the local level. This process resulted in a reshuffling of the existing power structure and a loss of place and privilege among the old elite. Causing further unrest was the rise of mercantilism, in which new wealth came from trade, not land. Moral values of the past were being put aside as trade became all-important and profit became an end in itself.

Andros's accomplishments in New England were significant because he brought a united government to a wide territory, extending from Maine to New Jersey. As governor-general, his most important task was the defense of England's American provinces from incursions by other European powers. Andros's appointment "created (in the hands of an experienced soldier and on the eve of a great contest with France) a single military command embracing almost the entire northern frontier of the

English colonies."[17] Andros proved the wisdom of a united military front in the Maine campaign of 1688–89, when he resisted French encroachment of Massachusetts's borders. He enjoyed success until after the Boston version of the Glorious Revolution, when the interim provincial government of Massachusetts recalled the troops. The French and Indians made continued and severe attacks on English frontier settlements in New England and New York, leading Andros to urge King William to send reinforcements before all England's North American territories fell to the French.

As Dominion governor, Andros imposed a fair system of taxation, tried to revive New England's economy, suppressed pirates, extended the vote to all qualified Christian (Protestant) voters, instituted religious toleration in a region that had never seen such a policy, and brought a united government to a diverse population in a far flung territory. When the Dominion was extended to include New York and New Jersey, Yankees and Yorkers were united for a short time. This brief example of a united government was not to be seen again in America until after the American Revolution.

Puritans valued their local culture, and anyone, monarch or governor, who "disturbed the fabric of local society," did so "only at their peril."[18] If the Dominion of New England represented the "most complete expression of the British colonial policy in the seventeenth century,"[19] then Sir Edmund Andros was the vehicle by which that policy would be implemented. Despite the overthrow in Massachusetts of the Dominion government, the process of Anglicization begun by Andros in New England continued even after he returned to England. Centralization was effected, forever shaping the course of Anglo-American history. The Puritans were never again permitted to resume their exclusive control of religion and government. Nor could Puritans deny either the vote or freedom of worship to all but their co-religionists. Although the Church of England was not established, the Anglican King's Chapel, whose construction was begun during Andros's administration, survives to the present day.

If there was any proof needed after the Glorious Revolution in England that it was still business as usual as far as colonial administration, it was in the reappointment to colonial posts of key Dominion executives, such as Edmund Andros, Francis Nicholson, Joseph Dudley, James Graham, John Palmer, and Edward Randolph. In fact, Andros profited from the change in monarchs by securing a better, higher-paid, more prestigious post in Virginia (1692–98), where the majority of the population largely shared his political and religious sentiments.

The Glorious Revolution had dramatic results in England, securing the rights of the English elite and bringing a strong Dutch influence to English politics. The effects of the Revolution were less dramatic and less evident in the American provinces. There was little change in the conduct of colonial affairs or the power of the monarch over the colonies. While the power of parliament slowly but inexorably increased after the Revolution, colonial assemblies, which considered themselves the provincial equivalent of parliament, had to struggle for every advance. Massachusetts did get a new charter, but despite Increase Mather's resigned comment that it was the best that could be expected, it did not please the more radical Puritans. The charter granted by William III gave only the standard privileges enjoyed by all royal colonies, except that the assembly had the right to nominate councilors. Under its new charter, Massachusetts could no longer think of itself as or act like an independent commonwealth. New Englanders found that even that charter was subject to revision. In 1726, the Massachusetts assembly was forced to accept further limitations on its charter privileges or run the risk of having it again recalled. In 1774 Massachusetts found to its dismay that many of its charter privileges were altered. The Glorious Revolution did not bring significant benefits to the provincial elite, as it had to the English elite. There was little, if any, liberalization in colonial administration.[20]

While the Glorious Revolution prompted rebellions in New England, New York, and Maryland, it had little or no effect in Virginia. In 1680, the crown had moved to prevent further unrest after the upheaval of Bacon's 1676 Rebellion by reducing the power of the lower and middling sort, represented by the house of burgesses. Charles II had ensured that the power of the assembly would be circumscribed by insisting that the burgesses pass a permanent revenue bill to cover all ordinary government expenses, including the governor's salary. This assured that future governors would not be dependent for their daily bread on the good will of the assembly and thus would not be inclined to make concessions to that body. Andros had little difficulty in working with the Virginia Assembly, even though he was burdened with heavy wartime expenses for almost all of his tenure there. In fact, his greatest contribution as governor-general of Virginia was as a military officer, protecting both Virginia's coast and its frontier. He assisted New York governor Benjamin Fletcher in defending

New York, recognizing the importance to the empire of protecting that colony from French incursions. Andros offered sanctuary to roving bands of Seneca Indians and preserved peace in Maryland following the death of Governor Lionel Copley.

The opposition Andros faced in Virginia came not from the assembly but from within the Church of England. The most virulent attacks came from the priest James Blair, who did not believe Andros supported the establishment of the College of William and Mary. Blair was fully abetted by Copley's successor as Maryland governor, Francis Nicholson, who wanted to succeed Andros as governor of Virginia, a more lucrative post than that of Maryland. Despite the turmoil caused by these two men, Andros kept internal dissension down, commanding the respect and loyalty of most Virginians. Andros, worn down by age, illness, and the political backstabbing of his enemies, resigned in 1698. Queen Anne appointed Andros to his last official post as lieutenant governor of his home island of Guernsey.

In all three of his American governorships, Andros was adversely affected by political events in England, which showed the close relationship between the Old and New Worlds. Puritan/ Whig attacks on the duke of York in England led to Andros's recall from New York; the 1688 overthrow of James II in England fomented a rebellion in Boston that caused a parallel overthrow of the Dominion of New England; the Whig ascendancy during the War of the League of Augsburg (1689–97) led the Whig-dominated Board of Trade to engineer the resignation of the Tory Andros from his Virginia post.

The problems that plagued Andros's governorships, rooted in colonial policy, were endemic in colonial administration. These issues were never resolved throughout American colonial history. The home government in England periodically determined to impose better control over the provinces but whenever a change of administration occurred, or there was a necessity to concentrate on events in Europe, that policy was abandoned. Failure to reinstitute the Dominion government, despite obvious defense and administrative needs, was typical of the pattern followed in colonial administration.

For provincials, the arguments advanced by New Englanders in opposition to Andros's government were essentially the same arguments that were to be later advanced by American patriots against British policy in the 1760s and 1770s. To Englishmen at home, the colonies were considered subordinate to the mother country, existing primarily to benefit England. Provincials had rights, but those rights were inferior to those of Englishmen at home. Representative government was seen as a privilege, not a right, and one that could be withdrawn at any time. Colonists, on the other hand, believed the colonies were established primarily to benefit them and their endeavors. Far from accepting a subordinate status within the empire, they were intent on proving that their local government institutions, particularly the colonial assemblies, were on a par with their English counterparts. Their rights, they believed, were the same as those of Englishmen at home. The two views were to prove irreconcilable.

To Edmund Andros, as to most Englishmen, the preeminent position of the home government was logical and necessary. Caught in the shifting winds produced by Calvinist thought, Andros could not foresee that the ideas advanced by the Puritans during the Civil Wars would prevail, ultimately leading to the separation from Great Britain of the colonies he had governed.

A skilled statesman, diplomatist, and soldier, Andros's career unfolded during the first attempts by the English crown to draw the colonies closer into the imperial orbit. While struggling with provincial resistance on the one hand and an inefficient bureaucracy on the other, his experiences anticipated those of future generations of imperial administrators who tried to create an efficient and workable system of colonial management. As was true of many of his gubernatorial successors, he epitomized a military imperialism that provincials disliked. Yet, Andros and others like him, with their commitment to imperial values, fiscal responsibility, defense measures, and economic growth, were in many ways responsible for shaping the character and attitudes of both England's provinces and the future United States. Edmund Andros, through his career, provided a better defined, more secure empire for England and helped to shape the future American nation.

1

Civil Wars and Restoration, 1637–1674

Holland, that scarce deserves the name of land,
As but th' off-scouring of the British sand; . . .
This indigested vomit of the sea
Fell to the Dutch by just propriety.
    —Andrew Marvell, "The Character of Holland"[1]

Holland, or more precisely the netherlands, figured largely in Edmund Andros's life. Like the exiled king and members of the royal family, the Andros family and other courtiers sought refuge there during the Interregnum. Despite the close family ties that bound the English royal family to the Dutch, the fact remained that the English were jealous of the Netherlands's economic prosperity. After the 1660 Restoration, Charles II was as anxious as any of his courtiers or any English merchant to usurp Dutch trade and appropriate Dutch possessions. The success of Charles's attempts to increase England's economic and territorial hegemony at the expense of the Netherlands provided opportunities for advancement for Edmund Andros, who was named in 1674 as governor of the former Dutch territory of New Netherland, renamed New York.

Training for his colonial career began, not in the scene of his first gubernatorial appointment, but in the experiences of Edmund Andros's early childhood and youth. It was then that he absorbed the lessons of empire and recognized the role of force in maintaining that empire. Nurtured by civil wars, his family persecuted, his mother incarcerated by religious zealots, and enduring exile with its accompanying uncertainty, poverty, and the anxiety that characterizes the life of an émigré, Andros early absorbed the lesson that "force gives the law to law."[2]

Edmund Andros was born in London on 6 December 1637, but the family was from the Channel Island of Guernsey. Andros was the son of Amias (Amice) and Elizabeth Stone Andros, who gave birth to nine children. Besides Edmund, the only others to survive infancy were one sister, Carterette, and two younger brothers, John and George. The family was in London at the time of Edmund's birth because of Amias's 1632 appointment as master of ceremonies to King Charles I. Originally from Northamptonshire, the first Andros (or Andrews) to go to Guernsey was Edmund's great-great-grandfather, John, sent to the island as lieutenant governor to Governor Sir Peter Mewtis. John's 1543 marriage to Judith de Sausmarez (Saltmarsh) brought to the Andros family, and passed on to future generations, the title of seigneury of Sausmarez. At Edmund's birth, his father held that title as well as the hereditary titles of cupbearer to the duke of Normandy (the English king) and keeper of the castle of Cherbourg.[3]

The families of both of Edmund's parents had long associations with and service to the Stuart royal family. His mother's brother, Sir Robert Stone, was cupbearer to James I's daughter, Elizabeth Stuart, queen of Bohemia. His father's post as master of ceremonies to Charles I meant that young Edmund's early years were spent in the company of the numerous children of Charles and his queen, Henrietta Marie. Two of Edmund's paternal uncles died in Stuart wars, one in 1618 in the service of Elizabeth's husband, Frederick V, elector of Palatine, and the other in 1644 fighting for Charles I during the English Civil Wars. Another paternal uncle, Charles, sustained five wounds while fighting for the doomed king and then, after Charles's execution, fought in France under the command of James, duke of York.[4]

At the 1641 outbreak of the Civil Wars, the Andros family returned to the largely French speaking and continent-influenced Channel Island of Guernsey. Geographically closer to France than to England, Guernsey was, and is, an island of great natural beauty and superb vistas. Its principal town and the oldest settlement on the island, St. Peter Port, is known for its picturesque cobbled streets and granite houses. Castle Cornet, built by King John to guard against Norman raids, today continues to guard the town and harbor.

On Guernsey, where the majority of the island's population favored parliament, the Andros family was part of a royalist minority. When the island's Presbyterian faction besieged the royalists in Castle Cornet, Edmund's mother fled by boat. Though captured and returned to the parliamentarians on Guernsey, she finally escaped in October 1645 to the nearby island of Jersey. From there, Elizabeth Andros wrote to Guernsey's royal governor, Henry Percy, to ask that her husband be permitted to join her, a request that was denied. In May 1646, Amias Andros was still helping to defend the citadel for the king. Amias asked Prince Charles for permission to join him on the island of Jersey, but Charles ordered him to remain on Guernsey. The prince praised Andros's devotion to the royal family, promising "to remember the same to your advantage." Amias Andros defended the castle for nine years and was still on Guernsey when Charles I was executed on 30 January 1649. Charles II, the king in exile, good to his word, rewarded Amias for his loyalty by naming him bailiff of Guernsey. If Amias, still besieged at Castle Cornet, enjoyed his new position at all, it lasted only until the castle fell to Oliver Cromwell, along with Castle Elizabeth on Jersey, the Isle of Man, and, in the New World, Barbados and Virginia. Whether Edmund and his siblings remained on Guernsey with their father or fled with their mother to Jersey is unknown. What is fairly certain is that these years molded Edmund Andros into a man who was "a reserved, ruthless, militant monarchist."[5] What is also certain is that Edmund took to heart Charles I's statement at his trial; "If power without law may make laws, may alter the fundamental laws as of the Kingdom, I do not know what subject he is in England, that can be sure of his life, or anything he calls his own."[6]

The Andros family was certainly unsure of their lives and their property when they were forced to follow Charles II into exile after Cromwell's 1651 triumph at Worcester. Preceded by several of the Stuarts, Amias Andros and his family went to The Hague in the Netherlands. Among the Stuarts was the princess Mary, who was the sister to the English King Charles II, the widow of Prince William of Orange, and the mother of William's posthumous son, also named William, who was born on 4 November 1650. Edmund Andros met the young prince at The Hague and later, William, as king of England, would fondly recall that early association. In the Netherlands, young Edmund joined his uncle Sir Robert Stone, who was serving in the household of Elizabeth, queen of Bohemia, also known as the Winter Queen. He later told an aide that he had been "brought up in the [royal] family (as Page) to the late Queen of Bohemia."[7]

Having chosen the military as his career, Edmund Andros served as an officer in the infantry, cavalry, and dragoons. His training began in the elitist cavalry, the military's most aristocratic arm. In 1656, at the age of nineteen and still in exile, Edmund Andros was apprenticed to his uncle, Sir Robert, a cap-

Elizabeth, queen of Bohemia (1596–1662). Daughter of James I and
Anne of Denmark, Elizabeth in 1613 married Frederick, Elector of the
Palatine. Frederick was briefly king of Bohemia in 1619 only to be
displaced by the Emperor Ferdinand II, earning Frederick and
Elizabeth the titles of the Winter King and Queen for their brief reign
in Bohemia. After Frederick's 1632 death, the queen lived in The
Hague and then London, where she died. Portrait by Gerard
Honthorst, courtesy of the National Portrait Gallery, London.

tain of horse. Edmund served with Sir Robert for three years at the rank of ensign, while his father served as captain of a troop of cuirassiers. Both Edmund and his father served under the command of Prince Henry of Nassau, whose Dutch army helped the Danes against the forces of Sweden's Charles X.[8]

Edmund endured two brutal winter campaigns in Denmark, first in 1655–56 and again in 1657–58, participating in the siege of Copenhagen and witnessing the devastation war brought to the Danish people. This continental experience and his early residence on the island of Guernsey later benefited Edmund's colonial career by perfecting his military skills and enhancing his leadership abilities. He also acquired a fluency in French, Swedish, and Dutch. On his return to The Hague, Andros returned to the queen of Bohemia's service, where he was named a gentleman of the household. After the 1632 death of her husband, Frederick, Elizabeth depended on the generosity of her brother, Charles I, and that of Sir William Craven, later the earl of Craven.[9] The queen's connection to Craven also benefited Edmund Andros, now a member of her household. Serving directly under Craven in the Netherlands, the men became friends and throughout his life Craven remained Andros's patron.[10]

With the 1660 Restoration, life for the Netherlands-based émigrés changed rapidly for the better. The flags on the ships sent to carry home the king and his two brothers, James, duke of York, and Henry, duke of Gloucester, were hastily redesigned to remove all vestiges of the commonwealth government.[11] Much to the joy of the exiled court, the fleet, under the command of Admiral Edward Montagu, arrived at The Hague on 14 May 1660. The fine clothing worn by Admiral Montagu and others was in stark contrast to the shabby attire of the king and his courtiers. The emissaries were appalled to find "what a sad, poor condition for clothes and money the King was, and all his attendants. . . . And how overjoyed the King was when Sir. J. Greenville brought him some money." Just prior to the fleet's return to England on May 23, "The King, with the two Dukes [Charles's younger brothers, James and Henry], the Queen of Bohemia, Princesse Royalle [Mary], and Prince of Orange [the future William III], came on board" the flagship and "dined in a great deal of state" on the *Naseby*, hastily renamed the *Royal Charles*.[12]

With the Restoration, Edmund Andros's family was able to return to its ancestral home in Guernsey. Islanders then sent Amias to London as one of the deputies to Charles II with a petition for a royal pardon for their guilt in supporting Parliament during the Civil Wars. The king granted the pardon on 13 August 1660, but deliberately excluded Amias, his brother Charles, and his son Edmund. These men had no need of a pardon, the king said, because they had "continued inviolably faithful to his Majesty." In 1661, Amias was renamed as bailiff of the royal court in Guernsey and major of the island's forces. Continuing his family's tradition of service to the Stuart royal family, Edmund remained with Queen Elizabeth at The Hague and then accompanied her when, after forty years in the Netherlands, she decided to visit London in May 1661. Andros continued to serve the queen at Craven's London town house on Drury Lane and then in the queen's own house on Leicester Square until her death on 13 February 1662.[13]

Seeking other employment, Andros was commissioned on 4 June 1662, as an ensign of Captain Sir John Talbot's company in the First (Grenadier) Guards, the king's household guards commanded by Craven. The Guards had loyally served Charles I throughout the Civil Wars.[14] The need to maintain a small but effective military force of a few thousand men was reluctantly acknowledged by both the king and his brother and heir, James, duke of York. At the time of Charles's death in 1685, the army in England had increased to 8,865 men, with 7,500 additional troops in Ireland and 2,199 men in Scotland, for a total of 18,564.[15] The duke, as Lord High Admiral, saw to the defense of England's coasts and created the Navy Board in 1660. The Royal Navy that year consisted of 156 warships that mounted 4,642 guns.[16]

A military presence and a strong naval force were needed not only because of internal problems and the threat of foreign invasion, but also because of the expansionist inclinations of both the king and the duke. These tendencies became obvious in 1663, when the Royal African Company was founded, with James as governor and Rupert, Elizabeth of Bohemia's son, as a member of the council. It was a belief at the time that the trade of the world was static and that if a country wanted to expand its commerce, it was necessary to take over the share of another country. To accomplish this end, the company, in 1663–64, sent two warships under the command of Sir Robert Holmes to West Africa to seize a Dutch trading post there. Their success infuriated the Dutch and delighted the English, who now had a base for the lucrative slave trade.[17]

The intent of the English was to provoke a war with the Dutch. In November 1664, the duke of York authorized two governors in the West Indies to order attacks on Dutch shipping in the area.[18]

The Dutch had earlier been harassed by another expedition that sailed from England on 15 May 1664, carrying three hundred soldiers in four ships. In command of this expedition was Colonel Richard Nicolls. Nicolls, with his fellow commissioners Sir Robert Carr, Colonel George Cartwright, and Samuel Maverick, was assigned to the capture of New Netherland, the North American territory controlled by the Dutch that neatly bisected the New England provinces from those in the Chesapeake. Controlling an unbroken stretch of North American coastline was essential to the English strategy, as was the prospect of profiting from the natural resources of the area. The English attacks in Africa and the West Indies, in concert with the conquest of New Netherland on 27 August 1664, brought swift action from the Dutch as the Second Anglo-Dutch War broke out in 1665. The French and the Danes allied with the Dutch, posing a formidable threat to England.

In September of that year, Andros was sent with one hundred guardsmen to the Isle of Wight to help the captain, Thomas Lord Culpepper, to guard the colony against Dutch and French incursions and a possible uprising by discontented islanders. Such an uprising was deemed likely because residents there hated Culpepper, a military, not a civil, commander. The islanders complained to the king that Culpepper "doth exercise an arbitrary power in the said island, frequently intermeddling in the civil government thereof." The king responded through Lord Clarendon that he wanted to remove Culpepper to "some employment fitter for him," but he would not be swayed by complaints from his subjects.[19]

An uprising did indeed occur shortly after the arrival of Andros and the guardsmen. The island's militia was the first to rise against Culpepper, seizing the bridle of his horse as he rode out from Carisbrook Castle, the same castle used to imprison Charles I during the Civil Wars. Culpepper managed to escape, and Andros's guardsmen rounded up and jailed the leaders of the dissident factions on the island, including the local mayor. To invest Culpepper with more authority, Charles named him civil governor as well as military captain. Charles also reinforced Culpepper's authority with three militia units from England and a cavalry troop. The events on Wight left Andros highly suspicious of the loyalties of local militia.[20]

Successful on the Isle of Wight, Andros returned to London to serve as part of the king's royal escort as he traveled to Oxford to meet Parliament. In 1666, Andros was garrisoned at his home in

Guernsey, where he fitted out a privateer to attack Dutch tobacco ships and French coastal vessels. While there, Andros moved to secure his financial well being by obtaining a license to ship wool to the island. He returned to London in time to help his regiment fight the Great Fire of 1666.[21]

While London was in the beginning throes of rebuilding, on 11 February 1667, Andros was commissioned a major in Colonel Sir Tobias Bridge's Barbados Regiment of Foot. This promotion from ensign to major reflected the trust placed in him by his military superiors and the king. As major in the Barbados Regiment, Andros was given the opportunity to gain administrative experience that would serve him well during his later career. The assignment to fight in the West Indies was fraught with peril, both from disease and enemy forces. Nevertheless, if he survived, his experience in Barbados would guarantee Andros's "rank and reputation," while "his new duties taught him the limits and direction of Atlantic empire."[22] In the regiment, Andros was part of a unit that was comprised of six companies with about eight hundred English and Irish soldiers to stop French encroachment into the English West Indies where the French had already attacked St. Christopher, Antigua, and Montserrat.[23] On 11 March 1667, the regiment sailed for Barbados with that island's newly appointed governor, William lord Willoughby, who, in addition to the soldiers, was bringing arms and ammunition to the island.[24]

The regiment, arriving at Bridgetown on 23 April 1667, found the island in near rebellion as rival factions struggled for dominance. Islanders were also experiencing economic difficulties, which had begun with Cromwell's Navigation Acts that limited the island from trading certain commodities with nations other than England. The relief the islanders expected with the Restoration did not materialize because the Restoration Parliament repassed the acts. Barbadians could only sell their major export product, sugar, to English merchants. When the price for sugar declined, planters blamed London merchants, although the cause of the decline was more likely over production, when more and more planters turned to sugar cultivation. Wartime increased distress on Barbados because few merchant ships could reach the island. Even the trade with the American mainland was disrupted, cutting off a major source of food, as well as the potential for profit. Andros's time on Barbados made him acutely aware of the importance of an integrated Atlantic economy.[25]

Willoughby calmed discontent and then ordered Colonel Bridge to retake the island of St. Kitts. They failed in this bloody attempt but did manage to hold Nevis for England. It is unknown whether Edmund Andros took part in the futile attack on St. Kitts or whether he remained on Barbados.[26] In July, Willoughby, militant and aggressive, ordered troops to seize the French island of Cayenne and retake the now Dutch-held Surinam.[27] The troops were successful in taking both possessions, but much to Willoughby's outrage, by the terms of the Treaty of Breda that ended the Second Dutch War, Surinam reverted to the Dutch.[28]

Willoughby used the Barbados regiment as agents against the Carib Indians on Santa Lucia and St. Vincent, the Caribs on those islands having allied with the French during the war. There was no battle on Santa Lucia since the Indians, awed by the presence of British regulars, agreed to sign a treaty acknowledging themselves as subjects of the English king.[29] From this experience with the Caribs, Andros learned that it was far better to ally with the Indians than to fight them. Indians would not only help fight enemies, their presence made it easier to claim and hold territory. Andros also learned that because people would create chaos if left to their own devices, order had to be imposed from above.[30]

With order restored on Santa Lucia and St. Vincent, the regiment returned to Barbados, arriving on 21 April 1668. They found they were most unwelcome, particularly because Barbados, still suffering from a poor economy and war-related expenses, had endured a devastating fire in Michaelstown, with damages estimated at over £300,000. All the taverns in town, which could have been used to house the soldiers, were destroyed, along with the military magazine. Willoughby, with "very great difficulty," managed "to persuade the Country to receive the Soldiers." The assembly reluctantly "ordered quarters for the Soldiers" but only on the payment of security. While the enlisted men were housed, the officers were not as fortunate since the assembly refused "to take the least notice of any of the officers."[31]

As Willoughy had no orders either to disband or maintain the regiment, both officers and men, Andros among them, were in sad circumstances—unpaid, ill-clothed, and uncertain about their future. Bridge was at a loss as to the future of the regiment, unwanted in Barbados, which was already heavily populated. Nor did Bridge, any more than Willoughby, have the authority to disband the men or send them back to England. Bridge made his plea for assistance to the king in the form of a letter that he entrusted to Major Edmund Andros for delivery. It was undoubtedly with great relief that Andros left Barbados.[32]

Arriving in England in August 1668, Andros stayed with the earl of Craven. From his base in Craven's house, Andros secured and shipped money and new uniforms to the regiment. He was not reimbursed until 19 January 1671, when a royal warrant was issued to pay him £673.6s.8d. for the clothing. This was followed in May 1671 by another warrant, directed to Sir Charles Wheeler, instructing him to pay £2778.10s.8d. to Edmund Andros for the Barbados Regiment. The regiment was ordered disbanded in June 1671, with its soldiers given the option of returning to England or receiving land in Jamaica or the Leeward Islands. The enlisted men were to receive fifty acres and the captains four hundred.[33]

Andros was not idle during the three years he spent in London securing pay for the regiment. In February 1669, King Charles sent Andros to welcome to England Cosimi de'Medici, prince of Tuscany. In August of that same year, Charles ordered Andros to salvage an English ship loaded with Cornish tin that had sunk in August 1665 in the Netherlands's Ostend Harbor. To succeed at the salvaging operation, Andros needed both diplomatic and mechanical skill, both of which he had in ample reserve. He secured the permission of the Spanish governor, the mayor, and the port officials at Ostend to salvage the wreck, then quickly learned enough of the necessary techniques to supervise the operation and the divers. Successfully concluding the operation, he made the necessary pay-offs to Spanish officials and to the governor's wife. For his efforts, Andros was rewarded with a gift of £250 from Charles and promises of continued favors from the royal family.[34]

Recognizing Andros's intelligence and devotion to duty, Lord Willoughby nominated him for the governorship of the Leeward Islands, but Andros was passed over for this post when Sir Charles Wheeler was named instead. Now considered an expert in colonial affairs after his sojourn in the West Indies, a colonial governorship was likely, but its bestowal was delayed. Andros received other marks of Stuart favor in September 1671 when the recently returned Barbados regiment was reorganized into four companies, with Andros as major and captain at a salary of 13s. a day.[35]

The Stuarts again acknowledged Andros's diplomatic skill when the duke of York, widowed by the March 1671 death of Anne Hyde, sought a new bride at the king's order. Charles's wife, Catharine of Braganza, had remained childless. Of the king's two younger brothers, Henry had died shortly after returning to England. This left as Charles's heirs James, who was suspected of being a Catholic, and his two Protestant daughters, Mary and Anne. Charles ignored the advice of his courtiers that he divorce Catharine and remarry. Instead, he urged his brother to seek a new wife in the hope he would produce a male heir. One potential bride was the princess of Holstein, a relative of the king of Sweden. In October 1671 the duke took advantage of Andros's diplomatic and linguistic skills, including fluency in Swedish, by sending him to Sweden to assess the advisability of such a match. When that arrangement fell through, the duke married, by proxy in September 1673, the Italian Catholic princess, Marie Beatrice d'Este, daughter of the duke of Modena. The marriage was arranged by Henry Mordaunt, earl of Peterborough.[36] James, never a popular figure in England, was unacceptable to most Protestants as a future king because of his personality and his conversion to Catholicism. James's marriage to a Catholic brought the specter of a perpetuated Catholic monarchy, should the duchess give birth to a son, who would be raised as a Catholic.[37]

Concerns about heirs had been put aside temporarily when Charles II, in accordance with the Treaty of London executed in 1670 with France's Louis XIV, started a third war with the Dutch on 17 March 1672. Perennially short of cash and needing money to finance that war, Charles had no choice but to call parliament in February 1673. That body, averse to Charles's policy of religious toleration made tangible by his 1673 Declaration of Indulgence, refused to vote funds unless Charles approved the Test Act, the primary intent of which was to bar the duke from the succession by forcing him to acknowledge publicly his Catholicism.[38] The act required all holders of civil and military offices to take oaths that they had received communion in a Church of England service during the past year and that they denied the transubstantiation of the Roman Catholic mass.[39] The act's motivating force was an irrational public fear that the Stuarts would try to reimpose Catholicism on England.

Protestant suspicion of James was confirmed when on Easter Sunday, 30 March 1673, the duke, by avoiding the customary communion at a Church of England service and much to the consternation of his brother, publicly acknowledged his conversion to Catholicism.[40] In June 1673, rather than take the Test Act, the duke resigned his post as lord high admiral, although he retained his place on the king's council and his seat in the House of Lords. He also unofficially retained a good part of his influence in the management of the government.[41]

Andros was aware of this public drama but in 1672 chose to concentrate on more personal and pleasant matters. In February, shortly after his return from Sweden, at age thirty- five, Andros married the thirty-seven year old Marie Craven, niece of the earl of Craven, thereby cementing his relationship with that family. A proprietor of the Carolinas, Craven obviously approved of the match and gave the couple 48,000 acres there as a wedding present.[42]

Andros also took part in the Third Anglo-Dutch War (1672–74). Additional troops were raised by the revitalized Barbados unit, now incorporated into a regiment of dragoons under the command of Prince Rupert, son of Andros's former patron, the queen of Bohemia, with Lieutenant Colonel John Talbott as second in command. Traditionally mounted infantry, the dragoons served as military police, often against civilian populations. Under the later Stuarts, dragoons were considered more as cavalry troops than as mounted infantry.[43] The Barbados Regiment, resplendent in blue coats, was the first in England to be equipped with bayonets. Rupert and Talbot remained in London when the regiment was sent to Yarmouth in 1672 under Andros's command to fend off an expected attack by the Dutch. His younger brother George and subordinate officer Anthony Brockholes assisted Andros. Andros fortified and policed the town with dragoons and established lookout posts along the coast in anticipation of a Dutch offensive.[44]

Despite rampant fears, the Dutch did not invade England. They did, however, attack, and in 1673 retook, their former possession of New Netherland, now New York. The English governor since 1668 was Colonel Francis Lovelace, who was at the time of the attack en route to Connecticut to visit that colony's governor, John Winthrop, Jr. On his return to New York, Lovelace, along with the commander of the New York fort, Captain John Manning, and the English soldiers, was sent back to England in August. The disconsolate Lovelace was thrown into the Tower of London until April 1675 when he was released, only to die shortly thereafter.[45]

The English, particularly the duke of York, were as disconcerted as Lovelace was at the Dutch victory in New York, whose location made it strategically essential to English interests. Sir John Knight urged Anthony Ashley-Cooper, the earl of Shaftes-

William Craven, first earl of Craven (1606–1697). Knighted by Charles I in 1627, Craven was named Viscount Craven and earl of Craven in 1664 by Charles II as a reward for his loyalty to the Stuart monarchy. Craven protected Andros's interests throughout his life. Portrait attributed to Louise, Princess Palatine, courtesy of the National Portrait Gallery, London.

bury and Charles's lord chancellor, to send a fleet to retake the colony. As Knight pointed out, Dutch possession of that area meant that New England would once again be isolated from the Chesapeake colonies. A Dutch presence in North America also threatened Virginia and Maryland tobacco exports, which brought the king £150,000 of revenue from customs duties each year.[46]

The signing of the Treaty of Westminster on 9 February 1674 eased English fears. This treaty ended the war between the Netherlands and England and gave New York back to the English. With peace, Prince Rupert's dragoon regiment was disbanded, except for the four remaining companies of the Barbados Regiment of Foot, now to be stationed in Ireland.[47] In February 1674, Andros received a commission as major and captain of the now Irish-based Barbados Regiment. As courtiers marveled at "the great favour" bestowed by the king on "the young Andrews," Andros realized even more rewards were in store for him. A month after the signing of the Treaty of Westminster, Charles II again granted New York to the duke of York. A governor was needed to replace the now discredited Lovelace. The duke's choice, announced on 24 March 1674, was his trusted servant, Edmund Andros.[48]

Andros was an excellent choice for the governorship. He was fluent in Dutch, the language of choice for the majority of New York's settlers; he also spoke Swedish, which would enable him to converse easily with the settlers along the Delaware. He was fluent in French, the principal language of Guernsey and of French Canadians, the latter with whom he would have military confrontations and diplomatic negotiations.[49] During his continental missions, Andros had perfected his diplomatic experience as an envoy for both the king and the duke. His military experience in the West Indies exposed him to colonial concerns, where he also learned how to win over and use the Indians to benefit the empire. The royal brothers could be certain that Andros would implement crown policy, maintain order in both settled areas and the frontier, and achieve crown goals even if at the expense of local elites.[50]

Philosophically, and from the duke's standpoint, Andros reflected the commitment of both the king and the duke to an imperialistic military regime for colonial government. Andros's competence, effectiveness, and bravery as a military officer were beyond reproach. As attractive as the new office was, Andros's immediate concern was a personal tragedy. On 28 March 1674, only four days after he was appointed to the New York post, his father Amias died, leaving Edmund as heir to the seigneury of Sausmarez and his father's other hereditary titles on the island of Guernsey. Charles II granted Edmund Andros his father's post as bailiff, against the wishes of the Guernsey governor, Christopher Hatton, who insisted that he, not the king, had the power to dispense of that post and other offices. The king, disagreeing, warned Hatton "not [to] disturb the said Major Edmund Andros in the admission to, and execution of, his office of Bailiff of the island of Guernsey."[51]

Andros came to Guernsey on June 19 to assume his post as bailiff and to impose the royal prerogative there. The problem on the island was related to the determination of the local elites to retain their place and privileges while resisting the efforts of the king to reduce their status and to centralize government authority. Andros, on arrival, informed local judges he carried with him an order from the king giving him or his lieutenant direct power over all Guernsey residents. Local judges were strident in their opposition to the order, but ultimately accepted the situation.[52]

When the royal court convened on July 4, Andros as judge decided whether each cause would be tried by English common law or by Norman law. He was also solely responsible for sentencing those found guilty, much to the outrage of locals who complained about Andros's "arbitrary judgement and punishment." Andros ignored his critics, imposing his own interpretation of the law in court, supported in England by both the king and the lord keeper, Daniel Finch, later earl of Nottingham. As the king's personal appointee, Andros accomplished his task of strengthening the royal prerogative at the expense of local elites. His position as bailiff secure for life, Andros named his uncle, Charles Andros, as deputy. He then sailed from the island for London on July 10 to prepare for his gubernatorial career in New York.[53]

In London, Andros found that in his absence a royal commission and instructions for the governorship of New York had been prepared for him at the order of the duke, who observed he had "conceived a good opinion of the integrity prudence ability and fittnesse of Major Edmund Andros to be employed as my Lieutenant there." Andros was also commissioned as captain of a company of foot in New York.[54] The fear of another Dutch attempt to retake New York, despite the haste with which they willingly ceded the territory back to the English in exchange for the Spice Islands, convinced the duke that it was necessary to maintain a garrison there. To ensure the safety of the province, Andros was to take one hundred soldiers with him, to be raised "by beate of Drum or otherwise in our Citty of London or parts adjacent and then so levyed to transport to Our said Towne of New York." The force was to become "an arm of Andros' authority, a policy which reflected James's belief that government had to be fully subordinate to the royal will." Andros's annual salary was £400 as governor, £145.12s. as captain of the New York company, and £227 as captain of the Barbados Regiment, plus what he could expect in fees and gifts. The duke assumed the expense of maintaining the garrison and ordered the treasurer to pay £1300 to Andros for their equipment and other expenses.[55]

The governor's commission and instructions constituted the only legal instrument of government in New York, a colony that lacked a charter throughout its existence. As Nicolls and Lovelace had, Andros was to govern with the assistance of a ten-man council. The Duke's Laws were reimposed with all power vested in the executive. There was not to be a representative assembly. Andros's instructions also demanded he exert government jurisdiction over the full range of the Dutch boundaries, or "ye maine land betweene ye two rivers wth ye said river called Hudsons River and all ye land from ye West side of Conecticut river to ye East side of Delaware Bay." The duke's secretary, Sir John Werden, later confirmed in a letter to Andros that "the Duke is intitled to all that the Dutch had in those parts."[56] The Dutch ambassadors at London informed the States General in the Netherlands of Edmund Andros's appointment as New York governor on 7 July 1674 and noted he was "ready to proceed thither in a ship." The ship was also to carry new English colonists to somewhat alter the ethnic balance in New York, which was then four-fifths Dutch. The Dutch governor, Anthony Colve, informed that Andros was en route, notified local officials in New York City of the order to surrender the colony to Andros.[57]

Seeing to last minute details of the trip, Andros's departure was somewhat delayed. On August 12, Andros was instructed officially by the king to take possession of New York from the Dutch by virtue of article six of the Treaty of Westminster and to follow the duke's orders as to its government and the collection of revenues. The latter were indeed a sore subject for the duke, particularly the income he had lost while the colony had been in Dutch hands. To recoup his losses, the duke on August 6 issued a warrant to Andros authorizing him on arrival in New York to seize Colonel Lovelace's estate there to satisfy a debt of £7,000 in lost revenue to the duke.[58]

Andros sailed on the *HMS Diamond,* one of two warships sent to New York. That ship, and the *Castle,* carried some, if not all, of the one hundred men raised for the garrison. Both vessels were crowded. Personal servants accompanied Andros and his wife. Also on board the ship was Anthony Brockholes, Andros's trusted subordinate at Yarmouth and now first lieutenant of the New York garrison, along with newly commissioned officers Christopher Billop as lieutenant and Caesar Knapton as ensign.[59] On the ship was another relative, Andros's cousin and East New Jersey governor, Philip Carteret. Other members of the shipboard party were Church of England chaplain John Gourdon and collector of customs revenue William Dyre. On board, too, was the luckless Captain John Manning, who was being returned to New York to face a court martial for surrendering the town to the Dutch. Also on board were the emigrants and dozens of auxiliary personnel.[60]

As he sailed, Andros was prepared to apply the lessons of empire to a largely hostile population. Being loyal, courageous, and obedient, he represented the values and philosophy of the monarch and the duke. These virtues were at once his greatest strengths and his greatest weaknesses. Andros was too literal minded and, in enforcing the royal prerogative, lacked an ability to compromise. To him, the center of empire was omnipresent, embodied in his person as governor-general. To provincials, the center of empire was distant. The governor was only one man whose appearance might have inspired awe, particularly when clothed in a splendid uniform, mounted on a fine horse, and surrounded by a military guard, but only one man whose tenure in the colony was limited. But Andros, having personally witnessed the dire results when legitimate authority was challenged, was determined to maintain that authority and to enforce the royal and ducal will. Thoroughly loyal to the Stuarts, he was determined to protect that colony from all threats, whether domestic or foreign.

2

New York: Securing the Duke's Province, 1674–1675

Still keep thy sword erect:
Besides the force it has to fright
The spirits of the shady night,
The same arts that did gain
A power must it maintain.
—Andrew Marvell, "Horatian Ode Upon
Cromwell's Return"[1]

WHILE MOST CERTAINLY NOT AN ADMIRER OF CROMWELL, ANDROS shared the sentiments expressed in Marvell's ode. The territory he was sent to govern was attractive not only to the Dutch but to other European nations. Andros and his garrison were responsible for defending New York from potential foreign invaders and from internal threats, whether those threats rose from local Indians or from provincial malcontents. Indeed, "the same arts that" gained New York for the English were deployed to retain it against all enemies, whether domestic or foreign.

The fleet carrying Edmund Andros and his party arrived in New York Harbor on 22 October 1674. The view that presented itself to Andros and his shipboard companions was magnificent. New York City itself could hardly compare to a European metropolis, but it was an area full of natural wonders. Like the Dutch before them, the English found the land to be "very fruitful, and fortunate in its fine woods. . . . The oak trees are very large; from sixty to seventy feet high." Indigenous people had regularly practiced "bush-burning," to "render hunting easier . . . [and] to thin out and clear the woods." Fish and wildlife were abundant, with bear, buffalo, deer, wolves, foxes, raccoons, otters, beaver, minks, rabbits, eagles, falcons, and hawks. New York Bay "swarms with fish, both large and small, whales, tunnies and porpoises, whole schools of innumerable other fish, and a sort like herring . . . and other kinds, which the eagles and other birds of prey swiftly seize in their talons when the fish come up to the surface."[2]

With the fleet anchored off Staten Island, Andros sent a letter to the Dutch governor, Anthony Colve, carried by Ensign Caesar Knapton, East New Jersey governor Philip Carteret, and Mathias Nicolls, asking Colve to arrange an immediate surrender of the island and its government. Andros and his party were anxious to set foot on firm ground. Colve told Andros he and his troops would be ready to leave in approximately eight days.[3]

Three Dutch representatives were sent on board the ship to welcome Andros and to discuss the final terms of surrender. The men, Johannes van Brugh, Cornelius Steenwyck, who was New York's mayor under Colve, and William Beekman, wanted assurance that the Dutch would be free from impressment in wars against their own countrymen. Andros told them he had "neither Orders Nor directions for any pressing whatever," which more than likely meant, as subsequent developments showed, that the Dutch would not be subject to impressment in the royal army or navy. Anxious to secure the peaceful surrender of the city, Andros probably was deliberately obscure in his response to disguise the fact that he considered all able bodied men in the province, including the Dutch, liable for militia service should the need arise. Nor was it possible that there was a linguistic misunderstanding between the English governor and the Dutch burghers because Andros was fluent in Dutch. When Colve later voiced similar concerns, Andros assured him that he did not "desire their bearing Armes against their Nation." Perhaps Andros did not "desire" it, any more than did the Dutch, but he certainly would call up the Dutch if they were needed in the militia.[4]

Andros further assured the representatives that all the Dutch would "participate in the same privileges as those of the English nation." On 31 October 1674, Colve officially turned the province over to Andros and formally absolved the Dutch from their allegiance, "ordering that the 5 banners of the Out people together with the Cushions and Table Cloth now in the City Hall should be taken Charge of by the Bargomaster Johonnes van Brugh."[5] Andros promised Colve that all sentences and judgments he had made would be honored, "pursuant to law," and that present owners would be permitted to keep confiscated property. When Colve raised the issue of religious toleration for the Dutch, Andros agreed that the Dutch would be permitted to worship as they pleased. Terms agreed upon, Colve prepared to leave but presented Andros with his magnificent coach and three horses prior to his departure. Andros graciously thanked him and as Colve boarded ship to sail for the Netherlands, wished him a "good & prosperous voyage." [6]

Colve's concern about religious toleration was valid because of the large number of sects in the province. The Dutch Reformed Church had the greatest number of members, but there were in addition churches of "all sorts, one Church of England, several Presbiterians, and Independents, Quakers, and anabaptists of several sorts, some Jews, but presbiterians and Independents most numerous." Under Dutch rule, the official religion had been Dutch Reformed. While tolerance was granted to other sects by the Dutch, only the English and French reformed churches were permitted the open practice of their faith. There were less than ten thousand people in all of New Netherland and perhaps fifteen hundred in its principal city of New Amsterdam, situated on the tip of Manhattan Island. The population in the province was mostly white, with few white servants or black slaves. Both servants and slaves were desperately needed, and a few slaves were imported every year from Barbados to be sold in New York for £30 to £35 each. [7]

New York was valued for more than its strategic location and size. With an excellent harbor and a major river that gave access to the hinterlands, New York was already a lucrative center for the fur trade. Following the initial 1664 capture of the city from the Dutch, Nicolls had sent Sir George Cartwright up the Hudson River to Fort Orange to secure its surrender and to offer a treaty of friendship to the Five Nations of the Iroquois Confederacy of Indians. Both the Dutch in New Netherland and the English in New York enjoyed good relations with the Iroquois and both recognized the strategic power of the Five Nations. Andros was only one of a long line of New York governors who worked to maintain good relations with the Iroquois. Cartwright was successful in both endeavors, and Fort Orange was renamed Albany, in honor of James, who was duke of York and Albany. [8]

Nicolls had to secure borders for the duke to the south as well as to the north. To achieve this end, he sent Sir Robert Carr to the Delaware River to effect the surrender of the Swedish and Dutch settlements on the west bank of that river on territory that was also claimed by Maryland. Carr was also successful, but only after he used brute force to quell token resistance offered by the colonists, killing three and wounding ten. Having achieved his mission, Carr renamed the town of New Amstel as New Castle. Later, Andros would have difficulty in persuading Maryland's proprietor, Charles Calvert, Lord Baltimore, that the Delaware area belonged to the duke.[9]

Part of the problem Andros faced was that technically, Carr and Nicolls had overstepped the southern and western boundaries of the duke's patent, which ran only to the Delaware (South) River, not to territory on the west side. The patent, or at least the area claimed by the duke, covered an area from the Connecticut River to west of the Delaware River that today encompasses the states of New York, New Jersey, Pennsylvania, Delaware, and half of Connecticut, as well as parts of Maine, Vermont, and New Hampshire, plus all the islands from Cape Cod to Cape May except Block Island at the entrance to Long Island Sound. Even before Nicolls landed, the duke had given a substantial portion of the territory to two courtiers, John Lord Berkeley and Sir George Carteret, the latter distantly related to Edmund Andros. The territory bestowed on Berkeley and Carteret was renamed New Jersey, in honor of Carteret's ancestral home on the island of Jersey. The courtiers promptly split the territory into two sections, East and West New Jersey. The duke almost immediately regretted ceding away such a large and vital portion of his grant and tried unsuccessfully at least to regain control of New Jersey's government through his agent, Edmund Andros.[10]

The province of New York itself, as the governor reported to the duke, consisted of over twenty-four towns, villages or parishes, the bulk of its houses being made of wood, but "some lately Stone and Brick," with some "good Country houses." New York City was situated on the tip of Manhattan Island, between the Hudson (North) and East rivers, with most of the city's docks on the East River, which "affords a safe and convenient passage." In 1664, and probably little changed by 1674, the walled triangular city was mostly contained south of present day Wall Street. Only a handful of buildings were north of the wall, the gates of which opened at daylight and closed at 9 P.M. The wall itself remained until 1699, finally being demolished as a nuisance, with its stones used to build a city hall. Architecture in New York City, as in the rest of the colony, reflected the Dutch influence, with typical Dutch stepped, steep-gabled, or gambrel roofs, resting on tall, narrow buildings. Most of the houses in 1674 had their own gardens and most faced the East River, with much of Manhattan Island farms or wilderness.[11]

Andros found a deteriorating fort defending New York City, a square stone structure with four bastions and forty-six guns. One of the first buildings constructed by the Dutch in 1626, it was originally named Fort Amsterdam. Andros renamed the building Fort James, and one of his first tasks as governor was to oversee the rebuilding or repair of its buildings, which included a chapel, barracks, storehouse, armory, kitchen, and governor's residence. The construction of the latter was begun, but never finished, by former English governor Lovelace. Most of the fort's buildings suffered from water damage. Andros ordered the governor's residence to be refurbished and the other buildings to be razed and rebuilt. Until the governor's house was ready in spring 1675, Andros and his wife lived in the house built in 1660 by Peter Stuyvesant, the former Dutch governor.[12]

The province was to be defended by an independent company of the royal army, the one hundred men brought by Andros from England, and the colony's militia, numbering about two thousand men of whom 140 were on horse—a small force with which to defend so large a territory. Effective resistance to a well planned attack whether by land or by sea was questionable because the militiamen were "all indifferently armed with fire-armes."[13] There were two main roads on Manhattan: one from the fort to the East River and the ferry to Brooklyn and the other, which was later known as Broadway, heading to the north from the fort. The city was dirty, as were all colonial cities, but Andros was determined to clean it up as much as possible. Owners of vacant lots or dilapidated buildings had either to build on their lots or improve existing structures to avoid their property being sold at auction. Tanners, whose byproducts polluted air and streams, were required to move outside the city limits to Maiden Lane, then a marshy area. Slaughterhouses, offensive to the sensibilities and dangerous to human health, were moved from the city to a new building constructed over the East River at the end of Wall Street. To improve trade, the weekly market first established by the Dutch found quarters in a new market house at the foot of Broad Street. In 1677, seven public wells were dug, principally to provide a water supply to douse the numerous fires that often resulted from open hearths in wooden houses.[14]

The improvements effected by Edmund Andros, done with the intent of increasing trade, would benefit not only New Yorkers but also its proprietor, the duke. He had been eager to secure the return of New York from the Dutch both for the prestige it would restore to the Stuarts and to England and for the revenue he expected the province would bring to him. James, like his brother, needed money, but if the duke expected an immediate profit from New York, he was to be disappointed.[15] When the fleet

Jacobus Secundus Dei Gratia Anglæ,
Scotiæ Franciæ et Hiberniæ Rex. &c.

S. Pe Largilliere Pinxit.   I. Smith fecit   Cum Privilegio Regis   Sold by Alex Browne at the Blew Balloone in little Queen street:

James II (1633–1701). The second son of Charles I, James' youth was disrupted by Civil War. Captured by parliamentary forces in 1646, he fled to Holland in 1648. Deposed in 1688, James, after futile attempts to regain his throne, died in France. Portrait by John Smith, courtesy of the National Portrait Gallery, London

carrying Andros sailed to America, the duke had already spent
well over £2,000 to outfit and transport the troops and was committed to pay their salaries, as well as those of Andros and other
government officials. He had lost revenue for the year the province had been back under Dutch control.[16] If nothing else, the
duke hoped to recoup the cost of maintaining the garrison.
Andros had been instructed by him "to lessen ye chardge of ye
government without weakening it or hazarding it." The duke
expected to "reape from thence some advantages, in return for ye
great expence and trouble I have been at in protecting that Colony." In February 1675, Sir John Werden, the duke's secretary,
anxiously asked Andros "how far ye publique revenues are likely
to suppurt ye publicke chardge."[17]

Revenues were meager. Quitrents, rarely collected, were a
small source of income, as were the revenues from the weigh
house, liquor licenses, and the liquor excise. The little money
raised by such means was used to resupply the garrison and for
other public expenses. Local taxes, imposed by the magistrates
and assessed on land and animals, were used for local expenses
and for such incidentals as Indian gifts. Magistrates could also
impose special taxes for extraordinary expenses incurred during
wartime. Provincial taxes were largely raised by customs duties
and most of the duke's revenue came from these, with rates
established every three years and then renewed. Even customs
revenues were low and, as the duke's secretary acknowledged,
the customs alone were not "likely to amount to neer so much as
shall defray the charge of the government." The rates established
by the duke as proprietor imposed a duty of 2 percent on goods
from England and other English colonies, and 10 percent on foreign goods. Furs and tobacco were the only exports taxed, fur
pelts at 1s. 3d. and tobacco at 2s. per hogshead each.[18]

Anxious to make New York a prosperous colony not only for his
own benefit but also for the benefit of New York's residents, the
duke ordered Andros to do everything possible "for the encouragement of Planters and Plantations and the improvement of
trade and commerce."[19] New York's principal export crop, rapidly
replacing furs, was wheat, with some sixty thousand bushels
exported each year, along with "pease, beefe, port, & some Refuse
fish, tobacco, beavers, peltry or furrs from the Indians, Deale &
oake, timber, plankes, pipestaves, lumber, horses, & pitch &
tarr." Imports from England and the Netherlands included a
wide variety of manufactured articles and such Indian trade
goods as blankets and duffels. Customs income remained low

because New York's overseas trade was still small, rebuilding slowly after being interrupted by the Third Anglo-Dutch War. Only ten to fifteen ships a year entered New York Harbor, as compared to one hundred or more sailing yearly into Massachusetts. As Andros later recalled, "At my first comeing to New Yorke I found the place poore, unsettled & without Trade, except a few small coasters . . . and severall parts of the Governmt never before well subjected under his Royll Hs. . . ."[20]

The immediate revenue problem was insufficient trade, hampered by English trade restrictions. As was true of Barbadian and other West Indian planters, New Yorkers claimed the Navigation Acts adversely affected them by restricting trade in certain enumerated commodities and forcing colonists to sell only to English merchants. In addition, only Englishmen could serve as factors in England's plantations. All foreign ships were to be excluded from colonial ports, specifically those from the Netherlands, formerly New York's chief and most profitable trading partner. Prior to the enforcement of the Navigation Acts, goods were shipped from New York and other colonies directly to Dutch ports and then reshipped to other ports. The province was officially confined to trading at much less profit with England and England's colonies.[21]

Responding to the pleas of Dutch merchants in New York, the Privy Council committee on trade in England had agreed in 1667 that for seven years New Yorkers could send three ships yearly to the Netherlands. The next year, a new, merchant-dominated trade committee successfully recommended to the Privy Council that this privilege be rescinded, making the colony subject to the same trade restrictions as other English colonies.[22] The Navigation Acts were enforced more strenuously after March 1675, when Charles II formed a new special committee of the Privy Council to "have the Intendency of all affairs formerly under ye care of ye Councill of Trade." Members of the committee included the earl of Craven, who was sure to look out for Andros's interests. Regardless of Craven's concern, the fact remained that the committee's main purpose was the enforcement of the Navigation Acts. The duke anxiously inquired of Andros "what effects you find from our late moderateing ye customes" and if the small direct trade previously allowed between New York and Holland was the "secret to rayse ye Customes."[23] Most New York merchants continued the Dutch trade but observed English customs regulations by first putting into an English port on the way to and from the Netherlands. The result was lower profits and less trade. Andros petitioned the duke for permission to allow merchants in New York to ignore temporarily the Acts so they could resume their direct trade with the Netherlands. The duke, hard pressed by enemies in England, could not grant that permission. His secretary, Werden, informed Andros that "whilst the Act of navigacon stands in the way it cannot be obtained, to have Ships trade directly from Holland, to yr parts."[24]

On occasion, Andros did ignore the Navigation Acts. He may have had the power to do so by virtue of the duke's instructions to the Collector of Customs, William Dyre, which gave Andros the authority to change customs regulations as necessary to accommodate local conditions.[25] Andros early had formed partnerships and friendships with such leading Dutch merchants as Frederick Philipse, Nicholas de Meyer, and Stephen van Cortland, who in addition to being business associates, were also his closest companions. Philipse, probably the richest man in New York at that time, was a favored friend, according to Jaspar Dankers and Peter Sluyter, visitors to New York who were not great admirers of Andros. They claimed that Philipse enjoyed "privileges . . . above the other merchants in regard to his goods and ships." Andros also vainly tried to favor Philipse's wife by asking the duke's permission for her to buy a Dutch ship "in hopes to make her free" of customs regulations.[26]

Having lived so many years in the Netherlands, Andros was quite comfortable forming business and social relationships with these elite Dutch merchants, and he was pleased to favor them and their interests. If these partnerships also meant that the governor allowed his Dutch friends to engage in illegal trading with the Netherlands, so be it. The governor's business associates did not pay any duties on imported items, since collector Dyre ignored incoming ships flying their flags. This courtesy was not extended to middling merchants, who were assessed at the full legal rate and whose cargoes were often subject to long and thorough searches.[27] Andros's business activities were varied, his critics saying he owned a retail shop in the city. According to Jasper Dankers and Peter Sluyter (whose testimony seems heavily biased and thus suspect), Andros was "also . . . a merchant, and keeps a store publicly like the others, where you can buy half a penny's worth of pins."[28] Such trade added to his wealth and also indirectly to that of the duke and, ultimately, of England.[29]

Also expanding the colony's wealth was the introduction into New York's economy of British merchants with mercantile connections in the home country and the West Indies. These merchants, such as John Robinson, George Heathcote, Lewis Morris, Sr., William Darvall, James Graham, John West, and Jacob Milborne, came to New York to promote their interests and oversee the sale of their merchandise. While Andros formed firm and lasting friendships with at least two of their number, Graham and West, other English merchants irritated Andros, not because they were English but because he considered them troublesome, ill-mannered, and divisive. Controversy with them began with the construction of a mole on the East River, a breakwater constructed of earth and rocks. Planned and designed by Andros to encourage trade, the mole offered a safe and protected dock for shipping. The result of its construction was that "Navigation increased att least tenn tymes to what it was." Though in the long run, the mole increased trade, in the short run it created a public debt. Five of the English merchants and twenty other people threatened to leave New York rather than pay their assigned share of the tax assessment for the mole, despite the obvious benefits it would accrue to them. These merchants, John Robinson, Edward Griffeth, George Heathcote, James Robson, and James Lloyd, also challenged the authority of New York's municipal court. Andros was offended by the men's behavior, particularly their attempt to leave New York before paying their assessment.[30]

Andros waited for an opportunity to even the score. His first target was George Heathcote, who, in 1676, was charged with illegal trade. Heathcote personally and vociferously protested in public to Andros about the charge at New York's customs house. He had the bad taste to upbraid Andros about the illegal and open sale of Dutch goods in Albany, which was hurting his business. Heathcote was charged with "scurrilous" speech, tried by the court of assize, found guilty, and fined £20 plus the exorbitant sum of £61.5s.6d. in court costs. The indignant Heathcote promptly left New York.[31] Andros's next target was the English factor, John Robinson, who complained to Andros about the sale of illegal Dutch goods. Robinson had been forbidden to trade at Albany on the grounds that he did not live in that city. Eventually making his peace with Andros, he established himself as a successful New York merchant.[32]

While the mole, the source of Andros's problems with these merchants, resulted in increased shipping, Andros also took other measures to build trade. Wheat, the principal export, seemed the key, but New York wheat sales were hurt because European or West Indian merchants could not rely on consistency in its quality. To improve quality, Andros restricted the processing of wheat to a central location in New York City, bringing that city added prosperity and growth but hurting the economy of Albany. Not only were millers attracted to New York, but also artisans whose crafts and talents supported the wheat industry. New York City was also granted a monopoly to process meat for export. The establishment of these industries in a central location considerably eased Dyre's task in collecting customs duties.[33]

To further lessen Dyre's responsibilities, Andros had requested that ships be permitted to clear customs in outlying "ports without being strictly searched." Permission was denied, as the duke's secretary explained to Andros, because customs officials in England strenuously opposed such a policy. All ships could only clear customs in New York after a thorough search, a regulation that irritated colonists in outlying areas. The duke's secretary also pointed out in a letter written a few days later, that none of Andros's predecessors in New York had permitted "any Forreigners vessells to pass up ye river of New Yorke to sell their goods up at Albany or elsewhere." Instead, such ships had to sell their cargoes in New York City, "secureing better the publique dutyes . . . and of keeping the Beaver trade within the hands of the inhabitants of our owne Colony."[34] Andros was instructed to forward his reasons for "proceeding different." Andros had no choice but to ban all trade on the Hudson River after 14 April 1677, except for that which was licensed by him. Irritated by this measure were rural New Yorkers who could no longer trade directly with either Europe or traders from other colonies, particularly, "the Bosteners and other strangers."[35] Andros himself protested this decision, arguing that trade "would be more if next neighbours of our own Nation . . . might without distinction, supply each other with our owne produce."[36] New Jersey governor Philip Carteret vigorously protested Andros's ruling, which was made at the duke's order, that required New Jersey bound vessels to clear customs in New York. The New Jersey governor claimed that Sir George Carteret's patent gave him the right to establish a port there. At a hearing held 11 July 1677, the New York court ruled that Carteret's patent did not include a grant for a port or harbor in New Jersey, declaring all "Shipps or Vessels" were to "enter and cleaer att the Custome house" in New York City.[37]

Customs collections particularly hurt middling merchants because they had difficulty finding the gold with which to pay the duty. To solve the problem, a perennial one in all the colonies, Andros asked the duke for permission to coin money. The duke refused, arguing persuasively, "It would soone by carryed away againe from you." In the absence of either specie or paper money, the most popular currency was wampum, supplied by the Indians, with its rate fixed by the New York City common council.[38]

When such measures as granting trade monopolies still did not raise sufficient revenue, Andros took further steps to diversify New York's economy by establishing and encouraging new industries and building an exchange and a covered market. Most important was the need to increase population. Andros's predecessor, Francis Lovelace, had granted two patents for manors, and Andros's successor, Thomas Dongan, was to issue several more. Andros did not grant a single patent while New York governor, reasoning that large, undeveloped patents discouraged settlement. Though manor lords tried to attract tenants, most colonists wanted their own land. Andros and the council ruled that every freeman who settled in New York would receive sixty acres, with an additional fifty acres for his wife and each child. Indentured servants would receive fifty acres upon achieving their freedom.[39]

To guarantee a steady market for New York's crops, Andros standardized weights and measures and, in 1676, prohibited the distilling of wheat in New York except for that portion of a crop that was damaged. The resultant dearth of alcoholic beverages led to a greater importation of rum from the West Indies, on which customs duties could be collected. The ban also increased the amount of exported grain. As the consumption of imported rum increased, the duke saw fit to raise its duty, a condescending attempt to prevent the devastating "pernitious consequences" of heavy drinking, often "fatall to ye health of many of his Mats good subjects." Better control of customs was further ensured on 20 May 1678, when Andros was granted the power to appoint admiralty judges.[40]

New York's economy boomed during Andros's administration, but again, the gains were not equitable, causing some discontent at all levels of society. Understandably bitter were middling craftsmen or laborers forced to move their places of business, those who lost business or were inconvenienced because of trade restrictions, and middling and small merchants who paid full duties while Andros's elite friends paid none. Andros ignored his critics, arguing that the measures he took to improve commerce would ultimately work to the benefit of all inhabitants, rich or poor. He might well have been right, for during his administration, "the Navigacon increased att least tenn tymes to what it was, and plenty of money (hardly seen there before) and of all sorts of goods att reasonable rates" flowed into New York.[41]

Andros was successful in increasing trade but was not permitted by the duke to extend traditional English government institutions to New York, which was considered a conquered colony. As such, the duke felt free to impose on it any government he chose. Andros reimposed the Duke's Laws, originally instituted by Richard Nicolls. This meant that Andros ruled alone, with the advice of a council not to exceed ten men. Although he had the authority to appoint that number, he at first named only four trusted English subordinates as councilors: John Lawrence, Mathias Nicolls, Anthony Brockholes, and William Dyre. The Dutch were temporarily excluded from high office, although Andros introduced them in subsequent years. In 1676, Andros appointed as mayor of New York City, Nicholas DeMeyer, a Dutch born merchant, and in 1677, merchant Stephen van Cortland was named mayor.[42] Frederick Philipse joined the council in 1675 and Stephen van Cortland in 1680. These three men, all wealthy merchants, formed the nucleus of the governor's court party. They retained their influence even after Andros left New York and was replaced by Thomas Dongan. Despite the presence of these men on the council, the Dutch remained a minority in government. Meeting every Friday morning, the council had the authority to enact and enforce laws. All laws had to be submitted for final approval to the duke; if not approved by him they were only in effect for one year. The governor also appointed all New York City magistrates, including the mayor, the twenty-three aldermen, and the colony's judges, sheriffs, clerks, secretaries, and revenue collectors.[43]

If the English colonists were optimistic that the new regime would mean the institution of representative government, they soon found out otherwise. Nevertheless, Long Island's Jamaica residents sent a petition to Andros, received on 1 December 1674, in which they informed him that shortly after the English conquest, Nicolls had assured them, "We should Enjoy as great priveledges as any of his majesties subjicts in America." They reasoned that since "few if any of his Majesties subjects ar debared of the liberty to have their deputys which are represenatiffs of theire townes to sitt In there High Courts at the least once A yeare with the governer and his councill and have there Votes in the making and Repealling such laws and Orders as they concieve may Conduce to the publicke good," they too should be accorded this privilege by "your honor." They were disappointed.[44]

Residents of the Dutch communities of Hurley and Marbleton sent a petition to Andros dated 4 January 1675, asking for reassurance that past "Rights and Priviledges" would be respected. Andros responded that he intended to do so but warned them that in return he expected "a punctuall obedience, for his Royall Highnesses service, and the good of all the Inhabitants, and that you beware of any Partyes, factions or discontents, amongst you, which I shall in no ways Suffer."[45] While determined to maintain order, Andros was not personally opposed to an assembly, believing it might be easier to impose and collect taxes with a representative body. He suggested as much to the duke. The duke, whose family had long had problems with recalcitrant houses of commons, later advocated to his brother as king the use of military force against parliament.[46] He told Andros he remained opposed to such an assembly, "wch ye people there seeme desirous of in imitacon of their neighbour Colonies, I think you have done well to discourage any mocon of yt kind." Nor did the duke see "any use of them." An assembly, the duke continued, was not "consistent with ye forme of governmt already established, nor necessary for ye ease or redresse of any greivance yt may happen." Colonial complaints could be "addressed to you at their Generall Assizes (wch is once a yeare) where the same persons (as Justices) are usually present, who in all probability would be their Representatives." If not at assizes, complaints could be handled "either at the Quarter Sessions or by other legall and ordinary wayes, or lastly by appeal to myselfe."[47]

Neither the duke nor Andros could have viewed the assize court, which met annually in October, as an adequate substitute for a representative assembly. The governor appointed the judges to the thirteen courts in the duke's domain, seven in New York, three in the Delaware River communities, and one each on Martha's Vineyard, Nantucket, and Maine. To form the assize court, Andros ordered each of the courts to elect two of their appointed judges to serve as its members. The court itself, "composed of the Governor & Councell & all the Justices & Magistrates [met] att New Yorke once a year," and functioned in both legislative and judicial capacities. In its legislative role, it approved taxes to pay for public works.[48] In its judicial capacity, the assize court tried such cases as those involving accidental deaths.[49]

Whether the assize or quarter sessions were, in the eyes of colonists, comparable to a representative assembly is questionable.

As far as the duke was concerned, they were sufficient. The duke distrusted assemblies, which tended, he said, "to assume to themselves many priviledges which prove destructive to, or very oft disturbe, the peace of the government." He remained open to Andros's suggestions, however, and said if his governor still advocated the establishment of an assembly, he was "ready to consider of any proposalls you shall send to that purpose." Andros was wise enough not to pursue the matter further.[50]

Particularly disappointed by the absence of representative government in New York were residents of eastern Long Island. Opposed to New York rule, the predominantly Puritan residents had petitioned Connecticut to be taken under its jurisdiction. In May 1674, the Connecticut general court approved the request for annexation of the three Long Island towns of Southampton, Southold, and Easthampton. Connecticut admitted Long Island representatives to its General Court and appointed magistrates for the towns. This brought the towns into conflict with Andros because he believed all of Long Island was part of the duke's grant.[51]

The towns ignored Andros's order to elect officials under New York's jurisdiction, voting to stay under Connecticut's control. One leader, John Burroughs, wrote a letter to Andros denying his authority and that of the New York court of assizes. On November 18, three representatives from the towns visited Andros in New York City. When the men continued to deny New York's authority over their towns, the council declared them rebels. The issue was decided with a show of force when Andros sent Captain Sylvester Salisbury to the towns to demand their surrender. Salisbury was to administer oaths of allegiance, reinstate English law, and hold elections to replace the officials named by Connecticut.[52]

Andros also wrote a polite note to Connecticut governor John Winthrop, Jr., son of the founder of Massachusetts, in which he reasserted the towns in question were part of the duke's domain. Andros then moved to suppress any further dissent on Long Island, personally visiting the towns accompanied by fifty armed soldiers to reinforce his message that the towns were indeed under New York jurisdiction. Governor Winthrop was not inclined to dispute the claim of the king's brother. In fact, Winthrop had sent his son Fitz-John and Samuel Willys to New York to welcome Andros as governor. The Connecticut governor's son and the New York governor, who shared not only a common vocation as soldiers but also common interests, became friends.[53]

In December, the rebellious Long Island towns capitulated. Andros pardoned the rebels, except for the three leaders, who were arrested and brought back to Fort James to be tried for sedition. Found guilty, two were subject to no further indignation than to be tied to the public whipping post on market day, but Burroughs was whipped and jailed. The duke, on 6 April 1675, told Andros he was well satisfied with his performance and "yor conduct in reduceing to obedience those 3 factious townes at ye East end of Long Island."[54]

Having secured the submission of the Long Island towns, Andros proceeded to draw other dissident factions into the orbit of English government, the most numerous of which were the Dutch. Andros, anticipating their mistrust and suspicion, allayed Dutch fears by confirming by proclamation on 9 November 1674, "All former Graunts Priviledges, or Concessions; heretofore granted, and all Estates Legally posses't by any under his Royal Highnesse, before the Late Dutch Government, As alsoe All Legall Judiciall Proceedings during that Government to my arrivall in these parts." With all laws again in force, the Dutch, like all other Protestant denominations, were guaranteed the religious liberty of their Reformed Church. The duke had ordered Andros "not to disturbe them [the Dutch] in their possessions, but on the contrary," to assure them "that your comeing is for their proteccion and benefit."[55]

While there was little resistance from the Dutch to Andros, religious tension existed in New York between Protestants and Catholics and among Protestants of different sects. An early disagreement pitted the Dutch minister, Nicholas van Rensselaer, against wealthy German born merchant, Jacob Leisler, and his future son-in-law, English born Jacob Milborne. Van Rensselaer, ordained in the Church of England, came to New York after the Third Anglo-Dutch War. He was part owner of Rensselaerswyck Manor, a vast patroonship established during the Dutch period. The Van Rensselaers had recently petitioned the duke to renew their patent to the patroonship, which the owners insisted included all of Albany. Granting of the request would injure both private and public interests in Albany. Not only had people invested time and money in developing the town, which was the second biggest in the duke's territory, but Albany had emerged as a major fur trading center.[56] Tensions against the family rose when the duke of York, despite Nicholas van Rensselaer's ordination into the Church of England, appointed him to serve with the Reverend Gideon Schaats in the Albany Dutch Reformed church.

Indignant Calvinist church members claimed he was not qualified to perform the rites of their church.[57]

Dutch Reformed opposition to Van Rensselaer was not based on his religious training alone, but rather that the governor had appointed him at the direct order of the duke. This action violated the basic tenets of Calvinism, which insisted that authority for both church and civil government came only from the people, each congregation having the right to choose its own minister. Opposition centered on accusations against Van Rensselaer lodged by Leisler and Milborne in August 1676, both men openly disagreeing with Van Rensselaer's interpretation of original sin. The infuriated minister promptly brought countercharges against the two men. On August 23, the Albany court required Van Rensselaer to post £1,500 security "to the end that he may make good his accusation and charge against the defendants." Van Rensselaer first agreed and then refused to pay the bond, a stand that led Milborne and Leisler to request Van Rensselaer's arrest. The Albany church elders stepped into the situation on August 29, calling the three men to church where they agreed to forget the matter while acknowledging the others as honorable men. Not quite ready, as it turned out, because when Leisler and Milborne demanded Van Rensselaer pay all court costs, the minister refused.[58]

On September 2, all three men were back in court and Leisler and Milborne requested Van Rensselaer be ordered to post the bond, an order with which the minister complied on September 4. Van Rensselaer then appealed to Andros and the council, giving his power of attorney to his brother-in-law, Stephen van Cortland. On September 15, Andros, the council, and the ministers of New York City considered the case, deciding that because van Rensselaer had posted bond, Leisler and Milborne should also pay £5,000 for security. The money was to be paid before noon on the following day.[59]

Andros was highly critical of the manner in which the case had been handled by the Albany magistrates and infuriated that religion had become a divisive issue. "I Canott tell you," he wrote Albany officials, "howe sensible and troubled I am att itt." He said, "As Chri[sti]an magistrates," they were to use their "utmost indeavour to asuage & prevent all animosity whatever & to that End stop all disputes." On September 18, when Andros was informed Leisler had failed to post bond, he ordered the sheriff of New York to take him into custody. The matter was resolved on September 23 before the governor, the mayor and aldermen of

New York City, and the ministers of the city. The decision was that if all the parties would stand by the amicable determination reached by the Albany church elders and let the governor decide who should pay court costs, the issue would be closed. The parties agreed, and on October 23 the governor in council issued an order that Leisler and Milborne "doe pay the whole charge both at Albany and here . . . and that Do[mini] Renslaer bee freed from bearing any part thereof."[60]

Andros's decision against Leisler and Milborne was not surprising. Both represented the extreme Calvinist branch of Protestantism, as had the Puritans and Presbyterians who had disrupted Andros's childhood. Throughout his life, Andros retained a loathing of such extremism. The Dutch Van Rensselaer was related to Van Cortland, one of Andros's closest friends, and Andros had an affinity for the Dutch. Van Rensselaer was also an ordained minister in the Church of England, though he ministered in a Dutch Reformed church. Andros, as head of the Church of England in New York, was sworn to uphold that church and its ministers. But neither Leisler nor Milborne were likely to forget the insults to their pride, even though all costs were eventually canceled by Andros.[61]

Despite such tensions within the Albany Dutch church, the Dutch were seemingly unaffected by the change to English rule. At first, there was little opposition to Andros based on religious principles or on ethnic lines. This changed on 16 March 1675, when Andros required all Dutch men to swear an oath of allegiance to Charles and James and to promise aid to the king against his enemies. The governor's close Dutch associates, Philipse, de Meyer, and Van Cortland, all signed the oath without question. The oath was a direct contradiction of Andros's former promise that he would not impress Dutch residents to fight against their countrymen. Eight prominent Dutch burghers, all municipal government officers led by former mayor Steenwyck, objected to the oath and refused to take it unless Andros, in turn, swore he would not impress them in the event of war with the Netherlands. The request was one they had made to previous New York governors, who had granted this privilege. Perhaps unaware of the custom, Andros refused. The eight Dutch men continued to refuse to sign the oath, even when called personally before Andros. The burghers explained that they were "willing to take" the oath, but requested Andros to confirm that they enjoyed "the right of exemption from being impressed."[62]

Andros again refused the request, ordering the imprisonment

of the men until they posted bail. Those charged were Cornelius Steenwyck, Johannes van Brugh, Aegidius Luyck, William Beekman, Nicholas Bayard, Antonio de Milt, Johannes de Peyster, and Jacob Kip. Facing prosecution, Johannes de Peyster gave in and took the oath. The remaining burghers complained to the States General that Andros had "laid before them . . . a formula of an oath he hath drawn up according to his opinion." They explained that they asked Andros "to allow them a proper time to depart with their families and property . . . promising on oath to be faithful." The only condition they made was that they not be "forced to take up arms against their own nation." Yet Andros "rejected their humble and civil petition, and denounced them as disturbers of the King's peace, placing them . . . in close confinement, from which they have been released, under bail, and ordering them to be tried."[63]

The Dutch ambassador to England, Van Beuningen, brought the matter to the attention of the duke of York, asking that the Dutch in New York "should not be oblidged to beare armes against the Hollanders." If they were not granted exemption, he asked that they be permitted to leave New York. The duke, on 28 January 1676, urged Andros not to force the Dutch to serve in war, but added that they should not be exempt from bearing the expense of the military. If not content with this compromise, they should be permitted to leave New York. The duke wanted "all persons whatsoever treated with all humanity & gentleness."[64]

By the time the duke made his decision, Andros, willing to resolve the matter, permitted the men to conduct their businesses and readily agreed to the Mayor's Court recommendation that bail for each be set at £200. He was also willing to accommodate the merchants after the court of assizes, on 6 October 1675, found the seven men guilty of "not being obedient to his Majesties Laws," and ordered their goods seized and forfeited to the king.[65] The men were summoned before the council on October 29 when Nicolas Bayard, the Dutch born nephew of former New Netherland governor, Peter Stuyvesant, complained so vociferously of his treatment that he was ordered to be held "prisoner in the Hole in the Fort." Released on bail, Bayard promptly fell ill. In early November, the recalcitrant Dutch merchants were ordered to appear before the council.[66] The men considered an appeal but finally sent a petition to Edmund Andros asking for a pardon "from the Previous severe sentence." All rejected the idea of either an appeal to England or a new trial, and all submitted to Andros. They were ordered to take the required loyalty oath

and "if not then done to have Execucion against their Estates."
When they did, their property was restored, but only after court
costs were deducted and after they also swore they would not
leave New York. The men quickly reestablished themselves in
trade and in politics. Despite the duke's stand on clemency, he
was pleased in August 1676 to learn the Dutch in New York had
capitulated and taken the oath. The duke informed Andros that
he "was very well satisfied with your care and prudence in quelling and composing those disorders with soe much calmness."[67]

Having won the however unwilling allegiance of the Dutch,
Andros next turned to extend the duke's authority over the New
Jersey and Delaware territory. The duke had given away New
Jersey to Berkeley and Carteret, but now claimed he had conveyed only the land, not the rights of government. When the king
reconfirmed James's title to all land in 1674, James reconfirmed
Carteret's patent to East New Jersey, but Berkeley had already
sold his share to two Quakers. Legal entanglements meant that
the patent for West New Jersey was not to be confirmed until
1680.[68]

The duke's secretary cautioned Andros in 1675 that he should
not act in East New Jersey because "we have as yet done nothing
towards ye adjusting Sir George Carterett's pretentions" there.
The Carterets acknowledged, at least tacitly, the duke's control
of government in East New Jersey, as did the proprietors of the
western part of the colony. Andros issued all land patents for both
East and West New Jersey, and all ships bound for New Jersey
continued to clear customs and pay duties in New York City.[69]

Andros's most pressing problem in the spring of 1675 was not
control of New Jersey, but rather the necessity to secure Delaware against being annexed by Maryland.[70] Andros knew that
Maryland had periodically raided the Delaware River settlements, granted land there, and ignored the duke's jurisdiction.
Shortly after his arrival in New York, Andros wrote to the lieutenant governor of Maryland, Thomas Notley, an appointee of
Lord Baltimore, the colony's proprietor, informing him that the
Delaware territory was part of the duke's grant. On arrival,
Andros had moved quickly to assert the duke's claim to hegemony over the area by authorizing the continuation in office of
all officers and magistrates who had been serving at the time of
the Dutch takeover.[71] To ensure the defense of the area, Andros
commissioned Captain Edmund Cantwell and William Tom to
take possession of the fort at New Castle. Cantwell was also to
serve as sheriff of the area. Andros also informed Lord Baltimore

and Sir William Berkeley, governor of Virginia, of his actions, further assuring both Chesapeake governors that he would "take all possible care upon this change, to prevent or redresse any kinde of injuryes to the neighbouring Colonyes."[72]

Andros was pleased to hear that Cantwell's takeover in the Delaware area was accomplished with little resistance and "that people are generally so well satisfied with the change."[73] Andros visited Delaware in early May. His purpose of traveling to New Castle in Delaware was to implement the duke's government there. Andros saw to defense, having cannons remounted to protect the duke's possessions. As he had in New York, he issued land grants of sixty acres to each head of family, fifty acres for wives and each child, and fifty acres to each freed indentured servant. He spurred the economy by ordering grist mills repaired and forbade the distillation of grain both to increase the amount of grain available for trade and to force colonists to buy imported spirits. To facilitate the bringing of goods to market, Andros ordered the building of highways. When it was obvious they could not be built because of marshy land near New Castle, Andros ordered the immediate construction of two dikes.[74] In mid May 1675, with government established and the economy given a much needed boost, Andros returned to New York. Maryland had been shown that Delaware was not up for grabs but was clearly part of the duke's domain.

Still to be settled were disputes over governmental authority in New Jersey and the resolution of conflicts over land titles there.[75] The Quakers in West New Jersey who had purchased land from proprietor Berkeley contested the titles issued by Andros. The Quaker John Fenwick now owned one tenth of West Jersey. Fenwick, during the Civil Wars, had fought under Cromwell, serving as a major in the New Model Army, and in that capacity, had supervised the execution of Charles I. This last fact alone would have led Andros to despise him. To Andros, Fenwick represented the very worst aspects of Puritan republicanism that had been so destructive to social order during the Civil Wars.[76]

In June 1675, John Fenwick sailed up the Delaware River with 150 settlers. He demanded Andros recognize him as the proprietor and governor of West New Jersey, ignored the land patents that Andros issued for that area, confiscated the land of Andros's patentees, and then sold it to other people. Andros, when Cantwell informed him in August of Fenwick's activities, ordered Fenwick's arrest. In a warrant issued on 25 September 1675, the governor charged that Fenwick "graunted Land extravagantly, dispossessed persons in those parts, sold their land, arrogating to himselfe a power of Judicature." Andros said Fenwick had no right to hold land in New Jersey because he had not had his title recorded in New York. In addition, Fenwick had permitted direct trade on the Delaware with foreign vessels. Such actions were not "to be allowed in any Case to the smallest vessel, boat or person." Fenwick was summoned, Andros reported, "to appeare without delay to answer the same before mee and my Councill in this place."[77]

When Fenwick ignored the order, Andros, on 8 November 1676, ordered Captain John Collier and the justices at New Castle to send him to New York, authorizing the use of force if necessary. Collier asked Fenwick to go voluntarily to New York, but he refused. Collier went to Fenwick's house and repeated the order, but Fenwick would not open the double bolted door, speaking through a "small scuttle hole at the end of the house." The Quaker firmly rejected Andros's authority and said he would only obey direct orders "from his Majesty the King or his Highness the Duke of York."[78]

Collier levied twelve soldiers from the militia to seize Fenwick. The men had "full power and authority to pull down break, or burn, or destroy the said house," should Fenwick refuse to surrender. As Fenwick reported, the capture was harrowing, the governor's men coming "in the middle of the night," to break down his door. A loaded gun was aimed at Fenwick's chest, while a pistol shot flew past his head. He was sent as a "prisoner in the depth of winter by sea" to New York City where he was tried in January 1677 with Andros "himself being judge." Fenwick was fined £40, and sentenced to prison for two years and three months, even though, as Fenwick complained, he had not "broken any of the King's laws."[79]

Andros realized that Fenwick's disobedience was setting a bad example for other colonists. Proof of this came in March 1677, when some of Fenwick's co-religionists decided that "no taxes, customs or duties were to be imposed" on West New Jersey without the approval of the assembly of that colony. Despite the Quakers' defiance, Andros relented and ordered Fenwick released on parole after he posted a £500 bond that he would not assume government powers. When he did so, the council, in Andros's absence, ordered Fenwick's arrest. Fenwick was again determined to resist arrest, claiming "no man shall take him alive—no—not if the Governor came himself." The New York council, unimpressed, again ordered the use of force if necessary.[80]

The order to seize Fenwick was conveyed to Captain Christopher Billop, lieutenant of the New York regulars, who either sympathized with Fenwick or disliked Andros. Contention between the governor and the captain began when Andros refused permission to Billop to resign his commission so he could develop a recently acquired estate on Staten Island. The duke agreed with Andros that Billop should not be permitted to resign. The duke's secretary, Werden, instructed Andros that Billop was to continue in his "former service . . . as long as he performed." Billop obviously did not perform very well, at least as far as Andros was concerned. Andros sent him to Delaware in 1677, but Billop, unhappy there, took pains to illustrate his discontent. The justices at New Castle reported to Andros in 1678 that they had "several complaints concerning several strange actions of your Commander Captain Billop, which hath occasioned some disputes and differences between us and your said Commander." Among those complaints was a charge that Billop was "a great friend to Major Fenwicke."[81] Whatever his wavering loyalties, Billop prevailed on Fenwick to surrender and, by 24 July 1677, he was in New Castle en route to New York. Thrown in jail, Fenwick was to be held prisoner until 12 March 1679. Billop was recalled to New York and dismissed in September 1678 because of his neglect of duty.[82]

In England, the duke, aware of the legal uncertainty caused by his insistence that he had not relinquished the rights of government in New Jersey, decided to investigate his legal status in the matter. His secretary wrote to the secretary of state asking if the duke's grant to the Quakers in New Jersey did indeed give them the power "to set up distinct Governements . . . or whether they are not still lyable . . . to the Lawes established in New Yorke." Until a decision was handed down, the problem of maintaining order in East and West New Jersey remained with Andros.[83]

Order was also difficult to maintain in the north, where the duke's territorial claims clashed with those of Massachusetts in Pemaquid (Maine), Martha's Vineyard, and Nantucket. Thomas Mayhew had acquired Martha's (or Martin's) Vineyard in 1641. In 1644, Massachusetts had moved to bring these islands under its jurisdiction. The islands came under New York's jurisdiction in 1664, and in 1671, Governor Lovelace appointed Mayhew as governor. Other islanders on Martha's Vineyard disputed the rule of the Mayhews during the Third Anglo-Dutch War when the

Dutch temporarily reclaimed New York. After the English take-over, Martha's Vineyard was again put under New York's protection. Andros promptly restored the Mayhew family to dominance, much to the relief of most residents there who complained they were being ignored by Massachusetts authorities. Andros planned to move against Pemaquid when given the opportunity but his more immediate target was a near neighbor, Connecticut.[84]

Before leaving for Delaware on 1 May 1675, Andros took time to write to Connecticut governor, John Winthrop, Jr., and the Connecticut assembly to inform them that the duke's patent ran as far to the east as the Connecticut River. The Dutch had initially believed New Netherland extended to the Connecticut River but acknowledged that the disputed territory was "mostly in the occupancy of the English nation," and had ceded their claim to the land with the 1650 Treaty of Hartford. After the English conquest, Nicolls, realizing that the loss of its most populous half would ruin Connecticut, agreed to a boundary at the Mamaroneck River. James refused to ratify the new boundary at that time, but in a letter dated 6 April 1675, told Andros that he had been informed that "ye bounds of those of Connecticut are to be on ye edge next ym of ye river Marrimac northwards as far as they please, provided they leave yt river where it inclines Westerly, soe as at noe time to approach neerer yn 20 miles to any part of Hudson's river."[85]

Andros could not have received this letter before the day he wrote to Winthrop and the Connecticut assembly. The Connecticut assembly insisted the Mamaroneck boundary was valid even after Andros pointed out it had never been confirmed. How could it be, he asked, when the boundary drawn from the river, which runs in a northwesterly direction, would encompass "Albany, Esopus, and in effect all Hudson's River?" To add weight to his claim, the governor sent to Connecticut a copy of the duke's patent, but the Connecticut authorities did not respond. Despite the duke's early admission that Connecticut's boundaries were settled on the Mamaroneck, on 28 January 1676, the duke's secretary wrote Andros that James approved of his demand for all land west of the Connecticut River. Nevertheless, the duke asked Andros not to press his demands since he hoped to settle the boundaries legally in England.

By the summer of 1676, after less than a year in New York, Andros had quelled dissension with the Puritans on Long Island, the Dutch in Manhattan, the Quakers in West New Jersey, and the Calvinists in Albany. He had successfully asserted the duke's claim to Martha's Vineyard and Nantucket and to the Delaware territory and had defended the duke's authority in New Jersey. He had also given notice to Connecticut that he would not easily give way on the border issue. Andros had taken positive steps to ensure the prosperity of the duke's colony by instituting economic reforms and imposing trade regulations that would eventually turn New York City into a thriving metropolis. Under Andros, the duke's territory was now more secure than ever before.

3
The Iroquois and the Governor:
The Covenant Chain, 1675–1678

Part 1: King Philip's War

New England in their last [King Philip's] Warr with the Indians had been ruined, had not Sr Edmund Andros sent some of those [Five] Nations to their assistance. And indeed they are soe considerable that all the Indians in these parts of America are Tributareys to them.

—Thomas Dongan[1]

NEW ENGLAND, AND POSSIBLY NEW YORK, MIGHT VERY WELL HAVE been "ruined" by King Philip's War if the Five Nations of the Iroquois had allied with the Wampanoag chief. That the Iroquois did not do so is due in large measure to the efforts of Edmund Andros. In fact, under Andros's direction, those same Iroquois launched decisive attacks against King Philip and his allies that soon brought an end to the war. Thomas Dongan, who succeeded Andros as governor of New York, appreciated his predecessor's role in ending this conflict. To ensure they would not join marauding New England or southern Indians, Andros had negotiated an alliance with the Iroquois and enlisted their aid in repelling the New England Indians from New York. Andros then forged a permanent and symbiotic alliance between England and the Iroquois to prevent their joining with the French. Called the Covenant Chain, it remained mutually beneficial to the Iroquois and the English until the mid-eighteenth century.[2]

Not long after Andros's arrival in New York in 1674, he became acutely aware of the power and prestige of the Five Nations. As Dongan observed, the Iroquois were the "bulwark between us & the French & all other Indians."[3] Cadwallader Colden, one of the Iroquois' early historians, reported in the eighteenth century that they were "the Fiercest and most Formidable People in North America," but they were also the most "politick and Judicious as well can be conceiv'd." In Edmund Andros, the Iroquois met not only a man who was willing to offer them respect, but also one who was their diplomatic equal.[4]

The Iroquois Confederacy consisted of five tribes with a population of approximately twelve to fifteen thousand. The Mohawks occupied territory north of Albany. To their west on the shores of Lake Oneida, were the Oneidas. In the geographic center of the confederacy, near present day Syracuse, were the Onondagas. Further west were the Caiugas, near present day Ithaca. The Senecas, on the shores of Lake Erie, were the most western of the tribes. The confederacy had probably been formed during the previous century for mutual self-protection and to eliminate warfare among the tribes.[5]

Having first welcomed the Dutch as trading partners, the Iroquois were just as happy to trade with the English. Tolerance of the Iroquois toward the English continued, probably because English settlement remained sparse in New York, unlike the intrusion of the Puritans in New England. The Iroquois quickly became dependent on English manufactured goods, for which they traded pelts. They took their furs by canoe down the Mohawk River to Schenectady, and then carried them overland the sixteen miles to Albany, bringing prosperity to that city.[6] Although the fur trade was less profitable by the 1670s than it had been at mid-century because of declining demand in Europe, it remained a lucrative business throughout the colonial period. The Iroquois, although facing a shortage of fur-bearing animals in their territory, found the trade essential to keep them supplied with iron axes, chisels, knives, kettles, and other useful items.[7]

The Iroquois in 1642 had begun a series of brutal wars against the numerous and powerful Hurons in the Great Lakes region. The Iroquois may have been motivated by the introduction of European weaponry, which gave them a significant edge over traditionally armed enemies to the northwest, or by the need to seek fur-bearing animals beyond their own territory. The Hurons and other Great Lakes tribes traded primarily with the French in Canada. Historians have speculated that it was the intent of the Iroquois to divert the Great Lakes fur trade to themselves, thereby becoming the middlemen between the Great Lakes tribes and the Dutch (later the English). When, by 1649, the Hurons, with a population of around twenty thousand, had been destroyed, the Iroquois attacked the Petuns, the Neutrals, the

Eries, and any other tribe that stood in their path or who refused their authority. Enemy survivors were often incorporated into the Iroquois tribes to replace those who had died in war or from sickness.[8]

As the Five Nations sought control of the fur trade, their string of conquests eventually gave them hegemony over a vast territory, or so they claimed. The territory ranged from the Great Lakes to as far south as the Carolinas and west to the Mississippi River, making them, by 1675, "the strongest military power on the continent."[9] Those tribes that offered resistance were given the choice—either extinction or subordination. As their reputation for ruthless warfare spread, many potential targets simply gave up. The spreading influence of the Five Nations made them an ally worth courting by the English, particularly New York's governor, Edmund Andros.

Andros, before the outbreak of King Philip's War in 1675, planned to visit leaders of the tribes in Albany in early summer 1675. His departure was delayed when, on 29 June 1675, in New York City, he received word from Connecticut governor John Winthrop, Jr., of Indian trouble in New England. On 24 June 1675, Wampanoag Indians, under the leadership of the sachem Philip, attacked English colonists in Swansea.[10]

Rhode Islanders, sympathetic to the Wampanoags, tried to negotiate a peaceful resolution to the problems that had led to the attack on Swansea. They proposed to Philip that the English and Indians negotiate. The Indians were to choose one of their leaders to speak for them, with Edmund Andros representing the English. Before arrangements for such negotiations could proceed, the Plymouth governor informed Rhode Island that his colony was intent on subduing Philip by force. Once negotiations broke down, Rhode Island was quickly drawn into the conflict.[11]

Andros received confirmation that war had broken out in a second dispatch from Winthrop and the Connecticut general court. Later that same day, Andros sent word to Connecticut authorities that he was distressed to hear "of the Indyans being in Armes in Plym. Colony, and their having destroyed severall Christians Plan[tation]s to the Eastward of you as neare as Narrogansett." The news, he said, caused him to "have hastned my coming to your parts" with "a force to bee ready to take such Resolucions as may bee fit for mee upon this extraordinary occasion." In fact, Andros said he considered the crisis so severe that he planned to "sett out this Evening, and to make the best of my way to Conecticutt river, his R.H.'s bounds there." Unfortunately, at that time the fighting was nowhere near either the Connecticut River or the Narragansett territory, but Andros chose to ignore these facts. He then informed East New Jersey governor Carteret and other governors of the "outrages committed by the Indyans in Plimouth Colony, and as farre as Narrogansett," apparently repeating the information sent him by Winthrop.[12]

Whatever the location of the uprising, Andros saw in the war an opportunity to assert the duke's claim to western Connecticut. The New England colonies were sources of constant irritation to the Stuarts. Both Charles I and Charles II had attempted to curb the tendency of New Englanders to ignore limits imposed by the monarchy. Charles II, irritated by New Englanders' failure to proclaim him quickly as king, sought to deal with the problem in 1664 when he dispatched Richard Nicolls to North America. Nicolls had a two part mission: the first was to take New Netherland; the second part of the mission, and equally important, was to bring within the royal fold the troublesome and defiant Puritan colonies in New England, particularly Massachusetts. The king was determined "That the Inhabitants of the Massachusetts Colony shall have their immediate dependence upon ye Crown of England." New England colonial authorities were informed Nicolls was coming but were not told the full nature of his mission.[13]

Nicolls's task was to persuade all New England colonies to give up their charters, a first step in imposing a direct royal control on New England, with the king approving all governors. Nicolls was also instructed to get royalists in office and himself named as governor of Massachusetts. Charles's intent was to unite New England under a single government with the newly conquered Dutch territory to the south. This proved impossible in 1664, as the Massachusetts Puritans had ignored Nicolls's threats and blandishments.[14]

While the Connecticut Puritans were not considered quite as radical as those in Massachusetts, they too resisted Andros's attempt at imposing direct crown control and were determined to avoid becoming part of the duke's colony. Seizing half of Connecticut for the duke could be seen as a first step in subduing all of New England. The Puritans were well aware of the crown's intent. Hence, when on July 7, Andros again informed Connecticut authorities he was on his way with troops, the news was greeted with alarm.[15] Recognizing Andros as an even greater threat to their security than were Philip and his Indian warriors, authorities in Connecticut acted quickly. Militia Captain Thomas

Bull was promptly sent to Saybrook at the mouth of the Connecticut River with orders to repel any aggressive act with force if necessary. On July 8, the governor and council heard that Andros
had arrived at Fort Saybrook in two sloops with a force of men.
The governor ordered Captain Thomas Bull "to inform Major
Andross that" he was not needed, since "the authority here hath
taken the best care they can sufficiently to defend the plantations." If Andros wanted to be of service in this Indian war, he
was told he should take his troops "toward Seacunck for the
reliefe of the good people there whoe are in distresse . . . for there
is the seat of war." If Andros persisted in his determination to
land, Bull was ordered to treat him with "all due respects," but
to request his troops not be allowed to disembark. If it were necessary for the troops to land, they were asked to leave their weapons on board ship.[16]

Andros did, in fact, land on July 8 with two or three of his men,
only to be met by the Saybrook militia, which was soon to be reinforced by the Hartford militia. Andros claimed he had come only
to visit and to help the Puritans against the Indians. His real
intent was to take possession of the fort, "intending when he had
done it, to keep possession," and then control of all of Connecticut west of the Connecticut River.[17] The Puritans, discerning his
true intent, again politely informed him his help was neither
wanted nor needed.

Andros and his party returned to the sloop, but the fleet
remained anchored nearby. On July 10, Deputy Governor William Leete and the general court of Connecticut issued an order
to all "his Maties subjects of this Colony of conecticutt . . . to
refuse to attend, countenance or obey the sayd Major Edmond
Andros." On July 13, Andros and "his Gentlemen" landed again.
Before the assembled townspeople, Andros "forthwith did in his
Majestyes name command his Majestyes Charter to be read, and
after that, his Highnesses commission." He then stated he would
sail away immediately unless the people preferred that he
remain. Andros found, to his dismay, that the New Englanders
did not want him. Their response was to read the general court's
protest of Andros's landing. After hearing it, Andros called the
protest "a slander," but, as Captain Bull reported to the general
court, he "departed peaceably." The Puritans were taking no
chances. Andros found the road to the dock lined "with the
towne-souldiers to the water-side." Andros knew when to cut his
losses. He set sail immediately but the sloops had to drop anchor
when faced with contrary winds and an incoming tide.[18] On July

22, Governor Leete complained that Andros's fleet was "still hovering thereabout." In an official letter of complaint to the king, the Puritans pointed out that Andros "would overturn what hath been thus settled, by clayming the goverment of us . . . o[u]r charter . . . must give way to the Duke's charter." If the colonists refused to honor the duke's claim to all territory west of the Connecticut River, Andros would consider their actions "rebellion and we rebells."[19]

Although he had no luck with the Connecticut colonists, Andros wanted to assure the defense of his own colony against Indian attack. A vicious war had indeed followed Philip's assault on Swansea.[20] Andros was not about to take the chance that the conflict might spread to New York. Hence, on the way back to New York City from Connecticut, he stopped at the eastern end of Long Island and sent the arms and ammunition originally intended for Connecticut's defense to Nantucket and Martha's Vineyard. He then proceeded through Long Island to New York City, on the way disarming the Long Island Indians. Once back in New York, he sent for the New Jersey and Delaware tribal sachems, who "all againe renewed their submissions."[21]

It was now necessary to secure the allegiance of the Iroquois to prevent any possibility of their allying with Philip, as had several New England tribes. New York, sparsely populated and poorly defended, could not withstand an Indian uprising within its borders. Nor could Andros risk the Iroquois allying with the French in Canada, an alliance that might also spell the end of New York's survival. On 5 August 1675, Andros set sail up the Hudson River to Esopus, arriving there on August 7. There he met with and secured the allegiance of the Mohegan Indians. Then Andros sailed on to Albany for his long-delayed meeting with the Albany burghers and the Iroquois sachems. In Albany, Andros established a general court of five or more magistrates. Being given a monopoly on the highly lucrative fur trade mollified Albany merchants, still irritated by being banned from the European trade, a measure that favored New York City.[22] To ensure Albany remained the fur trade center, Andros instructed Schenectady officials to exclude Indian trade in that city.[23]

Andros dealt effectively with Iroquois affairs while in Albany, reestablishing alliances with the Iroquois. He created a board of Indian commissioners with Robert Livingston, the secretary, responsible for keeping the board's records. He again met with the Iroquois sachems at Tinontougen, one hundred miles west of Albany. As a courtesy, the Iroquois bestowed on him the name

Corleaer, after the highly respected Dutchman, Arent van Curler, who had died in 1667. Andros was pleased to have the Iroquois renew "there former Allyance, and now submitted in an Extraordinary manner." By binding the Iroquois firmly to him with promises to protect them and a guarantee of a steady market for their furs, Andros ensured their loyalty to the English.[24]

As war in New England escalated in the fall of 1675, alarm spread among New Yorkers. Andros was aware of the risk posed by enemy Indians. On his return to New York City, he had the Albany garrison reinforced by "his first Lieut with more recruites" and ordered the building of blockhouses in "several Townes & places within this Government." Andros also sought to help Rhode Island, the only New England colony with which he maintained good relations during the war. He sent to the governor there six barrels of powder and "some match," which were "thankfully accepted" by the Rhode Islanders.[25]

As several Algonquin tribes joined Philip, the Puritans became convinced God was punishing them for their sins, particularly when, in September 1675, the war spread further to the north.[26] When Maine's Abenakis attacked English towns, the New Englanders found themselves fighting on two fronts. Unrest among the Indians was caused by increased English settlement in that area and by the ban on the sale of arms and ammunition to the "North Indians," the Abenakis, Pennacooks, and Sokokis from present day Maine, Vermont, and New Hampshire. The ban, imposed by the Massachusetts General Court, was devastating to Indians who had come to rely on European weaponry for hunting. These northern tribes turned to the French for assistance, which was readily provided since the French sought to oust the English from Maine. Urged by the French to attack, the Indians complied, particularly after being subjected to many acts of betrayal by the English. In one incident, colonists seized two hundred Indians who had come in good faith to discuss a treaty with the English at Pemaquid. The result of this and similar acts were all-out Indian attacks on Maine's villages. Hundreds of English colonists fled in panic, first to Monhegan Island off the Maine coast, and then to Boston, Salem, and Portsmouth.[27]

Whatever the cause of the Indian uprisings in neighboring New England, New Yorkers feared local Indians would join Philip's braves. This was particularly true on Long Island. Andros investigated, but concluded "there appears no Evidence or cause for such reports, but the contrary." He judiciously advised that blockhouses to be kept in good repair, not only for whites but also

so that "our Indyan women and Children, [who] come in & submitt, shall be received to live under the protection of the Government and that the Governr will bee there as afore, where any of
them may freely come and speake with him." Andros urged calm
among New York's residents, reminding them to treat Indians
fairly. As he realized, peace would continue, despite the threat of
the New England Indians, as long as "all our Indyans bee friendly
treated, and have equally Justice, according to Law."[28]

Although King Philip's War reduced neighboring colonies to
ashes, Andros's policy of fair treatment for all Indians meant that
peace reigned in New York. When Long Island Indians in May
1676 complained that the English were stealing fish they caught,
they asked Andros for permission to sell their fish to whomever
they pleased at the best possible price. He ruled that they be permitted to "dispose of their effects as they thinke good."[29] In
another instance, Long Island Indians complained to Andros that
land was taken from them without payment. On 13 March 1677,
he ordered the town of Hempstead to "Come to an agreement
with and make Satisfaccion to the said Indyans . . . within the
time of three Months . . . The which if you neglect to do, I shall
undertake the matter my selfe at the Public Charge." When
Andros visited Long Island later that month, the local Indian
sachems paid him a social call and assured the governor they had
"no particular businesse" but merely wanted to "visitt and to
declare the continuance of their friendship." After they gave
Andros a present of wampum, he assured them they were welcome even without gifts. He again told them they would be com-
pensated for their stolen land within three months.[30]

Andros's policy of equitable treatment was designed to prevent
an Indian uprising in New York. To make such an event even
more unlikely, the Council resolved to prohibit the selling of powder and lead to any Indians at Albany except "it be to ye
Maques & Sennekes" or to the Mohegans, and then only one-
quarter pound for hunting purposes. Despite the ban, the Puritans charged that New Yorkers sold arms and ammunition to
New England's Indians. The first complaint came from Connecticut, where the deputy governor informed Andros that New
England's Indians were armed by the French and also boasted
"of getting supplyes elswhere." Connecticut officials suspected
the "elswhere" was New York, with either the "mowhakes or others" in or near Albany supplying the weaponry and ammunition.[31]

The second accusation came from Massachusetts. In December

1675, charges were printed in Boston that Dutch merchants in Albany were engaged in arms and ammunition sales to the New England Indians. Although probably accurate (Albany traders continued to sell weapons and ammunition to enemy Indians and even to the French in Canada until well into the eighteenth century), the accusation infuriated Andros.[32] The governor had specifically given orders that no ammunition or arms were to be sold by the Albany merchants to Indians, except for purposes of hunting, and he sent representatives to Boston to so inform the Puritans. On 11 March 1676, Andros ordered the Albany magistrates to seize and hold William Loveridge, who had said the Dutch in Albany were selling ammunition to enemy Indians, "notwithstanding the Law and strict Prohibicion." Loveridge was jailed until he posted bail and was ordered to appear at the next court of assizes, scheduled to convene in October.[33]

Whether or not Albany merchants were guilty of arms trade with Philip, alarm rose in New York in November 1675 when word was received that Philip and his braves were within forty miles of Albany. The burghers, about to be hoisted on their own petards, were saved by Andros's prompt action. On 5 January 1676, Andros wrote to Connecticut Deputy Governor, William Leete, and informed him "that late last night I had inteligence that Philip & 4 or 500 North Indians, fighting men, were come within 40 or 50 miles of Albany northerly, where they talke of continuing this winter."[34]

Andros had also heard that New England troops had "marcht against the *Narrogansett* Indyans," who had allied with the Wampanoags. The report claimed a "great Success, but no certainty." The victory was a certainty, as Andros soon found out. The Great Swamp Fight of 19 December 1675 followed the attack of the Puritan army on a Narragansett village. When the New Englanders set fire to the village, many Indians were burnt to death in their homes. The survivors fled to a swamp, where the English soldiers surrounded them. The women and children were permitted to come out, and then the Puritan soldiers systematically killed every warrior.[35]

Despite the Narragansett loss, Philip was still at large and a serious threat to the colonists' survival. Philip had succeeded in uniting several Algonquin tribes and now moved toward New York to enlist the aid of the Mohawks against the English. In Connecticut, Leete was delighted to hear Philip was moving toward Albany and Mohawk territory. The Mohawks, he believed, could "destroy these bloody upland Indians without adventuringe any of Majesty's subjects in the designe." Leete was convinced that the Mohawks would attack Philip if Andros so ordered, since Andros had "settled soe firme a peace with the Mohawks" and urged Andros to do so. He was certain they could "with much facillity uterly extirpate this bloody generation, in the winter season, who have imbrued their hands in the blood of soe many of his Majesty's subjects."[36] Complete annihilation was what he had in mind. Leete then expressed his confidence that the New York governor would be able "to restraine the supplying the comon enemy with either armes or amunition, especially the Dutch people, who you know are soe much bent upon their profit"[37]

Andros was incensed by the accusations in Leete's letter and promptly wrote him so. Leete and his council "supposes & conclude many things,"Andros said, "without any grounds." According to the letter, if the Connecticut settlers were involved in a bloody Indian war, it was most likely their own fault. It was clear, Andros continued, that they "doe not understand or know the Maquaes [any] better then yo[u]r owne Indyans." Andros was astounded that the Connecticut Puritans, "having refused and slighted the assistance of this Government" when he came to Saybrook with armed troops, should now expect him to undertake such "an extraordinary great charge" and "expect me to bear expense & risk." The governor was also irate over the ethnic slur the New Englanders had hurled at the Dutch and the implication that New Yorkers of Dutch extraction were selling weapons to Philip, "in which you seeme to make mee a complice." He demanded an "explanacon, and to name the guilty, there being none in this Government but his Maties subjects, which obey all his lawes."[38]

On 4 February 1676, Andros's determination to stop the spread of the Indian war required him to take a softer tone with Leete. If he did send the Mohawks against Philip, Andros wondered "weather you would . . . admitt our forces, Xtians or Indians, perticularly Maquase & Seneques, to pursue such enemies, unto any part of yr Colony." After hedging a bit, on 7 March 1676 the Connecticut Council agreed the Mohawks and the Senecas were certainly welcome to come "into our towns for refreshment." Shortly thereafter, the Connecticut council asked if they could negotiate directly with the Iroquois, by sending "some agents of o[u]r owne to pass up to Albany." Andros refused.[39]

The Mohawks, disinterested in allying with the Algonquins, were willing to attack them at Andros's order. Andros acted because he was sworn to protect the colony and was alarmed by

exaggerated reports that Philip's force had grown to 2,100 warriors, supplemented by another five or six hundred Indians allied
with the French. Andros was unable to go to Albany personally
because the Hudson River was frozen solid. Nevertheless, he sent
word to the Mohawks by messenger asking their help against the
New England Indians. The Mohawks complied and later acknowledged that Andros was "incouraging us to goe out aginst them
and killed some and Putt the Rest to the flight."[40]

Andros reported he "supplied our Indians with ammunicion,
armes and all they wanted and received old Maques Sachems,
women and children into our townes." Happy to oblige while at
the same time pleasing Andros, the Iroquois used King Philip's
War as an excuse to rid themselves of a persistent problem and
an old enemy. The surprise attack by the Mohawks on Philip's
warriors in February 1676 was brutally efficient. As one contemporary observer reported, "King Philip and some of these Northern Indians being wandered up towards Albany, the Mohucks
marched out very strong in a warlike Posture upon them, putting
them to Flight, and pursuing them as far as Hossicke River . . .
killing divers, and bringing away some Prisoners with great Pride
and Triumph . . . did very much daunt and discourage the said
Northern Indians."[41]

To ensure Philip's braves remained on the run, Andros left for
Albany with a military force in six sloops as soon as the ice-
choked Hudson River opened.[42] On arrival there on 4 March
1676, Andros found about three hundred Mohawk warriors who
had just returned from attacking Philip. The Mohawks had with
them "some prisoners & the crowns, or hayre and skinne of the
head, of others they had killed." Philip and the survivors had fled.
The Mohawks wanted to pursue them, but Andros tried to discourage them from following Philip into Connecticut. Andros had
another plan in mind for Philip and his braves. He authorized
Lieutenant Gerrit Teunise to go with an Indian guide "to the fur-
thest pairt of the Government or as farr as Coneticut river,"
which Andros still insisted was the eastern limit of the duke's colony. Teunise was "to finde out Phillip or other north Indians,"
who had recently been in New York and taken prisoners there
and to give Philip messages from Andros. Andros ordered that
after meeting with the Indians, Teunise was to "refresch and rest
your self, and without delay to return and make the best of your
way to me."[43]

When Teunise met with the southern New England Indians, as
instructed by Andros, he demanded the return of some one hun-

dred prisoners they held, to which the Indians agreed. Teunise warned the New England Indians not to attack New York. He then conveyed to them Andros's offer of asylum in New York. This offer was ultimately accepted by hundreds of Indians. Perhaps the first to come to New York were from the Wayatanoc, Wickerscreek, and Stamford tribes, whose home territories were near Connecticut's Stratford River. The sachems of these tribes visited Andros on 17 April 1676, giving him deer, bear, and beaver skins. In return, Andros gave the sachems coats and a promise of protection and safety within New York's borders. In May, the council decided all New England Indians who came to New York were to be protected and kept safe from both the Mohawks and the New England colonists. Word was again sent to New England Indians that all who "come in & submitt" would "live under the protection of the Government."[44]

Andros's offer of safety to Philip's followers infuriated Connecticut authorities. They repeatedly asked Andros "that such of o[u]r enemis as had made theire escape into your parts might be surrendered" to them. The Connecticut council also repeated its request to send "agents to treat [with] the Maques." The purpose, the council explained, was to "renew that ancient league of friendship" with the Mohawks "that hath been between the English of New England." The Puritans voiced concerns because many of "o[u]r enemies are resigned up to the Maques over whom you have seemed to have commands."[45]

In May 1676, Rhode Island Deputy Governor Easton informed Andros that white refugees from King Philip's War were stranded in Rhode Island. Andros promptly sent sloops there to offer them land on Long and Staten islands.[46] The fleet carrying the Rhode Island refugees returned to New York on 28 May 1676, and the passengers reported to Andros that Massachusetts wanted to make treaties with the Maine Indians. The Maine Indians occupied territory that was claimed by both the duke and Massachusetts. If Massachusetts were permitted to negotiate a peace with those Indians, they would take control of the disputed land by treaty. Such an action would spell the end of the duke's dominion over Maine. Andros was more determined than ever to secure an immediate peace on his terms.[47]

As New Englanders continued to fight against both the southern and northern Indians, Andros sought to save the Maine Indians as he had many southern New England Indians, by offering them asylum in New York. Word was sent to the northern Indians that all who "come in & submitt, shall be received to live under the protection of the Government." Several northern Indians did indeed take Andros up on his offer and were seen crossing the Hudson to seek sanctuary in New York.[48]

Andros also made Connecticut an offer of his services as a peace negotiator in the spring of 1676 when he met with two Connecticut representatives. Andros told the men that he would negotiate "an honorble and safe peace" with Philip and his allies on their behalf if they wanted. To show his good faith, he offered to "suspend all further demands of that part of yor Colony claymed by his Royall Highnesse" until "a determination" was made in England. Despite his offer, he "had no answer" from the Puritans.[49] Since the war continued, in July 1676, Andros ordered Gerrit Teunise to lead three hundred Mohawks against enemy New England Indians.

Andros told the Connecticut council that he had given asylum to a New England Indian named Cospechy and fifteen other braves, as well as several women and children. The Connecticut council demanded the immediate return of Cospechy and the death of other enemy Indian leaders now in New York. When Andros refused the Connecticut suggestion, they asked if they could send their own soldiers into New York to kill the Indians. The answer was, of course, no.[50] Offering protection to New England's enemies gave Andros the opportunity to frustrate the Puritans' plans for revenge, while at the same time adding to the number of fighting men in New York, who were all loyal to him.[51]

Connecticut authorities, furious that enemy Indians were being given asylum in New York, again urged Andros to have the Mohawks kill them. They offered a compromise that if Andros would not kill all the northern Indians, perhaps he could see his way clear to kill the Indian leaders. Andros again refused. A promise of protection was just that and was not to be violated for personal revenge.[52]

The New Englanders may have been denied the privilege of murdering those Indians who escaped to New York, but they wreaked their vengeance on Philip, the Wampanoags, and their allies. On 12 August 1676, Philip was found in a swamp near Swansea, where the war had started, by an Indian guide and an English soldier from Plymouth. The soldier shot Philip dead. As soon as the Puritans realized the dead Indian was Philip, they "cut off his Head and Hands, and conveyed them to Rhode-Island, and quartered his Body, and hung it upon four Trees." Philip's wife and child were seized and sold into slavery. Other Indians were disposed of in a similar fashion, with more than "three thousand Indians, men, women and children destroyed" during the course of the war and its aftermath. Colonial official Edward Randolph later pointed out that these Indians "if well managed would have been very serviceable to the English." Despite the Puritan victory, New England was devastated. Damages were estimated at "unto one hundred and fifty thousand pounds . . . about twelve hundred houses burnt, eight thousand head of Cattle . . . killed, and many thousand bushels of wheat, pease, and other grain burnt."[53]

News of Philip's death reached Andros in late August 1676, immediately followed by renewed demands from New England to surrender escaped Indians. The Wampanoags and their allies were defeated, but New Englanders in Connecticut and Massachusetts were determined to punish all Indian leaders involved in the war. In October 1676, Puritan officials made another attempt to bypass Andros and deal directly with the Mohawks to secure the return or the murder of émigrés. The New York council refused, stating "that the *Maques* [Mohawks] are our Indians . . . and will be of ill Consequence for the *Maques* to treat or to make application to another Governmt, the which will breede a distraction amongst them."[54]

While Indian war ended in southern New England with Philip's death, it continued in Maine. That same fall of 1676, the Abenakis near Kennebeck drove the colonists from the area (present day Scarborough, Maine), burning that town and virtually every other English town in Maine. Residents complained to Andros that Maine had been "neglected by Boston, who had usurped itt." Not able to defend the area, Massachusetts authorities "told the Inhabitants 'twas the Dukes and nott their businesse." In December 1676, Andros sent a sloop to Boston, offering free passage to those English colonists driven out by Maine Indians, but the Massachusetts government would not permit the people to leave for New York.[55] The same month Philip was killed, the Puritans unwittingly ensured Indian unrest would continue when they sent an expedition to destroy the ripening corn in the fields of the Maine Abenakis. Beset by continued attacks and facing starvation, the Abenakis fled, some to New York, others to Canada where they united with the French.[56] Despite the continued protests of Connecticut authorities, the New York council ruled that "all strange Indyans, which came in, may live & be incorporated under ye *Maques, Mahicanders, Esopus* or other our Indyans and bee equally protected." Andros set aside land in the eastern part of New York for the defeated immigrant Indians, while others fled west to live with the Senecas. In New York, the many surviving Abenakis and refugees from other tribes, such as the Sakokis, formed a new community called Schaghticoke near the mouth of the Hoosic River.[57]

To resolve their problem with refugee Indians, New England officials persisted in demands to meet personally with the Iroquois. Andros finally and reluctantly agreed to such a meeting early in April 1677. The Connecticut council appointed Major John Pynchon to join Massachusetts's representative, James Richards, at Albany, "there to meet the Honble Governor of New Yorke." According to the Connecticut council, the purpose of the meeting was to conclude "a league of freindship and amity between the English of New England and the sd Maquaes." Its purpose was also to persuade the Mohawks to turn over to them or to "dispose of" the enemy Indians now sheltered by their tribe. Andros did not agree that the latter purpose would be addressed.[58]

Andros and the New England representatives arrived in Albany on 11 April 1677. At Andros's insistence, the meeting between the Puritans and the Iroquois took place under his supervision. When New Englanders insisted enemy Indians who escaped to New York should be killed, Andros refused, saying that they had already been incorporated into the Seneca tribe. Thwarted, Richards and Pynchon said they would "represent the same . . . to the respective Councills of our Colonyes . . . then your Honr would be pleased fully to answer theire desire." Andros, unfazed by this prospect, had gotten the better of the Puritans, but they were unlikely to forget. [59]

The agreement finally concluded between the Iroquois and the New England colonies was one of amity and friendship, the first of the Covenant Chain treaties. As the Mohawks acknowledged, "the Governr Genll & you of New England & we are in one triple Allyance with another."[60] The Covenant Chain was a metaphorical symbol of the commitment of the Iroquois and the English to the interests of the other. The symbolic chain represented "a multiple alliance binding tribes and colonies in a 'silver' chain of friendship." Forged out of a need to resolve the warfare of the mid-1670s, it guaranteed the "integrity of New York's eastern boundary." In succeeding years, the Iroquois frequently confirmed that "We are all One—One Heart, One Head & the Peace is made so Strong that it cannot be broken."[61]

Despite obtaining the Covenant Chain agreement, the Puritans were not entirely happy since their negotiations with the Iroquois had been conducted according to Andros's terms. In fall 1677, when enemy Indians continued to attack Connecticut settlements, the council there implied it was Andros's fault for refusing to deliver to them "those barbarian enemyes." Nor did Andros permit the Puritans to pursue their enemies into New York. The Puritans also complained that at the treaty talks conducted "in yo[u]r psence & wth yo[u]r inspectio & advice," Andros would not let New England representatives demand from the Mohawks the surrender of captured New England Indians. The result for New England was a continuing threat of Indian attack. They reminded Andros that "if the eggs cannot be timely crushed, the brood of vipers may grow too strong" to be extirpated. If Andros did not act, the Puritans threatened to take matters into their own hands or, as they put it, Andros had better destroy the Indians "before we be inforced to use other endeavors to p[ur]sue o[u]r Enemyes where ever they bee to be found."[62]

The New Englanders did not invade New York, having enough on their hands fending off the attacks of the Maine Indians. In June 1677, Andros decided the time was right to bring a stop to the fighting by ousting Massachusetts from Maine. He sent "a force and strong fram'd Redouth in four good sloops to take possession and settle in his Royll Highnesse right at Pemaquid and defend or secure the ffishery giving notice thereof to Massachusetts." Andros learned the Maine Abenaki Indians wanted to end the war, but their hatred of the Massachusetts authorities was so intense that they refused to surrender to them. Instead, they surrendered to Andros with the promise to return about forty English captives they had taken during the war. Andros ordered a fort built at Pemaquid, the area to be defended by its seven guns. Once there, Andros's commanders negotiated the Treaty of Casco with the Abenakis in April 1678—the treaty that officially ended King Philip's War. Massachusetts at first refused to accept the Andros peace and sent an expedition to Maine on June 28 to fight the Abenaki. When the Puritans lost, with high casualties, they finally accepted the peace negotiated by Andros.[63]

This treaty was later to be criticized by Puritan minister, Cotton Mather, as being too merciful to the Indians. The minister would recall with satisfaction the fate of the southern New England Indians after King Philip's War when there were "Extinguished whole Nations of the Salvages at such a rate, that there can hardly any of them now be found under any Distinction upon the face of the Earth." Mather bitterly regretted that "the Fate of our Northern and Eastern Regions in that War was very different," because, thanks to Andros, "a sort of Peace was patched up." This peace allowed the Maine Indians again to build their population, restock their farms, and sow their fields.[64]

Despite Mather's negative assessment, with Andros's treaty, the long sought peace finally came to New England. Surviving southern New England Indians who managed to make their way to New York were fortunate, as were those who fled to Canada. The French also gained since they were able to make good use of disgruntled New England Indians and their descendants in future wars against the English. New England tribes in Plymouth, Connecticut, and Massachusetts had been thoroughly destroyed as had those in Rhode Island, despite its largely Quaker pacifist population and that colony's commitment to dealing fairly with the Indians.[65]

As Edmund Andros astutely observed in 1678, "the advantages" gained by King Philip's War "were none, the disadvantages very greate and like to be more, even in the loss of said Indians."[66] Not only were the southern New England Indians eliminated as a threat—Indians that might well have fought as English allies in future imperial wars—but the northern Indians were alienated by Puritan perfidy and cruelty. King Philip's War, which may have been fomented deliberately by the Puritans to gain land, was almost as devastating for them as it was for the Indians. Little or nothing had been gained by any of the participants. In fact, in terms of casualties, it was the costliest war in proportion to population ever fought by Americans. Crops had not been planted, fishermen had not put out to sea, and trade was depressed. In Massachusetts alone, the war debt of £150,000 resulted in a dramatic increase in taxes.[67] A majority of Massachusetts's towns were burnt to the ground, and few, if any, land gains were made.

Additionally, the turmoil in New England had caused the king to look more closely at the governance of the continually defiant Puritan dominated New England colonies. Edward Randolph had visited Massachusetts in the midst of King Philip's War to observe conditions there. His report was so negative that the king and Privy Council felt compelled to take action. An order was issued to Massachusetts to send agents to London to answer to the charges brought by Randolph.[68] On 16 May 1678, the attorney general recommended that the Massachusetts Bay Colony charter should be voided. The Lords of Trade and Plantation agreed that *quo warranto* proceedings would be initiated.

Massachusetts stood in stark contrast to New York as far as

Indian relations were concerned. Due to the efforts of its governor, Edmund Andros, the relationship of New York to the powerful Iroquois confederation and other Indians within the duke's territory was excellent. The governor had extended that friendship to Indians in neighboring colonies. Not only New York, but New England had benefited, first from Iroquois help against enemy Indians and then by inclusion in the Covenant Chain, forged at the behest of the governor-general, Edmund Andros.

4

The Iroquois and the Governor: The Covenant Chain, 1675–1678

Part 2: Bacon's Rebellion

> The Governor Genll and we are One, and One heart and One head, for the Covenant that is betwixt the Governor Genll and us is Inviolable yea so strong that if the very thunder should breake upon the Covenant Chain it would not breake it asunder.
>
> —Mohawk speaker, Albany[1]

THE WORDS OF THE MOHAWK SPEAKER EMPHASIZED THE CLOSE AND symbiotic relationship that existed between the Five Nations of the Iroquois and the governor-general of New York as a result of the Covenant Chain. The relationship was particularly close because Andros fully realized it was preferable to have Indians as allies and trading partners than to engage them in futile and costly wars. As the Iroquois sphere of influence had grown, he recognized that the Iroquois empire might better serve the interests of England if it were united with all the North American English colonies. The Covenant Chain agreement that had been extended to New England in the spring of 1677 would, in the summer of that same year, include the English provinces in the Chesapeake. The agreement was an important step in further binding the Five Nations to the English.

The expansion of the Iroquois empire inadvertently led to a major Indian war in the Chesapeake, the immediate cause being the pressure brought by white settlement and Iroquois encroachment on the territory of the southern Indians.[2] The war that ensued pitted the Senecas against the Susquehannas and the colony of Maryland. This war, together with King Philip's War in the north, raised the fears of Edmund Andros and other colonial governors of a panIndian uprising whose purpose might be to cast the English into the sea. The Seneca-Susquehanna war also sparked an Indian war in Virginia that quickly turned into a civil war and then a revolt against crown authority, named after its leader, Nathaniel Bacon.

The chain of events began in 1663, when the Senecas sent eight hundred men to attack the Susquehannas, who were raiding Seneca trading routes. In retaliation, and to eliminate competition in the fur trade, the Senecas were determined to eradicate the Susquehannas, who, in 1661, had allied with Maryland. The Susquehannas' territory bordered the river that bears their name in present day Pennsylvania. Their total population, severely depleted by illness and warfare, was only about two to three thousand. When the Seneca attacks began, Maryland, in 1664, seeking to defend its ally, declared war on the Senecas.[3]

The Susquehanna and Maryland war against the Senecas was bitter and on-going, but in 1674, Maryland, anxious to end the hostilities, forged a treaty with the Senecas, leaving the Susquehannas to fight on their own. The Senecas then came south to attack both the Susquehannas and English frontier settlers. In 1675, when Maryland tried to stop the Senecas' incursions, Maryland authorities urged the Susquehannas to move out of Pennsylvania and away from the Senecas. The Susquehannas agreed and moved en masse. In February 1675, the tribe arrived at St. Mary's, then the capital city of Maryland, demanding to know the location of their new territory. The government finally assigned them land just to the south of present day Washington, D. C., bringing the Susquehannas close to Virginia and its burgeoning population.[4]

By 1675, the Susquehannas, now deprived of Maryland support, were willing to end hostilities with the Senecas. The Mohawks also wanted the Senecas to make peace and informed Andros in April 1675 that they were ready to repatriate seventeen Susquehanna captives to their own tribe. The Mohawks were anxious to maintain their ties to New York, and Andros was equally committed to preserving their loyalty. He asked the Albany commissaries to inform the Mohawks "that if they been not wanting themselves, I shall not on my part, in continuance of the friendship."[5]

Andros was very much aware of the unsettled relations between the Senecas and the Susquehannas and how those relations had affected white settlement in the Delaware River area. In the spring of 1675, he was informed by Captain Edmund Cantwell of the murder of a Dr. Rhodes and his servant by an Indian. Despite Andros's order to Cantwell to arrest the Indian who was responsible, the tribes refused to turn over the murderer. Instead, they complained that an Indian had drunk himself to death at a tavern owned by James Sandyman (or Sandyland) near the Raritan River, while another Indian died after English colonists broke his ribs. Andros acknowledged that these deaths might well be the "cause of their present actings."[6]

Andros knew that fear of Indian attack was rampant in the area. Cantwell informed Andros that two colonists had been killed on April 8 near New Jersey's Millstone River. In response, Andros reassured Cantwell that peace could well be at hand because on April 20 three sachems and about twenty tribal members of the Delaware (Lenni Lenape) nation visited the governor at Fort James. They "did not onely conclude a peace," but, in addition, promised to shun "our [Indian] enemyes." To appease the Indians, Andros urged Cantwell to bring to trial the tavern owner responsible for beating the Indian to death. Aware of Indian unrest and colonial fears, he ordered Cantwell to "let there be as little noise or talke of the Indyan concernes in yor parts as may be."[7] Andros preferred friendly persuasion but was not averse to a show of strength against Indians if all else failed. On hearing that the Delaware Indians who murdered the two settlers were rumored to be in league with the Esopus (New York) Indians, Andros had Secretary Matthias Nicolls inform Delaware authorities that if this proved to be true, he would "be obliged to use force to bring them to Reason."[8]

Indian unrest made all settlers in nearby colonies anxious. Cantwell's letters conveyed to Andros "how much you are alarmed in yor parts, and persuaded of the Indyans Intention to do mischiefe." Much of the mounting hysteria was caused by false or exaggerated reports of Indian attacks. In one instance, after Andros had received word that Indians murdered two messengers in New Jersey, he told Cantwell the men were safe and had been with him on the very day they were supposed to have been killed.[9]

Since the very survival and ultimate prosperity of the duke's territory in that area depended in large part on maintaining good relations with the Delaware Indians, Andros was determined to meet with tribal sachems when he went there in the spring of 1675, intending to assure them he meant to bring justice to all. Shortly after his arrival in Delaware, Andros called a meeting with four sachems, including sachem Renowewan, on 13 May 1675 at New Castle. In his opening speech, Andros asked for the help of the Indians and expressed his desire "to be kind, to those that will live quietly and well." In response to colonists' complaints that Indians had killed or injured their livestock, Andros asked the Indians to desist.[10] When the governor concluded, Renowewan rose and began to pace the room while he considered Andros's speech. Then, picking up "a band of sewant [wampum] hee measured it from his neck to the length downward & said his heart should bee so long & so great to the Gov." With that, he took the "belt of wampum, throwing it at the Gov. feet," an action that must have caused some slight apprehension on the part of the governor. Renowewan then gave Andros another belt of wampum and in return Andros gave each of the four assembled sachems a coat and a lapcloth, concluding the traditional exchange of presents.[11]

Always respectful and polite to Indians, Andros enjoyed their esteem in return. Schooled at court and raised among the royal princes, this courtesy was innate in Andros. Realizing that Indians who were treated courteously were less likely to bring death and destruction to English colonists, he continually urged his subordinates to be fair and just in their dealings with Indians. Renowewan was recognized by Andros as being an influential sachem. Andros instructed Cantwell to "be just to them on all occasions and kinde to Renowickam in particular."[12] Cantwell, reflecting his superior's concern that the Indians be treated fairly, was aware of the negative consequences of mistreatment. He noted to Andros the actions of fur trader Peter Smith, who had insulted the "imperor of those indyans." Cantwell observed that "such fellows might be ye occasion of shedding much blood, who coms there for one month or two and care not what happens to ye people when they are gon."[13]

To illustrate to the Indians his determination to be fair and impartial to all, Andros convened a general court in Delaware to deal with the problem of the drunken Indian who died after being ejected from the tavern by the owner, Sandyman. Since tavern owners were held liable if an Indian became drunk, Sandyman was tried for manslaughter. Several Indians were invited by Andros to attend the trial and to testify, but despite their testimony, Sandyman was found not guilty by the sympathetic all-white jury.[14] Furious at Sandyman's acquittal, Andros had him retried on May 17 on some unspecified but "scandalous businesse of James Sandyland & Laurens Hulst," leaving the nature of the scandal to the individual imagination. For this crime, Sandyman and Hulst were found guilty and fined three hundred and two hundred guilders respectively. In addition, Sandyman was relieved of his commission as militia captain.[15]

Andros's efforts to seek justice for Indians were prompted both by a sense of fairness and by his determination to preserve peace throughout the duke's province. Before he left Delaware for New York, he had negotiated treaties with three southern Indian tribes. Nevertheless, unrest continued in nearby colonies. In Virginia in July 1675, Doeg Indians, feeling pressure from other Indian tribes and from increased white settlement, stole some hogs and fled to Maryland. The Virginia militia pursued the Doegs onto Maryland's soil. The Virginians killed all Indians they found, including the Susquehannas, who had long been allied with the English. Their actions brought death and destruction to English settlers in the Virginia and Maryland backcountries when the Susquehannas attacked to avenge the murders. Among those killed was "Mr. Bacon's Overseer . . . and One of his Servants, whose Bloud Hee Vowed to Revenge if possible."[16]

In contrast, Andros's relations with the middle Atlantic Indians remained good. In September 1675, he was visited at Fort James by a delegation of New Jersey Indians. Telling them about King Philip's War in New England, he assured them that affairs were "well & quiet" in the duke's colony. The Indians left happily with Andros's promise that he would visit them on his next trip to Delaware.[17] In October 1675, Andros wrote to Lieutenant Governor Thomas Notley in Maryland to inform him that he had obtained a promise from the Mohawks and the Senecas not to hurt white settlers "in yor parts Southward, in their Warrs with the *Susquehanna's*." Andros reported that the Mohawks favored peace with the Susquehannas, but he found "the *Sinneques* wholly adverse to it; desiring their [the Susquehannas'] Extirpacon." Andros urged the Baltimore governor to send the Susquehanna chiefs to him "so I may Order Matters accordingly."[18]

Maryland officials did not accept Andros's offer to negotiate a treaty. In December 1675, Andros wrote again to Notley to express his sorrow that the Susquehannas were involved in Maryland's war, having "had the repute of being perfect friends to the Christians." Andros noted, with more than a touch of pride, that the only Indians who remained true to the English were the Iroquois, particularly "the Maques, and by their meanes the Senneke." The Mohawks and the Senecas, being the two most powerful tribes, influenced the "younger brothers," the Caiugas and the Oneidas, and "the keepers of the council fire," the Onondagas.[19]

The Iroquois may have remained friendly to Andros's government, but not to the Susquehannas or the Chesapeake colonists. The Susquehannas were now besieged from the north by the Iroquois and from the south by the Virginia and Maryland colonists. The Indian war accelerated after Virginia planter, Nathaniel Bacon, still angry over the murder of his overseer, accepted the leadership of a vigilante group of backwoodsmen, united in their desire to kill any Indian they saw, whether friend or foe. The action turned into a civil war when Virginia governor, Sir William Berkeley, refused to legitimize Bacon's vigilantism by giving him an official military commission. Virginia was split by the war between those who supported the governor and those who supported Bacon. The civil war turned into a rebellion after Bacon denounced the governor as a traitor, called for a colonial union and free trade, and demanded that his followers resist any force sent from England to quell them. The culmination of the war came in September 1676 when the rebel forces seized and burnt Jamestown, Virginia's capital city, to prevent its recapture by the governor's forces. Bacon died the next month, but the rebellion continued under the leadership of Bacon's second in command, Lawrence Ingram.[20]

In London, Charles II perceived correctly that this backwoods rebellion was not only a threat to the security of his crown, but also would wipe out his revenue from the highly profitable Chesapeake tobacco trade. The king, determined to put down Bacon's Rebellion as swiftly as possible, ordered an armed force of 1,300 men to be raised promptly and dispatched to Virginia. Once there, Governor Berkeley was to be advised that he was recalled to England. A three-man commission was dispatched to Virginia consisting of Colonel Herbert Jeffreys, who had orders to oust Berkeley and govern in his stead as lieutenant governor. Also on the commission were Sir John Berry and Colonel Francis Moryson. The commissioners were charged with quelling the rebels and restoring order to Virginia. The ships carrying the commissioners and troops were already underway to North America by 30 November 1676, when the duke's secretary warned Andros not to admit any of Bacon's accomplices into New York. By the time the fleet arrived in Virginia early in 1677, Berkeley had put down the rebellion and had launched his own personal reign of terror as he sought bloody revenge on his enemies. The commissioners were appalled at Berkeley's actions, particularly when the governor, reluctant to give up the power he had held so long, refused to leave Virginia despite the king's order to do so. Finally, the commissioners, on 29 May 1677, forcibly put Berkeley aboard a ship bound for England.[21]

Civil war and rebellion in Virginia were played against the backdrop of an ongoing Indian war. The Senecas' raids on the Susquehannas and other southern tribes were also devastating to the colonists. Some settlers in the Chesapeake claimed the Senecas, accompanied by several French men dressed as Indians, robbed Maryland and Virginia plantations and killed livestock. In Maryland, the Senecas even stole the colony's public records for a second time. Shortly after the first theft, Governor-General Andros had managed to persuade the Iroquois to turn the records over to him, and he returned them to Maryland officials. Despite the long-standing enmity between the Susquehannas and Senecas, the Chesapeake colonists feared they might unite against the English, much as the northern colonists feared an Iroquois-Algonquin union. Governor Andros was aware of this possibility and moved quickly to keep the Iroquois loyal to him. He then tried to make peace between them and the Chesapeake colonies, as well as with the Susquehannas.[22]

In June 1676, the Susquehannas, weary of war and with their manpower seriously depleted, agreed to send two sachems to meet Andros in New York City. When the men described their suffering during the war with the Chesapeake colonies, Andros told them "hee is sorry from his heart at their Troubles, and would willingly help them out." Andros offered them protection in New York from Virginia and Maryland colonists. The Susquehannas were free to "goe and live with" the Mohawks in the east, as far away from the western Senecas as possible. The Mohawks had already promised the Susquehannas safety and protection and looked on them as "their brothers & children." Andros also offered to negotiate a peace between the Susquehannas and their enemies, the Virginians, the Marylanders, and the Senecas.[23] The Susquehanna chiefs, impressed with the offer of asylum, promised to consider it but first asked permission to return "to their folkes," since they could not make the decision by themselves. Andros agreed. The offer was enthusiastically received by the tribe and also by the Delawares, with whom the Susquehannas had first taken shelter. Many members from both tribes prepared to flee to New York, as did other embattled and now landless southern Indians, escaping the ravages of war and continuing English frontier expansion.[24]

Maryland did not want the Delawares or the Susquehannas either to ally with the Five Nations or move to New York. The

Iroquois were under New York's control. Such a union would bring an Iroquois presence (that is New York, the governor, and the duke) to the Delaware region and further confirm the claim of the duke of York to land coveted by the Maryland proprietary party. Hence, Maryland moved to make its own separate peace with the Susquehannas in a vain attempt to reestablish their control of the Delaware region. Maryland authorities were ready to resort to arms to detain the Susquehannas and other Indians in Maryland, reasoning that keeping allied Indians in the area would secure Maryland's hold on the Susquehanna and Delaware river valleys.[25]

Despite Maryland's protests, many of the Susquehannas moved north to join the Mohawks. By August 1676, Maryland Lieutenant Governor Notley complained that the Susquehannas had fled and were "at Ease and out of our reach."[26] Andros sent Captain John Collier, the newly commissioned commander of Delaware, to privately tell the Susquehannas to continue their flight to the Mohawks in New York where they would be under the governor's protection.[27] Many Susquehannas were slow to avail themselves of the Mohawks' offer of protection, but others left quickly when, in September 1676, Andros warned that the Senecas would attack. In December 1676, the Senecas launched devastating attacks against the remaining Susquehannas. In March 1677, the Iroquois met with the Delaware sachems and Andros's representative, Captain Collier, to decide where the few surviving, defeated, and disheartened Susquehanna survivors could go.[28] The next month, Andros told the Susquehannas that if they promised "to leave off ye Warre," they were free to live in the duke's territory as long as it was not "in ye South [Delaware] River it being not safe for them."[29]

In May 1677, Andros was informed that Maryland authorities, still fighting the Senecas, were unhappy that the Susquehannas had submitted to the Iroquois. They reluctantly accepted Andros's offer to mediate peace between them and the Five Nations. Just as he had with New England, Andros insisted the treaty negotiations with the Iroquois take place in New York and under his direction. Maryland's delegate was Colonel Henry Coursey, instructed by Maryland "to treat with and Conclude a firm peace with the said Susquesahannahs, Cinnigos [Senecas] or any other Indians." Armed with a formal set of instructions that outlined Maryland's objectives in the treaty talks, Coursey was to travel to New York City, since the Iroquois lived "within the Territory of his said Royll Highness." Once there, he was to "treat with Edmond Andross Esqre Seigneur of Sansmarer and Governr Genll under his Royall Highness James Duke of Yorke and Albany." Coursey was to seek permission from Andros to travel to Albany "and to request his assistance in the procuring of a firme peace" with the Indians. Since Marylanders knew it was customary to give the Iroquois presents at the beginning of a conference, Coursey was told to buy appropriate gifts.[30]

Coursey's first stop was New Castle, where he was ordered by Notley to obtain information from Captain Collier as to the whereabouts of the Susquehannas. Coursey was dismayed on his arrival to find that Collier had told Andros that Marylanders were determined they "would make warr or peace att their owne pleasure and this hath incensed Governor Androes." Lieutenant Governor Notley claimed he was misinterpreted and misrepresented.[31]

The Marylanders also asked Coursey to convey to Andros their lingering sense of outrage at their ongoing war with the Susquehannas. Apparently, according to the peace treaty negotiated in 1674, the Susquehannas "were obliged to give us Twenty daies warning of their Intentions to warr" on them. Marylanders made no mention of their own or of the Virginians' culpability in initiating the war. They ignored the fact that colonists had killed innocent Indians. They did not mention the murder by the English of five Susquehanna chiefs who came out to parlay under a flag of truce. Coursey was also instructed to make provisions for Maryland's Indian allies, the Piscataways. The concern of Maryland officials was not only for the safety of the Piscataways and other allied Indian tribes, but also their realization that Maryland colonists would "never [be] safe from the Northern Indians as long as they have any pretence of warr with our ffriend Indians."[32]

Andros was indeed annoyed at Maryland's refusal of his assistance. To avert his anger, Coursey, who arrived in New York on June 6 and acting on the instructions of the Maryland government, was "to make a present of one hundred pounds Sterl" to Andros "as a token of his Lordshipps thankfulness for his care and kindness shewn to this Province." This may have been an attempt to buy Andros off, for Maryland had already started granting land in Delaware that the duke considered his. Since the previous winter, Andros had been hearing reports from Delaware residents of Lord Baltimore's determination "to Heave this pleats agin." By early June 1677, Baltimore had put his plans into action and begun surveying "Severall thousand acres the

which Land Lyeing within the Limitts of these governmt." Baltimore continued to grant land in Delaware, between 1670 and
1682, awarding 19,000 acres there to forty-five people.[33]

Whether the bribe was either accepted or rejected by Andros
(no evidence exists), Coursey went on to discuss with Andros the
terms he would present to the Iroquois. Andros was appalled. The
Maryland government placed all blame for the war between them
and the Iroquois on the Susquehannas, who had attacked Maryland settlements and then blamed the attacks on the Senecas,
"thereby to engage us in their quarrel with you." The Marylanders "fell upon them [the Susquehannas], and have now so near
destroyed them that they are forced to seek shelter under y[o]u
who were before their Enemies." Such an assertion would surely
have amazed the Senecas, who were largely responsible for the
defeat of the Susquehannas. In addition, the Marylanders
demanded that any Susquehannas "as shall come under yo[u]r
protection may by y[o]u be obliged not to do any violence or
wrong to any Xian inhabiting either in Maryland or Virginia, or
to any Pascattaway Indian, or other Indian in amity with the
Christians of Maryland or Virginia." If there were any incidents
involving the Susquehannas "living under the protection of you
the said Cinnigos, or by any of yor own Nation, You shall deliver
them up to us, or to the Honble Governr Genll of New Yorke, if
Wee desire it to be proceeded against, according to his demeritts,
and the nature of his offence."[34] This last statement was the
equivalent of New England demanding the return of enemy Indians or the right to negotiate directly with the Iroquois. Andros
refused to permit this invasion of the duke's prerogative by Maryland, just as he had refused demands from New England. Andros
instructed Coursey on how to proceed and arranged a meeting
between him and the Iroquois sachems.[35]

Despite requests from the Iroquois to come to Albany in July,
Andros was reluctant to go until August, probably because he had
just returned from Albany, where he had supervised treaty talks
between the Iroquois and New England representatives.[36]
Coursey and his party sailed up the Hudson River laden with
appropriate gifts for the Iroquois, meetings with them beginning
in July.[37] Coursey, acknowledging the Iroquois were "of this government [New York], & faithfull & Constant friends to ye
English," admitted past grievances on the part of both the Iroquois and Marylanders but hoped they would be "buryed & forgott."[38] The final version of the propositions presented by
Coursey to the Iroquois was an abbreviated document that was

significantly different from the earlier version Coursey showed
Andros. Gone were all attempts to place blame for the war on the
treachery of the Susquehannas and all mention of the Marylanders' single handed victory. Gone, too, were demands that any err-
ing Indian be returned to Maryland for punishment. What
remained in the document Coursey was permitted to offer the
Iroquois was a simple promise "that all what is past be buried
and forgott." A request (not a demand) was made that they would
not in "the future injure any of our persons," or the persons of
Indians allied with Maryland. If this was done, Coursey, on behalf
of Maryland, promised that "we shall alwaies esteem and treat
you as our good neighbours and friends."[39]

The document was acceptable to the Iroquois but they nevertheless insisted any future meetings would be held in Albany. The
Mohawk speaker noted "that the Governor Genll hath been
pleased to destinate and appoint this place to speake with all
Nations in peace, finding this a fitt place for the same, for which
we doe returne his Honor hearty thanks, especially that his
Honor hath been pleased to grant you the priviledge for to speake
with us here." The Mohawk speaker went on to delineate the particularly close relationship between the Mohawks and the governor. The "Governor Genll and we are One," he said, "and One
heart and One head, for the Covenant that is betwixt the Governor Genll and us is Inviolable yea so strong that if the very thun-
der should breake upon the Covenant Chain it would not breake
it asunder." The Iroquois promised that if the Marylanders did
no further hurt to them or their dependent Indians "living
w[i]t[h] us," the Mohawks were prepared to "Esteem and treat
you as our good Neighboures, and friendes." The Onondagas also
promised not to harm the Marylanders. The Oneidas informed
Coursey that twenty of their braves had gone to fight Maryland
Indians. They asked that "if they doe any harm that it may be
excused this tym" because the braves were ignorant of the peace
talks. Each of the Five Nations noted that although there had
been "some discontents or Injuries . . . between us hertofore,"
they were prepared to let the "past, be buryed & forgott." The
Covenant Chain was to be extended to the English in the Chesapeake, said Garacontie, the Onondaga speaker. "We doe make
now an Absolute Covenant of Peace, wch we shall bind with a
Chain," he promised. The Mohawks declared they wanted peace
with Maryland and "wee desyr yt ye matter may be moderat &
composed betwixt us, and wee do Ingage for o[u]r parts to give

Satisfacn to you for any Eveill that o[u]r Indians might happen to doe." With that, Coursey and the Iroquois signed a peace treaty.[40]

The creation of the Covenant Chain, which had begun with the signing of the alliance with the New Englanders the previous spring, was completed on 21 July 1677 with the signing of a pact with the Maryland representative. Andros was in personal attendance as the talks reached their conclusion in early August.[41] For England and its American colonies, the agreement has been termed "the most important diplomatic event in North American history," since the Covenant Chain "ultimately dictated the victory of English language, culture, religion, and economy." For the Iroquois, the Covenant Chain gave them "such a commanding position" that even today they are "the most influential Native Americans east of the Great Plains."[42] For the French it was also significant, for as Lewis Henry Morgan observed, "To this Indian League, France must chiefly ascribe the final overthrow of her magnificent schemes of colonization in the northern part of America."[43]

The Covenant Chain, which proved "integral to the growth and shaping of modern American society as a whole," provided "an example of accommodation and cooperation between peoples of different ethnicity, different cultures, and different social and political structures." It was a model which the world might be wise to emulate today, since "the sharing of spaces among different ethnic groups" remains a problem. There is truth in these assessments. England did persevere over the French because of this alliance, the Chain guaranteeing the survival of the Iroquois and their commitment to the English. In an age when genocide was the rule, with whites exterminating entire tribes who stood in their way, the Covenant Chain guaranteed Iroquois and English could work together in peace toward a common goal. There were betrayals, but despite this, the friendship persisted even if the alliance was brought about because of mutually practical concerns.[44]

The immediate impact of the Covenant Chain on eastern Indians was considerable. Hundreds, and perhaps thousands, of Indians, dislocated by war in New England, the Delaware region, and the Chesapeake, or by advancing white settlement, were forced to relocate. Some moved to what is now western Pennsylvania, but many others sought refuge along the Hudson River in New York or in the Susquehanna and Delaware river valleys. The Iroquois claimed the Susquehanna River territory as a result of conquest, placing it under New York's hegemony in 1679. The Chesapeake

Indians who settled there were under the control of the Iroquois, who were now firmly allied with the English. The Iroquois welcomed the southern tribes into the Susquehanna Valley, particularly since their presence temporarily protected the Iroquois from further pressures by white settlement.[45]

The result of the Covenant Chain on relations between the Iroquois and the Chesapeake colonists was less dramatic. Those Indians who had already left New York when Coursey arrived did not know of the treaty and continued their raids on Maryland and Virginia frontier settlements and on Maryland Indians. Many colonists were killed or taken prisoner, while marauding Indians attacked backcountry settlements in the Chesapeake. Hence, despite the Covenant Chain agreement, relationships between the Iroquois and the Chesapeake colonists remained unsettled for several years.[46]

Andros, however, had achieved a significant victory, not only in securing the Covenant Chain agreement but also in protecting the duke's claims to Delaware. He had stopped Maryland from invading the sovereignty of New York and had limited the expansionist tendencies of Lord Baltimore, just as he had of the New England Puritans. It is a small wonder that Baltimore despised Andros, as is evident from his comment to colonial official William Blathwayt in 1682. Baltimore noted that, "When I was last in England I met with Sir Edmund Andros at St James,' and he was very apprehensive least I should have made some complaint to His Royal Highness against him, for the great obstruction he had given Colonel Coursey in his negotiation at Fort Albany, and had he not made great asseverations of his future readiness to serve Maryland whenever we should have occasion to renew those same (by his meanes) articles, that had been made by the said Coursey, I had certainly complained to his Highness of him." The duke was fully aware that Andros had hindered Baltimore's determination to invade New York's sovereignty, but Andros retained the duke's territory—at least for a time—and preserved the peace there.[47]

While in Albany in August 1677, Andros received word from the duke that his request to return to England to oversee his personal business was approved. The duke suggested that Andros sail at the end of the summer, "soe as having the winter to yourselfe, you may be ready to returne to your government with the first ships that goe hence in ye spring."[48] The duke was delighted, as well he might be, that Andros had kept New York quiet, despite "the late troubles yt have beene in yor neighborhood." The duke's secretary, Werden, urged Andros to keep the "people in due obedience and subjection, and all inclinations towards mutiny severely supprest."[49]

Andros kept the news of his impending departure a secret until the October meeting of the Assize Court. He then asked the opinion of his council as to the wisdom of his leaving the colony at that time. The council decided that since "all was in peace and Countrey as well settled and quiett as could bee expected," the governor could safely leave.[50]

Andros sailed for England on 16 November 1677, leaving Captain Anthony Brockholes in charge of the province and his wife in charge of his personal affairs. Andros did indeed leave New York in peace—a peace that was sustained because of his policy of fair treatment toward the Indians.[51] Edmund Andros put his nearly three years in New York to good advantage for the duke. He avoided war and rebellion; he reasserted the duke's authority in West New Jersey; secured Delaware, Maine, Martha's Vineyard, and Nantucket for the duke; and, by offering sanctuary to hundreds of New England, Delaware, and Chesapeake Indians, increased New York's manpower. He spurred New York's economy, heightened its defenses, improved its fortifications, and reapplied the Duke's Laws. He also blocked Massachusetts expansion, and, to end bloody wars, negotiated agreements between Massachusetts and the Maine Indians, the Puritans and the Iroquois, the Susquehannas and the Iroquois, and Maryland and the Iroquois.

Above all, Andros had made through the Covenant Chain, a long lasting alliance with the Five Nations, the most powerful group of Indian tribes in North America. He had also made separate alliances with other tribes in Maine, New York, New Jersey, and Delaware. Andros could not have realized the lasting importance of the Covenant Chain in 1677. Like most administrators, he had simply reacted to the situation as it developed, in this case the situation being the rapid expansion of Iroquois hegemony. Andros's instincts told him it was better to befriend the Iroquois and win them as allies than to alienate them and create enemies. These Iroquois allies, recognizing they owed allegiance to the English monarch, also controlled a vast territory over which the English could claim ultimate control. The duke and the king had good reason to be well pleased with the services of Edmund Andros.

5

Andros and Imperial Machinations, 1678–1680

Of these the false Achitophel was first,
A name to all succeeding ages curst:
For close designs and crooked counsels fit;
Sagacious, bold, and turbulent of wit.
                    —John Dryden, "Absalom and Achitophel"[1]

THE "ACHITOPHEL" DESPISED BY DRYDEN, WAS ANTHONY ASHLEY-Cooper, earl of Shaftesbury, who, by the late 1670s, was the leader of the Whig, or opposition, party in England. Shaftesbury and his followers did not want Charles's brother James to succeed as king. As the Whigs worked to weaken the duke's influence in England, their machinations directly affected Andros. Until the effects of Shaftesbury's "sagacious, bold, and turbulent" efforts were felt in the colonies, Andros continued in his imperial assignment to take control of the government of East New Jersey, the proprietary colony owned by his distant relatives, the Carterets.

Andros may have gauged the growing hostility to the duke when he returned to London early in 1678 to find a city in political turmoil. He arrived just a bit too late to see his childhood acquaintance, William of Orange, nephew to the king and duke of York. William, as chief stadtholder of the Netherlands had been involved in a long and costly war with the French. He was in London briefly to discuss peace negotiations with his uncles, since it was apparent by the fall of 1677 that the Netherlands was defeated. England had already signed a peace treaty with the Netherlands in 1674 to end the Third Anglo-Dutch War. Prince William was also in London to marry James's eldest daughter, Mary. Charles favored the match because he believed it would illustrate that he was not pro-French.[2]

James's wife, Mary of Modena, gave birth on 7 November 1677 to a son, who died on December 12 of small pox, shortly before

Anthony Ashley-Cooper, first earl of Shaftesbury (1621–1683). During the Civil Wars, Shaftesbury fought first for the king and then for parliament. Pardoned at the Restoration, Ashley-Cooper was named earl of Shaftesbury and lord chancellor in 1672. Shaftesbury lost royal favor when he opposed the succession to the throne of the king's brother, James, duke of York, the future James II. Shaftesbury fled to the Netherlands in 1682. Portrait after John Greenhill, courtesy of the National Portrait Gallery, London.

Andros's arrival. James was distraught over the death. Added to his grief were ever increasing criticisms of him and the king from Shaftesbury and his followers in the opposition party. The Whigs, presumably named for Scottish bandits, believed in a limited monarchy and supported parliamentary power. Whigs, representing the new, modern capitalist order, were particularly fearful that Catholic James would outlive his brother and inherit the throne. Some Whigs, but not necessarily Shaftesbury, favored as the king's heir either Charles's Protestant niece, Mary, or his illegitimate feckless, charming, undisciplined eldest son, James, duke of Monmouth, widely popular and Protestant.[3]

The king, while feared and resented by Whigs, did not lack supporters even though he and his court were growing increasingly isolated from the people he ruled. The king's close associates formed a "court" party that became known as the Tories, believers in the divine right of kings. Tories represented the old, traditional, land owning wealthy, who scorned trade and capitalism. Obvious exceptions existed to these partisan generalities. Andros, for instance, was a royalist, yet had no compunction against associating with merchants or engaging in trade himself.[4]

While in London, Andros again stayed at the Drury Lane house of the earl of Craven. In England, primarily to attend to his private affairs, Andros also tended to business, informing the Privy Council committee of trade about conditions in America. He outlined his dealings with New York's Indians, his efforts to protect and secure the duke's territory, his attempts to help Connecticut early in King Philip's War, and his rebuff by the Puritans there. Andros discussed his plans for New York's defense during the war and his successful efforts to conclude alliances among the belligerents.[5]

On April 8, the Privy Council committee asked to speak with Edmund Andros about New England. The attorney and solicitor generals wanted to determine if Massachusetts's charter was still legal, since Charles I had initiated *quo warranto* proceedings against the charter several years before. The feeling among members of the Privy Council was that even if the charter was legal, Massachusetts had forfeited it because of misadministration.[6] The committee's questions ranged from requests for population figures to details about fortifications. Andros answered to the best of his ability their inquiries about the number of ships trading in each colony, whether the Navigation Acts were observed, and what were the causes of King Philip's War.

In response to the question about the cause of King Philip's

War, Andros replied that New England officials had not made him acquainted with the "originall cause" of the war but noted that the New England colonies had spurned his offer of "supplyes & assistances." As far as the New England colonies observing the Navigation Acts, he admitted he had no direct knowledge of the situation, but added, it "is generally beleeved not to be observed in ye Collonyes as they ought, there being noe Custome houses." On April 18, Andros gave the Council an account of the assistance New York had given to New England during the war, including his role in urging the Mohawks to attack Philip and his braves, help given despite the fact that the Puritans had earlier spurned his offers of assistance. When Philip neared Albany, "wee however supplyed o[u]r Indyans with ammunicon, armes & all they wanted . . . & though refused by o[u]r neighbours the latter end of ffebruary fell upon killed & took severall & drove sd Phillip & other Indians with him quite away." It was through his efforts, he said, that the New England Indians were defeated.[7]

While Andros was still in London, Jacob Milborne, a few English merchants, and some malcontents, including Christopher Billop, William Pinhorne, and Edmund Tudor, brought charges against him for obstructing English trade in Albany, persecuting English factors, and giving special trading privileges to his Dutch friends, particularly Frederick Philipse and Stephen van Cortland. English merchants charged that Andros ignored the Navigation Acts and, to the indignation of New York's English inhabitants, had installed a Dutch whipping post in place of the English type. The duke, obviously satisfied with Andros's performance in New York, was far from being swayed by the complaints or from condemning Andros's actions. Instead he urged Andros to return quickly to his post. To further show the royal brothers' approval of Andros, the king granted him a knighthood.[8]

Sir Edmund sailed for New York on the *Blossom* on 27 May 1678, accompanied by the Reverend Charles Wolley and several English merchants and factors intent on establishing markets in New York. The merchants were to be successful, at least in terms of the number of English merchant ships that began trading between London and New York. In 1676, there was only one English ship and none in 1677, while there were to be five in 1678 and four in both 1679 and 1680.[9]

On his arrival in New York after a nine week passage, Andros "found things quiet, tho' much allarmed with rumours of [Indian] war." Maryland authorities complained of "mischiefs done by strange Indians," probably the Senecas, on colonists in the Virginia and Maryland backcountries. Andros found such reports difficult to believe, the "said Seneques as well as Maquas, having been always very good and faithfull to this Government and kind to all Christians." This "kindness" did not extend to New England Indians. Soon after his arrival, Andros learned that there had been trouble during the summer in Massachusetts, where Mohawk warriors had attacked a band of Natick Indians six miles from Sudbury and taken twenty-two prisoners, most of whom were women. In late June, Captain Silvester Salisbury, commander at Fort Albany, was startled to see sixty Mohawks converge on the fort with their prisoners. The Mohawks assured Salisbury they would not harm the Naticks, who Salisbury was convinced were Christian "Praying Indians" and under Massachusetts's protection. Salisbury informed acting New York Governor Brockholes of the problem and the latter told him to get the Mohawks to surrender the Naticks to the Mohegans. A worried Salisbury reported to Brockholes that he thought most, if not all, the captives had already been burned to death. Salisbury acknowledged that Brockholes's earlier suggestion to have the Naticks surrendered to the Mohegans was sound but one he could not implement because the Mohawks were "not those sorte of people, yt Deliver up ther prissoners."[10]

Massachusetts authorities were outraged by the capture (they had yet to learn of the horrific murders) and sent Commissioners Samuel Ely and Benjamin Waite to New York to secure the release of the captives. Ely and Waite went to Albany in late July and, taking advantage of Andros's absence and Salisbury's inexperience, convinced the latter they should go directly and alone to the Mohawks' village to meet with the sachems. When Ely and Waite confronted the Mohawks, they were told that the captives had been taken by some overly enthusiastic young braves, "who are like wolves, when they are abroad." They reminded the Puritans that the Mohawks had fought New England's enemies ever since Andros had persuaded them to pursue Philip. The sachems explained that the braves involved in the incident were ignorant of the fact that the Natick captives were converts to Christianity and under Massachusetts's protection. The sachems rejected the representatives' suggestion that the Iroquois go to Hartford or Boston for future meetings. Andros chose Albany as the site for meetings between the Iroquois and the English. The Mohawks, confirming the continued existence of the Covenant Chain, acknowledged that "The Governor Genll & you of N. *England* &

we are one in one triple Allyance with another" and reaffirmed that the pact made the previous year "is as fast firm & Inviolable as ever it was."[11]

Brockholes was appalled when he heard that Salisbury had permitted the New England representatives to negotiate with the Mohawks alone and without supervision, telling Salisbury he should have "putt them off." Brockholes reminded Salisbury that when Pynchon, Richards, and Coursey came as representatives of their colonies of Massachusetts, Connecticut, and Maryland respectively, the meetings with the Iroquois were held with "The Go: being allwayes present, & Managing the discourse on all hands that they might not prove prejudiciall to the Interest of his R.H.s in this Province." Brockholes warned Salisbury that the governor was certain to be angry when he heard of the incident upon his return.[12]

Andros was indeed incensed by the news, particularly after he received two letters from New England officials complaining of the Mohawk action and asking Andros to do all in his power to have the surviving Indian captives returned. Andros responded promptly to the letters but politely refused to intervene since the Puritans had already made a "treaty with the Maquas . . . without my knowledge or notice to any here in my absence." As the Puritans had proceeded without his help, Andros believed it "not adviseable for me to deale with sd Maquas on yor accompte" now. If other details needed to be ironed out, the Puritans should send another representative to talk with the Mohawks. Governor Leete of Connecticut wrote personally to Andros, agreeing to send a representative and again asking that Andros order the Mohawks to return "those poore prayeing Naticke Indian captives." Delivery of the letter was delayed, and when it finally reached Andros in mid-November, he informed Leete that it was much too late in the season for anyone to travel to Albany.[13]

Andros acknowledged to the home government that permitting representatives from other colonies to deal directly with the Iroquois had been a tactical error. As a result, the Iroquois, after negotiating directly with the New Englanders, were now "rude and insolent" in their dealings with all the English. Indian unrest and belligerence would continue as long as each colony "hath or assumes absolute power of peace and Warr, which cannot bee managed by such popular Governments as was evident by the late Indian Wars in New England." Decisions made by "popular" governments would necessarily favor local interests over imperial interests. Only a disinterested party, concerned for the welfare of all the colonies, was in a position to make impartial decisions. Andros was such an imperial official, his broader approach to Indian relations being significantly different from that of colonists who were concerned mainly with their own communities and who treated Indians as foreign enemies. Colonial governments, seeing Indians as alien and enemy, found it necessary to make treaties to ensure peace. Andros did not make treaties with New York's Indians because they were an integral part of that colony, not foreign powers. Because of this view, he could ensure that New York would be free of Indian war.[14]

Andros wrote to Blathwayt that New Englanders had not learned any discretion from King Philip's War as to their land grabbing efforts. Puritans were "as high as ever," he said, claiming "and disposing of Narraganset country," even though it was not theirs. That area was "wholy distinct from and not under any [of] their Colonies and by the King's Commissioners in 1664, called King's Province and put under Rhode Island," where it properly belonged. The ministry agreed, and in 1679 the king informed Rhode Island that he was "pleased to give his Royall determination . . . to confirm the jurisdiction and government of the Narragansett and Niantick countrys unto" Rhode Island.[15]

In November 1678, Colonel Jeffries in Virginia notified Andros that the Iroquois had again attacked Chesapeake settlements and taken prisoners. Andros immediately sent two English agents to visit each Iroquois nation and demand the return of the captives. The men traveled to Mohawk, Oneida, and Onondaga villages and sent Indian messengers to the Caiugas and Senecas before severe winter weather forced them to turn back to Albany. The messengers conveyed to the Iroquois Andros's order that all captives be promptly surrendered to him. The Oneidas did indeed have English captives—two women and four children. They surrendered one woman and two children, keeping the others until Iroquois prisoners held by Chesapeake colonists were returned.[16]

The men found the Iroquois extremely bitter, claiming that the trouble started when eighteen Virginians on horseback attacked thirteen Oneida Indians. The Oneidas returned fire, killing two men and two horses. The Iroquois agreed to surrender whatever prisoners they still held, sending word to Andros of their continuing allegiance to him. The Oneidas addressed Andros as "Father Corlaer," assuring him they were still his "Children," while the Mohawks, who had always enjoyed a particularly close and symbiotic relationship with the English, considered themselves "your Brethren."[17]

On 24 May 1679, the Oneidas, as promised, delivered their prisoners to the commander at Albany, expecting the return of those Iroquois held by the English. When it became apparent that none of the Indian prisoners were to be returned, the Iroquois were irate. Saying the entire fracas was the fault of "the People of Virginia," who sent "their Men so far abroad," the Iroquois added that if they continued to do that, "dangerous Consequences might follow." A warning was also delivered to Andros through the commander at Albany. The sachems observed that "Corlaer governs the whole Land, from New-York to Albany, and from thence to the Sennekas Land; We who are his Subjects shall faithfully keep to the Covenant chain: Let him perform his Promise, as we have perform'd ours, that the Covenant Chain be not broken on his side."[18] They added that "If Corlaer will not hearken to us in this Affair, we shall not hereafter hearken to him in any way."[19] In an effort to resolve the matter, Andros agreed that Virginia representatives Colonel William Kendall and Colonel Southley Littleton could meet with the Iroquois in mid September 1679. The governor was about to depart for Maine, but planned to supervise the meeting upon his return. Andros sailed for Maine with the first favorable wind to establish Pemaquid as the chief place for trade in that area.[20]

While the threat of continued Indian unrest was serious enough for Andros, it was events that began in England even before Andros set foot in New York that had the most dramatic effect on him. They centered around opposition leader Shaftesbury, who, with the judicious use of propaganda, had heightened popular fears of Roman Catholics in general and of the duke of York in particular. The furor began with an sometime-cleric called Titus Oates who, perhaps at the instigation of Shaftesbury, uncovered an extensive but invented Catholic plot to assassinate the king. Althought it was imaginary, the plot was widely believed, heightening anti-Catholic sentiment. James also sought to calm hysterical fears of a Catholic takeover plot by resigning from the king's Privy Council and giving up his seat in the House of Lords.[21]

Despite these gestures, the Whigs would not let the matter rest. Rather, they continued to bombard the country with literature designed to heighten Protestant fears of a Catholic takeover. Fanned by this deliberate propaganda, the Oates plot spread to include several people, who were accused of complicity, in the king's and duke's households. Andros in New York must have felt a bit uneasy when he learned the duke's past secretary, Edward

Coleman, was tried, found guilty of treason, and executed on 3 December 1678. The king's servants were also sacrificed, with the earl of Danby to be held prisoner in the Tower of London for five years. As had been proved during the Civil Wars, monarchs were often powerless to save loyal servants. Both the king and the duke knew the charges against Coleman and others were false but could do nothing to stem the tide of hysteria that engulfed the nation. Indeed, any attempt to do so might have been as fatal to the royal brothers as it had been in 1649 to their father.[22]

In January 1679, the king dissolved the Cavalier Parliament and ordered elections. The elections brought an active and vocal Whig majority to what would be known as the first Exclusion Parliament. This body met in March with the clear purpose in mind to exclude the duke of York from the succession to the throne. A majority of Whigs now favored the succession of James's Protestant daughter, Mary. Just a few days before Parliament met, James, at Charles's strong suggestion, went into voluntary exile. Andros, his patron out of power and unable to protect himself or his servants, was in a precarious position.[23]

Reluctant to leave England, James had a more practical solution for the Whigs. He reminded the king that he "had enough of the army which was not yet disbanded to protect him if he pleased."[24] When Charles refused to use armed force to quell Whig opponents, James left England, going first to visit his daughter and son-in-law at The Hague and then to Brussels. Parliament's attempt to pass the Exclusion Bill failed on its first and two subsequent attempts, but Charles insisted his brother stay out of England.[25] On September 24, the duke and duchess of York went to Edinburgh, where the Scottish people warmly welcomed them. In England, a new Parliament continued to be recalcitrant, trying and failing to pass another Exclusion Bill. The king prorogued it and did not call another Parliament for a year.[26]

All these events in England had a dramatic impact on Edmund Andros's personal and public life. In the fall of 1679, Andros was in Maine. He had not been idle during his five-week stay. In that time, he had recovered the area from the Indians and laid out a small town at Pemaquid. On his return to New York, Andros proceeded swiftly to Albany to meet with Virginia representatives, Kendall and Littletown, and with the Iroquois sachems. Kendall's approach to the Indians was hostile, but the Iroquois, perhaps in an attempt to avert his wrath, were solicitous of the Englishman, the Mohawks inquiring about "your long Journey." The Mohawk sachem said to Kendall that such a trip could not have been accomplished "without much Fatigue, especially to you who are an Old Man." The speaker acknowledged that he, too, was "old likewise, and therefore I give you this Fathom of Wampum, to mitigate your pain." For their part, the Mohawks were determined to keep the "[Covenant] Chain, which cannot be broken, clean and bright."[27]

Neither rhetoric nor presents distracted Kendall. He voiced what would become a pet peeve among representatives from other colonies who came to New York to deal with the Iroquois. Virginia officials wanted the Iroquois to come to Virginia to negotiate, but the Iroquois explained they could not go to Virginia because smallpox raged "Violently in our Countrey." Kendall informed them that theirs was "a weak Excuse," complaining of Iroquois attacks on Virginia settlers in which Indian braves not only destroyed goods and killed people but also took captives, mostly women and children. Although Virginians were irate at these incidents, Kendall said that because of the great respect he had for Andros and the report he "hath given us that you have quietly and Peaceably, delivered to him, the Prisoners you had taken from us," the Virginians were willing to "forgive all ye Dammages you have done our People."[28]

The Iroquois explained that the warfare between them and the Chesapeake colonists was the result of a misunderstanding. According to the treaty they signed with Coursey in 1677, the Iroquois had permission when traveling in the Chesapeake to go to plantations for food. Having signed a treaty to that effect, the Iroquois expected to be welcomed and fed, but when they "came there & gott nothing, then wee took Indian Corn and Tobacco, whereupon the English comeing outt shott some of our People dead, and afterwards wee defended ourselfs." The Iroquois agreed to stop the attacks, but asked that they be given "Victalls when wee goe a fighting agst. Our foresd Enemes."[29] Despite tension and complaints on both sides, on 16 February 1680, Andros concluded an honorable peace between the Iroquois and the Chesapeake colonists.

After returning to New York City in December 1679, Andros was visited by customs collector, Edward Randolph, who was in transit to Boston to enforce the Navigation Acts. In January 1680, Randolph wrote to the ministry that Boston residents were still ignoring English trade laws and claiming they were not subject to English law. Randolph returned to England to urge the king to recall the Massachusetts charter.[30] Randolph's negative report was reinforced by the reports of Andros and other imperial observers. Coupled with the loss of control by New Englanders as exemplified in King Philip's War, the reports caused the king and the Privy Council to consider seriously reorganizing colonial administration. A first step to reorganization was to gain royal control of proprietary and charter colonies. In addition to Massachusetts, the Carteret proprietary of East New Jersey was among those targeted. The crisis in New Jersey followed Carteret's decision to declare free ports so that ships docking in New Jersey would no longer be required first to clear customs and pay duties in New York.[31]

While in England, Andros may have been given orders from the duke and possibly the king as well to proceed against Carteret, for it would not be expected that he would have acted as he did without such orders. Visiting missionaries, Dankers and Sluyter, speculate that Andros sent his trusted aide, William Dyre, to England specifically "for the purpose of obtaining instructions on this point" and only after receiving these orders would Andros have proceeded. Andros undoubtedly had reservations about initiating any action against his cousin and friend, Philip Carteret, but Carteret's flaunting of the duke's prerogative powers could not go unchallenged. Andros certainly realized that all good feelings that existed between him and Carteret would evaporate once he acted, but he was trained to obey orders and proceeded on his assignment.[32]

The death of Sir George Carteret on 13 January 1680, provided the impetus needed for Andros to challenge the Carterets' control of East New Jersey's government. On 8 March 1680, he sent a letter to Philip Carteret, asking him "to forbeare and not presume further to assume or exercise (distinct or) any Jurisdiction over his Majesties Subjects or any person within any bounds of that his Majesties patent to his said R. Highness's."[33] Andros also told Carteret he was preparing to build a fort at Sandy Hook in New Jersey. In his response, Carteret told Andros not to bother him and that he would stop any construction that Andros initiated at Sandy Hook. Andros just as promptly responded that Carteret was acting without legal authorization in governing East New Jersey.[34]

Andros next issued a declaration stating that he confirmed all present New Jersey constables in their posts. Carteret said he had "not plunged his Majesty's Subjects into any disturbances, so I intreat you not to molest me." He denied that the duke had any jurisdiction over New Jersey and warned Andros that he had put the province "in a Posture of Defence." On learning that Andros had ordered the New Jersey assembly to meet, Carteret countermanded the order. He accused Andros of behaving "in a sinister way" in his attempts "to subvert the Minds of his Majesty's Subjects here." Irritated by reports that Andros had sent spies to New Jersey to observe his actions, Carteret told Andros to desist or he would appeal directly to the king.[35]

On 6 April 1680, Andros left for New Jersey to deal with Carteret, but "in a friendly way." The next day Andros and his party "went ashoare," only to find they were faced with a militia company that obligingly made "a passage for us" as they proceeded to greet Carteret. Andros ordered "the Kings patent" read, with orders to him "to receive the place and Countrey from the Dutch." The patent was read "in the open field without the stockadoes, that all his Majesties subjects there present, might heare the same." This done, Carteret asked Andros to return to the governor's house, where he would show him the "lease from his R. Highness to Sir George Carteret." Sir Edmund looked at the documents but "insisted upon his Majesties [official] lettre . . . as being of greater force than the Kings private Lettres."[36]

A month later, on 1 May 1680, Andros issued a warrant to Captain John Collier for the arrest of Philip Carteret. Andros later claimed that Carteret "had all Kindness" shown to him when he was arrested and once in New York City, was given the "liberty of ye town."[37] Carteret told a different story. Andros, Carteret said, "sent a Party of Soldiers to fetch me away Dead or alive so that in the Dead Time of the Night broke open my Doors and most barbarously and inhumanly and violently halled me out of my Bed. . . . Indeed I am so disabled by the Bruises and Hurts I then received, that I fear I shall hardly be a perfect Man again."[38] Not permitted to dress, the naked Carteret was forced into a canoe, without even a "cap or hat on his head." On landing in New York, he was given "clothes and shoes and stockings" before he was taken to the fort's prison, where he became ill.[39]

After a five week incarceration, Andros had Carteret tried by a special court of assizes over which he presided on May 27 and 28. The son of Charles I's master of ceremonies, Andros knew the value of symbolism and spectacle. Each time he entered the courtroom, three trumpeters preceded him. To illustrate his exalted position in the colony as the personal representative of the duke, he "caused a seat to be erected in the court room up above all the others, and higher than usual; on which he sat." Carteret was charged with "misusing the king's name, power, and authority, and usurping the government of New Jersey."

Carteret countered that the court had no "power to try him."[40] In his defense Carteret offered the logical argument that he was indeed a legally appointed governor and Andros himself had acknowledged that by sending him "several letters . . . all addressed to the governor of New Jersey." Andros responded that "although I have done that, can I, therefore make you governor?" "No," replied Carteret, "but the king has made me governor."[41]

Carteret reported that when the jury came in with the verdict of not guilty, Andros "asked them Questions and demanded their Reasons—which I pleaded was contrary to Law for a Jury to give Reasons after their Verdict given in nevertheless he sent them twice or thrice out, giving them new Charges, which I pleaded as at first to be contrary to Law." The third time the jury was sent out, "the governor became very angry" and warned them to "look to what they did." Much depended on their reaching the right verdict, Andros said. In fact, "their entire condition and welfare" rested on their bringing in a guilty verdict. Despite Andros's strong arm methods, the jury insisted for the third time that *"the Prisoner at the Bar* [was] *not Guilty."*[42]

Andros had no choice but to free Carteret after warning him that he was "not to assume any Authority or Jurisdiction there, Civil or Military" but rather to live as a private citizen. Perhaps in an attempt to appease Carteret, Andros gave the East New Jersey governor a fine send off, personally accompanying Carteret back to New Jersey "attended by his whole retinue of ladies and gentlemen." Carteret was escorted with "great pomp, home to Achter kol [Elizabethtown]." The attempt at appeasement did not work. Carteret promptly wrote to England to complain of his harsh usage at Andros's hands.[43]

Andros's action was unpopular among colonists. One Long Island Puritan, John Curtis, made "railing Speeches against Sir Edmund Andross saying what a pox had Sir Edmund or any belonging to Yorke to try Governor Carteret, and that he did like a pittiful fellow to take him [Carteret] away soe Cowardly." A warrant was issued on 11 June 1680 to take Curtis into custody.[44] John Curtis was not alone in his condemnation of Andros's actions. Doctor William Taylor of New Jersey was also outspoken, calling Andros "A Rogue and a Traitor" who "dealt treacherously" in arresting Carteret. A warrant was issued for Taylor's arrest. After he was thrown in jail, Taylor, "committed for abusive language agst Go: & Governmt," quickly saw the light. He was brought before the council, posted security against his future good behavior, and abjectly craved pardon for his past errors.[45]

The entire Carteret incident was ludicrous. The wisest course for Andros would have been to ignore the duke's orders. Governors throughout the colonial period found ample excuses not to implement impractical measures conceived by the king or the proprietor. Instead, Andros put all personal feeling and common sense aside to follow an order his instincts undoubtedly told him was wrong. Colonists were rightly appalled by Andros's actions and not likely to forget his blatant display of ducal and gubernatorial coercion. They were further offended by Andros's autocratic manner and his attempts to interfere with the verdict of a jury. Andros, consciously or not, was trampling on what colonists considered basic rights and privileges and thereby giving colonists the opportunity to define these rights.

Shortly after the trial, Andros and his entourage left for New Jersey, where Andros convened the New Jersey Assembly in Elizabethtown. In his welcoming address to the assembly on 2 June 1680, Andros ordered them to choose a speaker and suggested Isaac Whitehead. The assembly refused, claiming it was their right to elect the speaker of their choice. When they elected John Bonne as speaker, Andros sent for Bonne and other assembly leaders. The men "held an argument of neare 2 houres, pleading their rights & priviledges" with the governor and, in addition, refused to accept the sovereignty of the duke in their colony. The assemblymen declared that they "dare not grant his Majesties Letters Pattents . . . to bee our Rule." The only authority they recognized was "the great Charter of England (alias Magna Carta)," all that was necessary, they believed, for the "joint Safety of every free borne English man." Mindful that Andros governed New York without an assembly and aware of the duke's dislike of representative bodies, the New Jersey Assembly further passed a resolution that the holding of an assembly was a "principall wherof is as of Right belonging to every free borne Englishman." They further objected to being called in the spring rather than in the fall when the assembly usually met. They complained that this assembly was to be "Called once a yeare . . . according to our useuall Custome for the making of all Such peculiar Lawes as Shall be necessarie for the good of the province."[46] The assembly refused to cooperate with Andros and on June 12, the New York council resolved "That nothing offered by the [New Jersey] Assembly is for the K[ing] or country's service, but the contrary particularly reflecting upon his Majties L'res patents & the Authority thereof . . . Resolved. That the Assembly bee dissolved."[47]

Discontent spread among other East New Jersey residents, still resentful of Andros's arrest and trial of Carteret and reluctant to be taken under New York rule. Woodbridge, Middletown, and Shrewsbury residents refused to appoint magistrates when ordered to do so by Andros.[48] They saw no need "to make choise of any men," they told the governor. Andros ordered the arrest of Samuel Moore on August 4 for signing a paper in which he refused to implement the order to choose officers. The arrest of Samuel Dennis was also ordered for refusing to serve as a clerk of the county court of session, as Andros had ordered. Moore, seized and imprisoned in the fort, quickly agreed to acknowledge his errors.[49]

Resistance to the duke's rule also came from West New Jersey. Andros had earlier imposed on all of New Jersey the duke's order that ships for that colony had to clear customs in New York City, but West New Jersey Quaker proprietor, Edward Byllnge, protested this practice. On 28 July 1680, the king's attorney general, Sir William Jones, gave an opinion that the duke could not "legally demand that or any other duty [from] ye inhabitants of West New Jersey." In effect, the ruling caused the duke to release all claims to West New Jersey, including that of government. The decision also brought into question the duke's rights in East New Jersey. Following Carteret's death, his widow sold the land to twelve men. Early in 1681, the duke's secretary, Werden, informed Captain Brockholes in New York that the duke was "pleased to Confirme and Release to the Proprietors of both Moyetyes of *New Jersey* all their and his Right to any thing Besides the rent reserved." James issued a formal deed of release for East New Jersey on 14 March 1683.[50]

The duke's territory was further reduced following Charles's 1681 grant to Quaker William Penn of the land that would become Pennsylvania. That land grant was made in recognition of William Penn's father, Admiral Sir William Penn, who had proved of great service to the Stuarts and had loaned Charles money. Charles was unable to repay the debt to Penn's heir, William, Jr., instead granting the younger Penn land in America. On looking at his territory on a map, Penn was alarmed to see that it ended twelve miles north of New Castle in Delaware, leaving him no access to the sea. Consequently, he asked the duke to release Delaware to him. The duke, a close friend of Penn's, hesitated, but only briefly, before he agreed to have the territory transferred to Penn. On 22 March 1682, the duke officially surrendered to Penn "all that Town of New-Castle otherwise called Delaware and Fort thereunto lying between Maryland and New Jersey in America."[51]

Edmund Andros's attempts to take control of East New Jersey for the duke were far from a rousing success. Resistance came from all sides against the policies of a proprietor who was increasingly seen as arbitrary and autocratic. The duke's policies were not popular on either side of the Atlantic. A more tactful approach on the part of the duke or his deputy might have eased the duke's efforts to regain control of East New Jersey. The inability of both the duke and the governor to present a degree of flexibility in public affairs worked to their detriment. On the positive side, Andros had ensured the continued allegiance of the Iroquois Confederacy to the English, despite enmity between Chesapeake colonists and the Five Nations.

6

The Trial of Sir Edmund Andros, 1681–1685

I doe find all the Imputacons upon my selfe to be totally untrue, and deny every part thereof, Humbly submitting to consideracon whether the matter thereof be not a consequence of former practices under pretence of his Royll Highns service against the Authority there to overthrow his Royall Highns Revenue and Authority, in the sd parts.

—Edmund Andros[1]

ANDROS, IN 1681, CORRECTLY SPECULATED THAT ATTACKS ON HIM AND other servants of the duke of York were meant primarily to weaken the duke and to remove him from the succession to the throne. Parliament had made several unsuccessful attempts to exclude James as the king's heir, but the crisis that ensued was a familiar one for the Stuarts and their courtiers. The developing contest between king and parliament bore some resemblance to the struggle that preceded the Civil Wars, but the outcome in 1681, thanks to Charles's political acumen, was decidedly different. This time, the king's parliamentary Whig opponents were put on the run while most of the king's men, including Andros, were restored to favor.

This outcome was still very much in doubt in 1680. Edmund Andros's patron, James, duke of York, was an outcast in Scotland, permitted by Charles to return to England only briefly when Parliament was not in session. James, disgruntled at what he considered his persecution by the rabid Whig faction, was further upset when complaints reached his ears that his governor in New York was alienating some English merchants who the duke needed as allies. These merchants also told the duke that he should be making more profit on New York than he had been able to realize to that point. When his own persecution reached the point where he was incapable of protecting himself, much less his servants, Andros fell victim.

In England during the summer of 1680, the king's and duke's

troubles continued. James, having been recalled from Scotland in February 1680, spent the spring and summer in England. Charles became increasingly fearful that parliament would attempt to impeach James. To ensure his brother's succession in the event of his own death, Charles, under oath, swore that he had never married Monmouth's mother. Hence Monmouth had no claim to the throne. Tension between the king and the opposition rose when Shaftesbury had James indicted as a recusant. Under existing penal laws, two thirds of James's estate could be seized if he was convicted. The case actually came to trial but the jury was discharged as unfit. By 20 October 1680, James returned to Scotland because parliament was scheduled to meet the next day and he remained fearful of impeachment. James now had an official position as governor or high commissioner of Scotland. Before he left London, James asked his brother for a general pardon but the king refused, despite the fact that he had offered one to the earl of Danby. The king told James that he was determined to break parliament. Skeptical, as well he might be, James remembered all too well the fate of his father, who had been equally determined to subdue parliament.[2]

The duke wanted to keep the friendship and support of the few powerful men he had. Andros's enemies in New York and New Jersey took advantage of this fact. Within a short time of Andros's arrival, it had been obvious that the governor and his small circle of friends, or Andros's "court" party, would do very well for themselves. Members of the elite who did not prosper were those excluded from the governor's inner circle. Middling merchants in New York were discontented because Andros seemed to favor elite merchants. Those English merchants who had incurred Andros's wrath were similarly annoyed. Throughout provincial history, the "country" opposition mounted campaigns against governors who did not favor them by getting their candidates elected to the assembly. This was not possible in New York, where there was no assembly for most of the seventeenth century. Instead, the opposition had to rely on personal complaints, letters, and petitions. Though this procedure for registering complaints was more difficult, in the long run it was just as effective. Andros's opposition relied on contacts in England to bring pressure on the proprietor, James, duke of York.

Among those who were discontented was the Carteret family. East New Jersey governor, Philip Carteret, wasted no time in complaining to his family in England about Andros's actions in arresting him and bringing him to trial. The Carterets, appalled by Andros's actions, complained to the duke, the very person who had ordered Andros to proceed against Carteret.[3]

Some London merchants lodged false complaints that Andros favored Dutch merchants. These London merchants were strong supporters of the duke of York, "who had always promoted commerce and overseas trade." Other malcontents added their complaints to those of the merchants. The father of regular army captain, Christopher Billop, angry at his son's dismissal from service, was particularly vocal. In March 1679, the same month that James was sent into exile, the duke's secretary, Sir John Werden, wrote a letter to Andros, telling him that the senior Billop had complained strenuously to the duke about the governor's "usage" of the young man. Even though the duke approved "your decision to suspend" Billop and to promote Captain Silvester Salisbury to that position, the duke could not afford to alienate the Billop family. Their complaint was added to the charges against Edmund Andros.[4]

As a Roman Catholic, the duke was a nonconformist and needed the support of other nonconformists, such as the Quakers. He was alarmed when London Quakers added their complaints about Andros to those of the Carterets, the Billops, and the London merchants. The Quakers claimed that Andros was persecuting their fellows in New Jersey and interfering with their government and land titles. Quakers in West New Jersey were annoyed with Andros because of his challenge to John Fenwick and other proprietors. New York Quakers on Long Island were equally irritated because Andros imposed fines when they refused to serve in the militia or contribute to the support of Church of England ministers.[5] The duke could not ignore the charges brought against Andros, even though the policies that Andros was implementing in New York were the duke's.

To these charges was added the allegation that revenues in New York were much higher than Andros reported. It was this last factor that caused the duke and the duke's secretary to write to Andros that his conduct as governor was under investigation. Though the duke's profits from New York were slight, he was pleased in 1677 to learn that he had gained a profit of a little over £126 from New York's revenue, raising his hope that in time profits would increase substantially. When that did not happen and when London merchants hinted that the revenue should be several times higher, the duke was willing to listen. In May 1680, the duke wrote Andros that he needed more information on New York's government and revenue and thought "it necessary yt you repaire hither by the first convenience" so that Andros could convey that information directly to him. Werden, in a separate letter, told Andros that merchants had offered "calculacons" as to what New York revenue should be that were "vastly differing from your accts."[6]

James was not the only member of the royal family concerned with colonial revenue and finance in 1680. At Charles's order, Governor Lord Culpepper in Virginia persuaded the house of burgesses to pass a permanent revenue bill. This bill guaranteed a perpetual government income to cover all normal expenses, including the governor's salary. This demand by the king was part of the crown's determination after Bacon's Rebellion to reduce the power of the provincial assembly, which represented the people of Virginia, while increasing that of the governor and the elite council, the king's appointees. In May 1680, the same month that the duke ordered Andros recalled, the king appointed William Blathwayt as surveyor and auditor general of all revenue in America. Blathwayt, as did all future imperial executives, shared the king's determination to reduce the power of provincial assemblies. The assemblies' control of money left provincial royal officials dependent on their good will and weakened the royal prerogative. But more to the point was the fact that much of the king's income from the colonies was never collected and thus never seen by the king. Blathwayt was responsible for supervising all government accounts in the royal colonies. With this royal emphasis on finding lost revenue, it was logical for the duke to investigate his chronically low revenue in New York.[7]

Andros was urged to return quickly to England so "you may vindicate your selfe from these chardges," which "relates to your behaviour in your government, whether ariseing from complaints of some private men, or anger of ye Quakers, or Captn. Billop or from suggestions of yor favoring Dutchmen before English in trade, or making by Laws hurtfull to ye English in generall, or detayneing ships unduly for private reasons, or admitting Dutch ships imediately to trade with you, or tradeing yourselfe in ye names of others." The most serious charge was the suspected misappropriation of New York's revenue.[8]

The charges brought against Andros were to be investigated in New York by an agent, John Lewen, who was commissioned by the duke on 24 May 1680. Lewen was hardly an unbiased observer, being a merchant in his own right and one who had traded with both New York and New England. In addition, he was a partner of Robert Wooley, an English merchant operating in

New York. Lewen arrived in New York on 16 October 1680 to find the governor absent in Boston, where he had gone at the invitation of Virginia governor, Lord Culpepper, whom he had served in 1665 when Culpepper was governor of the Isle of Wight. Culpepper, on his way back to England, had gone to New England to avoid the sickly southern summer season and to await transportation back to England.[9] While in Massachusetts, Culpepper had investigated Puritan attempts to ignore the Navigation Acts. Andros returned promptly to New York when he received word of Lewen's arrival. On his return, Andros was as inhospitable and uncooperative to the duke's representative as he dared to be. He prepared to surrender the government to his aide, Anthony Brockholes. He left New York for England in January 1681, leaving Lady Andros in New York.[10]

Lewen found several New Yorkers more than willing to talk to him about Andros, and even willing to paint him in a negative light. He also found many supporters of the governor, such as Stephen van Cortland, who warned his sister not to say anything against Andros, "even if you should have reason thereto." Van Cortland also asked that she "admonish Mr. Marten Gerritsz not to say anything to the detriment of Sir Edmund, but to say that all he did was for the best interest of the entire province."[11] Other friends of Andros put up impediments to hamper Lewen's investigation. Frederick Philipse complained that Lewen had no legal right to take depositions, while others charged that Lewen's actions were illegal.[12]

Shortly after Lewen began his investigation, Titus Oates's *Narrative of the Plot*, an expose of the Popish Plot, was published in England on 19 November 1680, increasing anti-Catholic hysteria. Among the early victims was William Howard, Viscount Stafford, a Catholic and friend of both the king and duke. Stafford, tried for treason on 30 November 1680, was a harmless old man. He was found guilty of treason and sentenced to be hanged, drawn, and quartered. The king signed the execution order, but reduced the sentence to beheading. The earl was executed on 29 December 1680, much to the outrage of James, who was surprised his brother had signed an execution order for a guiltless old man. On 18 January 1681, the king dissolved parliament. A new parliament was called, but the king decided that this parliament would meet, but not in the Whig stronghold of London. This parliament would meet in the Tory town of Oxford in March.[13] Charles, fearing an uprising in the capital city, ordered the guns on Tower Hill moved into the Tower to prevent their being seized by angry mobs. To ensure peace was maintained, the king left his trusted aide, the earl of Craven, Andros's uncle by marriage, in command of the guards. Craven's orders were specific, to keep the peace in London, if necessary by "killing, slaying or otherwise howsoever destroying those who shall so resist in the disturbance of the public peace."[14]

It was in this climate that Andros returned to London in early March. The news of the earl of Stafford's execution must have been particularly disturbing to Andros. If the king had to sacrifice a loyal friend, what chance did Andros have that the duke would protect him from his enemies. But whatever despair he felt at this news must have been quickly leavened when Craven imparted to him his knowledge of what the king had planned for the Oxford Parliament. Charles had, in fact, decided to be rid of parliament once and for all. If Whigs in London objected to the king's actions, Craven was ready with troops to put down any disturbance by whatever means.[15]

In Oxford, the king ordered his soldiers prominently posted on the streets as the members of parliament made their way to the chamber to open the session. The message and implied threat were not lost on the representatives. When the already cowed members of parliament met, the king suggested as a compromise that new limitations be placed on James if he became king. This effort to calm fears of a Catholic takeover on his death was rejected by Shaftesbury, who wanted James completely excluded from the succession. On March 28, for the third time parliament discussed an Exclusion Bill. Charles had had enough. He summoned Commons to Lords. As the members stepped into the chamber, they were astounded to see the king in his official robes, an indication that he was about to dissolve parliament. Fear rose among the representatives as they recalled the hundreds of king's soldiers lining the streets. After Charles dissolved parliament, the members fell over each other in an attempt to reach the doors, running through streets that were still lined with the king's soldiers. The king never called another parliament, having earlier signed a secret treaty with Louis XIV of France that brought him sufficient cash to permit him this luxury. Louis agreed to pay Charles two million crowns immediately and 500,000 crowns a year for two years.[16]

The actions of Charles II were reassuring to Andros because it was now obvious that the king was determined to regain control of the government and to reduce the influence of the Whigs. But a trial was still necessary to clear Andros of the charges brought

Charles II (1630–1685). Once restored to the throne, Charles was determined to exert royal control over the American colonies, as exemplified by the Dominion of New England. Hindered by Whig opponents who sought to exclude Charles's brother, James, from the succession, Charles dissolved parliament in 1681. Portrait after Sir Peter Lily, courtesy of the National Portrait Gallery, London.

against him, and also necessary to clear Andros's trusted subordinate, customs collector, William Dyre. The latter case arose because Brockholes, left in charge of New York by Andros, had proved ineffective in enforcing the governor's policies. Rather than offend middling merchants who did not want to pay customs duties, Brockholes failed to renew the duke's customs duties, imposed for a three-year period, which had expired just after Andros left New York. Despite Brockhole's inaction, Dyre continued to collect the duties, much to the outrage of local merchants. When a London ship arrived in May 1681, Dyre demanded customs duties, but merchant Samuel Winder refused to comply. When Dyre seized the cargo, Winder brought charges of treason against him. He reasoned that Dyre's act in imposing customs duties was tantamount to his assuming royal powers and was contrary to both the Magna Carta and the 1628 Petition of Right. At his trial in New York in the spring of 1681, Dyre challenged the authority of the court to try him. Hence, local authorities sent him to England for trial, along with Winder who would continue his suit there.[17]

It was obvious in England during the summer of 1681 that Charles was determined to eliminate parliament and to subdue his Whig opponents. More succinctly, Charles wanted to reduce local autonomy and enhance central power. There was little resistance from Whigs and no angry popular uprising. Any such defiance would have been quickly put down since the king had a loyal army and his brother controlled the Royal Navy.[18] To ensure popular support for himself, Charles issued a declaration to be read in every Anglican church, justifying his dissolution of parliament.[19]

A particular royal target was Shaftesbury, charged with treason for intending to make war on the king. Arrested at the order of the king on 2 July 1681, he was sent to the Tower. When Shaftesbury's case was heard by the grand jury, the Whig sheriff of London packed that body with like-minded Whigs. The carefully picked jury in November 1681 decided there was no case against Shaftesbury. The jury decision convinced Charles, if he needed further convincing, that Whigs had to be removed from positions of authority, particularly in London. To accomplish this, corporate charters had to be recalled, since Whigs dominated the governing boards of these corporations. Shaftesbury, exonerated by the grand jury but still fearful of Charles's vengeance, fled to the Netherlands after his trial and died there in January 1683.[20]

Despite Shaftesbury's success before the grand jury, it was

clear by December 1681 that the tide was beginning to turn against the Whigs. Many Whigs were now on the run, the Tories (and the king) sensing triumph. It was in this improved climate that the trial of Sir Edmund Andros began in December 1681, with Colonel John Churchill, the duke's solicitor general, presiding. Churchill and Andros had a long acquaintance, having served together in 1672 at the Yarmouth garrison. The duke was not present, still in Scotland awaiting his brother's permission to return to England. Lewen, Andros's accuser, was in attendance, as was Andros's customs collector, William Dyre.

On arrival in New York, Lewen had promptly allied with middling merchants who resented the favors shown by the governor to the Dutch elite. They could only prosper if the governor's power and the power of the royal prerogative he represented were reduced. It was mostly members of this group who had provided information to Lewen. Lewen said Andros had misappropriated tax money to make improvements on the fort and to build a mole and exposed other irregularities in his administration. Lewen claimed that Andros and his friends enriched themselves at the expense of the duke. Andros, Lewen said, extended favors "to some few Dutch Merchants vizt ffredrick Phillipps & Stephanus van Cortlandt the Govrs Trustee there both in regard of Trade." In addition, Lewen complained, Andros's associates in New York had hampered his investigation by using "all their cunning practices to give mee all the trouble they could." Lewen reported that an English merchant, Edward Griffeth, who had already initiated a separate suit against Andros, had told him that Dyre had admitted to him that the combined total customs for 1675, 1676, and 1677 was over £14,700, or "almost double the sume I can find." The customs revenue should be well over £5,600 a year, he reported. Lewen also complained that the governor had refused him permission to inspect the disbursement of revenues until he had the books transcribed. By the time they were turned over to him, he did not have sufficient time to examine them thoroughly.[21]

Andros answered each of Lewen's charges. He explained he had been visiting Lord Culpepper in Boston when Lewen arrived in New York on 16 October 1680. He returned to New York to find Lewen there and extended to him all possible cooperation. Andros said Lewen was quite blunt in his dealings and promptly informed the governor that he "was never to returne" to New York. Lewen was a magnet, Andros said, for "all the malecontents (with whom he most kept company) to bring in their Informacons."[22]

New York, the governor said, had benefited from his use of tax dollars. There was now a weigh house, improved fortifications, and a new mole, all measures designed to improve trade. The governor carefully pointed out that he had no responsibility for the actual collection of taxes or customs duties, that being left to local sheriffs or collectors. He denied any favoritism in his dealings with "mr ffredreicke phillips and Capt. Cortland," both of whom were "very eminent men there, & were heretofore magistrates of the Citty; & were since taken into the Councill." He strenuously denied that he had extended to either "of them or any others wtsoever" any favored treatment. In New York, "equall justice and countenance being given to all the inhabitants, merchants, sojourners, Traders or Strangers, without respect of persons, nation or quality w'soever."[23]

Andros pointed out that New York had prospered under his governance. "At my first comeing" he said, "I found the place poore, unsettled & without Trade." Since his administration began, New York was "greatly increased in people, trade, buildings & other Improvements," and navigation had increased "att least tenn tymes." Andros reminded the court that he had kept New York free from the Indian wars that had ravaged New England and the Chesapeake colonies. "Noe disaster happened in any part of the Governmt during my command there," he said, and, in addition, New York was "constantly serviceable to our English Neighbors." It was through his efforts, he told the commissioners, that the war ended. He recalled that he was the "principall instrumt" in negotiating that peace and was the person responsible for freeing "neare one hundred of their [New England] Captives," or colonists held by the Indians.[24]

Not only did peace reign while trade and revenue increased in New York, but population had also risen when the many Englishmen and Indians driven out of other colonies by war and unrest chose to settle there during his administration while "very few (if any) have quitted the place during my being there." All the charges against him, he said, were "totally untrue." He denied "every part" of Lewen's accusations.[25] Andros defended his fiscal management of New York by pointing out that his accounts were "all before His Royll Highness transmitted from time to time, examined, auditted and signed by sworne Auditors of the best reputacon." Anglo-American politics were one, Andros pointed out, with events in Europe directly affecting events in the colonies. The charges brought against him were part of a much larger Whig plot that originated in England to undermine the influence of the duke, reduce his power, and eliminate him from the succession. Andros wondered whether "the matter thereof be not a consequence of former practices under pretence of his Royll Highns service against the Authority there to overthrow his Royall Highns Revenue and Authority, in the sd parts." He also denied the charge that he told provincials "that their Privileges hung on a slender thread & that he was chidden for giving them such liberties."[26]

The Commissioners agreed with Andros's interpretation of events in New York, and concluded that the mole and other improvements were necessary and served to better the city. Lewen had offered little or no proof for his other accusations, the commissioners decided. Lewen had charged that Andros "did so influence & overcome the Councill that none of them durst contradict him," but offered no evidence that this was so. Similarly, Lewen had heard that Andros ordered the head customs searcher, Dyre, "not to be too strict what goods came to ffrederick Phillips but to be very strict in searching what goods came to Pinhorn & Robinson & to give them all ye obstructions he could in ye entryes," but could not substantiate this charge.[27]

In the absence of corroborating evidence for these and other charges, the commissioners declared that "wee do not think it is made out that the Governr hath misbehaved himself or broken ye trust reposed in him by his Royll Highness . . . nor doth it appear that he hath in any way defrauded or mismanaged his Revenue." Dyre was also cleared of mismanaging the duke's revenue and, for good measure, the commissioners added "that both Sr Edmond and Capt Dyre have behaved themselves very well in their sevll stations."[28]

Although exonerated by the duke's court, Andros faced other legal action, this time in a suit brought by Jacob Milborne, Andros's old adversary from New York. Milborne filed suit against him in London, charging that Andros had had him beaten and thrown in prison. The incident occurred upon Milborne's return to New York in 1678 after an absence of two years. Like all incoming travelers, Milborne was called before the governor and council "to give an accot from whence he came." When Milborne refused to do so, he was jailed at the order of the council "for his rude and insolent behaviour." Milborne won his suit and was awarded £45 in damages.[29]

Merchant Edward Griffeth, a business partner of Jacob Milborne also brought suit against Andros. Griffeth's family had, earlier in 1678, unsuccessfully sought to detain Andros in London so that they could bring charges against him. In December 1682, Griffeth tried again, charging that Andros did "prohibitt restrayne and hinder" him "from Carryeing or Transportinge any of his Said goods or merchandizes to Albany," causing him to lose more than a thousand pounds on the merchandise. Griffeth also observed that Andros "himselfe deriving a trade to Albany as a Merchant and designeing to get and Engrosse the whole trade thereof to himself And other his Confederates did to that end restrayne and hinder" him. In his response to these charges, Andros claimed he simply did not recall the details of the incident. He pointed out that Griffeth's problem was with the customs regulations and the customs officers, not with him. Andros, for his part, "did never prohibit nor restrein any person or persons whatsoever to his remembrance who might trade" in New York. He also denied that he ever "exercised the trade of a Merchant or traded as such tho he knows of no restrein or prohibition to the contrary," or that he ever tried "to enrich himself or discourage any lawful trades." Griffeth was hard pressed to prove otherwise.[30]

One person who was completely convinced of Andros's gubernatorial ability and competence was the Quaker, William Penn, undoubtedly influenced by the duke in his high opinion of Andros's ability. Penn's comment on Andros's recall from New York was that "he has no easy game to play yt comes after Sr Ed. Andros for tho he was not without objection he certainly did great things more than both his predecessors." Penn thought so highly of Andros that he offered him the governorship of Pennsylvania and the command of three companies there. As an inducement, Penn offered Andros ten thousand acres in Delaware, the same area that Andros had previously secured for the duke. The ethical Penn, committed to fairness in Indian relations, was also aware of Andros's commitment to treat Indians fairly. Penn knew that Andros could provide the kind of leadership a new colony needed. Andros declined the generous offer.[31]

Neither the king nor the duke needed any further proof of Andros's innocence, nor was royal favor lacking. After the duke returned from Scotland in January 1682, he decided not to return Andros to his post. Instead, Thomas Dongan was appointed governor-general of New York on 30 September 1682. On 13 April 1683, Edmund Andros was sworn in as a gentleman in ordinary of the king's privy chamber, giving him continual and direct access to the person of the king. The next year, still further proof of the king's favor came with a ninety-nine year grant to Sir Edmund and Lady Andros of the island of Alderney for the rent of £13.6s.8d. Andros promptly leased the island to his Uncle Charles.[32]

The duke, perhaps realizing an assembly in New York would facilitate the collecting of money, permitted Dongan to call a representative assembly. There was a sizable condition imposed in that an assembly would be permitted only if "the Inhabitants will agree to raise money, to discharge ye publique debts, and to settle such a fond for ye future, as may be sufficient for the maintenance of ye garrison and government." What the duke wanted was the guarantee of a permanent revenue from New York, such as the Virginia House of Burgesses had been coerced into guaranteeing to Governor Culpepper in the aftermath of Bacon's Rebellion. The New York Assembly passed such a measure as well as a Charter of Liberties, or constitution. The permanent revenue was accepted, but the charter was soon rejected.[33]

While the exonerated Andros and the duke dealt with New York's fiscal affairs, another colonial official, William Dyre, was still awaiting trial in England. His treason case was first heard on 14 September 1681 by the king and council. On trial for his life, Dyre was saved when merchant Winder, also in London to press charges, fled London after he was accused of reneging on a promise to a woman. Dyre asked for acquittal and return of his bond. By July 1682, Winder remained missing, despite numerous attempts to find him. He was believed to be in Southampton, whose mayor placed an advertisement with an order for Winder to appear in one month's time. In the interim, Dyre's bond was returned to him so he could be free to file charges against Winder. On 30 September 1682, when Winder had still not appeared, the case against Dyre was discharged.[34]

Andros and Dyre were exonerated, but Whigs in England were resentful of the Tories and continued plotting against the king. Charles was aware of the plots and, to guard against any future threats, the king in July 1683 ordered the garrison at Tangier to return to England. Such protection was needed, since only a month earlier, in June 1683, a new plot against the royal brothers had been discovered, this one with more substance than the Popish Plot. Implicated in what was called the Rye House Plot was James, duke of Monmouth, the king's own son.[35] The king promised Monmouth a pardon if he confessed and gave information about his co-conspirators, to which Monmouth agreed. The leader of the plot, Sir Thomas Armstrong, was executed in 1684 without benefit of a trial. Lord Russell and Algernon Sidney were tried, convicted, and executed. Monmouth was sent into exile, where he was joined by other Englishmen and Scotsmen who were all discontented with Stuart rule. The Whigs were indeed on the run.[36]

Central to the king's program to destroy the power of the opposition was the recalling of the charters of Whig dominated cities, towns, and provinces, particularly that of London. That city had long been "virtually a republic" that elected its own municipal officials, had a fairly broad electorate, and had its own treasury and trained bands of militia. On 18 June 1683, the London charter was recalled by the king. It was formally surrendered on 4 October 1683.[37] The king promptly ousted all those Whig officeholders who opposed him and replaced them with Tories loyal to him. New commissions for a lord mayor and several new aldermen were issued in the fall of 1683.[38]

London was not the only city affected. Before the process of recalling charters ended, several hundred charters were canceled, among them the charter of the Massachusetts Bay Company. The decision to recall the Massachusetts charter was based on the reports of several colonial administrators, including Sir Edmund Andros, Lord Culpepper, and Edward Randolph, all appalled at Massachusetts's blatant flaunting of the royal prerogative. Culpepper, after meeting with Andros in Boston, wrote a report to the Privy Council Committee on 9 August 1681. To deal with Massachusetts, Culpepper suggested installing a competent customs officer there and backing him with "all possible Countenance & Encouragement" in what was sure to be "a Station attended with many difficulties." Culpepper was outraged that Massachusetts dared to coin its own money, a practice he considered "extreamly prejudicial" to England's monetary soundness.[39] Randolph had urged that the power of customs officers be strengthened and that offenders of the Navigation Acts be punished.

In October 1683, Randolph arrived in Boston with a writ of *quo warranto* order against the charter. He conveyed to colonists the royal declaration that if the colony submitted, the king would change the charter only as necessary for the purposes of effective government. Moderate Puritans prepared an address of acquiescence on 30 November 1683, but the Massachusetts general court refused its approval, resulting in *quo warranto* proceedings being initiated in England. The grounds on which the charter was vacated were solid and included a list of Massachusetts's transgressions: that the colony did not impose duties on English imported goods, that Massachusetts taxed all residents but let only Congregationalist church members vote or hold public office, that the government there imposed its own rules on granting freemanship, and that it had set up its own admiralty courts.[40] The charter was vacated on 23 October 1684.[41]

Under an imperial scheme, all the colonies of New England would be united under a single, crown appointed governor. The first governor-general named by Charles II was Percy Kirke, former commandant at Tangier who ordered that city burnt when he and his troops abandoned the garrison there. The Massachusetts colonists were horrified at the threat of direct royal control and even more horrified by the prospect of Kirke as head of a centralized government. Massachusetts governor, Simon Bradstreet, asked Randolph if the king would forgive Massachusetts's past sins and merely send a governor to ensure their compliance. Bradstreet pointed out that King Philip's War had devastated Massachusetts's economy. New Englanders had learned their lesson, Bradstreet said, and would reform as far as illegal trading. In addition, they had done his Majesty a service by expanding his kingdom through conquest. The king was not persuaded by Bradstreet's argument.[42]

In England, by the winter of 1684–85, Whig power was significantly reduced and the royalists were in command. William Penn, returning to England in 1684 from his new colony of Pennsylvania, noticed the change in manner of both the king and the duke. The brothers, he said, were now "sour and stern and resolved to hold the Reins of Power with a stiffer hand than heretofore, especially over those that were observed to be State or Church Dissenters." In other words, Whigs and Puritans were now the targets, an attitude that did not bode well for New England. During those years, Andros saw and absorbed the new belligerent attitude of the royal brothers.[43]

Andros and the rest of the court suffered through London's winter, which was so unusually severe that trees split "as if lightning-strock," with "men & Cattell perishing in divers places, and the very seas so locked up with yce, that no vessells could stirr out, or come in." One observer wrote to Andros that "great quantities of fish especially conger, have lately been found dead," while wild animals froze to death. In London, the air became so foul with coal smoke "that hardly could one see crosse the streete, & . . . one could scarce breath." The Thames froze so solid that shopkeepers were able to display and sell their wares on the ice.[44]

The severe weather may have contributed to the sudden death of the king. Charles, having enjoyed his years as ruler since dissolving Parliament and subduing the Whigs, was in good spirits and in apparent good health prior to his last illness. Nothing prepared the king, his family, or his gentlemen in waiting for the sudden onset that began early on the Monday morning of 2 February 1685 and ended with his death between ten and eleven o'clock on the morning of Friday, 6 February 1685, "in the 36 yr of his reign & the 54 of his age." Among those in attendance during those final five days when the king hovered between life and death were the duke of York, "continually kneeling by his bed side, & in teares," as well as the king's gentlemen of the chamber, including, most likely, Sir Edmund Andros. To ensure a peaceful succession, James, on the night Charles died, ordered to London the royal Regiment of Dragoons, recently formed from the Tangier regiment.[45]

The same day the king was buried, "the Herould proclaimed His Majesties Titles to the Imperial Crowne, & succession according to the forme . . . then by coach according to rank to Temple bar, then to Exchange in Cornhill & then returned." Sir Edmund Andros's patron, James, the duke of York, was now King James II.[46] A proclamation was sent to all the colonies informing them that on the death of Charles II, the "Imperial Crowns of England, Scotland, France, and Ireland, as also the Supream Dominion and Sovereign Right in the Plantation and Province of New York . . . rightfully come to the high and Mighty Prince James, Duke of York and Albany, his Majesties onely Brother and Heir." On 5 March 1685, the Privy Council Committee informed Governor Thomas Dongan that with the ascension of James II to the throne, the "Propriety of the said Province of New York is now wholy devolved upon the Crown," making it a royal colony.[47]

James II was crowned on 23 April 1685, but his reign was opposed by many Protestants in Britain, some of whom favored the rule of the king's illegitimate son, James, duke of Monmouth, still in exile in the Netherlands.[48] With Monmouth was the ninth earl of Argyll, under sentence of death for treason in Scotland. After Charles's death, the men plotted to take the crown from James II, Monmouth's uncle. The first step in this plot was Argyll's landing in Scotland in May 1685. When the Scottish highlanders and lowlanders ignored Argyll's appeal for followers, he was captured and executed. Andros again absorbed a lesson of empire that opposition to legitimate authority could not be tolerated.[49]

Monmouth landed in England at Lyme Regis with 150 men on 11 June 1685 to promptly "set up his standart, as k[ing] of England." The duke had considerably more success in England's west country than had Argyll in Scotland, attracting many members of the trained bands, who flocked to the standard of the popular and charismatic duke. Monmouth's followers were, for the most part, "poor Clothworkers of the Country, no Gent: of account being come to him." Monmouth, pronouncing himself king, charged his uncle with usurping the throne. James, in turn, declared Monmouth a traitor and offered a reward of £5,000 for his death or capture.[50] Trusted subordinates led James's army, including Sir Edmund Andros, who had been commissioned to command a troop of cavalry on 6 June 1685. Andros and Sir William Stapleton, former governor–general of the Leeward Islands, were sent to the west country by James to ensure that any potential rebels were discouraged from assisting Monmouth. Despite their efforts, Monmouth's rebels soon numbered around five thousand, the large number of rebels reflecting the personal appeal of the old king's natural son, who had inherited much of his father's charm if not his aptitude for political survival or his common sense.[51]

A highly professional force met Monmouth's unprofessional and untrained army. James, who realized militia was unreliable, depended mainly on the regular army. The decisive battle of the uprising was fought at Sedgemoor on 6 July 1685, and word was promptly sent to James in London of Monmouth's "Utter defeate." Monmouth, trying to escape after the battle, "walked 16 miles on foote, changing his habite with a poore coate," but despite his shabby dress was found in a ditch on July 8, "cover'd with fern-braken." Monmouth was so altered by his harrowing experience that he might not have been identified except for "his George" garter, given to him by his father.[52] Monmouth, whose popularity was undiminished, was tried for treason in London. Although he blamed others for his actions, he was found guilty and sentenced to death. The executioner, Jack Ketch, "made five Chopps before he had his head off, which incens'd the people, that had he not ben guarded & got away they would have torne him in pieces."[53]

The rebellion gave James the opportunity (or excuse) to increase the size of his army, which in February 1685 numbered 8,865 in England, with another 7,500 in Ireland and 2,199 in Scotland. As Shaftesbury had aptly observed, "There is no prince that ever governed without a nobility or an army. If you will not have the one, you must have the other, or the monarchy cannot long support or keep itself from tumbling into a democratical republic." James had no desire to have a democratic regime in England any more than in New York. By June, the army doubled to 15,710 in England; by December, it had grown to 19,778, with regiments still being raised and almost ten thousand men remaining in Ireland and Scotland. Nor were any of the regiments disbanded when it became obvious that the rebellion was thoroughly crushed.[54]

And crushed it was. Andros played a significant role in putting down the rebellion and seeing that it did not erupt again. Undoubtedly, he and his men were ruthless, but not as ruthless as General Percy Kirke, who believed in immediate retribution, particularly when suspected rebels did not meet his demands for heavy bribes. Kirke imposed no restraints on his men who raped, pillaged, and plundered at will. Kirke, an advocate of swift punishment, needed only a post or a tree and a length of rope. In the first week after the victory, Kirke's men and others summarily strung up one hundred or more rebels. Kirke obviously did not act alone. All of James's officers and regiments had a hand in punishing the rebels, and James himself encouraged revenge. He told Commander Feversham, after the latter passed through a rebel stronghold, "you might have done well to have hanged any persons you found deserving it there, as he would have you do in other places if you see cause." Feversham did not make the same mistake twice and promptly ordered four rebels "hanged in Chains." In addition to the rebels disposed of by Kirke and others, another fifteen hundred were killed in battle, and some fourteen to fifteen hundred were taken prisoner. Of these, a thousand were sent as indentured servants to the West Indies for a ten year term, a veritable death sentence. Another three hundred were tried, convicted, and were hanged, drawn, and quartered. Beginning 5 September 1685, Chief Justice George Jeffries and the assize court dispensed these judicial punishments. The court wreaked a terrible vengeance in the aftermath of Monmouth's Rebellion. James approved of the slaughter and named Jeffries as lord chancellor as a reward for his services.[55]

The king also acknowledged Andros's diligence in subduing rebels on 30 July 1685, when he was named lieutenant colonel of a new regiment, the Princess Anne's Cavalry, commanded by Robert Leeke, earl of Scarsdale.[56] The duke's army was led by men like Andros, who personified the new breed of officer now that the old era of the gentleman officer was over. The new offi-

cers in James's army were, like Andros, "professional career soldiers from Tangier, the colonies, France, the Spanish
Netherlands, and the United Provinces." Andros's career also
illustrates the dependence of this new officer class on the monarch "for its livelihood, progress, and very existence upon obedience to the royal command." A corps that was responsive solely
to the king would not be particularly sensitive "to the prejudices
and vested interests of the English gentry," much less to the
interests of the provincial gentry.[57]

Andros's role in restoring peace and his loyalty to the Stuarts
were to be further rewarded. The king deprived Kirke of the
Dominion governorship, not because of his brutal and sadistic
execution of rebels, but because he had disobeyed orders and sold
them pardons. In addition, colonial officials were appalled by
Kirke's brutality. Edward Randolph believed Kirke should be
replaced after "the great carnage he has made in ye West" of
England. The king, looking for a man who was competent and
with an imperial vision, chose for the post of governor of the
Dominion of New England the former governor-general of New
York, Sir Edmund Andros.[58]

7

The Dominion of New England, 1686–1688

Part 1

> An entire new model of government was intended, but there
> was not time to perfect it.
>
> —Thomas Hutchinson[1]

> This people are riveted in their way and I feare nothing but
> necessity or force will otherwise dispose them.
>
> —Edward Randolph[2]

HUTCHINSON WAS CORRECT IN HIS ASSESSMENT THAT THE INTENT OF the king was to alter completely the governments of Massachusetts and other New England colonies. Randolph was also correct in his prediction that New Englanders would resist change as long as they could. The intent of the metropolis was to exert its authority in New England, much to the dismay of local elites. The agent to effect this change was Edmund Andros. Every aspect of life would be affected, from young couples getting married, to witnesses appearing in court, to landowners who had bought land from Indians, to ministers who were in danger of losing their former power and prestige, to members of the elite who could no longer be certain their interests would be favored.

The task to which Andros was assigned as governor-general was difficult. The Dominion of New England in 1686 consisted of the colonies of Massachusetts, Plymouth, New Hampshire, and the Maine territory formerly under New York jurisdiction. It would soon include Rhode Island and Connecticut and later, New York and New Jersey. James had a specific purpose in mind in consolidating this vast territory under a single governor. Like most seventeenth-century monarchs, James wanted to centralize government authority to increase the power of the crown. The

134

implementation of centralization and the interference of government down to the local level by James in England, and by his governor Edmund Andros in New England, resulted in the displacement of the old, traditional ruling class.[3]

The opposition of this class to loss of status and privileges produced discontent, first against the king in England, then against his deputy in New England. In the latter, the old traditional ruling class lost power and influence as discontent among the lower orders of society increased, not only because of the changes in royal policy but also because of lingering debt from King Philip's War and the resultant uncertain economy.[4] Anxiety was heightened by the establishment of the Dominion of New England, modeled on Louis XIV's highly centralized Dominion of New France and on the duke's own province of New York, Andros's previous post. Conceived by Charles II and executed by James II, the Dominion was an imaginative system of closer colonial management, sadly needed in the seventeenth century and even more so in the eighteenth. The attention paid to the colonies by the later Stuarts reflected their new commercial importance as suppliers of raw products and consumers of manufactured goods and to meet the need for effectively defending those colonies from foreign threats. To exploit the colonies fully, it was necessary to draw them into the imperial orbit, but to achieve centralization it would be necessary to weaken the power of the local oligarchs.[5]

Local oligarchs in both England and the provinces were also offended by the king's religious policies. Thoroughly committed to Catholicism, the king lacked any discretion about practicing his religion or in trying to get his chief counselors and others to convert. Fears that James would force Catholicism on the nation acerbated when, in October 1685, Louis XIV revoked the Edict of Nantes, previously the century-long guarantor of religious toleration for France's numerous Protestants. They would now be forced to convert to Catholicism. News of the revocation and the persecution that followed quickly reached England. To escape further persecution, Protestants fled in great numbers from France to settle throughout Europe and the American colonies, with perhaps one hundred thousand going to Germany and England. In those countries, the Huguenots spread horrific tales of Catholic atrocities to the Protestant populations. In light of these, as fears rose in England that James would follow Louis's example and forcibly convert or expel English Protestants, resistance to James and his policies increased. Caught in the crossfire of this resistance was Sir Edmund Andros, governor-general of the Dominion of New England, and the one responsible for implementing James's policies there.[6]

Division among Protestants was also a religious issue in New England, where Calvinist residents were to be under the governance of an Anglican, in Calvinist eyes only a step away from a Catholic. James was determined to reduce the opposition to direct royal rule offered by chartered and proprietary colonies. Hence in 1685, Edward Randolph was dispatched to America with orders "to serve the Quo Warranto upon my Lord Baltimore, Proprietor of Maryland, and the Proprietors of East and West Jersey, and to serve two writs upon the Colonies of R. Island and Connecticott." Writs against Maryland and the Jerseys were ineffective, and although Rhode Island and Connecticut retained their charters, they also became part of the Dominion. Despite the Massachusetts charter having already been vacated, the Puritans there and in other New England provinces continued to defy royal commands. They shielded regicides, coined their own money, maintained exclusive control of both church and state, and persecuted and, in fact, killed the king's subjects in the name of religion. Only reluctantly did they swear allegiance to the king, while denying "any Dependance on His majy."[7] In addition, the New England colonies ignored English common law. Massachusetts refused to accept any laws except their own and limited the vote and the holding of public office to Congregational church members. They also imposed fines on people for not attending Puritan services or for observing Christmas or other holy days. Massachusetts fined ship captains who brought Quakers there, established their own mint, ignored the Navigation Acts, and refused to put the king's image on their stamps.[8]

Although the majority of those who settled New England could be described as Puritan, they comprised several sects. These included Separatists who settled Plymouth and who, believing the English church was beyond redemption, wanted nothing to do with it. The Massachusetts Puritans did not want to leave but to reform the Church of England. In fact, being distant from England assured that the Puritans would become separate, free from episcopal control and able to establish their own congregational churches, as confirmed by the 1648 Cambridge Platform. Religious discord fractured New England society, first from breaks in the leadership ranks of the Puritans and then from an influx of other faiths. These non-Puritans included Anglicans, Fifth Monarchists, and Quakers, all of whom were seen as threats to a Calvinist oriented church under the control of its congregation. The Calvinist or Puritan vision was of a church that "represented an entirely distinct religious tradition from the Anglicanism it opposed."[9]

Edward Randolph brought word of the charter dissolution to Massachusetts in May 1686. He would serve as the secretary and registrar, and later as collector, surveyor, and searcher of customs for the Dominion of New England. Sailing with Randolph was the Reverend Robert Ratcliffe, an Anglican minister sent to care for the spiritual needs of the Anglican governor, the garrison, and the four hundred or more Anglicans already living in or near Boston. Ratcliffe was the first Anglican priest in Massachusetts and certainly the first to perform services there. On his arrival, Ratcliffe held services in Boston's Town House with a portable lectern.[10]

In addition to a sizeable population of Anglicans, by the 1680s, other Protestant denominations were also present in Massachusetts. Quakers, initially expelled from the colony, were permitted to build a meetinghouse in Boston in 1679. Baptists also had made inroads in that city by the 1680s. Despite the presence of a significant number of people from different sects, many of whom had achieved economic prosperity, Congregationalists (Puritans) retained their firm hold on government.[11]

Although Puritans regarded Ratcliffe with alarm, even more alarming was the order to dissolve the general court that Randolph brought. He carried with him a commission for Puritan-born Joseph Dudley as head of a newly appointed council to serve until the arrival of the governor. Dudley, a wealthy farmer from Roxbury whose father was the second governor of Massachusetts, was a Harvard graduate.[12] Convinced that royal authority was necessary to maintain order in New England, Dudley had broken with more orthodox leaders. A convert to the Church of England, he was now one of a growing number of influential men in Massachusetts who welcomed royal intervention in the colony's affairs. These included William Stoughton, Wait Winthrop, Peter Bulkeley, Richard Wharton, and several other prosperous merchants and landowners. Many of them opposed the colony's largely orthodox leadership and a few, like Dudley, had even left the Congregational Church for the Church of England.[13]

The retention of control by the orthodox leaders was made difficult because of the social and financial chaos that fell on the colony following King Philip's War.[14] Puritans believed they were being punished by God for evil behavior. Or, in the words of Increase Mather, Puritans were "guilty before the Lord, of *Sig-*

nal Apostacy, Debauchery, and (above all) of nefandous Contempt of the Pure and Powerful Dispensation of the Gospel."[15]

The turmoil raised by unsettling events caused the more moderate Puritans, along with people from other sects, to reject orthodox leaders who no longer seemed capable of guiding the colonies. Many welcomed the king's governor. These men, who were mostly merchants, wanted to protect and expand their mercantile interests. They could only accomplish this goal by cooperating with English officials. Orthodox Puritans wanted nothing to do with England or the Stuarts or merchants, for that matter, who represented the new capitalist order.[16]

Both moderate and orthodox Puritans were present when Dudley, now president of the council, called a meeting of the old general court on 17 May 1686. It promptly rejected Dudley as president on the grounds "that there is no certain determinate rule for your administration of justice; and that which is, seems to be too arbitrary." The court pointed out that without a representative body, "the subjects are abridged of their liberties as Englishmen, both in the matter of legislation, and the laying of taxes." They urged Dudley "to consider whether such a commission be safe either for you or us." They acquiesced only to the point that although they denied their consent to the new government, they still hoped to "demeane ourselves as true and loyall subjects to his majesty."[17]

The Massachusetts General Court met for the final time on May 21. Refusing dissolution, it merely adjourned until the fall. Massachusetts's affairs were now in the hands of Dudley. The newly appointed council was largely composed of merchants. In addition to Dudley, the council included Edward Randolph, Richard Wharton, William Stoughton, Peter Bulkeley, John Usher, James Pynchon, Captain Gedney, Randolph's cousin Robert Mason from New Hampshire, and Wait Winthrop, who, with his brother Fitz-John, were both grandsons of Massachusetts founder, John Winthrop.[18] Dudley got along well with the merchant dominated council because he cooperated with them and favored their interests. He also deliberately courted Increase Mather, whom he correctly identified as the "spokesman of the real tribal heads of the native population."[19] Furthermore, Dudley approved grants for large tracts of land to councilors and gave them the most profitable offices. They had every reason to believe this practice would continue once Andros had arrived.[20]

Dudley's commission gave the Puritans some inkling of the substantial powers to be wielded by the incoming governor.

Andros's commission, dated 3 June 1686, spelled out these powers. He was "to be our [the king's] Captain General, and Governor in chief in and over all that our territory and dominion of New England, in America," including "Massachusetts Bay . . . New Plymouth . . . New Hampshire and Maine, the Narragansett Country, otherwise called the King's Province, with all the Islands." His administrative and civil powers included the right to appoint and suspend councilors, and "to make, constitute, and ordain laws, statutes and ordinances" with the advice and consent of that council. He also had the power "to impose and assess, and raise and levy such rates and taxes, as you shall find necessary for the support of government," with sole control of the disposal of that money. Andros could appoint judges, commissioners of oyer and terminer, justices of the peace, and sheriffs, and he could hear appeals in causes worth over £100, grant pardons, and impose quit rents. He had command of all troops, whether regular army or militia, as well as military power to "levy, arm, muster, command, or employ all persons whatsoever." Andros could impose martial law in times of war or rebellion and was authorized "to do and execute all and every other thing which to a Captain General doth, or ought of right to belong." The governor could build fortifications, erect admiralty courts, serve as vice admiral by virtue of a separate commission, appoint captains or other commanders, and punish or execute mutineers or those guilty of seditious behavior. To reward his efforts, the governor was to be paid £1,200 per annum in 1686 and 1687, and £1,400 in 1688.[21]

Andros's commission bestowed powers on the governor that would touch every single person in the Dominion by completely revamping government, religion, and society. Most important, these powers would eliminate the Puritan theocracy that had for so long controlled both church and state. The government that James wanted was a startling and efficient concept, but one that New Englanders were bound to resist. What the king tried to implement through Andros was an "entire new model of government . . . but there was not time to perfect it."[22]

Andros had been given the tools the home government believed necessary to bring the Puritans into line and had great leeway in the interpretation of his powers. The English church and army, both formidable and effective agents of Anglicization, further buttressed his authority. His rule was to be supported by the Reverend Ratcliffe as representative of the Anglican Church, and also by the presence of two companies of foot soldiers. The men, captained by Francis Nicholson, were the first regular army troops ever seen in Massachusetts.[23] The troops would help Andros establish royal authority, effect the centralization of government, and protect the colonies from foreign invasion.

In fact, defense was probably the most important consideration in forming the Dominion. Andros, with his extensive administrative and military experience, was considered by English authorities to be ideally suited for the task of governing New England. Also, Andros had dealt with New Englanders while governor of New York. The earl of Clarendon, on hearing of Andros's appointment, remarked that he "understands the people, and knows how to manage them."[24] To English administrators and the king, Andros's commission was a significant step forward in colonial administration. The Dominion was a long awaited and long needed advance in colonial management that was designed to bring recalcitrant colonies into line, provide adequate defense, and bind colonies more closely to the mother country.

To the Puritans, it spelled disaster. As one unidentified Puritan commented in the wake of the Glorious Revolution, Andros's "commission was such as would make any one believe that a Courtier in the time of the Late King *James* spoke true, who said Sir *E.A. was sent to* New England *on purpose to be a Plague to the people there.*" To the Puritans, who saw the divine hand in everything, Andros was seen as an instrument sent by God to punish them for their sins, just as had been King Philip's War.[25] Though more acceptable than Percy Kirke as governor, Andros was still feared because of his "arbitrary disposition" and his reputation as a "dictator." Even William Penn, an admirer, admitted that Andros's fault was "an over eager & too pressing an execution of his power when provoakt." Like his master, James II, Sir Edmund had never learned the art of compromise.[26]

Now armed with formidable powers, Andros sailed from England on 19 October 1686 on board the fifty gun *Kingfisher*.[27] He sailed without his wife, who planned to join him the next year. On 11 November 1686, the council in Boston ordered the top officials in the town to escort Andros into Boston on his arrival. They also ordered "the gunners at the forts [to] be ready to salute on signal from the townhouse, that the regiment be ready to receive him at the sea shore, and that the Castle company be ready to turn out at a quarter of an hour's warning." The king's colors were to be hoisted "on the Forts and Sconces," guns were to be fired, and the captain of the fort on Castle Island should be on hand "to meet & salute the Governour" as his ship made its way to Boston. Not forgotten by the council were the soldiers traveling on Andros's fleet. The council directed "that a Pipe of Wine be put in some convenient place nere the Towne House" for their refreshment.[28]

In early December, Andros's ship was off of Cape Ann, where it encountered severe weather but was "miraculously preserved from being cast away upon a rock."[29] By Sunday, December 19, the ship arrived in Boston Harbor, and the governor landed the next day, splendidly arrayed in full dress uniform with a "scarlet coat laced, and accompanied by several officers in their brilliant uniforms." Eight companies of the Massachusetts "militia in armes & a great concourse of people," all of whom were "well disposed for His Majts Service, received him." After Congregational minister, Increase Mather, invoked a blessing, Andros's commission was published, and the council, whose members would help him govern, was sworn. Throughout the ceremony, Andros stood, not humbly with hat in hand, but boldly with his hat on his head to underline his superior position in the colony.[30]

The new governor sought to ease any apprehension felt by the colonists on the arrival of royal government by making "high professions of regard to the public good and the welfare of the people, both of merchants and planters." He further assured the people that magistrates appointed by him would "administer justice according to the custom of the place." To show that there was continuity between the old and new regimes, all rates and taxes were to continue in force as would "all the colony's laws not inconsistent with his commission."[31]

Shortly after the ceremonies, Andros inquired of the local Puritan dignitaries whether he and other members of the Church of England might have the use of one of the three Congregational meetinghouses in Boston for services. The request was startling. The next day Puritan leaders, including diarist Samuel Sewall, met to discuss how to respond to Andros's request. On December 22, Andros, having taken lodging at Madam Taylor's house, was visited there by a small Puritan delegation that included ministers, Increase Mather and Samuel Willard. They informed the governor that they "could not with a good conscience consent that our Meeting-House should be made use of for the Common-Prayer Worship." Sewall reported that Andros did not seem insistent and, in fact, "seems to say [he] will not impose." The matter was dropped, and the governor's party continued to hold services in the Town House.[32]

With this religious issue temporarily resolved, Andros turned his attention to the other colonies in the Dominion. Of these, Plymouth was small in population and offered little resistance to being absorbed under Andros's government. Andros appointed eight Plymouth residents to the council, including a former governor Thomas Hinckley. New Hampshire colonists were relieved no longer to be under the control of their rapacious governor, Edward Cranfield. Andros appointed two New Hampshire men to the Dominion council.[33]

Although not part of the original Dominion, the intent of the crown was that both Rhode Island and Connecticut would be quickly absorbed into the new union. Rhode Island accepted Dominion status. On 12 January 1687, Andros's commission was published there, and he dissolved the existing government and broke the provincial seal but was not given the charter. He appointed seven influential Rhode Islanders as councilors, including former governor, Walter Clarke.[34]

Getting Connecticut to accept Dominion status was considerably more difficult. As the Connecticut governor and council wistfully observed, "Old rights and privileges are hard to give up."[35] Andros was authorized in his 13 September 1686 additional instructions to take Connecticut into the Dominion if they were willing to surrender their charter. He and Randolph both informed Connecticut governor, Robert Treat, on 22 December 1686 that a third writ of *quo warranto* had been entered against the colony's charter and that if Connecticut did not defend itself, a judgment would be entered on its nonappearance and the charter voided. Connecticut officials were warned that if this happened, it would not be "your choice how next to dispose of yourselves." The king would then impose on Connecticut any kind of government he pleased.[36]

The Connecticut general court wrote to the earl of Sunderland on 26 January 1687, saying they wanted to continue in their present state but if forced to accept a new government, they would prefer to be included in the Dominion of New England. They thought this "more pleasing than to be joining with any other province," namely New York. Connecticut continued to stall throughout the winter and spring of 1687, still insisting as late as 18 June 1687, that they would not join the Dominion until they heard directly from the king.[37]

Connecticut's stated preference to join the Dominion was spurred by New York's Governor Thomas Dongan, who wanted Connecticut annexed to that colony. The size of Dongan's domain had already been reduced in the spring of 1687 when he surrendered to Andros's control that part of Maine formerly belonging to New York. The transfer was effected when Andros, "upon notice from Col. Dongan," dispatched "an officer with a detachment of soldiers to receive Pemaquid, and keep a garrison in the fort there." Dongan was now extremely unwilling to lose Connecticut as well. He was unaware that the ministry in London had interpreted Connecticut's letter stating they would prefer to be part of the Dominion rather than New York as an agreement to be included in the Dominion.[38]

Andros was instructed to receive Connecticut into the New England government, and on 22 October 1687, Andros informed Robert Treat he would be in Hartford at the end of the next week. Treat decided to yield.[39] Andros was assisted in bringing Connecticut into the Dominion by Fitz-John Winthrop, who urged John Allyn, secretary of Connecticut, to capitulate speedily to Andros, warning that delay might cause them to be excluded from the Dominion council. Andros had already named Winthrop as colonel of the Rhode Island and Narragansett Country militias. After the annexation of Connecticut, Andros gave Winthrop command of the Connecticut militia, promoted him to major general, and appointed him to the council.[40]

Despite a bad cold that had lingered since the end of September, Andros traveled to Connecticut, arriving in Hartford with a retinue of about sixty men, including his friend Fitz Winthrop and "divers of the members of his Council and other gentl. attending him, and with his guard." Connecticut authorities accepted but were not pleased by the king's decision. Andros had his commission read, appointed Treat and John Allyn as Dominion councilors, and erected courts of judicature.[41] The ceremonies completed, Andros went on to New Haven, New London, Fairfield, and Greenwich, "every where chearfully and gratefully received," establishing courts and renaming those men previously in office as sheriffs, constables, or justices of the peace, "not one excepted." As Andros reported, Connecticut leaders "came to meett me & very readily tooke Comission[s] of the peace & militia." With the government ordered, Andros returned by boat to Boston, where he arrived on November 17.[42]

With this first phase of the Dominion established, Andros turned to government. The Dominion of New England did not have a representative assembly. All legislation would be adopted by the governor and council subject to the approval of the king. The king's negative attitude toward assemblies had been amply demonstrated in New York, where he permitted only one assembly to meet under Dongan. In New England, Andros was to govern with the advice of a council but without an assembly. Unlike Andros's own experience in New York, in New England he would attract significant opposition because representative government had been the rule there for several decades. William Blathwayt's assistant, John Povey, accurately surmised that it "will put Sir Edmund to his utmost dexterity" to govern Massachusetts without a representative body. Andros himself had no aversion to an assembly and in New York had requested the duke to permit him to call such a body.[43] The absence of an assembly was probably the chief reason underlying unrest in Massachusetts. Even before Andros arrived, Randolph had warned the Privy Council that he found "the country dissatisfied for want of an Assembly of Representatives . . . with power to raise money, and make laws, etc." Randolph's suggestions to provide representative government fell on deaf ears.[44]

The reduction of traditional rights and privileges resulting from the absence of representative government in New England was, Puritans realized, a dim reflection of events in England. Despite the fact that Monmouth's Rebellion was long since over and England was at peace, James still maintained a large standing army. Whigs protested its presence, citing cost and the fear that the army could be used to deprive them of civil liberties. But they had few avenues in which to protest since James called only one parliament during his reign and that parliament met only two times. The first session was in the spring of 1685; the second was in November 1685. When parliament protested James's appointment of several Roman Catholics as army officers, James prorogued parliament on November 20 and never called it again. On 23 November 1685, he issued a dispensation from taking the Test Act to sixty-eight Catholic army officers. Parliament was dissolved in July 1687. The king devoted his attention to packing the next parliament he would call with Catholics loyal to him. In England, James realized the need to call parliament. He felt no such necessity to have even token representative government in the Dominion of New England.[45]

On 30 December 1686, only ten days after Andros's arrival, the Dominion of New England council met for the first time under his regime. Andros inherited from Dudley a council consisting of fourteen men.[46] The council would eventually grow to forty-two men, with a quorum of seven needed, except in an emergency, when five would suffice. Representatives from Plymouth and Rhode Island were also present at the initial session. Those moderate Puritan merchants who had initially welcomed Andros's arrival in Massachusetts dominated the council. By offering him their support, they expected favors and concessions in return, as had been the case under Dudley's stewardship, but most were disappointed.[47]

The first issue to alienate the councilors from the governor was revenue. The councilors themselves were divided as to who should bear the burden of taxation. Merchants, the majority of the moderate faction, favored a tax on land, while landowners wanted the tax levied on trade.[48] The bill Andros proposed placed a tax of "a penny in the pound on all Estates personal or real, twenty pence *per* head as Poll Money, a penny in the pound for goods imported, besides an Excise on Wine, Rum, and other Liquors." Both landowners and merchants on the council objected to this measure, and the meeting adjourned without a decision being made. When the council reconvened the next day, 3 March 1687, the councilors found that the bill favored by Andros was already engrossed and signed into law by the governor without a vote.[49]

Andros, soon realizing the revenue being raised was insufficient for government expenses, requested and received permission from the king to raise the levies on customs and excise. On 15 February 1688, additional impost and excise duties were adopted on wine, rum, and brandy over the objections of several councilors who did not want to pay higher taxes or impose them on others. Even though taxes overall were lower during the Dominion government than they had been before or would be after, the net effect of both revenue bills was to alienate both merchants and landowners on the council.[50]

Further alienating the Puritan elite was the fact that Andros and his close friends controlled council meetings. The governor "had alway three or fo[u]r of his creatures to say yes to everything he proposed after which no opposition was allowed." Council meetings were poorly attended so that Andros frequently had no choice but to pass legislation whenever he had a quorum. Distance prevented many councilors from attending, as did the expense because councilors were not paid. Hence, the most frequent attendees were those men who lived in or near Boston, including Edward Randolph, John Usher, Joseph Dudley, William Stoughton, Wait Winthrop, Robert Mason, John West, and Francis Nicholson, the latter named to the council in August 1687.[51]

It also seems likely that Andros, despite his initial encouragement of dissenting opinions on the council, grew weary of what he saw as Puritan intransigence. He may well have forced through measures he deemed necessary or that he was ordered to implement by the king. There may have been some truth in the Puritan charge that those who disagreed with Andros "were seldom admitted to" council meetings "and seldomer consulted at the Debates." One councilor charged that "unrighteous Things" were imposed on Massachusetts "and the Governor, with five or six more, did what they would." Another councilor complained that "the Debates in Council were not so free as ought to have been, but too much over-ruled and a great deal of harshness continually expressed against Persons and Opinions that did not please." For the most part, it was Andros and his closest Anglican advisors who formulated laws for *"a Territory the largest and most considerable of any belonging to the Dominion of the Crown."* New Englanders said that discussion of bills was discouraged by Andros, and to avoid it he frequently had bills prepared and shown to the council when they were "too far promoted" to change. Nor did Andros usually bother taking a vote, so that *"there was never any fair way of taking and counting the number of the Councellors consenting and dissenting."*[52]

Facing continuing dissent from the Puritans on his council, Andros relied more and more on the advice of long time friends and associates, who were all outsiders and non-Puritans. This fact alone alienated the Puritan elite who, for the first time since settlement, did not control their own government. At the highest level of government, the governor was both an outsider and an Anglican. So too were his top advisors, most of whom had come from England or New York, not Massachusetts. Those closest to Andros were councilors John Palmer, Brockholes, Mason, Usher, Randolph, Secretary John West, Justice of the Peace Benjamin Bullivant, and Attorney General James Graham.[53] Excluded from the governor's inner circle were such moderate Puritans as Richard Wharton, Wait Winthrop, and William Stoughton, who initially supported the Dominion. The Puritans were angry that Andros conferred "preferments principally upon such Men as were strangers to and haters of the People."[54]

One of the most hated of Andros's advisors was his customs agent, Edward Randolph. Even more offensive to Puritans than Randolph, if that was possible, was the merchant James Graham, a Scot, who came to New York with Andros in 1674. Graham also followed Andros to Boston in 1688 to serve as attorney general, replacing Benjamin Bullivant. The latter, an apothecary and physician from London, was close to the governor, serving first as attorney general and then as justice of the peace. John Palmer was another friend who came to New York in 1675 and was favored both by Andros and by his successor, Thomas Dongan. The latter appointed Palmer to the New York council. When New York and New Jersey were added to the Dominion, Palmer moved to Boston and was named a judge in 1688. John West, a merchant, had also accompanied Andros to New York in 1674 and then followed him to Boston to serve as clerk of the court of assizes and town clerk. When West was in need of additional income, Andros, in the spring of 1687, persuaded Randolph to lease his office of secretary to West at a fee of £50 annually. This favor cost Randolph some £300 or £400 per year in fees.[55]

The Puritans complained that "of all our Oppressors we were chiefly *squeez'd* by a Crew of abject Persons fetched *from New York*," who extorted "extraordinary and intolerable Fees" from the Puritans "upon all occasions." Fees were often "arbitrarily imposed." Randolph himself had complained to John Povey in 1687 that West "extorts what fees he pleases" and had fought off attempts to establish a fee schedule. Andros tried to correct the fee situation by appointing a committee to establish a schedule, but it was never adopted because Secretary West "insisted upon Fees much more extraordinary."[56]

Palmer and West had consistently sought to profit from the American colonists. While the men were still in New York, Dongan had appointed them as commissioners to Maine and approved their purchase of land there. Concerned only with their own profits, Palmer and West immediately began to call into question the titles of colonists. Many were "Some of the first settlers of that Eastern country," telling them they "were denied grants of their own lands," while West and Palmer appropriated "the improved lands" for themselves. By 1688, they had leased land back to some 140 of the original owners, each of whom paid West and Palmer a fee of two pounds, ten shillings. When Andros went to Maine in the spring of 1688, the farmers complained, asking him to confirm their rights. Andros recognized "the whole proceeding" as "illegal," with new patents essentially worthless. The original Maine colonists, while not pleased to be included under the Dominion government, benefited by the transfer because Andros stopped the seizures of land. Andros was annoyed not only with West and Palmer but also with Dongan, who had permitted this greed. Randolph commented that it "was not well done of Palmer and West to tear all in pieces that was settled and granted at Pemaquid by Sir Edmund, that was the sceene where they placed and displaced at pleasure, and were as arbitrary as the great Turke."[57]

Despite their greed, Palmer and West, along with Graham, all Anglicans, formed the nucleus of the inner circle that ruled New England with Andros. Giving choice offices to close friends and relatives was a common practice in the seventeenth century and one with which the Puritans were well acquainted. What bothered the Puritans, particularly those who had initially supported Andros, was that they were now excluded from the offices that promised favor.[58] The opportunities these offices presented for pay-offs and bribes were considerable, so the Puritans' charges of greed and corruption against Andros's closest associates were undoubtedly true. No evidence exists, however, that Andros himself participated in the graft or that he used his position to acquire land, as did so many of his aides.

New Englanders, excluded from the profits of office and decision making by corrupt Anglican officials, resented the fact that Andros bestowed "Preferments principally upon such Men as were strangers to and haters of the People."[59] This charge and many others that were later brought against Andros and his friends were patently absurd, making it difficult to separate fact from fiction. But Andros did rely heavily on the advice of his friends, ignoring that from others. Randolph noted soon after Graham's appointment as attorney general that "now the Governor is safe in his New York confidents, all others being strangers to his councill."[60] Andros's rift from the New England elite is apparent in his failure to make friends there. Unlike New York, where Andros had no difficulty in befriending local Dutch merchants, several of whom he appointed to positions of power, he made few close friends among the New England Puritans, except Fitz Winthrop. Even Winthrop's friendship proved unstable because at best, Winthrop failed Andros when he needed him to defend the colony; at worst, Winthrop had knowledge of the Puritan plot to overthrow Andros's government and failed to warn the governor.

By putting trusted, like-minded friends in positions of authority, Andros's actions in New England were similar to those of James II's in England and raised as much, if not more, alarm. In both old and new worlds, the old ruling elite were ousted, replaced by outsiders who were personally loyal to the king or to the governor. These practices effectively isolated both the king in England and his governor in Massachusetts.

Of the many aspects of the Dominion government that irritated Puritans, perhaps the most galling was the loss of control over politics. Local government was lost with the requirement to bring all public records to Boston. No longer did Puritans dominate jury panels to the exclusion of all others. Although jury trials were guaranteed, Andros exerted a strong measure of control over jury decisions because jurors were appointed by sheriffs who were, in turn, appointed by the governor. Sheriffs were no longer required to be members of the Congregational Church any more than were other officials. In the court itself, there were visible reminders of the new regime, as Andros imposed English law and legal practices on a colony that had previously ignored both. Puritans had not sworn on the Bible when taking oaths, but preferred to "Swear with an uplifted Hand, agreeable to the ancient Custom of the Colony." It may have been a Puritan New England custom, but Andros's assignment was to make legal practices in the Dominion conform with those in England. Hence, Andros introduced the practice of swearing in court on the King James version of the Bible. Those Puritans who refused to do so were fined for contempt of court and thrown in jail if they could not pay the fine.[61]

In 1687, popular discontent raised by lack of representation and other measures became open defiance. On 28 September 1687, Andros informed the Privy Council Committee on Plantations that the people of three Essex County towns, at a town meeting, had refused to elect tax commissioners or assess tax rates. They claimed that only an elected assembly could take such action, stating that taxes instituted by Andros alone were "Illegal Taxes" because they ignored their rights as Englishmen under the Magna Carta. The Puritans complained long and loudly that their rights as Englishmen were being violated, conveniently ignoring the fact that an exclusively Puritan leadership elected by an exclusively Puritan electorate had for decades imposed taxes on members of other religious sects who were excluded from voting solely on the basis of their religion. Apparently there was no recognition that by doing so the Puritans had also denied people their English rights.[62]

If Essex County residents thought Andros would overlook their defiance or change his policies, they were mistaken. Andros, angry with this backwoods resistance, termed "the people of the countrey Jacks and Toms," and insisted "that he and his Crew had the Immediate dispose of our fortuns," or so the victims charged. He ordered the arrest of thirty protesters, who later complained they were "denied an *Habeas Corpus.*" John Palmer claimed their actions were "far from a peaceable objecting," and that in fact they behaved "in a *riotous manner* . . . next door to *Rebellion.*" For this behavior "they were Indicted, Tried, and Convicted." While it was true that "habeus corpus was denied in Major Appleton's case," Palmer said, this right was "limited to the Kingdom of *England.*"[63]

Most of the prisoners were soon released, but six leaders, including John Appleton and the minister John Wise, were bound over for trial before the superior court in Boston, where judges Joseph Dudley, William Stoughton, John Usher, and Edward Randolph presided. During the course of the trial, one of the defendants protested that the trial and sentence interfered with their rights as English subjects under the Magna Carta. The magistrate told him, "You have no more privileges left you than not to be Sould for Slaves."[64]

In his summation to the jury, Dudley told them that he was pleased to have "so many worthy Gentlmen of the Jury so capable to do the king['s] service, and we expect a good Verdict from you, seeing the matter hath been so sufficiently proved against the Criminals."[65] To no one's surprise, the verdict was guilty. The six defendants were returned to prison, where they were kept waiting twenty-one days for sentencing on October 24. The excessive fines imposed were a surprise. Wise and Appleton were fined £50 each and had to post bonds of £1,000 each to ensure future good behavior. Wise was silenced until he apologized to Andros, which he did in November. Four other defendants had fines imposed of between £15 and £30 and were required to post good behavior bonds of £500. In addition, each defendant was charged £16.19s.6d. in court costs.[66]

The issues raised by the Essex County revolt were fundamental to colonial/imperial relations and defined issues that would never be resolved. Essex County residents later claimed that they were only "peaceably objecting against raising of Taxes without an Assembly," objecting to being taxed without a representative assembly, the existence of which they considered a basic right due them as English subjects. Colonists believed their assemblies were equal in importance and influence to the British House of Commons, though Englishmen at home recognized no such similarity. To them, the rights of colonists were inferior to those of Englishmen at home. Colonial assemblies were established only for the convenience of the home government, and the existence of such assemblies were seen as a privilege that could be withdrawn at any time.[67]

The governor's attack on property denied Puritans what they considered a basic right. Puritans may have left England by choice but insisted they were "intitled to the liberties and immunities of free and natural born English subjects." Believing this, they declared "no monies ought to be raised from them but by their representatives." Without a general assembly, they believed their "condition is little inferior to absolute slavery." While colonists until the American Revolution continued to believe that they enjoyed, or should enjoy, all the privileges of Englishmen at home, English administrators believed colonial rights were circumscribed to only those rights of Englishmen living abroad, two diametrically opposed views that would never be reconciled. As Judge Dudley told one of the Essex County defendants who argued that taxes imposed by the Dominion government interfered with his rights as an Englishman, "They must not think the privileges of Englishmen would follow them to the end of the world." Andros may have had some sympathy with the colonists' demands for a representative assembly, but if he did, it was primarily because such a body would make it easier for him to impose and collect taxes. As far as the provinces were concerned, Andros shared the view of most English colonial administrators that the colonies were subordinate to the mother country and existed primarily for the benefit of England.[68]

While lack of representation and high taxes were disturbing, the most serious immediate threat posed by Andros was to landowners, because long held land titles were brought into question under the new regime. To Andros, with his empire-wide perspective, land titles should only be confirmed on valid purchases. It made sense to him that land companies should not be permitted to drive out colonists of modest means. Developers did not share imperial concerns. They wanted only to exploit their fellow colonists and the natural resources of the land. Support for the governor among moderates quickly faded when they realized Andros threatened their land holdings, since land was the basis of all other rights.

What New Englanders considered an attack on property began soon after Andros's arrival, when he startled landowners by informing them that their ownership of land had been voided by the revocation of the colony's charter. Land in the Dominion now belonged to the king, and landowners were required to petition the government for new titles. Land titles previously issued by towns, including titles issued to members of his council, were now deemed invalid. The concept that all land in New England, just as in England, belonged to the king was one Puritans refused to accept. When Andros visited Puritan minister Higginson and asked for his opinion, the minister argued that the land belonged not to the king but to the king's subjects who had occupied it for more than half a century. When the minister still refused to accept royal proprietorship, Andros put the matter squarely. "Either you are subjects or you are Rebels," he said. To Andros, there was no middle ground. People either accepted royal authority and obeyed orders without question, or they were no different than the parliamentary forces during the Civil Wars or Monmouth's followers during his rebellion.[69]

Although Andros bore the complaints, the decision to repatent all land was that of the home government. A simple and automatic repatenting of New England property was deemed impossible since so many titles were unclear, overlapping, or uncertain. Left to the discretion of the governor as to how to proceed, Andros decided all landowners, even those with long standing titles, had to apply to Attorney General Graham and offer solid proof that they were entitled to their land. Only then could they obtain title reconfirmation. Uncertainty was the result and New Englanders later claimed that the people were "every day told, *That no Man was owner of a Foot of Land in all the Colony.*"[70] The reconfirmation process entailed the paying of fees and bribes to government officials, including Attorney General Graham and Secretary West.[71] To encourage owners to develop their property, undeveloped land was subject to quit rents of 2s.6d. per one hundred acres. Further animosity was raised when Andros ruled common land was also the property of the crown, granting much of it to his coterie of friends.[72]

Many Puritans had bought land directly from the Indians and lacked any kind of solid proof of ownership. Such was the case with Joseph Lynde of Charles Town. When he explained his problem to the governor, he was told that his title "was [of] no more worth than a scratch with a Bears paw." Lynde, who had extensive land holdings, reluctantly agreed to petition for a new patent, only to be told by Secretary John West that he had to get patents for each county in which he claimed to own land. Lynde found "the thing so chargeable and difficult" that he delayed filing his petition. When much to his surprise, a writ of intrusion was served on him in the summer of 1688, Lynde applied for a patent.[73]

Others resisted applying for patents, not only because of the inconvenience but also because patent fees could be as high £50 for a small parcel of land. And the attitudes of Andros and his aides toward petitioners were often unnecessarily brusque. When petitioners told Graham they were determined to defend their claim to Boston property, Graham responded that "it might cost them all that they are worth, and something besides." One old and sick minister, Mr. Wiswall, had transcribed a document to clear an owner's rights to property. He was summoned to come to Boston to defend his actions. Though he protested he was incapacitated with gout in both feet, he was ordered to come immediately.[74]

Andros also raised animosity among New Englanders by his refusal to recommend the approval of large land grants to individuals or land companies. An early victim was councilor, lawyer, merchant, and land speculator, Richard Wharton, a moderate Puritan who was married to Wait and Fitz Winthrop's sister. Wharton, initially a supporter of Andros, was a member of the Atherton Company that claimed almost sixty thousand acres in the Narragansett country, disputed territory that had been placed under Rhode Island by Charles II. Despite the king's ruling, Connecticut and Massachusetts continued to claim jurisdiction over the area. Rhode Island's right to the land was thrown into doubt when the Narragansett country was included in Dudley's commission as part of the Dominion territory.[75] Members of the Atherton Company included colonials Simon Bradstreet, former Massachusetts governor, and John Winthrop, Jr., former Connecticut governor and father of Wait and Fitz. They were assisted in their petition to London by such influential Atherton Company members as Thomas Lord Culpepper and Edward Cranfield, former governors of Virginia and New Hampshire respectively, both known for their extreme greed. All stockowners believed that if the patent was approved, the company would realize a profit of £10,000 sterling.[76]

William Blathwayt was also a member of the company, a fact apparently unknown to Edward Randolph, who complained to him that the Atherton Company had nary "a notion of a title no wheres fixd either by Indian purchase or Grant from Any Go[ver]m[en]t and every way uncertain."[77] The company appealed for a royal charter for the land, requesting the land itself be put under the jurisdiction of Connecticut. When Andros was asked to give an opinion on the appeal, he decided strongly against the Atherton Company, reporting to the home government that the company's claims were invalid and the land not part of Connecticut at all, but part of Rhode Island. Andros granted Richard Wharton only a little over seventeen hundred acres, not the sixty thousand he originally claimed. Probably because of Culpepper's considerable influence, the Privy Council Committee on Trade actually recommended to the king that Andros be ordered to award a patent to the company for sixty thousand acres, but the recommendation was not acted upon.[78]

Wharton was also an investor in Maine land. He and fellow New Englanders, Joseph Dudley, Samuel Shrimpton, and others, bought a tract of land, the Million Purchase, that measured six by ten miles. Asked to rule on whether a royal charter should be granted, Andros again gave a negative report. He reasoned that "many others Lay Clayme to Great Tracts and parcells of Land In those parts . . . To the great Hinderance of the Settlement and Improvement of the country and prejudice of many his Majesties Subjects who are Desirous to plant and Improve the Same." Despite strong support from London investors, this claim was also rejected.[79]

Nor did Andros approve of a scheme to establish a manor on a half million acres Wharton personally owned in Maine. Undaunted, Wharton continued to pursue wealth through land investments, forming a joint stock company to exploit Maine's natural resources. Wharton, backed financially by Wait Winthrop, sailed for England in 1687 to enlist support for his plans. He found an ally in London mayor, Sir John Shorter. Wharton also tried to affect Andros's removal, but died before he could achieve his goal.[80]

By 1688, several provincials were in London to complain about Andros's administration, their number increasing as Andros continued to investigate land titles. He was particularly disturbed to find that many New Englanders had bought land directly from Indians, a practice that undermined the royal prerogative.[81] Samuel Sewall initially ignored the order to submit his claim to 498 acres on Hog Island for reconfirmation. He changed his mind when his tenant on the island, John Hubbard, informed him that "there is a Writt out against me for Hog-Island, and against several other persons for Land, as being violent intruders into the Kings Possession." Sewall's was one of only seven writs issued by the Dominion government. He was undecided about whether he should capitulate and file for confirmation. Samuel Shrimpton, also served with a writ, refused at first to petition for a new title. Sewall finally yielded and applied for a new patent in July 1688,

Samuel Sewall (1652–1730). Born in England, Sewall was educated at Harvard College. He was named a magistrate in 1684 and served as a judge at the 1692 Salem witchcraft trials, although he later regretted his participation in the trials. In addition to keeping a journal of events in Massachusetts, Sewall also published the first American anti-slavery pamphlet. Portrait by Nathaniel Emmons, ca. 1730. MHS image number 74. Reproduced by courtesy of the Massachusetts Historical Society.

asking "your Excellencies favour that he may obtain His Majesties Grant and Confirmation of the said Hogg-Island." Although Sewall obeyed, the majority of people in Massachusetts remained "very averse from complying with any thing that may alter the Tenure of their Lands, and," Sewall admitted, "look on me very sorrowfully that I have given way." In fact, resistance was widespread, with only about two hundred applications filed for patent reconfirmation. Even when initiated, the process was so slow that only about twenty titles passed the seal during Andros's governorship, but Sewall's was one of them. Sewall sailed for England in November 1688 to complain about Andros.[82]

Andros's land policy affected all landowners, Puritans and non-Puritans alike, and had the net effect of drawing alien groups and dissident factions together. When the opportunity for rebellion presented itself, Andros could count for support only from those few Anglican advisors who were closest to him and had benefited from their association with him. The net result of Andros's refusal to confirm large land patents or his inflexibility in confirming existing patents was to alienate both moderate and militant Puritans. Sewall and Wharton were only two of the Puritans who were initially willing to work with Andros but changed their minds when their property and profits were threatened.[83]

Also at issue were Andros's attempts to bring new ways of thinking and acting to people who had become set in their ways. As Andros himself acknowledged, it was difficult to make progress with people "so wedded to their old wayes & Customs." Edward Randolph also believed that any change was difficult because "this people are riveted in their way and I feare nothing but necessity or force will otherwise dispose Them."[84] Riveted they remained, despite efforts by Andros to bring them within the king's realm and in compliance to royal directions.

8

The Dominion of New England, 1686–1688

Part 2

> The Standing Forces were a crew that began to teach New
> England to drab, drink, blaspheme, curse, and damn; a crew
> that were every foot moving tumults, and committing insuf-
> ferable riots amongst a quiet and peaceable people.
>
> —Increase Mather[1]

IT IS DOUBTFUL IF NEW ENGLAND BEFORE THE ARRIVAL OF ENGLISH redcoats was free of the sins outlined by the Reverend Mather. Nevertheless, it was the first time that regular soldiers had been permanently stationed in Massachusetts. Despite the fact that their actual number was small, their presence was disturbing because of what an armed force represented. They were there not only to defend the colony from invasion, but also to assist Andros in his assigned task to bring New England society and practices into conformity with those of England. The governor-general was as determined that the New England provincials would adopt English values and standards as the New Englanders were to resist these demands.

Under the Dominion of New England government with Sir Edmund Andros as governor-general, the Puritans found daily reminders that they were part of England's empire. They had initially fled to New England to escape corruption in England and to establish a perfect utopian society in the New World. Such a community can succeed only with isolation and the ability to keep out all but the like-minded, two goals that proved impossible to achieve. By 1686, members of other sects had flocked into New England, and provincials had become dependent on England for trade outlets. The colonies were equally important to England, leading the king to draw the New England colonies more firmly under his control.

The governor of the Dominion was the first of the reminders that New England was part of England. The second arrived in Boston on 24 December 1686, when "About 60 Red-Coats are brought to Town, landed at Mr. Pool's wharf, where drew up and so marched to Mr. Gibbs's house at Fort-hill." For the first time, Boston heard the "rattling of guns" and, in this case, professional soldiers, soon to number one hundred, wielding guns with bayonets.[2] The men were under the command of Captain Francis Nicholson, who had served at Tangier under Lieutenant Colonel Thomas Dongan, now governor of New York. Nicholson himself reported to an efficient, dedicated, and experienced military officer who was now the governor-general. Provincials resented the fact that the soldiers were in Massachusetts "to support what was to be imposed upon us, not without repeated Menaces that some hundreds more were intended for us." It did not seem an idle threat since the Puritans were well aware that James maintained a large and prepared army of almost twenty thousand men.[3]

More immediately distressing to the Puritan majority was the fact that Andros reorganized the local militia, replacing many Puritan officers with members of the Church of England. Thus, "the colonial militias became an arm of Andros's authority, a policy which reflected James's belief that government had to be fully subordinate to the royal will." So had James II raised animosity in England when he replaced Church of England army officers with Catholic officers. Also offensive to Puritans was the thought that Andros could send their militia of 13,279 men to anywhere in English America. If the need arose, New Englanders were willing to defend their own colony, but they most certainly were not ready to send soldiers to die for New Yorkers or Virginians.[4]

New Englanders might resist efforts at centralization, but they could not ignore the immediate presence of English regulars in their midst. Not only were they not welcome, the Puritans blamed them for introducing sin, satan, and unrest to Massachusetts.[5] Well might provincials complain about the coarseness of the soldiers (most civilian populations had similar reactions to regulars), but the complaints extended to their commanding officer.[6] At least one New Englander accused Andros of "common Cursing and Swearing and Sabbath-breaking" and of heavy drinking with his "Knot of Counsellors" until "after midnight."[7]

Whether drunk or sober, Andros found the Dominion ill prepared for defense in the event of a French attack. There was a clear view of incoming vessels from the aging Castle Island fort, three miles distant from Boston. The fort there, Andros said, "commands the channel, hath four bastions, but very small and inconsiderate . . . the walls about ten foot high, and out of repair, and only guard rooms under the batterys of the curtains and a room over the gate." Militia officer, Wait Winthrop, commander of the Castle Island fort, lost his post when Andros appointed Francis Nicholson as its new commander. Winthrop, though distressed by the change, continued to wield influence as a council member.[8] Andros came supplied with some military stores but was dismayed on arrival to find only fifty "Old Match Locks at Boston and some few old Arms & Necessarys for the Great Guns at Castle Island." There were eighty iron guns and "no magazines of powder or other stores of war, no store-house or accommodation or lodging for officer or soldier, nor any good fortification."[9]

To improve defenses, Andros ordered the repair of the Castle Island facility, the construction of eight other forts at strategic locations throughout the Dominion, and the building of a new fort "at the South end of towne, called Fort Hill, very proper to command the Towne and comeing in both by land and sea." The proposed site was near "a good Channel close to the shore, where convenient Warehouses may be made, and as am advised," Andros wrote, "a Dry Dock if Occasion."[10] The site was leveled, and a 150 foot long square polygon fort with barracks was built by local militia units.[11] By the spring of 1688, the barracks were complete, or at least complete enough so that the governor could house the garrison there. The structure, named Fort Mary in honor of the king's elder daughter, flew the Dominion flag. St. George's cross was displayed on a white field with the initials JR and a crown embroidered in gold in the center of the cross, a reminder to provincials of the dominion of the king. Andros had few weapons to store in the fort and a year after construction began was still requesting ammunition and small arms from England to supplement the antiquated matchlocks. While the fort was necessary for defense, or at least so Andros believed, the Puritans resented it because they would bear the cost in the form of taxes of its construction and the cost of maintaining the soldiers as well.[12]

While Andros planned for his defense of the Dominion, he awaited the arrival of his wife. Lady Andros had remained in England for almost a year after her husband sailed. She embarked for New England in the fall of 1687 with her niece, Craven. After her November 17 arrival, Andros reported that his wife was "very well," but she and her niece understandably found "the Contrey very Cold."[13] It was too cold apparently for a person used to a more moderate climate. Weakened by the long ocean voyage, Lady Andros became ill, and by 16 January 1688, it was known throughout Boston that she was near death. Andros had also been ailing throughout the winter but was so distraught by the condition of his wife that he would neither eat nor drink nor sleep, raising fears in his friends that he would suffer a relapse of the illness that had lingered since the fall. On Sunday, January 22, prayers were said for Lady Andros in the South Meeting House, but Sewall noted that "About the beginning of our afternoon Exercise, the Lady Andros expires." Services were held in the meetinghouse on 10 February 1688, the coffin attended by mourning women, with numerous candles, torches, and ringing of bells. The hearse was pulled to the cemetery by six horses and was escorted by a military honor guard "to the great grief and sorrow of his Excellency and all that knew her." Lady Andros's niece, Craven, remained in Boston until April 1688 and then sailed home for England. At her departure, Andros moved "his very small family to fort hill" to live again the solitary existence of a soldier.[14]

Soldiers from the fort and sailors from Royal Navy ships in the harbor were constant reminders of the military might of the king, even accompanying the governor to religious services on Sundays and on Christmas day. It was offensive to Puritans to see Andros walking to the services with a red coat on the right and Royal Navy Captain John George of HMS *Rose* on the left. Christmas services were a further affront to the Puritans, who did not celebrate it or any saint's day. The Puritans went about their business as usual, with all shops open and craftsmen pursuing their arts.[15]

Ignoring Andros and Christmas as they would, provincials could not escape the changes that the Andros regime personified, reminders being evident all around them. Puritans were startled on 31 January 1687, the anniversary of the 1649 execution of Charles I, by the ringing of bells in Boston and the holding of two Anglican memorial services at the Town House. Sounded at the order of the governor to commemorate the execution, the bells were the first public expression in Boston of mourning for the deceased king. A further reminder that Puritans were now under the direct rule of the king came on St. George's Day, April 23, also the anniversary of the coronation of James II. A celebration was held in Boston at the governor's order. Many non-Puritans or moderate Puritans attached red paper crosses to their hats to indicate their loyalty to the king and the new regime. Orthodox Puritans were appalled by the public display of gunfire, bonfires, and fireworks. The latter echoed the magnificent fireworks display seen over the Thames the night of James's coronation, an event that was perhaps recalled by Andros, who probably had been one of the courtiers watching with the king at Whitehall.[16]

Puritans also felt their religious freedom was further threatened when differences developed concerning public support for the Congregational Church. When this matter was brought before Andros's council, several Puritans, including former Plymouth governor, Thomas Hinckley, urged the practice be continued. Andros and his close aides disagreed, Edward Randolph arguing it would be just as reasonable for Plymouth to be forced "to pay our minister of the church of England, who now preaches in Boston . . . as to make the quakers pay in your colony."[17] When the councilors voted to end public support of congregational churches, their ministers became dependent upon the uncertain charity of their congregations, now solely responsible for their support. This earned Andros the undying enmity of Congregational ministers, the most influential men in New England.[18]

Puritans also resented what they interpreted as Andros's efforts to take over Harvard College, established to provide an educated ministry in the first few years of settlement. Andros, suspecting misappropriation of funds, called "to account the Managers of the publick money of the Colledge" and insisted on auditing its accounts.[19] Randolph went so far as to suggest the dismissal of the Harvard president, Increase Mather, over this issue.[20] Andros further alienated Puritans when he personally attended commencement exercises and ordered Minister Ratcliffe to sit on the pulpit during the ceremonies. This was an unwelcome intrusion at the services, where Increase Mather presided.[21]

The king in England had made similar attempts to destroy the hold of the Church of England on Oxford and Cambridge. At the latter university, James dismissed the Anglican vice chancellor when he refused to accept a Catholic candidate for a master's degree. In Magdalene College at Oxford, in March 1687 the fellows rejected James's nomination of a Catholic, John Hough, as president. This act won them a royal visit in September 1687, during which the irate king berated the fellows for their defiance. Despite the royal tirade, the fellows held fast and continued in their refusal to accept a Catholic president. The result was that by March 1688, virtually all of the Anglican fellows at Magdalene had been dismissed. After this purge, Oxford was no longer under the control of the Church of England, the Catholic mass replacing Anglican services.[22]

The king, to implement his programs, had turned to other non-conformists for support, probably at the suggestion of the earl of Sunderland, who was virtually prime minister. The result was the first Declaration of Indulgence, issued on 4 April 1687. A ruse whose true purpose was immediately apparent to Anglicans at home, it suspended all penal laws against Roman Catholics, permitted public worship of nonconformist religions, granted freedom of worship, and eliminated the Test Act for holding civil or military offices. Most Englishmen viewed the measure with alarm because it seemed a signal that James was about to impose Catholicism on the nation. In New England, where Andros published it at the order of the king on 25 August 1687, it brought great joy to the colonists because it seemed an assurance from the king that Andros would not be permitted to establish Anglicanism there.[23]

James II, a dissenter himself, needed and sought the support of other dissenters. Preceding the Declaration, James, in March 1686, had offered a general pardon to dissenters and had freed Quakers from prison, stopping all criminal proceedings against them.[24] The Puritans in Boston, to show the king their gratitude for the Declaration, asked Andros if they could hold a day of thanksgiving. Andros, who recognized the slur to the Church of England and to himself, refused. When the ministers persisted in their demands, he informed them that "they should meet at their peril, and that he would send soldiers to guard their meeting-houses." The Puritans decided instead to ask Increase Mather to carry a personal letter of thanks to James, to which Mather agreed. By December, he was ready to embark for England, not only to carry the letter, but also, as Andros well realized, to convey Puritan complaints to the king.[25]

As Mather prepared to sail for England, Randolph charged him with defamation of character and sued for £500 in damages, undoubtedly an attempt by Andros and Randolph to keep him in Massachusetts. Randolph had uncovered a letter presumably written by Increase Mather in 1684 to Abraham Kick (or Keck), a fellow minister of the English church in Amsterdam, in which Mather criticized Randolph. Mather, on inspecting the letter, declared it to be a fake, accusing Randolph of the forgery. Randolph sued Mather for defamation, and Mather was arrested on 24 December 1687. On 31 January 1688, Mather's case was heard, but he was cleared of the charge, with Randolph ordered

Increase Mather (1639–1723). Born in Massachusetts and educated at Harvard College, Mather also attended Trinity College in Dublin. Mather was the minister of the Second Congregational Church in Boston. In 1685, he was elected president of Harvard. Portrait by John van der Spriett, 1688. MHS image number 1442. Reproduced by the courtesy of the Massachusetts Historical Society.

to pay court costs. On 18 March 1688, a triumphant Mather gave a farewell sermon as he prepared again to sail to England. Andros was still determined to detain him, and on March 27, an officer was sent to arrest Mather but was refused entry to Mather's house. Mather, escaping from the house in disguise, made his way to a ship in the harbor bound for England.[26]

Further alienating Congregational ministers and laymen alike was Andros's renewed demand in 1687 to hold Anglican services in a Congregational church. As spring approached, the governor became more and more weary of attending church services in the Town House, which Andros found in "no wayes Convenient." In late February 1687, Andros told Puritan leaders that he wanted Church of England services held every Sunday at 11 A.M. and at 4 P.M. in their South Meeting House, where Samuel Willard was the congregational minister. Though the Puritans did not use the meetinghouse at these times, they were aghast at the prospect. They refused the governor's request, but the governor ignored their refusal. On March 22, he sent Edward Randolph to look at three Puritan churches in Boston. After deciding on the South Church, Andros sent Randolph back to obtain the keys. Anglican services were held there two days later on Good Friday, and then every Sunday thereafter, "between eleven and twelve in the morning, and in the afternoone about fower."[27]

Andros's appropriation of a Congregational church was similar to James's actions within the British isles, except that Andros was not interested in conversions. James wanted to achieve not only acceptance of Catholicism but wholesale conversions. Andros's sole interest, however, was to provide for the spiritual guidance of members of the Church of England (and perhaps to irritate the Puritans). In 1687, James had sent Catholic soldiers to Andros's home island of Guernsey, along with a Franciscan priest, Richard Trappes, to deliver mass.[28] There was as much opposition to the priest on Guernsey as there was in Boston against Andros's holding of Anglican rites in a congregational church.[29] To New England Puritans, to conduct in their churches the very rites and rituals that they or their ancestors had fled England to avoid was an outrageous and ungodly intrusion. Anger increased on Easter Sunday, 27 March 1687, when the Anglican minister, Ratcliffe, who should have been finished with the service at 1:30 P.M., went on at length in his sermon, forcing the Puritans to wait outside before they could enter for their own service. In early June, members of the South Church held a private fast because of the difficult times thrust upon them by

Andros's use of the church. Despite the fast and the protests, on 12 June 1687, Sewall noted in his diary that the governor's use of the church for Anglican services posed "little hindrance to us save as to ringing the first Bell."[30]

Sewall's attitude of tolerance toward the use of the church by Anglicans changed in June 1688, after Andros decided he wanted services held earlier than the congregational service on Sunday morning. This followed another incident when Anglicans had been kept waiting until the Congregational services concluded. Andros sent John West to tell Willard that Anglican services would be held first. The governor's demand caused church members Samuel Sewall and Captain Frary to confront Andros, explaining that Willard had no authority to approve the change because the church building was owned by all the church members, who made decisions as a congregation. They further explained that the long service the previous week was because it " 'twas the Lord's Supper, and [the governor] had promised to go to some other House on such dayes." Randolph said he recalled no such promise and Graham was charged by the governor with investigating the legal aspects of church ownership. Andros was indignant at being accused of breaking his word, but peace was temporarily restored when the Puritans agreed that Anglican services would start at 8 A.M. and Andros agreed they would end no later than 9 A.M.[31]

In fact, the use of the church was only a temporary expedient. Andros, "understanding it gave offence," decided to raise money to build an Anglican church "at the charge of those of the Church of England." King's Chapel was the first Anglican church established in Boston. Samuel Sewall reported on 16 October 1688, that "the Ground-Sills" of the church were laid, "the stone foundation being finished."[32] The sight of the wooden chapel offered a new affront to Puritan sensibilities, particularly since Andros had it built on part of a Puritan graveyard.[33] They continued to show their distaste for the chapel, with the building "receiving the marks of their indignation and scorn by having the Windows broke to pieces, and the Doors and Walls daubed and defiled with dung and other filth." Puritans also showed their disdain of Anglicans by calling "them *Papist Doggs, and Rogues*, to their Faces." The abuse continued. Samuel Miles, who succeeded Ratcliffe as Anglican minister, wrote in 1690 that the chapel "is perpetually abused[,] the Windows broken as soon as mended."[34]

Adding immeasurably to the general discontent caused by the very visible Anglican presence in Boston was Andros's March

1688 ban on town meetings, a cherished tradition in most communities since first settlement. Such meetings presented a forum at which colonists could protest unpopular measures, such as taxation and quit rents. It was at a town meeting that the people of Essex County had first decided to flaunt Andros's tax measures. Consequently, Andros limited town meetings to only one a year and only for the specific purpose of electing civil officers. The governor's regulations reached every person and every person's pocketbook, even those of newlyweds. To marry, a couple had to post bond with Andros that would be forfeited if later there did "appear to have been any lawful impediment" to the union. Another blow to the Puritan practice of civil, instead of religious, marriage was Andros's threat to declare unlawful all marriages "but such as are made by ministers of the church of England." Puritans objected since they recognized only the sacraments of baptism and communion. Nor were widows and orphans free from harassment, or so the Puritans claimed. To raise money, new fees were established, such as a 50s. fee imposed on the probate of a will, which Puritans claimed was "a great burden upon widows and children."[35]

The effect of such measures was probably not overly dramatic, but Anglican influence was very obvious and growing steadily. Further evidence of Anglicization was provided by the presence of a Maypole in Charles Town, a symbol that was particularly offensive to Puritans. Angry Puritans cut down the Charles Town pole, but an even bigger one was put up. Its very existence was a sign that Anglican influence was becoming stronger and that the Puritans were losing control of their society. The Maypole represented only the tip of the Anglican wedge, soon to be followed by observance of Christmas and other holy days, and by card games, dancing, playgoing, and other activities previously banned by the Puritans.[36]

The Anglican influence that so irked Puritans was embodied in the person of the governor-general, who, like all royal governors, was quite conscious of his dignity and position. Sir Edmund Andros, son of Charles I's master of ceremonies, raised in the company of future monarchs, embodied the aristocratic attitudes that Puritans loathed. Incidents that underlined these qualities were later collected and circulated as evidence against the governor. Equally offensive to provincials was Andros's attitude toward Indians. In one case, two militia officers from Sudbury had said that an Indian named John James had charged that "the Governour was a Rogue and had hired the Indians to kill the

English." The men were ordered by the local justice of the peace to appear with the Indian before Andros in Boston. On arrival in Boston, they went to the governor's house but were kept waiting outside in the rain and cold for several hours. When they were finally admitted to Andros's presence, they were amazed to find that the governor, instead of punishing the Indian, was kind to him. Andros, who believed the two colonists had bribed the Indian to make his statement, ordered the men to take care of the Indian until he summoned them again. The two were burdened with the Indian in Boston as though he were an albatross around their necks. The next day, much to the amusement of Bostoners who directed "many squibs and scoffs" at the two men, they waited in the street from 9 A.M. to 3 P.M. to be readmitted to the governor's presence. When they were called, they were subjected to lengthy questioning by the council until finally permitted to go home.[37]

There was more involved in this incident than Andros's haughty manner in dealing with the Sudbury men. Also at issue was the determination of Andros to be fair, just, and kind in his dealings with Native Americans. It was this attitude, more than any other, that antagonized the Puritans, who had come to believe the only way to live in peace in New England was to exterminate the native population.

Adding to the discontent caused by Andros's autocratic behavior and his forced imposition of Anglican practices were poor economic conditions that were partly a result of King Philip's War and partly a result of a depressed global economy.[38] Expenses from King Philip's War had been great, and damages to personal property and to the population were extreme. Added to this were natural disasters that had taken their toll on Boston and the country at large, including two recent fires, and the wheat crop having been ruined for several years running. Poverty was rife, the fur trade had become almost nonexistent because the Indians were "very much diminished," and the province was ill defended.[39]

The economic depression worsened because of Andros's determination to rid Boston Harbor of pirates. They had previously brought valuable goods and specie to Boston, thereby sparking the local economy. Piracy itself was part of England's heritage. The situation was complicated by the fact that England and other European countries augmented their naval forces in wartime by legalizing piracy. After the wars, it was difficult for governments to persuade seamen to abandon a highly profitable career. The official English government position on piracy in America was that it was to end, as directed by the Treaty of Madrid, signed with Spain in 1670, and by the Treaty of Whitehall signed with France in November 1686. Trade could not flourish if the seas remained lawless.[40]

Signing treaties is one thing, but enforcing them in the outposts of empire, three thousand miles away from the centers of law and order, was quite a different matter. Despite the passage of laws to end piracy and the harsh penalties imposed, pirates remained popular heroes, and piracy continued to flourish.[41] In the summer of 1688, Francis Nicholson reported that eight pirates were in prison in Boston, the men off a pirate ship that had cruised along the Rhode Island coast selling its booty. Andros ordered the people who bought the pirates' loot to be tried, "butt the grand jury would nott finde the bill."[42]

Despite the popularity of pirates, Andros's duty as governor was to obey royal commands to suppress piracy. Hence, to discourage piracy, the *Rose* and the *Kingfisher* remained in Boston Harbor through the winter of 1686–87 for defense and to ensure that the Navigation Acts were enforced. In fact, as Andros reported to Secretary to the Admiralty Samuel Pepys in late June, the ships had been virtually useless most of the winter because they were ice bound. The governor recommended that ships be wintered further to the south. Trade remained depressed in 1687, primarily because the French prohibited English fishing off the coast of Nova Scotia, while Spanish pirates continued to seize English ships bound for New England loaded with salt from Tortuga.[43] To protect New England's maritime community, the *Rose* stayed near Boston, even after the *Kingfisher* was ordered home in September 1687. When not ice bound, the *Rose* was employed to patrol the coast between capes Sable and Cod, frightening off pirates and enforcing the Navigation Acts. The enforcement of the Acts meant that the former New England trade directly with Europe had to end. To achieve this goal, enforcement was tightened and trade adversely affected. Inevitably, the price of goods increased following the stricter enforcement of the Navigation Acts, another reminder to Puritans that they were now part of an empire-wide commercial system. A shortage of specie meant the slump in trade continued, and this, along with higher prices, made it all the more difficult for colonists to pay taxes, quit rents, and the higher import duties demanded by the crown.[44]

It was easy for officials in England to identify a problem and to make regulations applying to the colonies. It was much harder for them to see the on-site effects of their policies or to realize that literal enforcement of the Navigation Acts would ruin many New England merchants, or at least cut into their profits. Insensitive to these concerns, English officials continued to believe colonies existed primarily to benefit the mother country. Illegal trade might be good for colonists, but it deprived England of a substantial source of revenue. Hence, the Navigation Acts had to be enforced, and Andros did just that. But colonists were resentful at their financial loss, and the immediate target for their resentment was Andros.

Andros did all he could to improve New England trade. He realized it was necessary to ensure a steady, long term market in the West Indies and Europe for New England's goods. To accomplish this, the governor adopted "strict meanes" to ensure that "goods which are shipd off from hence to the West Indies (as beefe pork ffish Boards etc.)" were of a consistently high quality. In New England, as in New York where he had instituted similar measures, all exports were inspected by officers who would decide if commodities were "fitt for markett." Maintaining a market by the use of quality controls would boost the economy in the long run, but in the short run it left several farmers, fishermen, and lumberjacks with sub-quality merchandise on their hands.

Like James's regime in England, Andros's administration in New England had brought significant, but unwanted, changes to the provinces under his control. One historian points out that the changes initiated by Andros were the "most abrupt and sweeping changes attempted anywhere in the English-speaking world since the days of the 1640s."[45] Another historian says that Andros's actions in New England were "more radical than James II's parallel innovations at home, but because New England was a smaller society, her local traditions less virile, and Andros an abler man, he was able to accomplish more positive and lasting results." Certainly resistance to these changes was every bit as deep and bitter in New England as it was in England.[46] Andros may have been determined to drag the Puritans into the modern era, but the Puritans were every bit as determined to resist. Their desire was to return to the society they had enjoyed in the early days of settlement, one that they increasingly, if inaccurately, viewed as a perfect utopian society.

9

Andros, the French, and the Indians, 1688–1689

> The English are the principal fomenters of the insolence and arrogance of the Iroquois, adroitly using them to extend their sovereignty; uniting with them as one nation, in such wise that the English pretend to own nothing less than Lake Ontario, Lake Erie, and the entire Saguinan country, that of the Hurons if these become their allies, and the whole territory towards the Micissippy.
>
> —Jacques-Rene de Brisay, Marquis Denonville[1]

DENONVILLE WAS CORRECT IN HIS ANALYSIS THAT THE LATE SEVENteenth-century English North American empire was built on the back of the Iroquois empire. The Covenant Chain, negotiated through Andros's efforts in 1677, proved effective in keeping the Iroquois allied to the English. One of the unfortunate consequences of Andros's chain was that it rightly alarmed the French, who saw the economic ruin of New France if they were cut off from the fur trade. They not only recognized the military threat presented by the union of the English and the Iroquois but realized that Andros "took all the Iroquois under his protection as subjects of the Crown of England" and had further "prevented them" from making "peace with us." The French feared that the English and the Iroquois would combine to destroy them. The English urged the Iroquois to fight the French and to seize French forts at "Niagara, Michilimakinak," and other locations. If the Iroquois were successful, the result for the French would be first a loss of trade and then complete destruction. To avert this, the French and their Indian allies decided to seize the initiative by striking first, bringing chaos to the northern frontier.[2] Their dual targets were the Iroquois in New York and the English at trading posts and settlements in Maine. Andros, head of a united military force, was prepared to meet this threat.[3]

The 1686 Treaty of American Neutrality, negotiated between James II and Louis XIV, had guaranteed a temporary peace between the two nations in Europe, but this peace did not extend to America. James signed the treaty because he hoped to get Louis's help in imposing Catholicism in England. In fact, at least one of James's military aides, John Churchill, believed the treaty made it easier for Louis to expand his North American empire at the expense of England. Colonial official, William Blathwayt, along with Churchill, feared that the French had "tied our hands" through the treaty. The French tried to ignore English claims of hegemony over the Iroquois, insisting that the Iroquois were under French dominion by reason "of the Missionaries whom the [French] King first sent thither."[4] Dongan repeatedly told the French governors that the Iroquois were "under this Govermt" and had voluntarily delivered "themselves and their lands to it."[5]

The Iroquois themselves did not accept French domination and in 1684 had acknowledged to Dongan that they were English subjects. This was a significant achievement for Dongan, who had built on the base created by Andros. Not only could the English claim sovereignty over the Iroquois and their extensive territory but also over the many New England and southern Indians who became dependents of the Iroquois.[6] The French Canadian governor, Denonville, was fully aware of the English design, commenting that by uniting with the Iroquois "the English pretend to own nothing less than Lake Ontario, Lake Erie, and the entire Saguinan country, that of the Hurons if these become their allies, and the whole territory towards the Micissippy."[7] Allied with the English and refusing to trade with the French, the Iroquois continually invaded French territory, killed their Indian allies, and blocked the French from invading English territory. Afraid they would be destroyed, the French were determined to retaliate and to reduce or eliminate the threat presented by the Iroquois.[8]

In August 1687, Andros received word from Dongan that the previous month, Governor Denonville, frustrated in his attempts to achieve an alliance with the Iroquois, had decided to use force at the order of Louis XIV. Denonville, determined to "lower the pride of the Iroquois," had marched against the Senecas in July, destroying their villages and food supplies. Although casualties among the Senecas were slight, the devastation was complete because the French and their allied Indians spent several days "in destroying the corn which was in such great abundance that the loss, including old corn which was in *cache* which we burnt and that which was standing, was computed according to the estimate afterwards made at 400 thousand minots (minot equals three bushels) of Indian corn." Of the 150 or more Iroquois prisoners taken, the women and children were dispersed among Canadian tribes, some of the men were kept in Quebec, while others were sent to France at the request of the French government. Denonville asked that these latter Indians be kept "in a place from which they can be withdrawn," in case of a proposed prisoner exchange.[9]

By the fall of 1687, Dongan acknowledged that the situation in New York was dire. Expecting another French attack on Iroquoia during the winter, Dongan feared that the Iroquois would not be able to withstand the French, and the entire colony would be at risk. New York was in such a precarious position that Dongan, who had previously urged the home government to add Connecticut to New York, changed his mind. He now suggested that both Connecticut and New York be added to the Dominion of New England. The home government had already made the same decision. The French were also wary of an Iroquois counterattack, knowing that the Iroquois were "incited by the English." With a sparse population, the French were convinced that five hundred European-led Iroquois warriors could overrun Canada in three months.[10]

New York governor Dongan, aware that the French had sent three thousand troops to Canada and intended to continue their "warr with our Indians on this side the Lake," met with the Iroquois in Albany in October 1687. Dongan brought with him 450 soldiers, "to assist the Brethren if need be," and food in the form of "Corn and Provision for your wives and children when they come here." In Albany, the governor said, because the Iroquois were under English protection, "they need not fear the French or any of there Indians." He told each nation to send him two of their "wisest men with power from the Rest to give me their Advice . . . for I am Resolved to doe nothing without the Brethren."[11]

Meeting with "the Brethren," Dongan renewed Andros's Covenant Chain. When the Iroquois complained that the French had taken prisoners, Dongan assured them he would write to the French governor and tell him that the Iroquois were subjects of the English king, whom he was prepared to defend "to the Last man." He promised he would demand the release of all Iroquois prisoners held by the French, urging them not to kill or torture any prisoners, but merely to hold them for exchange. He also asked that they release captives, including a French woman and four children who were the offspring of a couple fleeing to the English from the French.[12]

James, also concerned about the attacks of the French on the New York frontiers, instructed Andros in November 1687 to provide military help to Dongan, if so requested. Andros was to raise and arm troops, who would be paid out of tax money. This decision was sure to cause further resentment among New Englanders, who already shouldered a heavy tax burden.[13]

On 18 November 1687, Dongan, who planned to stay in Albany for the winter of 1687–88, feared an all-out war with the French. He asked Andros to send him two hundred "of the youngest and lustiest of your militia, with good arms, and a hundred red coats, with fifty horse," as well as money for provisions. Andros was distracted from filling Dongan's request by the illness and death of his wife. Nevertheless, he complied, although, as he admitted to Blathwayt, he was "under hard Circumstances by the loss of my wife," the sole surviving evidence that the stoic governor admitted to a deep-seated grief.[14]

In an effort to end the conflict, James and Louis agreed to negotiate territorial disputes in North America. Although no decisions were reached because neither side could be persuaded to make concessions, the talks halted border hostilities for most of 1688.[15] One exception was Maine. Early in 1688, the Abenakis in Maine, probably instigated by the French, launched a war against the English. New Englanders remained convinced that peace could be achieved with the bellicose Maine Indians only at the point of the sword. Andros's Indian relations policies proved a major source of contention between the governor and the Puritans. As Randolph noted to William Penn, the New England Indians "were never civilly treated by the late [Puritan] government" which instead did "encroach upon their lands, and by degrees to drive them out of all." It was colonists' land greed, said Randolph, undoubtedly echoing Andros, "that was the grounds . . . of the last [King Philip's] war." Unlike New Englanders, Andros "has all along taken other measures with them," measures scorned by many colonists who favored total annihilation. Andros, on the other hand, believed "Indian confidence" in his fairness would "put a stop to their present rage." Andros insisted "the Indians had been treated with too great severity, if not injustice" by the provincials. He instead planned "to try mild measures, and endeavour to win them by good words and small courtesies." Mild measures or not, some Indians advanced into Connecticut, killing several people there. The Indians then fled north to Canada, where the French governor, Denonville, refused to surrender them. New England's borders were virtually unprotected, and Massachusetts was at immediate risk, as were the Maine settlements. A garrison did exist at Pemaquid, "but it was no security to the scattered settlements upon the frontier."[16]

In response to heightened French aggression against English settlements, in the spring of 1688, Andros went to Pemaquid in Maine to establish boundaries and see to defense, traveling some two hundred miles from Boston. He met with Indian sachems, who "were well treated with shirts, rumm and trucking cloath." The sachems were reassured that Andros intended to protect them from the French and he asked them to recall their young warriors. He also found that the baron of St. Castine, a Frenchman who sold arms and ammunition to the Indians, had settled, or squatted, in the area. Andros, determined to eject him from what he considered to be English territory, sailed with Captain George on the *Rose* to Castine's dock. The Frenchman declined Andros's invitation to talk. Instead, he, along with his houseguests, fled. Andros landed with his soldiers. He left untouched the "small altar in the common roome . . . and some pictures and ordinary ornaments," but took "away all his armes, powder, shott, iron kettles and some trucking cloath." The fact that Andros did not destroy the altar was later offered as proof by the Puritans of their charge that the governor was a Roman Catholic. The goods were taken to the fort at Pemaquid, and notice was sent to an Indian sachem who was Castine's neighbor that "all his goods [would be] restored if he would demand them at Pemmaquid and come under obedience to the [English] king."[17]

Massachusetts residents, ignoring the Maine colonists' provocation of the Indians, later attributed Indian unrest in that area to Andros's actions against Castine. The baron was reputedly so angry at the attack that he incited the Indians against the English.[18] What the Puritans chose to ignore was that Indian discontent in Maine was caused not by Andros's actions but by settlers' refusing to pay Indians the yearly gift of corn called for in the peace treaty. Also irritating the Indians was the practice of whites invading fishing areas reserved for Indians on the Saco River. Colonists physically abused Indians when given the opportunity, while Indian land was being patented to whites. Indians also complained they were given alcohol and then cheated in trade.[19]

After his raid on Castine's settlement, Andros returned to Boston in late May to find that on 23 March 1688, a warrant was passed in England for him to be governor of New York and New Jersey, as well as the New England colonies. Andros, determined "to do my duty . . . in so dificult a station," made immediate plans to go to New York and New Jersey. Militarily, the decision was important. Andros was now in charge of colonial defense from St. Croix to the Delaware River. As commander, he could call the militia from all colonies to defend any English borders under attack. The militia numbered over thirteen thousand men in New England, with another two thousand in New York.[20] Francis Nicholson was to follow Andros to New York in September 1688, remaining there as lieutenant governor.[21]

Andros left Boston on 31 July 1688, arriving in New York on Saturday, August 11. Relations between Andros and Dongan were poor. Part of the reason for Dongan's animosity was "his being disappointed of his great expectation of being Govr of New Engd."[22] Despite his dislike of Andros, Dongan welcomed him in suitable style, sending out "a regiment of foot and a troop of horse" to greet him. Once Andros's commission was read in the fort and then published at city hall, he asked Dongan for "the Seal of the late Govt which was defaced and broaken in Council."[23] Next, Andros with his large retinue crossed the Hudson to New Jersey to have his commission published in both East New Jersey on August 15 and West New Jersey on August 18. Andros reported with satisfaction that he was "now Crowded by freinds, and all sorts of Contrey people." He then returned to New York City to meet with the council on August 20.[24]

Andros was still in New York when he received word at 6 P.M. on August 27 of the 10 June 1688 birth of James's son, James Edward, prince of Wales. Andros immediately went to the fort, summoned Dongan, the council, the mayor and aldermen, and invited all to drink the prince's health. The great guns in the fort fired volleys and were answered by all the ships in the harbor. Bonfires were lit in front of the fort gates and several pipes of wine were opened, "which plentifully supplyed the whole Company runing ffrom one pipe to another." Two weeks later Andros and his retinue with fifty soldiers sailed up the Hudson for Albany. Halfway up, the governor ordered the vessel to anchor and went ashore for another celebration. Three great bonfires were lit and the party lasted all night, with drinking and the firing of guns. The celebration was repeated yet again when Andros arrived in Albany.[25]

The prince's birth had dramatic consequences in England,

where James continued his efforts to increase conversions to Catholicism. Protestants viewed with alarm the birth of a son, who would take precedence in the succession over his two half sisters, the princesses Mary and Anne, because the prince would be raised as a Catholic. This raised the specter of a long line of Catholic monarchs in England. Apparently unknown to James and his principal advisors, public sentiment against the king continued high after the birth. Rumors began immediately that the queen had not been pregnant and that the baby was smuggled into the queen's chamber in a warming pan. Public indignation against the king increased dramatically after the June 29 trial of the archbishop of Canterbury and six bishops. The prelates had been charged with seditious libel for refusing to order subordinates to read in their churches the king's second Declaration of Indulgence, issued May 1688. To almost universal jubilation, the sympathetic jury in the Court of King's Bench found them not guilty. Despite this public show of support for the bishops, in August 1688, the earl of Sunderland observed that "I believe there never was in England less thought of rebellion," perhaps voicing the sentiment the king wanted to hear.[26]

Like Sunderland in London, Andros that same month did not give much thought to rebellion. His more immediate concerns were Indian unrest and French encroachment. To deal with these problems, Andros went to Albany to offer manpower and "stores of powder and armes" to the Iroquois because the French continued to make "severall incursions" against them. The French were indeed moving closer, having built a fort at Niagara Falls in Seneca country, "upon an advantageous pass, neare the Indians hunting places, capable greatly to annoy and awe the Indians and obstruct and hinder the trade with them."[27] Dongan, on learning of the fort, had written to Denonville demanding he withdraw the garrison there. Denonville agreed "in order to contribute to a permanent peace."[28]

In Albany, the Iroquois, pleased to see Andros again, reassured the governor they had not allied with the French but were determined to maintain "the old Covenant" with the English. Andros urged the Iroquois to return any French captives. A Caiuga sachem objected to returning French prisoners because the chief warrior of their nation, Taweeratt, had been taken prisoner by the French and not returned. Two Mohawk sachems took exception to Andros's addressing them as "Children" instead of "Brethren," noting that the old "Sachems who spoke formerly with you, are dead, and wee have not soe much knowledge as they." As their ancestors wished, the "old Covenant" continued, they said, but when the agreement was made, "wee were called Brethren . . . therefore lett that of Brethren continue without any alteration." An aging Andros might well have looked on the younger generation of Mohawk sachems as "children," but diplomatically explained that "they are both words of relation and friendship, but Children the nearer." Anxious to retain good relations with Andros, the Caiuga sachem, seeing that Andros was "not well pleased w[i]th what he sayd about the French prisoners, stood up, and speaking to His Excelly againe, desired to be excused for what he had spoke amiss, and as for the prisoners they will deliver them." The next day, the Iroquois again sought out Andros to ask his help in securing the return of captive Iroquois still in the hands of the French.[29]

Andros promptly wrote to Denonville only to be informed that the Iroquois captives had been sent to France where they served as galley slaves. At Andros's request, Denonville promised to obtain their release and apparently was successful. Or so Andros's enemies later charged. New Englanders claimed that Andros's "unwearied Industry and Mediation procured of the *French* King the Return of those *Mohawks* which had been carried into France." This statement was not made in support of the governor but rather was used as confirmation of the Puritans' charge that Andros, because of his latent Catholicism, had influence with the Catholic French. Since he took undue pains to please the Indians, they reasoned he must be plotting with them against New Englanders. Since the French obliged him, it must be because they regarded him as one of their own.[30]

While in Albany, Andros got word that eleven French-allied Indians had killed five Massachusetts colonists near Springfield and six more at Northfield. Andros immediately wrote to Denonville to demand the surrender to him of the guilty Indians.[31] Realizing he would have to return to Boston to handle the situation personally, Andros sailed for New York City to make sure that Nicholson was in command there and matters were ordered. On October 4, Andros had to put New York problems out of his mind and assured William Blathwayt he was "hastening back to Boston." The reason for the haste was that Andros had received word that French Indians had also killed English colonists at Casco Bay in Maine, near the Kennebec River. Much to the governor's dismay, the Dominion council blamed Maine Indians for the attacks at Northfield. The council, in his absence and without Andros's authorization, raised militiamen and sent them to

Casco Bay. Andros knew that the presence of the militia in Maine was sure to aggravate the situation and lead to counter attacks.[32]

The Maine Indians who conducted the Casco Bay attack bragged the French assisted them and, indeed Castine, and two Jesuit priests had encouraged them. When Andros wrote to Denonville to ask his help in stopping the Indians, Denonville assured Andros of his determination to maintain peace, telling him he had already ordered the withdrawal of his forces from Fort Niagara. Denonville, by implication, blamed Andros for Indian aggression in Maine. He was "surprised," he said, "to learn [of] the violence said to have been committed by your orders on Sieur de St. Castin at Pentagouet. I should have supposed, Sir, had you any pretension to that place, it would have been better left to the decision of our masters, than to commit an act of hostility by pillaging his house."[33]

On the way back to Boston, Andros visited Indians in the Narragansett Country to reassure them of his protection. He also told them that if they feared attack by the French Indians, they were to go to the nearest English plantation. The Indians were thankful and asked for powder and balls, which Andros gave them.[34] Andros also made a point of talking to the colonists he met on the way and found the people "full of Extraordinary Apprehensions & feares of ye Indians." Some outlying plantations in North Yarmouth were deserted, the residents having gone to Falmouth. Terror had taken hold in Andros's absence, with houses on the outskirts of Boston fortified with "Pallasadoes."[35]

New Englanders, whose collective memories of King Philip's War were still vivid, were almost hysterical with fear, unwarranted as far as Andros was concerned. This fear was reflected in the acts of the English militia commander at Saco, Captain Blackman, who seized twenty-one Indians presumed to be enemies and sent them to Boston. Some of the Indians were so old and feeble that "they were forced to be carried when ashore, on others backs." The Maine Indians, on hearing that the twenty-one people had been seized, began to attack English settlements and took captives to be held hostage until the Indians were returned. Several Indians and colonists were killed in a bungled attempt at an exchange of prisoners. On 20 September 1688, Andros reprimanded Colonel Edward Tyng, Jr., a Maine landowner, for the actions of his subordinates. He told Tyng bluntly that "by your seizing and disturbing the Indians you have Alarmed all your Parts and putt them in a posture of Warr." The Maine Indians, Andros said, did not commit the murders at Northfield at all, but rather they were committed "by eleven stragling Indians from Canada." Andros, realizing the captured Indians were innocent, ordered their release, including one held by Increase Mather's son, Cotton. The younger Mather strongly protested and pointed out that the Indians should be kept as "a Guide into the Woods . . . to find out the Haunts of our Heathen Enemies." Despite Andros's efforts to appease the Indians, the situation had escalated, and colonists now demanded protection and revenge. [36]

To cope with increased perils on the frontier, the governor ordered two and a half companies of regulars drawn from the Massachusetts and New York garrisons to march to Maine. Nine militia companies from Massachusetts supplemented the regulars for a total of 709 men. Word soon came of the burning of New Dartmouth and Newtown. Andros realized that, like it or not, he had a full scale Indian war on his hands, a war that had been brought by the New Englanders' over reaction to a supposed Indian threat.[37] While Andros in the autumn of 1688 was aware of the increasing internal unrest that followed the birth of the prince of Wales in England, his more immediate concern was Indian war on the Maine frontier.

The campaign could not have come at a worse time, since it drew Andros away from Boston to a remote frontier where he would be unable to deal with public reaction to the increasingly unsettling news from England. Fitz Winthrop, once a loyal friend and probably privy to the fact that Puritan leaders in Boston were already contemplating a rebellion, used the excuse of illness to decline the command of the troops Andros raised to defend the Maine border. It may well be that Fitz's illness was feigned because he and his brother Wait wanted Andros out of Boston while events in England unfolded.[38] When Fitz Winthrop refused the assignment, Andros assumed command himself.[39]

Shortly after Andros returned to Boston from New York, he and the troops set sail for Maine, accompanied by the Reverend Robert Ratcliffe and Edward Randolph. The latter expressed some concern over the health of the governor, who was now past fifty. "His Excellence," Randolph observed, "discharges all offices: from Generall to Sutler: giving himselfe no tyme to eate or sleepe." The ever loyal Randolph was determined "to accompany him intending never to leave him, so long as I am able to follow." Despite his resolve, Randolph was back in Boston some time prior to the end of January 1689. Andros, remaining in Maine through the winter, was successful against the Indians, even though his men were poorly armed, and there was no way to add to the weapons for there were "none here to be bought."[40]

Gone were the days of appeasement and patience with the Indians. Faced with a determined enemy, Andros responded in kind, and since he commanded sufficient forces from a united Dominion, his response was highly effective. He ordered the building of new forts in Maine and waged an aggressive campaign against the Indians, "takeing and destroying their forts and settlem'ts, provision, ammunicion and canoes, dispersed and reduced them to the uttermost want and necessitys, and so secured the Countrey."[41] In fact, the Indians, now short of ammunition, were brought to the point of surrendering, reduced to the "use of their bows and arrows that they could not much longer hold out, but beg their lives upon any termes." Nor could the Indians expect any help from local French settlers who had been "plundered of all their Stores by the Privateers and [were] as necessitous as the Indians." Surrender might indeed have come during that winter if the Indians had not been re-supplied by "some merchants in Boston (Foster & Waterhouse) . . . [who] sent a vessell of forty tunns with supplyes of powder, shott, bread, Indian Corne, and English linnen and woolen manufacture to trade with those Indians and the French." Foster and Waterhouse, after loading the vessel in Boston, duped customs officials by falsely reporting that the ship was headed for Bermuda. Instead they "sent her Eastward" to Maine to trade with the Indians, exchanging Indian furs for ammunition and enough food to keep the Indians in action. The deeds of the merchants were well known by people in Boston, being "the publick discourse of the Town." The venture earned the merchants a £500 profit.[42]

Despite the interference of Foster and Waterhouse, Andros's success in Maine proved the effectiveness of a combined united military effort. As Viola Barnes notes, Andros's "military policy was the strongest feature of his administration. By his diplomatic dealings with the Indians and the French, his garrisoning of strategic points, and his rigorous warfare, he made New England formidable to its enemies."[43]

Even without a well supplied enemy, conditions in Maine were harsh for the Massachusetts soldiers, with brutal cold and short rations. Cotton Mather commented that Andros "and his Army underwent no little Hardship, thus in the Depth of Winter to Expose themselves unto the Circumstances of a Campaign, in all the Bleak Winds and Thick Snows of that Northern Country." Still, every privation that was suffered by the men was also suffered by their commanding officer. Even Thomas Hutchinson, a grandson of the John Foster who supplied the French and Indians and certainly not an admirer of Andros's, "acknowledged that he readily took to himself his full share of the hardships of the campaign, and that he was a kind and good general to the men under his command." Andros and his soldiers traveled in the dead of winter three hundred miles or more from Boston into the Maine woods in pursuit of the enemy.[44] The Puritan militia, in addition to suffering from the extreme cold, enemy attacks, and disease, also fell under the command of regular army officers, an experience that was an eye opener. Colonials were unused to the thoroughly brutal discipline inflicted on enlisted men in European armies. As regular army lieutenant, James Weems, told the men, "Hell is like to be your winter quarters and the Devill your Landlord" during the campaign.[45] Andros wisely distanced himself from the brutality, acting like "a father unto" the men, visiting "them in their Sickness." At night he went to every tent to be sure the sleeping soldiers were covered and "if he found them sleeping with their knee strings bound, would untie them himself."[46]

Andros's concern for his men was probably only slightly exaggerated by his adherents. Under the poorest of conditions, resentment among the militiamen grew to such a point that there were frequent desertions. The rapidly diminishing manpower led Andros in the winter of 1688–89 to call for an additional two hundred militiamen. Not only did the men go reluctantly to the frozen Maine backwoods, but also taxpayers were hard pressed to meet the added expense of paying their salaries and buying supplies. Over the course of the winter, many deserters began to spread stories about Andros's brutality and his indifference to the sufferings of his men. When this proved not enough to excuse their dereliction, they began to accuse Andros of fraternizing and conspiring with the French and Indian enemies. There were Puritans who were willing to listen.

Stories were also running rampant in England in the fall of 1688 about a massive military build up in the Netherlands. When these stories reached the king, he could hardly bring himself to believe that his daughter Mary and son-in-law William were amassing forces to attack him. Aghast when he realized the rumors were true, James prepared to defend himself and his kingdom. On 16 October 1688, he wrote to colonial governors, including Sir Edmund Andros, to warn them of a possible Dutch invasion and to order each colony to defend itself in the event of such an attack.[47]

In January 1689 at Fort Charles in Pemaquid, Maine, Andros received James's letter about the Dutch military build up. For the fourth time in his life and the third in his career, the Dutch were again a threat to England. In addition, Monmouth had launched his 1675 invasion from the Netherlands, so there was nothing unusual to Andros in being ordered to oppose the Dutch. He immediately published a proclamation throughout the Dominion, warning that "a great and sudden Invasion from *Holland*, with an armed Force of forreigners and Strangers, will speedily be made in an hostile manner upon His Majesty's Kingdom of ENGLAND." All civil and military officers throughout the Dominion were "to be *Vigilant* and *Careful*." In the event an enemy fleet approached the Dominion's shores, they were to "hinder any Landing or Invasion."[48]

In March of 1689, rumors from Virginia of a revolution in England reached Andros in Maine. He decided to go back to Boston on March 16, "leaveing the garrisons and souldiers in the Easterne parts in good condition." The two hundred soldiers remaining in Pemaquid Fort were under the command of Captain Anthony Brockholes and Lieutenant James Weems. The troops, both regular and militia, were left to defend the frontier while Andros proceeded to Boston with only a minimal guard. Once the governor left Maine, the discontent among the Maine militia troops escalated, as "Some of the Soldiers took Advantage from the Absence of the Governor to desert their Stations in the Army."[49]

As Sir Edmund Andros traveled wearily toward Boston over the frozen New England countryside, he was without any official account of dramatic events that had already transpired in England. Indeed, events in the colonies were dire enough. Despite the governor's best efforts to reduce friction between the French and the Iroquois, Andros saw that the latter were in danger of being exterminated by the French. If defeated, there would be no force to stand between the French and New York. In New England, Andros had imposed a temporary peace in Maine, but it was precarious, as he well realized. Even so, Andros remained confident that he could manage what had become a volatile military and political situation, though the twin crises would be a rigorous test of his executive skills.

10

The Glorious Revolution: England and New England, 1688–1689

Part 1

> For he was of that stubborn crew
> Of errant saints, whom all men grant
> To be the true Church Militant:
> Such as do build their faith upon
> The holy Text of pike and gun.
> —Samuel Butler, "Hudibras"[1]

IN ENGLAND, THE BIRTH OF A BABY AND THE TRIAL OF FIVE BISHOPS caused members of "the true church militant" to lead a revolution. In Old and New England, churchmen overthrew a legitimate monarch and his appointed lieutenant in the name of religion. In each case, the church relied "on the holy Text of pike and gun" to achieve its ends. The uprisings were spurred not only by anti-Catholic fears, but by friction among Protestant sects. It was as true in New England as it was in England that each rebellion was "a religiously driven military coup."[2] Both were indeed military coups, with the major actors, regular army officers in England and militia officers in America, spurred by religious considerations and more practical concerns.

The situation first proved volatile in England, where a bloodless coup was effected by disgruntled Protestant army officers. Fearing the loss of position and power, these men acted at the instigation of Anglican prelates. The new professional corps of army officers, comprised mostly of Protestants, was willing to support the king as long as he was Anglican or as long as he did not try to force Catholicism on the entire nation. When James did exactly that, Protestant army officers could not tolerate the situation and rebelled.[3]

In New England, a revolt was sparked by the events in England. Had the revolution not occurred in England, it is doubtful the Dominion government would have been overturned. In Massachusetts, the uprising was planned by and executed under the direction of Congregational ministers, who directed militia officers. To Congregationalists, there was little difference between Roman Catholics and Anglicans. Andros, raised in Guernsey, fluent in French, a servant of the Catholic King James, and a member of the Church of England, was suspected of being a Catholic. With this suspicion firmly established in many New Englanders' minds, militia officers had no trouble prodding their units to rebel. The intent of the New England elite was threefold: to end the Dominion of New England, to oust Edmund Andros as governor, and to secure the return of their old charter.

Ironically, James II, playing a double game, had given credit and encouragement to dissident factions in the New England colonies. On the one hand, he used Andros as his weapon to destroy the power of and impose centralization on the traditional ruling elite in Massachusetts. On the other hand, to secure his own place on the throne, he needed and sought the support of all nonconformists. Accomplishing one objective undermined the other.[4]

As discontent with the king's policies increased in England, James mounted efforts to secure the support of religious nonconformists. To garner that support, he sought to appease Puritan New Englanders' indignation over the fact that Sir Edmund had excluded them from government and had taxed them without benefit of a representative assembly. The most influential of the unofficial Massachusetts ambassadors to England was the minister Increase Mather, who arrived in London in May 1688 and was presented to the king by Stephen Lobb, a London nonconformist minister. The king received Mather several times over the course of that summer, during which Mather presented petitions detailing Puritan discontent with Andros. The governor, Mather charged, did "traduce the most peaceable and conscientious men as Seditious & dissaffected to royall Government." Puritans, the minister said, were not allowed days of prayer and thanksgiving and were threatened with punishment if they advocated public support of nonconformist ministers. They were fined and imprisoned at Andros's order for swearing "by lifting up their hands to Heaven, and not by the booke." In addition, Mather said, their lands were given to members of the Church of England. Whole towns were in fear of land seizure as Andros enforced his decision to repatent all land. Officials of the Dominion government had

told them "they are no better than Slaves, that they have no Title
to property or English Priveledges, and they are treated accordingly." All traditional English rights seemed lost as some Puritans were jailed without "assigning any cause." In courts,
arbitrary fines were set and they feared that Harvard College
"shall be taken from them and put in the hands of such as are for
the Church of England."[5]

By 16 October 1688, James promised Mather some redress for
New Englanders, with "a full & free Liberty of conscience & exercise of Religion, and . . . Possessions of Houses & Lands according
to their ancient Records and also their Colledge at Cambridge to
be governed by a President & fellows as formerly," a triumphant
Mather told his son in Massachusetts, minister Cotton Mather.
The most important issue to Increase Mather was the restoration
of the old charter. James was not prepared to grant that request,
nor did he promise the return of representative government.[6]

The king was willing to appease Mather to a degree because he
needed nonconformist support to counter rising antipathy to him
spurred by the birth of the prince of Wales. This antipathy
increased as members of the traditional English ruling class were
relieved of influential posts that were then bestowed on Catholics
by the king. In the summer of 1688, seven spiritual and temporal
lords, both Whigs and Tories, sent an invitation to James's son-
in-law, William of Orange, to invade England. Motivated by
dynastic, national, religious, and personal concerns, William
decided to act.[7]

Andros, isolated in New England, did not know until much
later that William had gathered together a military force of some
fifteen thousand men and was prepared to sail for England. After
numerous weather delays, the fleet got underway, presenting "so
dreadfull a sight passing through the Channell with so favorable
a Wind," one that kept James's admiral, the earl of Dartmouth,
from sailing out to intercept William.[8] On 5 November 1688, William set foot on English soil at Torbay to "put the King & Court
into greate Consternation, now employed informing an Army to
incounter their farther progresse."[9]

When news that William's forces had landed reached the king,
with a standing army of almost twenty thousand men, he was still
in a position to repel any foreign invasion. To James, the army
was a tool to be used to force order and obedience on civilian populations.[10] Although he had appointed approximately one hundred Catholics as officers, the great majority were Protestant
career officers, such as Andros, who felt that the king was

"threatening their pockets, careers, and dignities." James, by his actions, had "planted the seeds of his own destruction." Protestant officers feared James was "about to cleanse the English officer corps" of "political malcontents" to rid "the English army of all but the most devoted to his service."[11]

James, believing his officers faithful to him, prepared to fight, demoralized though he was by the betrayal of William and Mary. Most observers thought James would prevail over William, just as he had forcefully and successfully repelled Monmouth's army in 1685. William's army at fifteen thousand was considerably bigger and better organized than Monmouth's had been, but James was now much better prepared to defend his crown. When faced with further betrayals, James's determination wavered. Lord Lovelace, son of James's second governor in New York, was one of the first to desert but was soon captured and sent as a prisoner to London. His desertion was followed by that of the earl of Clarendon's eldest son, Lord Cornbury, who led his unwilling regiment to William's side as the latter advanced to London. The desertions among the officer class continued. The king received "the last and most confounding stroke" when he heard of the betrayal of the duke of Grafton, his own nephew and Charles II's son by the duchess of Cleveland.[12] This was followed by the desertion of the Lord Churchill, "him that I raised from nothing," as the king complained, "on whom I heaped all favours; and if such betrays me, what can I expect from those I have done so little for?" This betrayal was followed by that of Churchill's wife, Sarah, and James's own daughter, Princess Anne, and her husband, George, prince of Denmark. While both Tories and Whigs deserted the king, the most distressing betrayal was that of his daughter, Anne. The Anglican priest, Henry Compton, former officer in the Life Guards and one time tutor to Anne and her elder sister, had been deprived of his post as bishop of London by the king and now engineered Anne's flight, first to his house on Aldersgate Street and then to Nottingham. Compton, a member of "the true Church Militant," raised a regiment and then, in full military regalia, led his men to Oxford.[13]

Interestingly, although some of the officers were quick to abandon James, the great majority of the officer class remained loyal to the king, as did most of the rank and file. Despite the betrayals by a few Protestant officers, James retained a large army with enough loyal officers and men to conduct a massive assault against his son-in-law. He failed to act because he had lost heart. The betrayals of those nearest and dearest to him were devastating to a man who had previously proven his bravery in battle on numerous occasions.[14]

Demoralized and feeling his situation was hopeless, James sent his wife and young son out of England on 10 December 1688. James followed her two days later, running from Whitehall in disguise but taking with him the great seal, which he threw into the Thames. This act was a revenge on the usurper since no government business could be transacted without the seal, nor could a legal parliament be called. The king made his way to the channel and was actually on a ship ready to sail for France when some self-appointed papist hunters insisted on searching the ship and found him. James was returned to London to find that his absence of a few days had turned public opinion to his side. Londoners now saw James as a sympathetic victim and William as the unprincipled usurper. As the king was led through London streets on 17 December, the crowds turned out to cheer, light bonfires, and otherwise celebrate the return of the Stuart monarch.[15]

Andros's patron and relative by marriage, the still loyal and feisty earl of Craven, at age eighty-two was in command of the palace's Coldstream Guards. He visited James at 11 P.M. on the evening of his return to tell him the Dutch were near, with orders from William to take their posts at Whitehall. James realized there was no point in resisting and ordered Craven to withdraw his guards so William could take over without bloodshed. A distraught Craven begged the king on his knees to let him fight the Dutch, but James refused, thanking Craven for his loyalty and past service. The king went to bed, only to be awakened shortly after midnight by some Dutch soldiers, who told the king that he was to leave London the next morning. When the king asked to go to Rochester, William agreed.[16]

By December 19, James was imprisoned at Rochester in a house on the Medway with a very lax guard. William wanted James to escape. As had been shown with the London mobs, the king was still popular with many Englishmen, who looked on him as God's anointed monarch. As a prisoner and on English soil, the king elicited a good deal of sympathy. James represented a distinct threat to William. Even if James chose not to fight, as long as he was in England William would be faced with the problem of what to do with him. The best solution, as far as William was concerned, was for James to leave the country. As William hoped, James fled to France, and thus, as Louis XIV commented, became a lost man. James arrived at Calais on December 25. Once he set foot on French soil, he forfeited any chance to regain his throne.[17]

The Convention Parliament, illegally called and not a representative body, on 28 January 1689 decided that James, "having by the advise of Jesuites & other wicked persons endeavored to subvert the Lawes of church & state, and Deserting the Kingdome carrying away the Seales etc. without taking any care for the management of the Government, had by demise, abdicated himselfe and wholye vacated his right" to the throne. With the decision conveniently made that James, by flight, had "abdicated," parliament decided "to place the Crowne upon the next heires." The crown was bestowed "jointly" on William and Mary "during their lives."[18]

The Convention Parliament proclaimed William and Mary joint sovereigns on 6 February 1689. Word to proclaim the new monarchs and to continue in office was sent to all plantation governors on 19 February 1689. A letter was also prepared for

Mary II (1662–1694) and William III (1650–1702). Mary, daughter of James II and his first wife, Anne Hyde, married her cousin, Prince William, posthumous son of William of Orange and Mary, daughter of Charles I. For the sake of religion, she supported her husband's invasion of England and the ouster of her father as king. Named as joint monarchs by the Convention Parliament in 1689, the couple had no children. Mary's younger sister, Anne, succeeded William. Portrait by an unknown artist, courtesy of the National Portrait Gallery, London.

Andros, but William's secretary showed the letter to Increase Mather before it was mailed. Mather realized that if Andros was reappointed as governor-general under William, the chances were that he would not be recalled. Mather, wanting an end to both the Dominion and to Andros's governorship, told the secretary that *"New-England* would be undone, if that letter should come to them." The secretary then told William, who "Ordered him not to transmit that Letter to *New-England.*" Andros was thus the only English governor in North America who was not officially informed of the change in monarchy.[19]

Mather, aided by Massachusetts born treasure hunter, Sir William Phips, had not been idle in England during the winter of 1688–89. Both worked to convince King William that the Dominion government should not be restored. On 16 February 1689, a new committee of the Privy Council was formed to oversee trade and plantations. That committee, meeting on 22 February 1689 with Phips and Mather in attendance, requested a new governor for New England and that Massachusetts be granted a representative assembly. On 26 February 1689, the decision was made to "send forthwith another Governor to New England in the place of Sir Edmund Andros."[20] In addition to Andros's ouster, the Puritans wanted the restoration of Massachusetts's old charter. William was willing to institute a new government in Massachusetts but was not willing to let that colony revert to its former practices. The king "believed it would be for the Good and Advantage of his Subjects in that Colony, to be under a Governour appointed by himself." He favored "a Military Man," just as had his predecessors. Nevertheless, the king promised Mather he would "have Charter-Priviledges Restored."[21]

Even if the February 1689 order to all governors to proclaim William and Mary had been sent off immediately to Andros, he would not have received it until mid April at the earliest, since it took at least two months for a fleet to sail westward against prevailing winds. In fact, no official confirmation of William and Mary's accession to the throne came to Boston until 26 May 1689.[22] Andros may have heard rumors but he remained officially unaware of the accession, although he, of course, suspected there was trouble in England, as did other government officials in the American provinces.[23]

These rumors led Andros to return to Boston in March 1689, leaving the bulk of the army on the Maine frontier. He found no word from London of any change in the royal authority much less any orders on how to proceed. James II had appointed Andros to his post. Andros had watched his father protect Castle Cornet for James's father, Charles I. Andros's family had shared the exile of James and his brother Charles II. His loyalty to the Stuarts was lifelong. Ignorant of the situation in England and mindful of what had happened to Monmouth and his followers, Andros continued in his loyalty to James, knowing that the king was well defended by a large army. Even if there had been an invasion, Andros would probably have reasoned that the king would prevail, just as he had in 1685 when faced with Monmouth's rebels. There was simply no way for Andros to know what had happened in England or that, for the sake of self-preservation, it was time to change sides. In fact, if he had been in England in November 1688, he might well have supported William, as did his old regiment.[24]

When John Winslow arrived in Boston from Nevis, bearing news of the accession of William and Mary to the throne, Andros had him thrown in jail. Despite Andros's efforts to suppress rumors, news of events in England filtered through to the colonists and heightened serious unrest in Massachusetts. A reflection of Andros's concern was an act that he had the council approve on 15 April 1689, requiring ship masters on incoming ships to give him "a List of all passengers" and outgoing ship captains to post security guaranteeing they would not transport "out of this Dominion any person without a Tickett from the Governour." In a letter written on April 16 to Captain Brockholes, who was still in Maine, Andros told him of "a general buzzing among the people, great with expectation of their old charter, or they know not what."[25]

The troublesome Mathers caused part of the "general buzzing" in Boston. Increase Mather's son, Cotton, had proven particularly irksome in his father's absence. In January 1689, Andros issued an order to arrest Cotton Mather on a charge of seditious libel for an anti-Anglican tract published two years earlier, "A Brief Discourse Concerning the unlawfulness of Common Prayer Worship," an essay actually written by Increase Mather. Wait Winthrop was able to quash the order, but in February 1689, Andros had Cotton Mather charged with a breach of the Acts of Uniformity. Though Mather was not arrested, he lived in constant fear.[26]

Andros looked for another excuse to silence Mather. It came on 14 April 1689, when Mather preached a sermon in which he apparently justified rebellion. It was somewhat ambiguous, but Andros chose to interpret the sermon as advocating sedition by voicing anti-monarchical sentiments.[27] On April 17, Andros ordered Mather's arrest the next day. The governor was also determined to discipline the militiamen who had deserted their posts in Maine and on April 17 ordered their arrest the next day. The militia was determined to ignore the order to seize their fellows. The deserters with their "Friends began to gather together here and there in Little Bodies to protect them from the Governor."[28]

Neither the errant militiamen nor Cotton Mather were arrested on Thursday, April 18. Instead, at 5 A.M. on that day, twelve militia companies in Charles Town and Roxbury began a march on Boston. When they reached that city, the Boston Regiment, under the command of Lieutenant Thomas Treffrey, Blathwayt's cousin, was roused to defend the city. The militiamen demanded Treffrey surrender "his Colours and Drums" and "threatened to shoot him down" when he refused. The militiamen then stole the colors while Treffrey sought refuge in the fort. The men proceeded on their march, capturing and imprisoning any allies of Andros that they happened to meet. On taking their captives to the prison, they freed "a Crew of Privateers who were imprisoned for Piracy and Murder."[29]

The ranks of the invaders were swelled by the Boston Artillery Company, led by militia officers and merchants John Nelson, David Waterhouse, and John Foster. Nelson was a member of the Church of England, but his trade with the French in Maine and Acadia had been hurt by Andros's policies. This was also the case with Waterhouse and Foster, who were the proprietors of the mercantile firm that had so recently sold arms and ammunition to enemy Indians in Maine. By 8 A.M., Andros heard the threatening crowds on the street and sent for the sheriff, James Sherlock. The sheriff "assured him it was a false report," but it was true. At 9 A.M., "the Drums beat through the Town," alerting the people that trouble was brewing. The crowd that gathered quickly descended on the *Rose,* brought to the vessel at the instigation of its ship's carpenter, Robert Small, who had joined the rebels a few days earlier. Small had helped to raise public hysteria by spreading the rumor that Andros planned to fire the city, just as Percy Kirke had fired Tangier, and then would kill survivors with the ship's guns. The mob seized and arrested the *Rose's* captain, John George, as he stepped on shore, imprisoning him in a private home on the North End. That same hour, "the Drums beat through the town" and soon there were about a thousand men "in armes crying one and all; seizing and carrying to Prison whosoever they suspected would oppose, or disprove their designe."

By 11 A.M., most Anglican leaders were in prison, except those who had joined Andros in the fort.[30]

The mob, led by Nelson, Waterhouse, and Foster, marched on the fort where Andros was housed with Edward Randolph, John Palmer, Charles Lidget, John West, "and one or two more."[31] The crowd was numerous and armed, and its ranks swelled when "many of the Countrey came in, that there was Twenty Companies in *Boston*, besides a great many that appeared at *Charles Town* . . . (some say Fifteen Hundred)." Civilians, including small boys wielding clubs, further enlarged the mob. Andros sent Judge Dudley's son, Thomas, to the homes of four congregational ministers, including Cotton Mather, to request that they come to the fort. The governor hoped the ministers would be able to calm the tumult, but the four, otherwise occupied in plotting rebellion, all refused, saying the streets were unsafe.[32]

Andros had only fourteen soldiers and officers in the fort and perhaps another dozen men in the Castle Island fort. When he became aware that the mob was at Fort Mary's gates, he "rebuked" the guards "for not firing on our soldiers," said a New Englander, "and, as I am informed, beat some of them." Andros may or may not have upbraided the soldiers for not firing their muskets on the crowd, but he did not order the cannon fired on the mob. If the great guns had been fired, "they might have killed an hundred of us at once—being so thick together before the mouths of their cannons at the Fort, all loaden with small shot," said one Puritan rebel. The Puritans had fewer scruples about firing cannon if necessary, for they seized the battery guns and quickly turned them on the fort, "which did much daunt all those within." As the crowd gathered around the fort, the governor may have remembered a similar scenario from his youth when his father and other royalists occupied Castle Cornet on Guernsey and held it for the king, Charles I. To defend the castle against the Presbyterians on the island, the cannons were fired on the town. Andros's decision not to fire on the Boston crowd was undoubtedly a wise one since the crowd kept growing and soon numbered about five thousand. The ranks of the militiamen had been added to by "country people," who "came into the town, in the afternoon, in such rage and heat" that their number alarmed not only Andros and his followers, but also the townspeople who had nothing to do with the tumult.[33]

Lieutenant David Condon on the *Rose* was now in command after George's arrest. Aware of events on shore, he was determined to resist capture by the rebels. The lieutenant ordered the

Rose's seamen to "put out all her flags and pennants, and opened all her ports, and with all speed made ready for fight," with the lieutenant "swearing that he would die before she should be taken." Condon also tried to help the governor by sending a boat to the fort. Andros saw the boat and with "about half a score Gentlemen, were coming down out of the Fort," tried to make their escape, but were spotted by the Puritans. As they retreated, "the Boat being seized, wherein were small Arms, Hand-Granadoes, and a quantity of Match, the Governour and the rest went in again."[34]

At 1 P.M., John Nelson, with an orange flag flying over Beacon Hill as a backdrop, demanded the governor surrender himself and the fort. Andros came out to talk to the rebels and asked the reason for the demonstration. In reply, he was "presented with a paper" by Nelson and told that the Council was meeting at the Town House and wanted to speak with him. Unknown to Andros, early that morning, Cotton Mather and four other ministers had planned the action. The ministers included William Milborne, brother of Andros's old New York adversary, Jacob Milborne, and lately arrived from Bermuda where he had been a leader of the rebellion there against former Governor Richard Cony. The ministers were busily engaged in writing orders to the numerous crowd leaders in the streets.[35]

The Congregational elite, seeing a necessity to control the crowds, put aside their factionalism for once and temporarily united to oppose Andros. Fifteen people, including Wait Winthrop, Simon Bradstreet, Elisha Cook, John Nelson, John Foster, David Waterhouse, William Stoughton, Samuel Shrimpton, and others, signed the letter prepared by the ministers. Presented to Andros by Nelson, it claimed that members of the Dominion council were "surprized with the Peoples sudden taking to Arms in the first motion whereof we were wholly ignorant." They took control of the mob, they informed Andros, only "for the quieting and securing of the people . . . and . . . [for] your own Safety, We judge it necessary you forthwith surrender and deliver up the Government and Fortifications," promising Andros, his staff, and his soldiers their personal safety.[36] Andros refused to surrender either the government or the fort. The governor told Nelson that he knew of no council meeting and that he was the only person with power to convene the council. The crowd leaders informed the governor that "they must have the governmt in their owne hands; telling the Governor hee was their Prisoner."[37]

There was much truth to Randolph's later statement that the

"violent and bloudy zeal [was] stird up in the Rabble acted and managed by the preachers."[38] In this respect, the Congregational ministers were emulating their Anglican brethren in England, who during James II's reign had "engaged in extensive and concerted civil disobedience." As one Puritan leader acknowledged, the action was planned by a select few, with "not very many acquainted with the measures that were to be taken."[39]

The leadership role of ministers in New England society was traditional. As Randolph pointed out to the Privy Council committee of trade, prior to the establishment of the Dominion government, it was the ministers who directed all "matters of publique import." Denied their usual prominent role in New England society under Andros, the ministers were now active "in contriving & setting on foot this generall revolt and subversion of the government."[40] The ministers, Randolph said, "were the Cheife promoters of this Rebellion."[41] Andros, as well as Randolph, realized it was the old Puritan elite who were openly leading the mob, while Puritan ministers were busily engaged in writing position papers to justify the rebellion. The ministers were aided, Andros said, by the Puritan councilors who "combined and conspired togeather with those who were Magistrates and officers in the late Charter Goverment . . . and severall other persons, to subvert and overthrow the goverment, and in stead thereof to introduce their former Comonwealth; and having by their false reports and aspersions gott to their assistance the greatest part of the people." Men who had been militia officers under the old charter government led the crowd that marched on Boston.[42]

The scheme to overthrow the government was long in the planning. From the fall of 1688 on, it was commonly known throughout New England that "a plot [was] on foot in Connecticut, as well as other parts of the countrey, to make insurrection and subvert the Government." Increase Mather, in a letter they received early in January 1689, instructed the New England ministers to "prepare the minds of the people for a change."[43] Randolph charged "that the Revolt of this people was pushd on by their Agent Mr. [Increase] Mather, who sent his letter directed to Mr. Symon Bradstreet Govr. In which he encouraged them to go cheerefully to so acceptable a piece of service to all Good people."[44] Such an extremely militant stance was predictable for Increase Mather, who, since 1685, had preached that in the fight for freedom, *"The ministers of God must then stand in the forefront of the battle, and be the first that shall be shot down."* The

Anglican, Henry Compton, had taken precisely the same role in England. Increase may have encouraged his son, Cotton, and all other Puritan ministers to assume militant leadership roles. They may have complied because Cotton was suspected of holding a meeting "of Armd men" at his house on the evening of April 17. The Puritans themselves acknowledged that the rebellion was planned and not spontaneous when they commented of events on April 18 that "not very many [were] acquainted with the measures that were to be taken." Once the rebellion started, however, the news ran "like Lightning through the Town, all sorts of people were presently inspired with the most unanimous Resolution." The climate was indeed ripe for such a rebellion because Increase Mather in his letters had raised hopes "of a new charter."[45]

Far from the revolt being a spontaneous movement initiated by the masses, it was the elite who planned, led, and executed the revolution. They worked on the fears of the lower orders by spreading rumors that more redcoats were to be sent to Massachusetts and that the soldiers already in Boston were preparing explosives to destroy the city. Andros knew that the April 18 uprising was the work of a few. By exaggerating the fears of the lower classes, Andros said, the elite "gott to their assistance the greatest part of the people . . . undr the comand of those who were Officers in the sayd popular goverment."[46]

It was the masses, unpredictable and difficult to control, that Andros now faced outside the fort, further urged on by the Puritan leaders reading to the crowds a "Declaration of the Gentlemen . . . of Boston," dated 18 April 1689, from the balcony of the Town House. The declaration, probably written during the course of the day by Mather and the other ministers in the Town House, was a carefully considered document designed to justify the actions of the elite for instigating the rebellion. As a Puritan position paper, it offered a rationale for rebellion by spelling out the historical background of the Puritans' grievances against King James and his Dominion government. Their rights as Englishmen were first threatened with the Popish Plot, they wrote, which was engineered "by the great Scarlet Whore," the Roman Catholic church. The intent of Catholics was to reduce New England, the true Protestant state, to "Desolation." To achieve this, it was first necessary to "have our Charter vacated." The agent who accomplished this ruin was Edward Randolph, whose "Malice and Falshood [were] well known unto us all." With no opportunity to defend the charter, it was lost and the colony "put under a President and Council, without any liberty for an Assembly." The Puritans "made no Resistance" to Dudley's caretaker government, even though they believed "The Commission was . . . Illegal." Dudley's illegal government was superseded by one "yet more absolute and Arbitrary, with which Sir Edmond Andross arrived as our Governour."[47]

The document then reiterated Puritan complaints concerning non-representative government, arbitrary taxation, the rule of outsiders, and exorbitant fees. It complained of Andros's land policy that put all property in jeopardy. To remedy the situation, Andros had required owners to take out new patents "at excessive rates" and allowed no opposition at council meetings to his measures. As for the people of New England, they were told they were "all Slaves, and the only difference between them and Slaves is their not being bought and sold."[48]

As the declaration was being read to the crowd at the Town House, the militia surrounding the fort tried to persuade Andros to surrender. Andros, initially refusing to accompany Nelson to the Town House, returned to the fort where he burnt his papers. Then with his close associates, Randolph, Palmer, West, Graham, and Lidget, Andros agreed to be "conveyed to the Council-house." On his journey, Andros reported he passed several armed men, "yett none offered him or those that were with him the least rudeness of incivility, but on the contrary usual respect."[49] On arrival at the Town House, Andros's aides were seized and kept outside, and only Andros was permitted to enter. He found present there Simon Bradstreet, the last governor under the charter, as well as several of his council members and the five ministers. The first to speak was William Stoughton, who told Andros "he might thank himself for the present Disaster that had befallen him." When Andros demanded to know the meaning of their actions, one councilor said that "now was the time for them to look to themselves; that they must and would have the Government in their own hands, and that he was their prisoner." The governor's associates were admitted to the council chamber where they were insulted by the rebel councilors. All were then ordered to be imprisoned.[50]

The fort was still in the hands of the governor's regular soldiers. When the rebel leaders demanded that Andros order them to surrender, he pointed out that as a prisoner, he could give no orders. He "wondered at their Confidence, of him, saying, he would sooner dye than give any such order." The rebels held a loaded pistol to Edward Randolph's chest, "threatening to shoot

him, if hee did not goe with them to the ffort, and acquaint those
in it, as from the Governor, that it was his pleasure and direction,
that they should deliver it up." Randolph had no choice but to
obey. He was marched back to the fort, where he informed Lieutenant Treffrey that the governor had ordered him to surrender.
Treffrey refused, saying he took orders only from the governor-
general. He agreed to yield only when the Puritans promised that
the soldiers would not be arrested if they surrendered and would
be permitted to go to another post. The soldiers surrendered, and
the Puritans immediately ordered their arrest. At Castle Island,
Ensign John Pippon refused to surrender without orders from
Andros or another superior officer. The Puritans, deciding they
would have to use force, gathered together men and boats to
transport them from the mainland to the island. To avoid a blood
bath, the Puritans asked Treffrey to intervene. He agreed and
went to the island to order Pippon to surrender. Pippon and his
men were also thrown into the prison at Fort Mary. At the dock,
the *Rose's* lieutenant agreed to surrender only when "all the
guns, both in ships and batteries, were brought to bear against"
the vessel. Captain George, fearing the destruction of the ship,
ordered Lieutenant Condon to surrender. To ensure that the vessel did not leave the harbor, the Puritans took its sails with the
willing help of the *Rose's* sailors.[51]

Andros was taken "under strong Guard" to John and Elizabeth Usher's house to spend the night of April 18. Militia Captain
Waterhouse, fearful that Andros would escape, came that night
and insisted on seeing Andros in bed. To prevent his escape,
Waterhouse demanded the governor's socks and shoes. The next
day, a crowd came to Boston from the country "like soe many
wild bears. . . . All the cry was against the Governor and Mr. Randolph." They threatened to destroy Usher's house and tear
Andros "in pieces." The rebel leaders, alarmed, told Andros of
the threat to his personal safety. Andros, sick in bed, calmly
"replied with a smiling countenance, they should not bee so much
concern'd for him, but rather pity themselves, their wives and
children, their posterity and country, for they might assure themselves, there must be an account of that day's uproar." It was the
rebels' fault, he continued, that the crowds were out of control,
"and if they had raised the Rabble, which they could not govern,
it behoved them to look to it." Despite his illness, the governor
agreed to be transported to the fort. He was taken through the
crowds, but throughout the journey, "not one of the whole rout
opened his mouth against him," such was their awe of the king's

personal representative. Andros was incarcerated in Fort Mary while Randolph was imprisoned in Boston's common jail. West, Palmer, Graham, and Treffrey were sent to the fort prison on Castle Island.[52]

With the collapse of the Dominion government, the government officials who had been in office before Dudley's regime took power again. Simon Bradstreet, now at the advanced age of eighty-six, was president of the revolutionary Council of Safety, composed of the men who signed the letter delivered to Andros. The council, led by Simon Bradstreet, controlled the government for about a month, until assembly elections were held on May 22.[53] As word reached the other New England colonies, they too resumed their old charter governments, so that "New England, which yesterday was united and formidable, is divided into about ten little independent kingdoms, each acting as if it knew no superior power." As Andros observed, "The old charter Government tho' vacated in Westminster Hall, was reassumed without any regard to the Crowne of England, and they revived and confirmed their former laws contrary and repugnant to the laws and statutes of England." New Englanders quickly reverted to all their former bad habits.[54]

On May 20, Bradstreet sent a congratulatory letter to William and Mary on their "glorious enterprise against tyranny and slavery." Determined to link their rebellion to William's own usurpation of a legitimate ruler, Bradstreet informed William that "the people here, excited to imitate your example . . . resolved to seize and secure some of the principal persons concerned and most active in the ill management of the evil and arbitrary Government set up over us; and accordingly on the 18th of April we seized Sir Edmund Andros and other of his evil instruments and now keep them in custody pending receipt of your royal orders." In London, Increase Mather was delighted to learn of the overthrow of the Dominion government. But, as Increase Mather realized, the Puritans' action was rebellion. The minister tried to put a good face to the news by observing to the king, "I presume your majesty has bin informed of the great service which your subjects in New England have done . . . in securing that Territory." The Puritans did, indeed, have a strong hand. It would have been difficult for William to find fault with the Puritans' overthrow of the Andros government when he himself was guilty of toppling a divine right king.[55]

Andros in prison may have hoped for help from his lieutenant governor in New York, Francis Nicholson, but the latter could do little to assist his commanding officer because he had to contend with a major rebellion of his own. Nicholson first heard of the Boston revolt on April 25. The next day, he held a council meeting and ordered the news of the revolt to be given to other public officials.[56] The rebellion that began on May 3 in New York on eastern Long Island was also a militia-led revolt spurred by divisions between Protestant sects and anti-Catholicism. The New York militia, on hearing of events in Boston, announced they were determined to put their government into trustworthy hands. As unrest spread westward from Long Island and then to the north up the Hudson River, James's appointees, whether civil or military, were turned out of office. At this point, with the militia becoming increasingly belligerent, Nicholson received direct orders from Andros on May 18, carried from Boston by George Wedderburn. Nicholson was to send two council representatives to Boston to demand his release. He was also to keep Albany quiet and, ever mindful of the welfare of his men, Andros told Nicholson to send a sloop with supplies to the soldiers at Fort Pemaquid. Nicholson attempted to comply with these orders. On May 22, he summoned councilors Andrew Hamilton from East New Jersey and William Smith from Long Island to New York City and told them they were to go to Boston. When both men refused, Nicholson did nothing to change their minds. Nicholson did not deploy troops to Boston or even supply the garrison at Pemaquid because he himself now faced total rebellion.[57] Any military action on his part on Andros's behalf was hopeless, since half of Nicholson's New York City garrison had gone to Maine with Andros and were still there. Nicholson, not having enough regular soldiers to guard the fort, had to rely on the militia. This proved a serious mistake because on 31 May 1689, the militia demanded and received from Nicholson the keys to the fort. Militia captain, Jacob Leisler, Andros's old adversary, led the rebels. Leisler was appointed captain of the fort on June 28.[58]

After the New York phase of the Glorious Revolution, Nicholson did not linger to offer any assistance to Andros or to see if Leisler, who had assumed the rule of governor, could be dislodged. He boarded the first ship he could find back to England. Nicholson planned to sail with former governor Thomas Dongan on the latter's brigantine. The duo actually boarded the vessel, but Dongan became so seasick that he had to return to shore. Nicholson sailed on 24 June 1689 while Dongan returned to his Long Island estate only to be put under house arrest until he managed to escape to New Jersey.[59]

Members of Andros's old New York council, having been nominated by him to the Dominion council, were still in office when the rebellion occurred in New York. Andros's friends, Van Cortland and Philipse, along with several other elite merchants, became alienated from Leisler when they suffered financial losses. The losses followed Leisler's ending of New York's monopoly on the bolting of grain. He then placed heavy taxes on trade to cover the expenses during the War of the League of Augsburg (1689–97), known in the colonies as King William's War. The elite merchants plotted to oust Leisler, but he anticipated their actions and ordered the arrest of any person who had held office under the Dominion government. These merchants included Nicholas Bayard, Andros's former adversary, who had refused to take the loyalty oath in 1675 and had been jailed for his defiance. Bayard, a realist since 1675, had accepted English imperial rule and now refused to follow Leisler, who then threw Bayard, along with several other prominent New Yorkers, into prison. Others, including high church Anglicans and Roman Catholics, were forced into exile.[60]

Just as the Glorious Revolution in England sparked an uprising in Boston, so did that uprising lead to Leisler's Rebellion in New York. This, in turn, brought on Coode's Rebellion in Maryland and sparked populist movements among the Delaware River settlements.[61] The rebellion in New York, as in Boston, was not only Protestants against Catholics, but also Protestants against Protestants, or more specifically, Puritans against Anglicans, Presbyterians against Episcopalians, Parliamentarians against Royalists, Calvinists against the Church of England, and Whigs against Tories. In both Massachusetts and New York, Calvinists displaced and persecuted both Anglicans and Catholics. Religion may also have been a precipitating factor in Maryland, although economic concerns and resentment against the proprietor had long contributed to unrest there. One Maryland colonist, aware of the increased resentment of the proprietor's government, in 1687 warned Lord Baltimore that the leaders of the discontented faction "will be very apt to pretend religion the better to carry on their evill Designs." The Maryland rebellion, led by Protestant assemblyman, John Coode, overthrew Lord Baltimore's proprietary and Catholic government on 16 July 1689. Coode took control of the government until William appointed a royal governor.[62]

News of the spread of the rebellion was extremely distressing to Andros and those who shared his imprisonment. At Fort Mary with Andros were Charles Lidget and Joseph Dudley, the latter on circuit when the revolution occurred having been seized and sent back to Boston. Militia captain and merchant, John Nelson, was now in command of the fort and keeper of the prisoners. Nelson was suspect to the Puritans because he was an Anglican. The Puritan fears were confirmed when it became obvious Nelson was too civil to the governor, permitting "his friends to come and visit him."[63] Consequently, Nelson was relieved of his command and replaced by a nameless but "old, sullen, morose, single eyed hypochrite" who "denied" the governor "the service of his own cook to dress his meat, nor suffered [him] to speak to anyone except before two witnesses." Supervision was so close that Andros's food was searched to ensure there were no letters hidden there.[64] Randolph reported that when a packet of letters arrived for the governor "from Whitehall and letters of both publick and private concernes of his and mine," the correspondence was "opened by Sr William Phips," the treasure hunter who had recently returned from England. Phips said "the Governr is a rogue and shall not have his packetts nor letters."[65] From this confinement came the story, possibly true, that Andros attempted an escape dressed in women's clothes but was discovered because he had not changed his shoes. This and similar stories, said Anglican minister Ratcliffe, "have not the least foundation of Truth" and were all "falsehoods, and lies, the Inventions of wicked men spread abroad on purpose to render the Governour odious to his people."[66]

Andros may well have attempted an escape because on June 7, he was moved from Fort Mary to a more secure location. At the fort on Castle Island, he was "kept under very stricte Confinemt: tho no Cause asigned or any thing said to me," said Andros, "and then only passionate Expresions agt: the Arbitrariness of ye Comision." Andros knew, as did other imperial observers, that although he as governor drew criticism for his actions, the real animosity was directed toward the central London based government itself. This fact was also recognized by Randolph, who noted that "notwithstanding all the pretence of grievances and the cry of the Governor's oppression, it is not the person of Sir Edmund Andros but the Government that they design to have removed, that they may freely trade." Randolph, principally concerned with enforcing trade regulations, understandably emphasized this aspect. More than resentment at trade restrictions that angered Puritans, particularly the Puritan elite, was their loss of control of the government they had dominated since first settlement.[67]

In addition to their imprisonment, the prisoners at Castle Island, at Fort Mary, and in the common jail had one thing in common—all were members of the Church of England. Of the twenty-four arrested, only four were natives of New England. Those incarcerated were the outsiders who had thwarted the ambitions and threatened the profits of local leaders and merchants. Imprisoned Anglicans cynically observed that it was not surprising the Puritans became "Persecutors of the Church of England." They were simply reverting to past practices when "they punished with Fines, Imprisonment, Stripes, Banishment, and Death" any who practiced other religions. Nor was religious persecution the only example of Puritan perfidy. Despite their past complaints that their rights as Englishmen were ignored by the Dominion government, after the rebellion, the Puritans themselves detained prisoners without warrants, broke into houses and offices, seized and destroyed personal and official correspondence, and denied prisoners *habeus corpus*. As Palmer observed, the prisoners were kept ten months in prison "without any Mittimus, or just Cause."[68]

Also at the Castle Island prison since April 20 were John Palmer, James Graham, John West, and Thomas Treffrey. The prisoner population at Castle Island decreased when Treffrey was dismissed and West was ordered to the common jail in Boston. In July, Andros, Randolph, and Dudley, the three men deemed the most dangerous enemies of the Puritans, were each charged with a capital crime against the Massachusetts general court. The Puritans concluded that "any man" who did "Attempt the Alteration and Subversion of our frame of Polity or government fundamentally he shall be put to death."[69] In the eyes of the Puritans, Andros and his aides were guilty of treason because, in their opinion, "the very *Form* of Government imposed upon us" was "the *worst of Treasons*, even a Treasonable Invasion of the Rights which the whole *English* Nation lay claim unto." Most of the prisoners, including Andros, were also denied bail. In Andros's case, sympathetic supporters offered to post bail in the amount of £20,000 to gain his release from prison. Bail was refused.[70]

On Castle Island, Andros was put in an underground cell with James Graham and John Palmer. A small, damp room, it measured no more than seventeen by nine feet. After Palmer's transfer to Boston, the room contained "2 beddsteds, 2 close stooles, a table . . . and this is the whole accomodation allowed him [Andros] & Mr. Graham, to exist in day & night, there is no chimney in it nor candle when they have a fire they burn their beds:

when they eat they open the door and sett their table part out of ye Room: & not above 2 can sitt at it: it stands so low, that the Rain stands in the flower 5 or 6 inches & is sometymes higher." The cell was so damp that "their Shoes pull'd off at night, are all mouldy next morning." The keeper at Castle Island was Captain John Fairweather, described by Randolph as "a very strict zealot and Church monitor." Minister Ratcliffe, however, offered a slightly more charitable view of Fairweather, saying that he "was very respectful" to Andros and "gave him liberty to walk about the Island . . . and freely admitted his friends to him." Food was inadequate for Andros primarily because Fairweather had appropriated for his own use the rabbits Andros raised on Castle Island, along with the governor's milk cow. The Puritans, in defense of their actions in keeping the governor in such shabby accommodations, said Andros himself had chosen to be in that particular cell.[71]

The limited freedom of movement permitted to Andros on Castle Island was further restricted following his second escape attempt on August 2, this venture better documented by reliable sources than his earlier attempt in June 1689. The escape was effected after his servant "enticed the centinel to drink" and Andros "escaped from the castle" at about eleven at night. Andros was in Rhode Island the next day, perhaps hoping that he would rally to his side the Quakers there, who had no great love of the Puritans. Before he could contact the Quakers, he was spotted and captured by Rhode Islanders that same day and held at Peleg Sanford's house under twenty-four hour armed guard. Rhode Island officials immediately wrote to Bradstreet to ask how they should proceed. Bradford sent Captain Thomas Prentis with a guard to escort Andros back to Boston. Rhode Islanders were instructed to take the governor to Bristol and turn him over to former Dominion councilor, Major John Walley. Bradstreet knew, as Walley warned him, that it was not safe to leave Andros in Rhode Island because many "Quakers and some others are for his escape."[72]

By August 8, Andros was at Walley's house. Obviously sympathetic to the governor, Walley told Bradstreet "wee have been very carefull to avoid tumults and any incivility that might be offered, and wee hope the like care will be used in the other parts." Progress toward Boston was apt to be slow, Walley warned, because Andros was ill, "complaining of indisposition of body, and unable to ride swiftly." Walley asked Bradstreet if Andros "might be conveighed by way of Dorchester . . . to the Castle. It will be extremely well taken by him and I hope you will gratyfie him. . . . He desires, at least at present, that he may not come to Boston." The Dorchester route was not only shorter but would spare Andros the humiliation of being paraded as a captive through the streets of the city he had so lately governed. Back in the Castle Island prison, Andros was "denied the liberty of discourse or conversation with any person, his own servants to attend him, or any communication or correspondence with any by letters." After his recapture, he was "Confined to his roome," although the Puritans later claimed that Andros was allowed to walk on the island accompanied by two armed musketeers. The governor refused to accept this condition and so did not exercise. Andros himself complained of being kept "under severe and close confinement."[73]

Andros was in misery, but his imprisoned subordinates, particularly those in "the Common Gaol in New Algeires," as Randolph described the Boston jail, fared no better. John West, moved from the Castle Island prison to Boston jail on June 7, the same day Andros was taken to the island, experienced thirteen weeks of close confinement, though he was never charged with any crime. He talked to his keeper in September, and the keeper said he had no orders to hold West. West, believing he was discharged, left the prison but was forced back by armed men outside. Joseph Dudley complained that his lengthy prison stay destroyed his health. He was released on £10,000 bail and allowed to return to his home, but angry crowds surrounded his house, "broak down his ffence [and] fetched him to the Goal" again. Sarah Palmer petitioned Bradstreet to release her husband John from his prison cell at the Castle, since he was "very much troubled with the goute and other distempers of body, and is there confined in a roome with Sir Edmund Andros and Mr. Graham where noe fire can be made nor attendance upon his distempers require, to the great danger and hazard of his life." Edward Randolph complained that he was thrown into a cell with common criminals, one of whom "has lain 16 days rotting in his own excrement." Randolph requested that the poor wretch "might be taken and removed into some other warm place, that we be not infected with the vehement stench."[74]

As Dominion officials languished in prison, the northern Indians took advantage of the lack of unity in New England. There were virtually no defensive forces left in Maine because on April 27, Captain Savage arrived at the Pemaquid fort with orders from the Council of Safety to withdraw all troops. Bradstreet had asked regular army Lieutenant James Weems to come to Boston from Pemaquid to serve the Puritan government. Weems refused. "My Dependance is elswhere," he explained, "where I hope to be more servisable to my King and Countrey." Weems further told Bradstreet that "since you have seen cause to Displace the Governor and all Gentlemen under his command, I am resolved to take my fortune with them." Weems urged Bradstreet to "send your forces and take possession of this place, for I cannot promise to secure it, my men being all resolved to leave me, as some have done already." Brockholes and Weems requested permission to go to New York but were seized. Their captors "tied their hands behind their backs, brought them as the vilest malefactors to Boston, and immediately committed them to Gaol which was all the thanks they had for their winter's labor and service against the Indians."[75]

Throughout Maine, Indian attacks backed by the French accelerated after the Puritan elite recalled the soldiers. In May, the "French & Indians in warr with us, who are come into the province of Maine, kill destroy & burn what they left standing last winter, the present Govt having withdrawn all the forces left there in very good forts, well man'd by the Govr Sr Edd Andros & kept them under such restraint & want that the Indians would have been forced to sue for peace." Instead, with Andros and the troops gone, Maine was "now deserted and left to the ravage of the barbarous heathens, who are already come down, have destroyed and burnt some forts and severall dwelling houses and kill'd some of the people." One Maine Indian, sachem Dockowando, apparently unaware that the soldiers were gone from Maine, came to Boston to submit to Andros in June, but "seeing the Governor in prison and the land in confusion, has turned our enemy."[76]

On 2 August 1689, some three or four hundred Indians, encouraged and armed by the French, attacked English settlements. By the end of the summer, several hundred English settlers had been killed or taken captive. The French and Indians, having taken the fort at Pemaquid, were in command of most of Maine and went on to destroy part of New Hampshire. By September, the Indians had overrun the eastern country from St. Croix to Piscatagua, causing an estimated £60,000 in damages.[77]

In October 1689, Mohawk sachems came to Boston at the invitation of New England leaders. As it had been during King Philip's War, their assistance was needed to help subdue the northern Indians. When the Mohawks on arrival wanted to see Andros, the Puritans asked if he would permit the sachems to visit him on

Castle Island. Embarrassed to have the sachems see him as a prisoner, Andros refused, asking his keepers if they meant to make a show of him. The governor knew the danger in letting the Indians see "the disunion and separate goverments, and shewing them the countrey and disorders thereof."[78]

War damage was not confined to New England. On 9 February 1690 at 11 P.M., 250 French and Indians launched a major attack on Schenectady in New York, devastating the town, killing sixty and taking twenty-seven captives. The Indians burnt Schenectady to the ground, leaving only a few houses standing, the survivors scurrying to Albany for safety. In addition to the devastation of people and property, the fisheries and lumber industries were destroyed in New England, with the French taking masts originally slated for the use of the Royal Navy. As the Indian threat drew ever nearer to Massachusetts, soldiers who had returned from Maine, including the regulars from New York, were dismissed by the Puritans but were not paid. The government had no money, even though taxes were higher than they had been during the Dominion government. Nor was there any hope that the Puritans could soon raise an army to defend Massachusetts because they also lacked the authority "to presse men and see no way how they shall be paid." No wonder the returning soldiers were irate. One of their number was led to cry, "God Blesse King William god Bless Sir Ed. Andros & Dam all pumpkin states."[79]

Unrest was endemic in New England, with civil disorder following the overthrow of the Dominion government in Massachusetts as its society was restructured. The restructuring was only partially a result of the Dominion and Andros's governance. The old social fabric was already weakened by the debt and disorientation brought about by King Philip's War. The burdens imposed by the war caused formerly mute colonists to question local leaders. That, coupled with attempts by England to control trade, suppress piracy, weaken the power of local elites, and centralize government authority, led inevitably to the breakdown of local political culture. In its place, a new and more centralized government was to evolve.[80]

Had it not been for the Glorious Revolution in England, the Dominion would undoubtedly have survived, with or without Andros. Edmund Andros had made significant strides in the implementation of that government. While the absence of a representative assembly was a major thorn to colonists, such an assembly could easily have been established as it was in New York. In addition to more efficient colonial administration, the major advantage the Dominion provided was defense. A united military force under a single leader, such as Andros had commanded in the Maine campaign, was essential to guard the English colonies against Louis XIV's expansionist schemes. With that force absent after the fall of the Dominion, New England and New York faced several decades of bloody warfare on their northern frontiers. As the colonies reverted to their old separate governments and separate identities, defense was again splintered and colonies continued to be concerned only with their own problems, ignoring those of their neighbors. The rebellion in Boston had threatened not only the safety of colonists in Maine and Massachusetts, but also the very survival of all of England's North American colonies. Militarily, it would take the English almost a century to implement again the unified show of force mustered by Andros against the French and the Indians during the winter campaign of 1688–89.

Religion had provided the rationale for the Puritans to reject a government that the provincial elite saw as threatening their power and prestige. Although they had ousted the governor and ended the Dominion government, their success in regaining their old charter was still very much in doubt, as was the future of the imprisoned Edmund Andros.

11

The Glorious Revolution, 1690–1692

Part 2

When William our deliverer came,
To heal the nation's grievance
I turned the cat in pan again,
And swore to him allegiance.
—Anon., "The Vicar of Bray"[1]

THE GLORIOUS REVOLUTION CAUSED MANY PEOPLE, IN BOTH ENGLAND
and England's American colonies, to "turn the cat in pan." In
England, when it became obvious that James was no longer a
threat, allegiance was quickly extended to the new king and
queen. For people living in the remote reaches of empire, such as
Andros, it was at first difficult to know which side to support. The
rebellious New Englanders benefited from the English people's
ready acceptance of William and Mary. If the English at home
could depose a legitimate divine right sovereign, then how could
the people in New England be faulted when they then dislodged
that king's appointed governor? The similarities in the actions
caused some concern among members of the Privy Council Committee on Trade that heard the complaints of New Englanders.
Many councilors had themselves worked to overthrow James,
making it difficult to condemn the actions of New Englanders
who had overthrown their governor. Neither did the committee
want to condemn a governor-general, who represented the legitimate authority of the home government. Metropolitan interests
had to prevail, so the committee members looked hard for a legal
loophole and finally found one.

With the arrest of Sir Edmund Andros in April 1689 and the
overthrow of the Dominion of New England government, Massachusetts colonists may have believed they would be permitted to

resume their old charter government. The accession of William and Mary to the English throne in the place of James undoubtedly brought hope to elite colonists that they would again be secure in their religion and in their rights as English subjects and that privileges won by the upper class in England would now be extended to them. They were to be disappointed. The Glorious Revolution did indeed guarantee the rights of the English gentry. The upper classes, or "the men of property won freedom— freedom from arbitrary taxation and arbitrary arrest, freedom from religious persecution, freedom to control the destinies of their country through their elected representatives, freedom to buy and sell." These rights were not extended either to the lower orders of English society or to provincials of any class.[2]

The colonial elite may have been optimistic at first about the possibility of benefiting from the Glorious Revolution and its provincial counterparts. Part of that optimism resulted from the first reactions of officials in England to the 1689 Boston uprising. Initially in England, news of the overthrow of the Dominion government was received with approval and seen as a counterpart of events in England. This view quickly changed when details of the rebellion and its aftermath were received in London. A Boston Anglican merchant wrote to associates in England that he believed that the restoration of the Dominion government was the only hope for the survival of Massachusetts. He predicted that the reimposition of a Puritan government would bring ruination to the province. Certainly, the merchant continued, it would be the ruination of all Anglicans in Massachusetts, leaving them no choice but to flee from New England. Chaos reigned on the Maine frontier, other New England residents said, after the Dominion forces had been withdrawn, resulting in three hundred deaths and £40,000 in property damage.[3] Colonists who lived on the frontier of New Hampshire bemoaned the fact that they were now at risk of Indian attack, whereas during Andros's regime the governor had provided military protection.[4] In Boston, there were many people, both Puritans and Anglicans, who wanted the Andros government restored. City residents sent letters to London begging for the protection offered by English law. Others asked to be "delivered from the thralldom of a most extravagant and arbitrary government," such as that imposed by the Puritans after the rebellion.[5]

Also effective in swaying English public opinion were letters sent by concerned New Englanders describing the cruel imprisonment of the Dominion's governor and its top officials. Indignation mounted as stories circulated that the governor, personally known to the king and many courtiers, was being held in a small, dank, unheated cell that periodically flooded. News of his dire circumstances turned the public opinion of both Whigs and Tories, but particularly Tories, against the New Englanders, now seen as lawless rebels. It was the Tories who dominated government immediately after the Glorious Revolution.[6]

Andros's personal report of events in New England during the spring of 1689 was also effective in evoking antipathy against the uprising. John Riggs, Andros's subordinate, had brought the report to the king and the Council of Trade. The Reverend Robert Ratcliffe accompanied Riggs, carrying with him letters from Randolph to the Council of Trade and Plantations, to William Sancroft, archbishop of Canterbury, and copies of the Puritan manifestos. Ratcliffe's purpose in going to England was "to solicit for the enlargement of many of his constant hearers imprisoned for no other reason but because they were of the Church of England."[7] Both men arrived in London in mid July 1689. While Ratcliffe enlisted the aid of ecclesiastical officials, Riggs presented petitions to the king on behalf of Andros, assuring William that Andros "is and always was a Protestant." Riggs further assured William that Andros "would readily have obeyed your orders had he received them." Riggs conveyed Andros's desire to "be released from his present close confinement, where he is denied writing materials and any other convenience, and that he may be sent home to answer for any charges brought against him."[8]

On hearing of Andros's arrest, the king wrote immediately to Bradstreet on 30 July 1689 and ordered him to send Andros to England on the first available ship. The king warned the Puritans that Andros must be "Civilly used." The council of trade also sent orders to the Puritans to continue their present government until instructed otherwise.[9] The various petitions and letters sent by Andros, Randolph, and others to officials in London and elsewhere had the desired palliative effect in England.

The shift in public opinion against the New Englanders eventually worked against the efforts of Increase Mather to have Massachusetts included in the Corporation Bill, which restored the corporate charters of English cities and towns that had been vacated under Charles II and James II. Parliament ruled that the revocation of the Massachusetts charter was not comparable to the revocation of English town and city charters. The Massachusetts charter was voided "upon quite different reasons from those in England, these [New England] Charters being seized for the

abuse of their Power, in destroying . . . the very Laws and Navigation of England, and making themselves as it were Independent
of this Crown." Massachusetts was guilty of "imposing an Oath
of Fidelity to their Commonwealth . . . incroaching upon the
neighbouring Colonies, . . . Their making Laws against all other
opinions in religion except that of the Congregational Churches,
and more especially against that of the Church of England." In
other words, the monarch had changed, but the attitude toward
the colonies had not. Massachusetts was not to have its old charter restored.[10]

John Riggs returned to North America with the king's July 30
letter, landing first at Boston where, on November 24, he delivered the letter to Simon Bradstreet. Massachusetts authorities
also received, at that same time, a letter from Increase Mather
dated 2 September 1689. Mather assured the New Englanders
that the king had said *"That He did kindly Accept of what was
done in* Boston. *And* that *His Subjects in* New-England *should
have their Ancient Rights and Priviledges Restored."* The New
Englanders, reassured that they would not be regarded as trai-
tors, were hopeful that they would again be able to enjoy their
traditional liberties. But, as the Puritans were to find out, William's interpretation of those liberties differed substantially from
that of the Puritans. On December 12, the Puritans instructed
Captain Fairweather to read the king's letter to Andros and the
other prisoners.[11]

If Andros expected an immediate release after the receipt of
William's order, he was disappointed. Puritan leaders were hesi-
tant about sending Andros back to London until they had
amassed sufficient proof against him and his "Accomplices and
confederates" to justify their actions in overthrowing a legitimate
government. Officials throughout Massachusetts were ordered to
collect affidavits against Andros and his aides, impressive in vol-
ume if not in accuracy or even believability. As Randolph commented, "they know if they send us home & have nothing to
charge upon us, 'twill not sound well on their side." The Puritan
elite, since 18 April 1689, had lived in daily fear that a military
force would be sent from England to punish them for their rebellion, or that William would rename Andros as governor. Fears
were particularly strong among those merchants who traveled to
England and to other English colonies that they would be viewed
in those locations as "revolters from their allegiance."[12]

The main points against Andros in the Puritans' charges were
related to their conviction that the voiding of their charter was

illegal. Puritans considered this document their Magna Carta and pointed out that without the charter, they were without law. English law, they said, was designed for England and not suitable for Massachusetts. English law was, in fact, "unknown" in Massachusetts prior to the establishment of the Dominion, "and no *habeas corpus* granted" until Andros's regime. Next in importance was Andros's imposition of taxes without a representative assembly. Equally disturbing was Andros's threat to land titles, as shown in the complaints of John Higgeson and Samuel Sewall. Both were indignant with "Sir Edmund Andros his affirming that all the lands in New England were the Kings and not the peoples." Andros, with the assistance of those who were "joined with him in his Arbitrary Laws," did "make laws destructive of the Liberty of the People, imposed and levied Taxes, threatned and imprisoned them that would not be assisting to the illegal Levys, denied that they had any Property in their Lands without Patents from him." Andros's loyalty to William was also questioned because he had ordered all people "to oppose any descent" of William into New England and had stifled news of William's accession to the throne.[13]

Many of the charges against the governor were ludicrous. The Puritans said Andros was a Francophile who had schemed with the enemy to effect a French and Irish invasion of New England. They claimed the governor was a Catholic who prayed to the Virgin Mary. Andros planned to destroy Boston and its residents, the Puritans said. He had prepared explosives in the fort and had tunnels dug to achieve that end. Even more absurd was the charge that Andros, while in meetings with the Mohawks in Albany, had given a sachem £12 to attack Manhattan in April 1689. The governor, one witness said, "hired the Indians to kill the English" and gave presents and ammunition to Indians to achieve his purpose. The governor, while in Maine, charged a Puritan militiaman, "admitted the Squaws dayly to him." In one specific incident, the accuser said Andros consorted with four Indian squaws for two days and when the women left, gave each gunpowder and bullets. The governor "had more love for them, the Indians, then for his Majesties Subjects the English." Andros's innate politeness to the Indians also drew criticism. The militia soldiers who served under Andros in Maine were aghast that Andros had ordered Captain John Jourdan "to treat the Enemie Indians with all manner of Civility, and to accommodate them with what their store afforded if they came to the Garrison where he commanded." Andros alone, said the Puritans, was responsible for the outbreak of the Indian war in Maine, *"For he went (with the* Rose *Frigat,) and violently seized, and took and carried away, in a time of peace all the Household Goods and Merchandises of* Monsieur *Casteen a Frenchman* at Penobscsot."[14]

Puritans even sought evidence against Andros from Leisler in New York. Leisler obligingly tried to persuade "one Matthias, a servant or soldier," who had served Andros for two years while he was New York governor, to swear "that Sir Edmund was a papist, offering him twenty-four shillings in hand, with a promise that he should not want as long as he should live." Despite the offer of a bribe, Matthias refused to confirm what was clearly untrue.[15]

Examples of Andros's own quick temper were numerous and apparently were believed sufficient to justify rebellion. Joseph Wood complained "about [the governor's] threatning to hang him." On another occasion, the governor, on being asked how the constables should proceed in the event of a riot, "fell into a great Rage, and did curse them and said they deserved to be sent to Goale and indited and called them ill names and order Mr. Jno. West Deputy Secretary to take account of their names."[16]

Several militiamen spoke out about their ill treatment by Andros and his subordinate officers. David Foulton and Thomas Clark, who had served under Andros in Maine, blamed him for "the Cruelty of Sir Edmunds officers to Souldiers Eastward." Examples of Andros's own cruelty were forthcoming. Samuel Wright and six other men said that Andros "bid his Sergeant when they went upon the long march, to kill them Souldiers that were not able, or unwilling to tr[avel]." Two militiamen complained of the "millitary officers unhumaine destroying of souldiers that were here Imprest." Three other soldiers complained "about the more then ordinary Inhumanity of Capt: Jno: Jourdan to one of his Souldiers" and "about Capt. Geo: Lockers being the cause of the death of two of his souldiers by inhumaine usage." While charges of officers' cruelty to men were probably true, other charges were outlandish or bizarre. Andros was accused by Increase Mather in London of poisoning the soldiers in Maine with rum and deliberately planning the deaths of the several hundred New England militiamen he took to Maine "in the Depth of Winter on purpose to Sacrifice them there." The governor was deemed capable of such an action because he was known for the low regard in which he held Puritans, particularly those who were extreme Calvinists. He had been heard to say, *"They were a People only fitt to be rooted off the face of the Earth."*[17] The last statement was probably the most accurate piece of evidence the Puritans advanced. Andros did indeed despise the Puritans.

The necessity of New Englanders to justify their actions caused them to delay sending the governor to England despite the king's order. Andros, understandably annoyed, demanded that he be returned immediately, but the Puritans delayed until 5 February 1690. On that day, a warrant was issued to Captain Gilbert Bant to "safely convey" to England "according to his Maties Commands" Andros and his aides, Edward Randolph, Joseph Dudley, John Palmer, John West, James Graham, James Sherlock, and George Farwell. The men, having survived an imprisonment that lasted almost ten months, were put on board the *Mehitabel* at the cost of £20 for each passenger. Even though Andros left his wife in the churchyard of King's Chapel, he could not have sailed from Boston with any regret. The governor and his party willingly "endured all the Miseries of a Troublesome Winter Voyage" on a dangerously overloaded ship, said Palmer, arriving in London on 7 April 1690. The Massachusetts representatives, physicians Elijah Cooke and Thomas Oakes, preceded them to the capital having arrived March 30. They joined Increase Mather and Sir Henry Ashurst, a Presbyterian, Whig merchant. The four men were there to get the old charter restored, to press their charges against Andros, and to defend the actions of the Boston Puritans in overthrowing the Dominion government.[18]

Andros's immediate concern on his arrival in London was the trial that he was convinced would exonerate him and his subordinates. Increase Mather and the Massachusetts agents were perhaps a bit more apprehensive at the trial's approach. Andros and his party went immediately to the Privy Council, where they informed the members that they had returned as ordered by the king. The council members were delighted to see Andros and "received him very kindly and told him they would Informe the King of his arrival." Andros was equally delighted to find that nothing much had changed as far as the make-up of the government infrastructure after the Glorious Revolution. Daniel Finch, earl of Nottingham, was now secretary of state for the colonies. Nottingham had supported Andros in his role as bailiff on the island of Guernsey. William Blathwayt, an old friend and strong supporter, was the clerk of the Privy Council. Nottingham and fellow privy councilor, Thomas Osborne, marquis of Carmarthen (the former earl of Danby), both Tories, were now allied with William III. After a friendly greeting, the council advised Andros that until the Massachusetts agents appeared, the governor and his aides were "free to goe where they please, onely to attend the Counsill board when Called."[19]

On Thursday, April 10, the principals were summoned to appear at a hearing before the Privy Council committee, presided over by the marquis of Carmarthen. Present were Oakes, Cooke, Mather, and Ashurst, along with Andros and those associates who had sailed with him. The Massachusetts agents asked for an extension to give them time to prepare their charges against the governor. Andros was annoyed with the request for a delay, arguing that he and his aides had spent almost ten months in jail while the Puritans had tried to collect evidence against them. Surely, he reasoned, that had been sufficient time to prepare their argument. The sympathetic council agreed that the Puritans indeed had enough time but reluctantly permitted the agents a few days to formulate their charges. The document was to be delivered to the board the following Monday, with the council meeting again on Thursday, April 17, just one day short of the first anniversary of the uprising in Boston.[20]

The agents worked feverishly and the following Monday delivered the document of complaints to the council of trade. The numerous charges collected by the Puritans over the course of the previous year had been reduced to three. The first accused the governor of publishing a proclamation warning colonists to resist the invasion of William of Orange and of suppressing news of William's accession to the throne. The second claimed that Andros "made Lawes destructive of the liberty of the people," placed "illegal levies," refused to accept their titles to land and required them to apply for new patents, and supplied the Indians "with ammunition" and encouraged them to "make war upon the English." The third was directed primarily at Andros's aides who, the Puritans claimed, helped Andros achieve his ends and were guilty of extortion.[21]

The April 7 hearing was presided over by Carmarthen, who had spent several years in the Tower of London because of the Whigs. It was not to be expected that Carmarthen would have much sympathy for the New England Puritans. In addition to the Privy Council committee, the attendees included Andros and his colleagues with their attorneys and supporters and the four Massachusetts agents with their attorneys. The Whig, Sir John Somers, represented the Massachusetts agents. Sir George Treby and Sir Robert Sawyer defended Andros. The latter, as attorney general in 1683, had successfully prosecuted the crown's case against the Massachusetts charter. Sawyer, who had despised the Puritans in

1683, had not changed his views in 1690. Only two months prior to the hearing, Sawyer had convinced this very same committee that the revocation of the Massachusetts Bay Company charter was legal, thereby thwarting Increase Mather. A few months prior to that, Treby had informed the committee that Andros's imposition and collection of taxes in Massachusetts was within the law. On entering the room, Andros and his party moved to one side of the room, and the four Massachusetts agents and their attorney Somers moved to the opposite side.[22]

Sawyer, Andros's attorney, immediately took the offensive. They "came prepared with a charge against the colony, for rebellion against lawful authority, for imprisoning the King's governor etc." Sawyer also complained that his clients had suffered unduly during their incarceration and had incurred considerable expenses during that time. Somers, the Massachusetts attorney, admitted "the agents were upon the defensive part." Sawyer then went on to review "the pretended Crimes that Mr. Randolph had formerly suggested," which had brought *quo warranto* proceedings against the Massachusetts charter. Sawyer managed to detail virtually every one of the Puritans' past sins before he acknowledged that those past proceedings had nothing to do with the present case. Nevertheless, his point that these New Englanders were chronic troublemakers had been made with the committee.[23]

The defendants had received copies of the agents complaints before the hearing. The president of the council asked William Blathwayt to read the objections against Andros and the others. Two colonists, Dr. Cooke and Thomas Brinley, give two different accounts of what followed. Both were prejudiced observers; Cooke was an ardent Puritan intent on defending the actions of his coreligionists, and Brinley was a strong Andros supporter who had helped to found King's Chapel. The latter, in a letter to his father, said Andros did not respond to the charge. Sawyer replied that the proclamation issued by Andros was in response to an order that was sent to all government officials in both England and America. It had been sent to America well before William's landing in England. By publishing it, Andros "did butt his duty as being Governour their and Commandr in cheife." In Cooke's account, written in a letter sent to Simon Bradstreet several months after the trial, Andros denied ever issuing such a proclamation. His associates supported Andros, only to be embarrassed when the proclamation itself was actually produced by the agents. Since Andros was well aware that the Proclamation had at his order been widely circulated throughout the Dominion and copies of it sent to England, it seems unlikely he would deny its existence.[24]

At this point, Joseph Dudley, who, along with all the defendants, had a copy of the Puritan complaint, asked the assembled lordships of the council why the charges produced by the Puritans were unsigned. The committee also demanded to know why they had been presented with unsigned charges. The agents' attorney, Somers, replied that they brought the charges on behalf of the people of Massachusetts. When Carmarthen ordered the agents to sign the accusations, they refused. Carmarthen then "demanded their Credentials and who they came from." The agents refused to disclose this information. "Then my Lord President asked them if they Came from any Governor and Counsell or any General Assembly. They answered from the People." Carmarthen asked "From what People?" When the agents still refused to answer, Sawyer responded that the charges were originated "by the Rabble spirited by the faction to overthrow the Government."[25]

Carmarthen should have been sympathetic to the actions of the Boston citizenry in overthrowing the Dominion government. Somers's intent in phrasing his response as being the spontaneous actions of the people in Massachusetts was undoubtedly to remind Carmarthen of his own actions during the Glorious Revolution. Then, as earl of Danby, he had directed the spontaneous seizure of the garrison at Hull for William of Orange. Carmarthen faced a dilemma. If the Massachusetts people were rebels, then so were he and all other Englishmen who had opposed James. Looking for a legal loophole, he found it by demanding a signature on the complaints.[26]

Carmarthan said to the agents, "You say it was done by the country and by the people, that is nobody. Let us see A. B. C. D. the persons who will make it their own case." The agents again refused to sign, realizing that if they signed and lost, they would be liable for law suits by Andros and his colleagues. Somers replied, "My lord, we are here in behalf of the country, to manage their concerns, and not in the behalf of any particular persons." Carmarthen told the agents "if they Could not show any Credentialls nor who they came from they must withdraw, for then they came from nobody." The Massachusetts agents left the room. Carmarthen told Andros and his associates to attend the council on the next day, when they would be discharged. On April 18, exactly one year after the Boston uprising, the lords of the committee made a report to the king of the "Innocency" of Andros and his associates "and that their was nobody would stand to accuse them, and they were accordingly discharged." On April 24, the king met with the entire Privy Council, who reported that it was their humble "opinion to your Matie that the said Sr Edmond Andros and other persons lately imprison'd in New England . . . be forthwith discharged and set at liberty" since no complaint had been filed against them. The king agreed, ordering that Andros and his aides be "hereby discharged and sett at Liberty." William received Andros and his colleagues, who numbered seventeen or eighteen. "The King, hearing they were come, immediately left all the Court and came out to them, and they all kissed his hand. The King told them that he would take care of them all, and said he rememberd he had seene Sir Edmond severall times," as indeed he had when the king was a child and Andros was a courtier in the queen of Bohemia's household. As a result of that old acquaintanceship, "Sir Edmund is almost every day with the King and is sent for by him often. The Agents are never since seen about the Court."[27]

Puritans became the laughingstock of London, or, as Mather complained, the agents were "Exposed in the News Letters and ridiculed in the City and Countrey." Increase Mather himself admitted that "the Toreys insult [us] saying the N[ew]-E[ngland] Agents put in a Libell which the darst not signe and that the things were false that Sr. E was charged with." Mather explained that neither he nor Ashurst could sign the complaint because they had not been in Massachusetts and did not know if the charges were true; Oakes and Cooke said they were advised by their attorney Somers not to sign. Charles Mordaunt, the first earl of Monmouth, took pains to tell Increase Mather that the "King was offended at New England because they had Imprisoned their Governor and had cutt the throat of their own countrey."[28]

Andros, who had been silenced for almost a year by the Puritans, began to tell his side of the story to the Council of Trade. He emphasized that he was not, nor had he ever been, a Catholic. He had proven his loyalty during more than twenty years of service to the crown, "in severall parts of America in the Wars against the French in the Charibee Islands, and in the Government of New Yorke as well as in New England." Andros said that in New England, he had merely followed King James's orders in publishing the October 16 declaration. Nor had he imprisoned the bearer of the news of William's accession, explaining that John Winslow had been arrested not for bringing the news but for contempt when he refused to show the announcement to officials.[29]

Andros said that as governor-general of the Dominion of New England, he had not made any laws destructive of liberty, but had merely "by vertue of the power and authority given under the great seale of England," seen to the passage of "severall prudentiall Lawes and Ordinances as could be agreeable to the Lawes of England." In response to charges that he had weighted the Dominion council with outsiders, Andros pointed out that the council was, with the exception of two men, composed of the "inhabitants and Planters of New-England."[30]

In response to Puritan complaints that he had forced them to swear on a Bible in court, Andros noted that the courtroom procedures he introduced were all "agreeable to the Lawes Customes and Statutes of England." He had neither imposed any arbitrary taxes nor imprisoned any one who did not pay them, except for those few "who riotously and tumultuously combined together" to protest the levies. These troublemakers were indeed "proceeded against by due course of Law." Taxes were imposed with the authority conveyed to him in "his Commission under the Great Seale of England." The taxes he placed were moderate, and he noted that the present government had found revenue insufficient and had raised taxes "sevenpence half-penny in the pound." The Massachusetts government was so desperate for funds that they had even taxed imprisoned Dominion officials. All his actions, Andros said, had been authorized by his commission or by his instructions, including "confirming others where [land] Titles were defective." Andros had, in fact, followed to the letter the orders given him by James II. His commission gave him considerable leeway, in the interpretation of those instructions. Andros had used that leeway, although perhaps not always wisely.[31]

Understandably, Andros was indignant at the reports that he had armed the Indians, one of the most ludicrous of the charges brought against the governor. Andros called the charges "a vile and base aspersion, unworthy of an Englishman and a Christian, being without the least ground or colour of truth." In his defense, he again cited his long years of service to the crown and his record of peaceful and successful negotiation with the Iroquois. The war in Maine had started in his absence, he said, when an overly zealous council, which acted without his knowledge or authorization, had ordered troops to the frontier. The results were as disastrous as they were predictable. Faced with an all-out Indian war,

Andros, on returning to Boston, personally led his men to "above one hundred miles into the Desart further than any Christian Settlement" and had repelled the Indians. If his military policies had been followed, Andros said, the Indians would be at peace now. Instead, when the Puritans recalled all troops, chaos followed. Other observers from New England confirmed that the disasters on the frontier would not have occurred if Andros had remained in command.[32]

Andros detailed the events leading up to the 18 April 1689 rebellion, which, he said, came as a surprise to him. After the rebellion, Andros reported, New Englanders, "without any regard to the Crowne," simply reestablished their old governments, "tho' vacated in Westminster Hall." Nor did New England authorities permit any "appeales to His Matie." Since the uprising, Andros claimed, Massachusetts did "tolerate an unlimited irregular trade, contrary to the severall acts of Plantations, Trade and Navigacon, now as little regarded as in the time of their former Charter Governments." Consequently, the entire revenue that should have come to the crown was lost. Even more serious was the threat posed to England's colonies by France. The French, taking advantage of the disunity among the English, launched destructive attacks against the English colonies. Andros urged the king to act immediately to "put a stop to the French and Indians, and thereby prevent the ruine or loss of that whole dominion of New England & consequently of Their Majties other American Plantacons."[33]

Andros also submitted an account of his expenditures for a total of 709 men raised to defend New England. In his account of the conduct of the provincial troops, Andros was not complimentary. In this, he anticipated future generations of British army officers who threw up their hands in disgust when they had to rely on American militiamen. Andros charged that the men in Captain Withington's militia unit, stationed at New Dartmouth, were "debauched so that they carried their officer prisoner to Boston and deserted the fort." He reported that Major Thomas Savage "and most of the officers of the New England forces revolted, seized the Lieutenant-Colonel, drew off the men and deserted the forts." Despite their lack of discipline, the troops were effective in Maine and "the Indians were powerless." After the troops were withdrawn, the Indians did a great deal of damage. Nor could Puritan leaders persuade the militia to return to the frontier to defend the colony. The new government thus failed in a vital role.[34]

Oakes and Cooke drew up a reply to the charges to present to the Council of Trade. The agents took issue with Andros's reports, particularly because he had used such terms as "subversion of Government" and "insurrection" in describing the rebellion of April 18. They admitted that the situation on the Maine frontier was dangerous but disclaimed all responsibility. Andros himself caused the Indian attacks, the Puritans repeated, because of his seizure of Castine's property. Andros, they said, had not been at all successful in repelling the Indians; rather, they insisted, not one Indian was hurt by Andros's troops, and the entire undertaking was a waste of time.[35] They also commented that the forts Andros ordered built in Maine were useless, "mere fancies of his owne." The soldiers had been withdrawn, they admitted, but at "no prejudice to the Countrey." It was true that the Dartmouth fort and twenty houses had been destroyed, the agents said, but this was not because of the withdrawal of the soldiers. Oakes and Cooke said the destruction of Dartmouth was, in fact, Andros's fault since it was done to avenge Andros's destroying of Castine's home and goods in peacetime. The agents were summoned to appear before the council on June 14 but were not called on that day or any other, even though they waited for hours each day in the anteroom of the council chamber until mid July.[36]

The paper war between the Anglicans and the Puritans continued, as each side for years thereafter wrote, published, and circulated essays supporting their positions. John Palmer wrote one of the most illuminating pro-Andros tracts while he was in prison, publishing it on his return to London.[37] Palmer said that the form of representative government enjoyed by the colonies was not an innate right but rather was a privilege bestowed only "from the grace and favour of the *Crown*," and these colonies "may be rul'd and govern'd by such ways and methods as the Person who wears that Crown . . . shall think most proper and convenient." Representative government was a privilege that could be withdrawn at the will of the sovereign. Parliament had never confirmed any colonial privileges, but instead insisted that colonists were "not to have those Privileges and Liberties which England enjoyed." What remained entirely consistent until 1776 was the conviction among Englishmen in England that colonists had inferior rights to those of Englishmen at home. Equally persistent was the conviction that colonies could be governed any way the mother country chose. Privileges granted to colonies should not be considered permanent and could be withdrawn at any time.[38]

What also remained consistent was the insistence of colonists that they were entitled to the very same rights as Englishmen at home. Colonists believed their rights were based on tradition and custom and could not be changed. To colonists, their charters, or constitutions, whether written or based on custom, were equally inviolate. They also believed that one of their rights was that of a representative government and that only that body had the power to tax them. Colonists remained as convinced of these truths in 1776 as were the Puritans in 1689. Increase Mather shared the colonial view and pointed out in response to Palmer's essay an obvious truth in that "No Englishmen in their Wits will ever Venture their Lives and Estates to Enlarge the Kings Dominion abroad, and Enrich the whole English nation, if their Reward after all must be to be deprived of their *English Liberties*."[39]

As imperialists struggled with the definition of empire in London, turmoil continued in New York, where Jacob Leisler remained in control of government. Leisler, by usurping the government, persecuting Catholics and members of the Church of England, and assuming the authority of governor on his own volition, was aware that his position was shaky. To legitimize his government, Leisler sent Matthew Clarkson and Joast Stoll to London to obtain a charter, but they were relatively ineffective in lobbying. Sympathy for Leisler decreased when Andros's old associates, persecuted by Leisler, began writing letters to Andros in London, all critical of Leisler. Based on these reports, the king replaced Leisler with Henry Sloughter. The new governor experienced a harrowing journey during the course of which he was almost shipwrecked. Delayed at Bermuda, he was preceded to the province in January1691 by Major Richard Ingoldsby and his troops. On landing, Ingoldsby demanded Leisler surrender the fort and the government to him. Leisler refused and barricaded himself in the fort with three hundred men. The situation remained unchanged until Sloughter, on his arrival in March 1691, ordered the men of war in the harbor to turn their guns on the fort. Leisler capitulated.[40]

Sloughter allied with Andros's former allies in New York, the anti-Leislerian faction. Wanting revenge, they persuaded Sloughter to have Leisler, his son-in-law, Jacob Milborne,and other leading rebels tried for treason because of their refusal to surrender the fort. The presiding judge at the trial was none other than Joseph Dudley, who, with the support of Andros and Blathwayt, had been appointed judge and president of the New York council.

As expected, neither the anti-Leislerians nor Dudley, a victim of Boston mobs, had much sympathy for Leisler or Milborne. Found guilty, both were executed on 16 May 1691.[41]

While Leisler and Milborne paid with their lives for their part in the New York phase of the American Glorious Revolution, Massachusetts leaders were left unscathed, even though their crime was far more serious than that of the New Yorkers. The rebellion had started in Boston, with the governor and his top aides seized and imprisoned for almost ten months. In New York, while some of Andros's aides were imprisoned or exiled, the lieutenant governor was permitted to leave peacefully. The fact that the retribution that Andros threatened and the Puritans expected did not descend on Massachusetts was due to the efforts of Increase Mather. The minister, a most effective political propagandist, gave the Boston uprising the most favorable aspect possible from the very beginning. Then, too, there was no single identifiable leader of the rebellion in Massachusetts as there was in New York. Although Bradstreet resumed his role as head of government, he did not lead the rebellion, making it ludicrous to name the Boston uprising for him, as the New York rebellion was named for Leisler. In New York, the old ruling merchant clique that had served Andros and Dongan was still in existence, and they were allied with imperial, not local, interests. Abused and persecuted by Leisler, these men simply bided their time while using their imperial connections to denigrate Leisler and Milborne.

John Coode of Maryland, who effected the overthrow of Baltimore's government, was also a more fortunate rebel than Leisler. Coode's ostensible targets were Catholics, or at least the Catholic proprietor, Lord Baltimore. Since William, like his predecessors, wanted to eliminate proprietary colonies, Coode's actions were entirely acceptable to the king and Privy Council. In addition, Coode's seizure gave the home government the long awaited opportunity to royalize Maryland. The crown took control and in 1691 appointed the first royal governor, Sir Lionel Copley. The colony remained royal until 1715, when it was returned to the now Protestant Lord Baltimore. Even though Maryland was returned, the crown did not waver in its determination to seize and royalize charter and proprietary colonies. William Penn briefly lost control of Pennsylvania following the Glorious Revolution. The governing of Pennsylvania was assigned to New York until 1694, when Penn's proprietary rights were reconfirmed by King William. Despite these exceptions, by the time of the American Revolution, of England's more than thirty colonies, only Maryland, Pennsylvania, Rhode Island, and Connecticut were not royal colonies.[42]

With royal government reestablished in New York and extended to Maryland, several of Andros's aides returned to America and the profitable investments they had there. These men included James Graham, who returned to New York. When Sloughter brought instructions to permit New York to have a representative assembly, Graham was elected speaker of the assembly and was largely responsible for leading that body as it dealt with the aftermath of Leisler's Rebellion. On 13 May 1691, the assembly overturned the permanent revenue act passed in 1683. It then passed a charter, very similar to the charter earlier passed by Dongan's assembly. This earlier attempt to have the colony's rights confirmed was rejected by James II, and William III similarly rejected this second attempt.[43]

Massachusetts was also more fortunate than New York in regard to securing a charter, thanks again to the efforts of Increase Mather. The decision on the charter was delayed because of William's preoccupation with the war in Ireland against James II, resistance to William in Scotland, and the king's continental war against Louis XIV. Mather was persistent. Every time the king returned to England, Mather was waiting to see him. At one time, Mather saw William twice during a short two week period the king spent in London. William apparently liked Mather and was willing to please him, asking Mather, "What I would have to be done for New-England." Mather wanted the restoration of the old charter. The king, wisely relying on the advice of Andros, Randolph, and the Privy Council, refused. William finally, in 1691, ordered the draft of a charter to be prepared for Massachusetts.[44]

The Massachusetts charter was completed on 30 April 1691, ordered revised, and passed the great seal on 7 October 1691. Despite Mather's years of lobbying, the charter was in no way the equivalent of the old and was bitterly opposed by agents Elijah Cooke and Thomas Oakes. It did grant the Puritans some special benefits. For one, Plymouth and Maine were to be included as part of Massachusetts, the Puritans thus achieving part of the territorial growth they had sought for so many decades. While neither New Hampshire nor the Narragansett country were included within Massachusetts's boundaries, the province through its charter gained some significant benefits. The colony was guaranteed an elected assembly and the assembly had the right to elect councilors who were approved or disapproved by the governor. While both the governor and the king could veto legislation, there was a three year time limit for royal review. But religious freedom was granted to all except Roman Catholics, with the franchise now open to all freemen, not just members of the congregational church, who met the property qualifications. The crown would appoint the governor. Gone was the Puritans' exclusive control of government.[45]

The secularization and Anglicization of Massachusetts, begun with the 1684 recall of the charter and accelerated by Sir Edmund Andros and the Dominion government, was now well underway despite Mather's claim that he had secured "a Magna Charta" for Massachusetts.[46] As Michael Hall points out, the significance of the new charter lay in the fact that it "wiped out the political bases of the old colony." The franchise no longer required membership in a Puritan church, but was now "based on property." Even more significant, perhaps, was that authority for government originated not within the Puritan church, but in London. As Mather himself acknowledged, "nothing more or better could be expected."[47]

Once the charter was approved, all that remained was for the king to name a new governor. Many of Andros's New England supporters urged William to reappoint Andros, arguing that no one knew the Puritans better than he. Mather wanted Massachusetts to choose its own governor, as in the past. William was at first equally determined that he alone should appoint the governor and "that a Military Man should be set over them." When William asked Mather for his recommendation, the minister nominated his friend Sir William Phips, and the king agreed. The choice must have come as a surprise to Andros, who did not think highly of Phips, who, by all accounts, was a boisterous, belligerent adventurer.[48]

Free of Massachusetts's problems, Andros put the years in London to good use. Too old for active campaigning in William's wars, he nevertheless sought to serve the king as a spy. He offered to go to Paris on the pretext of seeing the deposed king. James continued as the guest of Louis XIV. Andros would pretend he offered William's pardon to James, but his real mission was to secure information on Louis's military plans. The plan was never implemented, sparing Andros the pain of becoming a secret agent.[49] In July 1691, Andros married for a second time. His choice was Elizabeth Crispe Clapham from County Kent, widow of Christopher Clapham. His wife had at least one son by her first husband for whom Andros had developed a deep affection.[50]

Although too old for active military service, Andros was still able enough to assume another government position. As a reward for his past service, he was in line for a new and prestigious government post. With the resignation of the governor of Virginia, Howard Lord Effingham, the desired opportunity presented itself in February 1692, almost two years after he returned to England. Effingham had returned to England in 1690 to appoint Francis Nicholson as his lieutenant governor. The Virginia council swore Nicholson in on 3 June 1690. At Effingham's resignation, Nicholson had, of course, hoped the position of governor would be his permanently, but the Tory government backed the leading Tory colonial official in England, Sir Edmund Andros. News of the appointment reached Nicholson in August 1692. Nicholson, also a Tory, was bitterly disappointed when he lost the highly lucrative post. Edward Randolph, appointed surveyor general of the American colonies, was in Virginia at that time and reported Nicholson was "in a high ferment." Randolph had long sensed animosity between Andros and Nicholson, which intensified on Nicholson's part as he waited unhappily in Virginia for Andros's arrival.[51]

Andros sailed from England with the newly appointed governor of New York, Benjamin Fletcher, who succeeded Henry Sloughter after the latter's sudden death in July 1691. Andros must indeed have felt fortunate to be spared having to deal with the aftermath of the Massachusetts and New York rebellions. His posting to Virginia was fortuitous. Virginia, with a permanent revenue and no serious Indian problems since 1676, looked to be a relatively easy governorship. The wealthiest and oldest colony, it promised the governor-general a handsome income.

Andros and his subordinates had either received appointments to choice colonial posts or resumed their profitable occupations in the provinces. On the other hand, Mather and the New England agents were not able to secure the return of the old Massachusetts charter, and the crown had not approved the New York charter. Nothing much had changed in colonial administration, despite the change of monarchs. To the English, the colonies were still viewed as subordinate, while colonial rights were seen as limited. Colonial administration under William and Mary remained essentially the same as it had been under Charles II and James II, particularly efforts to centralize government authority.

12
Virginia, 1692–1698

Part One

Virginia
Earth's only paradise.
Where nature hath in store
Fowl, venison, and fish,
And the fruitfulst soil
Without your toil
        —Michael Drayton, "To the Virginian Voyage"[1]

ONE DOUBTS IF MANY ENGLISHMEN WERE FULLY TAKEN IN BY Drayton's promise that Virginia would bring wealth and success "without toil." It was possible to make a healthy profit there from the cultivation of tobacco, but it was achieved only with backbreaking labor and at great risk to one's health. By the time Andros sailed to Virginia in 1692, the death rate had declined somewhat, so it was a relatively more salubrious place than it had been earlier in the century. In contrast to the turbulence of New England, Andros might well have anticipated that Virginia would serve for him as "earth's only paradise." In many respects, the Virginia governorship did fall in the realm of paradise, a somewhat flawed Eden.

Sir Edmund Andros was fifty-five when he was appointed governor of Virginia in February 1692. In Virginia, Andros would have a well ordered government, a permanent revenue that included a generous £2,000 yearly salary, and an established church. Despite the criticisms leveled against Andros by New Englanders, Virginians made no objections to his appointment on either political or religious grounds. Andros shared the religious convictions of the majority of Virginians, who were members of the Church of England. Francis Nicholson was correct in his assessment that most Virginia colonists were indifferent to Whig

227

ideals, but instead the "Inhabitants are for Monarchy and the Religion Established in the Church of England."[2] Charles II had at least temporarily crushed any egalitarian tendencies fostered by Bacon's Rebellion. His intent had been to curtail the popular elements represented in Virginia's House of Burgesses while favoring the elite, whose members usually formed the council. Neither were Virginians drawn into the turmoil that plagued other colonies in the aftermath of the Glorious Revolution. Alarm rose in the spring of 1689, when word was spread that James II had sent thousands of Indians to kill Virginians. The council, in Effingham's absence, calmed those fears, and William Byrd on 26 April 1689 proclaimed William and Mary as king and queen. [3]

In June 1692, Andros and the newly named governor of New York, Benjamin Fletcher, were at Deal awaiting transportation to North America. Fletcher came from a military family and had served with Andros in the Princess Anne's regiment.[4] The governors sailed on the *Wolf* and arrived in New York on 30 August 1692, Andros giving up "his halfe of ye Great Cabin" to Fletcher and his family. Andros "lay in a standing Cabin in the steerage that Coll ffletchers family might not bee streightened." On arrival, Andros remained in New York for a few days visiting old friends and reminiscing.[5] He then left for Virginia, arriving on September 13. Francis Nicholson put aside his disappointment at not being named governor to properly welcome Andros. On hearing that Andros's ship was approaching, Nicholson hurried to Jamestown, ordering out the local militia to accompany Andros into the town. On September 20, Andros met with his council for the first time. With Nicholson present, Andros's commission was read and the members of the council sworn into office.[6] Andros ordered that all civil and military officers should continue in office.

Nicholson, who was lieutenant governor of Maryland, went there briefly and then sailed back to England on the *Wolf*. After Nicholson's departure, Andros, concerned for the safety of the frontiers, which were still being harassed by wandering bands of Indians (probably Senecas), left immediately on an inspection tour. Vigilance was a necessity. As recently as 1689, William Byrd had complained of marauding Indians who killed livestock and murdered or kidnapped white frontier settlers. Unrest was so severe that Byrd abandoned his frontier plantation to live in the relative safety of Westover, his recently purchased Tidewater estate.[7]

Andros found Virginia to be sparsely settled, with a population

Sitter believed to be Francis Nicholson (1655–1728). Reports of
Nicholson's luckless pursuit of a Virginia woman followed him for the
remainder of his career, even to a 1715 play, *Androboros,* written by
Robert Hunter, one of Edmund Andros's successors as governor of
New York. Ousted from the Virginia governorship in 1705, Nicholson
continued to obtain colonial posts, the last as governor of South
Carolina. He returned to England in 1725 and died in London.
Courtesy of the Virginia Historical Society, Richmond, Virginia.

of 70,000. Its topography was considerably different from that of either Massachusetts or New York, particularly in the capital city of Jamestown, or, as it was rather pretentiously termed in the 1690s, James City. Just barely a city, it would be difficult to find a less suitable place as an urban or government center. Fifty miles up the navigable James River, Jamestown was surrounded by brackish river water. Burnt to the ground by Bacon's rebels in 1676, Governor Culpepper had rebuilt Jamestown three years later. In 1692, the town contained only a church, a state house, a jail, and a few dozen houses, almost all, except the jail and church, built of highly flammable wood.[8] Its climate was as unhealthy as its drinking water, with heat, humidity, and swarms of biting insects that carried malaria, which made the summers virtually unbearable. Small wonder that Andros in July 1693, after less than a year's residence in Virginia, found himself "much incomoded by the Excessive Heats." In fact, Virginia's average daily temperature was probably three and a half degrees less in the seventeenth century than in the twentieth century but, particularly when combined with high humidity, was still extremely uncomfortable.[9] To escape the heat, Andros requested and received permission from the king to spend two summer months each year in the more salubrious climate of Delaware or New York, as had his predecessor, Lord Effingham.[10]

No governor's house was available for Andros's use in Virginia, although he was awarded £150 a year by the assembly to cover the cost of renting a house. Both he and Nicholson had urged the assembly to authorize the construction of an official government house to no avail.[11] While Nicholson had lived in a rented house in Jamestown, Andros chose instead to live in "a small house att midle plantation" (Williamsburg) that he rented from Mrs. Page. The choice of Middle Plantation was a wise one since there were fewer insects and less disease there than in Jamestown. After his wife arrived in September 1693, the Middle Plantation house proved inadequate, and Andros began looking for "another house fitted for my family before winter." He wanted one near a town but found there were "none Convenient to be had," so the Andros family stayed in the Page house until the spring of 1695.[12]

Despite inconvenient housing, Andros did his best to organize Virginia's government, the colony benefiting from his skills. Andros was a "great lover of method and despatch in all sorts of business, which made him find fault with the management of the secretary's office." Records had been in disarray since Bacon's Rebellion. Andros insisted on a major overhaul of the office and "caused the loose and torn records of value to be transcribed into new books and ordered conveniences to be built within the office for preserving the records from being lost" and ensured papers would be kept "dry and clean."[13]

Andros found Virginia's economy different from that of either New York or Massachusetts. Both big and small Virginia planters cultivated tobacco for export. The nature of tobacco farming and the fact that many of the large plantations were built on navigable rivers with their own docks for ocean going vessels meant that there were no major urban areas in Virginia.[14] A very profitable crop, tobacco was planted by virtually everyone who owned land. Its chief export crop, tobacco made Virginia, the Old Dominion, a valued colony to the crown, bringing the monarch over £80,000 a year in revenue. Virginia also traded skins, furs, pipe staves, pork, beef, corn, and some tobacco to New England, New York, and the West Indies. Virginia imported rum, sugar, molasses, salt, and Madeira wine from other colonies. Manufactured goods were obtained from England.[15]

Andros recognized that the nature of Virginia agriculture meant that the colony needed a proportionately larger labor force than was necessary in either New York or Massachusetts. Slavery was the dominant feature of life in Virginia with whites' social standing usually determined by the number of slaves they owned.[16] Though slaves were also part of the labor force in New York and Massachusetts, they constituted a much smaller proportion of the population than they did in Virginia. Early in the century, the Virginia work force had been predominantly white indentured servants. When blacks were imported from Africa, they were originally used more as indentured servants than slaves, since many achieved freedom, and of those who did, several bought land and slaves of their own. This had changed by the time Andros took office in 1692. A shortage of white indentured servants and the participation of those servants in Bacon's Rebellion led Virginia plantation owners to rely more and more on slaves, who, because of their condition, could be more closely controlled than free lower class whites. To protect their financial investment in slaves and to protect themselves from the threat they saw in a large free black population, the Virginia gentry in the latter half of the seventeenth century codified slavery. By law, slavery was a condition inherited through the mother, was lifelong, and unchanged by slave conversion to Christianity.[17]

To control the growing slave population, the colonial assembly also passed several laws specifically designed to prevent uprisings. Andros, like all whites, realized the dangers presented by a large, deprived, and discontented labor force. He was concerned to find that the laws designed to prevent slave uprisings were not enforced and "Diverse Negroes and Slaves in Sundry parts and Counties in this Colony have Met, Congregated, and got together . . . being of dangerous Consequence." Virginia law prevented slaves from carrying any item that could be used for "Defence or offence," or from traveling away from their home plantation without a certificate. Sheriffs, justices of the peace, and constables were charged with enforcing existing laws. In 1694, Andros issued a Proclamation requiring previous slave acts to be read by ministers at church services and to be published two times a year in September and March.[18]

While slaves ensured the production of large crops of tobacco, during King William's War, or for most of Andros's tenure in Virginia, there was reduced trade between England and the colonies. The few ships that did sail during the war years had to wait for convoys. For some years during the war, no convoys at all reached Virginia; hence, very little tobacco was shipped.[19] The planters had no return for their investment, no cash came into the colony, and needed supplies were not delivered. By the summer of 1693, Andros was concerned that with another crop already planted and ready for harvest, the market would soon be glutted and the colony would suffer further economic reverses. Nor was there any illegal trade to offset the depression caused by wartime conditions.[20] In Virginia, as in Massachusetts, Andros would not permit pirates to trade. As in Massachusetts, the end of the pirate trade had a negative effect on the economy since it kept out a significant source of specie.[21] Since Andros would not condone an illegal trade, the economy in Virginia did not regain its former prosperity until 1697, when the war ended. That year, 150 ships carrying 70 to 80,000 hogsheads of tobacco sailed from Virginia to England, bringing £200,000 in customs revenue.[22]

Andros, recognizing the economic problems caused by dependence on a single crop, sought to improve the economy, as had several of his predecessors, by encouraging the establishment of manufactures. The need was intensified because of the war. The inability of English merchant fleets to reach the colony forced many people in Virginia to make their own linen and wool and to tan leather for shoes. Andros, aware of the shortage of fabric and other necessary materials from England, encouraged the cultivation of cotton. He also urged a Virginia artisan to make a gin, which he proudly showed to Francis Nicholson on one of the latter's frequent visits to Virginia.[23] Supporting the governor's efforts, the assembly ordered fulling mills built, encouraged the cultivation of cotton, and ordered ferries established "over Every River Creeke and Lake within this Government." All attempts at economic diversification were made without the approval of the home government. In fact, they were often made in defiance of established policy. If planters turned from tobacco to other crops or if they established manufacturing facilities, the English economy would suffer. Similarly, parliament tried to protect the colonial economy by such measures as prohibiting the cultivation of tobacco in England.[24]

Economic considerations were important to Andros, but with an ongoing war between France and England, his most pressing concern was for the defense of Virginia. Existing fortifications being "utterly ruind," Andros restored the platforms at the Jamestown fort and mounted twelve guns on new carriages and two more on old ship carriages.[25] He then ordered the building of a warehouse with a room to store powder, as well as repairs at the fort on Tyndall's Point and "made a most convenient Armory in one of the Garretts in the state house in James Town & furnished it with good arms, etc."[26] The platforms at the Jamestown fort did not long survive and in March 1695, Andros noted that they were "wholy ruined the brick being decayed." The fort was demolished, the guns moved to a better position to defend the James River. At the orders of the Treasury in March 1695, Andros hired ships to patrol the Virginia coast. He planned for Virginia's future defense by passing a bill to station soldiers at the heads of the major rivers. Andros notified English authorities that he needed additional powder and shot, complaining that the militia was poorly armed. With no regular soldiers under his command, Andros relied on the militia for defense against the constant threat of a French naval attack. In June 1695, Andros posted lookouts along the coast in response to intelligence that the French had fitted out several men of war to attack English colonies.[27]

Andros's commission conferred on him broad civil and military powers. As vice admiral, he was in charge of prizes, ships, and seamen, and could place embargoes. As lord treasurer, he approved the payment of all the colony's debts. As lord chancellor, he approved all land and office grants and decided all causes in chancery. Andros was also lord chief justice of the courts of king's bench and common pleas and lord chancellor of the exchequer, presiding over that court, as well as over the colony's council. Andros, appointed ordinary by the king, was also head of the Church of England in Virginia, which, like all colonial Anglican churches, was under the jurisdiction of Henry Compton, bishop of London. As ordinary, Andros had the power to appoint and confirm ministers, outranking all ministers in Virginia including the bishop of London's commissary, or agent, the priest James Blair.[28]

As he had in New York and the Dominion of New England, Andros governed with the assistance of an appointed council whose twelve members included the most prominent and influential planters in Virginia.[29] The governor and the council together constituted the General Court. Unlike New York or the Dominion of New England, Virginia had a representative assembly, or house of burgesses, with two representatives from each county and one from Jamestown, totaling 107 representatives in Andros's first assembly. As did most bills, money bills originated in the lower house, although the council or the governor could also initiate legislation. The permanent government revenue guaranteed by the Virginia House of Burgesses in 1680 at the order of the king raised money for all normal expenses, including the governor's salary and rent. Money was also raised by an export duty of 2s. per hogshead (500 lb.) and an import duty of 1s. 2d. per ton on merchandise and 6d. on each person entering Virginia. Neither Andros nor any other Virginia governor was dependent on the assembly for either his salary or ordinary government expenses. By special acts, the Virginia assembly retained the right to raise money for all extraordinary expenses, including defense, although Andros was authorized by the king to spend £1,000 for defense measures from Virginia's quit rents, which amounted to £4,000 annually.[30]

Originally, the assembly functioned as a court of justice, hearing appeals until 1682, when this right was taken from it by the king as part of his plan to curtail rising popular power. With the assembly denied appellate jurisdiction, the General Court, comprised of the governor and council, became the highest judicial power in Virginia. Unlike the assembly, whose members were elected by Virginia colonists, the king appointed councilors, usually at the recommendation of the governor.[31]

This was the first time Andros had worked with an assembly, except for his brief encounter with the New Jersey assembly. His relations with the Virginia House of Burgesses were cordial, although he disliked both the first speaker, Thomas Milner (1693–95), and his successor Philip Ludwell, Sr. (1695–96). Rob-

ert Carter, with whom Andros enjoyed a generally amicable relationship, succeeded Ludwell.[32] Andros, aware of the Virginia
assembly's long history, said "that he would be very glad to have
an Assembly."[33] He had advocated the establishment of an
assembly in New York, so he may well have been sincere in that
statement, particularly since he was not dependent on it for his
salary or day-to-day expenses. What tension there was between
the Virginia assembly and the governor sprang from a conflict
between provincial and imperial issues and from extraordinary
expenses resulting from the war.

While not dependent on the burgesses for his daily bread,
Andros was dependent on them for extraordinary war expenses,
and war persisted for almost the entire term of Andros's governorship. Shortly after his arrival, Andros, in November 1692, dissolved the existing assembly. He issued writs for an election, with
the assembly called to sit in March 1693. On meeting, Andros
appointed Peter Beverley as clerk and confirmed William Drum-
mond as messenger. The assembly protested Andros's actions,
claiming that the appointive privilege had been theirs in the past,
but Andros pointed out that his commission gave him the power
to confirm all government officers. The last clerk appointed by
the Virginia burgesses was Robert Beverely, who, in 1685, deliberately omitted an amendment added by the council to an assembly bill. After Governor Effingham informed the king of
Beverley's actions, James discharged Beverley as clerk and
ordered that in the future the governor would select the assembly
clerk.[34] On 22 July 1693, Andros notified Blathwayt that the burgesses accomplished little during the session, but they had
"y[i]elded the Contest of Chosing their clark." Andros apparently
retained the upper hand in dealing with the assembly, dissolving
it in 1698 when it insisted on its right to admit a Scottish member, contrary to the 1696 parliamentary act that specified only
those born in England, Ireland, or the plantations could hold civil
office. Andros was, however, willing to make concessions, frequently proroguing the burgesses at their request.[35]

Despite Andros's efforts at conciliation, conflict between local
and imperial concerns was inevitable. As the imperial representative, Andros was responsible for seeing that customs duties were
collected, that London merchants were not cheated, and that necessary defense measures were taken. The burgesses knew that
imperial interests often conflicted with their own and those of
their constituents. Consequently, they objected to two acts proposed by Andros at the insistence of Whitehall. The first con-

cerned the exportation of tobacco, the export duty of which was 5d. per pound for premium tobacco but nothing for damaged tobacco. Planters, to avoid paying duty, mixed damaged tobacco in with high quality and shipped it in bulk. Customs officials wanted shipments limited to small, five hundred pound hogsheads so the practice could be curtailed. Customs officials also wanted to limit the number of legal ports to prevent planters from shipping tobacco from their own unsupervised docks. Having all merchandise brought to one or two central locations would make enforcement easier. Planters wanted to protect their right to ship tobacco free of interference from customs inspectors. The assembly, composed of planters, refused to consider either of these measures.[36]

Andros's first assembly also was faced with another major task, since the colony's one hundred or so laws had to be revised. The burgesses had hardly begun this undertaking in the spring of 1693 when Andros agreed to prorogue them because of a measles epidemic in Jamestown. When the burgesses met again in the fall, they returned to the arduous task of the revision, but by November, they were anxious to return home, so Andros dissolved them on 18 November 1693, even though the revision was nowhere near complete. Neither had the burgesses addressed the bills that Andros had asked them to consider. The revision of the colony's laws proceeded slowly, not to be completed until after Andros's resignation as governor.[37]

During the two 1693 sessions, the assembly passed bills to encourage the establishment of fulling and grist mills and the manufacture of linen cloth. It also provided for the defense of the frontiers, established the site of the proposed college, and levied taxes. The assembly failed, however, to pass a bill to better provide for the support of Virginia's ministers. The Church of England and its ministers were sustained by money raised through taxes. Clerical salaries were paid in tobacco, as were most debts. By law, Virginia's ministers were paid thirteen thousand pounds of tobacco a year. A depressed economy caused by falling tobacco prices meant that their salaries had actually declined. In February 1693, the king noted that while thirteen thousand pounds of tobacco had previously been worth about £80, "the same is now fallen above one halfe, by reason of the low price of Tobacco, by w[hi]ch means the Ministers are not able to subsist." William urged "that a Competent Salary or Allowance, be Appointed, for the maintenance of Each Minister."[38] The bill to raise ministerial salaries was not approved before adjournment in November 1693.

The assembly protected the economic interests of its members and constituents, partly from greed and partly because there was little money to spare in Virginia during King William's War. Facing even greater threat of French invasion was New York. At the order of the king, Andros in 1693 sent £600 to New York's governor, Fletcher, because "of the danger that Albany is in and the incapacity that country lyes under of supporting the charge of that garrison without the help of their neighbours." With the king's approval, £500 of the £600 was taken from Virginia's quit rents.[39] Fletcher's reports of French incursions into Iroquois territory were cause for alarm. In January 1693, the French destroyed all the Mohawk villages and took three hundred Indian captives. As the Iroquois experienced wave after wave of French incursions with no help from the English, they became increasingly resentful that they alone were absorbing the full fury of those attacks. Devastation continued throughout the Iroquois nations, bringing a dramatic drop in population of at least 50 percent. The effects of this bloody war ultimately forced the Iroquois in 1701 to sign treaties of neutrality with both the French and the English. It was exactly to prevent the future loss of the Iroquois as English allies that Andros in the 1690s was more than willing to assist Fletcher. Andros knew that the future of all of England's North American colonies depended on that assistance.[40]

In November 1693, Fletcher asked for more money from Virginia, but the legislature refused to act on the request. By January 1694, Fletcher repeated his request, but there were no funds in Virginia on which Andros could draw. In April, the legislature agreed to send £500 to New York, but Virginia auditor, William Byrd, complained to Blathwayt that he was at a loss as to where to find the money. The colony's revenue, taken from a tax imposed of "two shillings per hogshead will not defray the ordinary charge of the government: and the remainder of the quit-rents are all the government hath upon any emergency of invasion or otherwise," Byrd complained. Revenue was in arrears because colonists had no money with which to pay taxes. Hence, the government could not pay its expenses. William responded to this complaint by authorizing Andros to take an additional £765 for New York out of the colony's quit rents. Fletcher also wanted men to defend New York, "there being great apprehensions that the 5 Nations of Indians having by some way or other deserted the interest of ye English Nation may fall upon the Western Plantations in those southern Go[vern]m[en]ts." Such reports added to a general climate of unrest around the Chesapeake in the spring and summer of 1694.[41]

On 18 April 1695, the burgesses, having met, initially refused Andros's suggestion that they send more money to New York because it was needed to defend Virginia's own frontiers.[42] The burgesses finally, but with great reluctance, agreed to send another £500 to New York, raised by placing an impost on liquor.[43] In 1696, the queen, responding to Fletcher's plea for soldiers, ordered Andros to send 240 men to aid in the defense of New York. Virginians hesitated because of the expense involved in raising, clothing, arming, and transporting the men. Andros argued to the home government that sending that many men out of Virginia would cost the crown money as well. He noted that these men all planted tobacco and harvested one to two thousand pounds of the crop each year, which brought the crown at least £10 to £15 in tobacco duty from each small planter. Neither was money available to transport the troops to New York, leading Andros to offer the colony a loan of £1,000 of his own money. Andros's loan proved unnecessary when, on 1 May 1696, the assembly voted to raise £1,000. Andros ordered Byrd to send the money to New York. The cost of defense was indeed dear, and in 1697, Byrd complained "the extraordinary charge of assisting New York, & maintaining a sloop . . . hath brought us in debt."[44]

Part of the economic problem in Virginia was caused by war and part by the Navigation Acts, the latter dictating that tobacco could be traded only to English merchants and taken only by English ships to England. The agency handling enforcement was the Privy Council Committee of Trade. On William's accession to the throne, the committee was composed of both Whigs and Tories.[45] In 1695, a Whig dominated House of Commons, influenced by negative reports on customs collections by Edward Randolph, called for reform.[46] Randolph, after four years as collector of customs in America, complained of repeated abuses of the Navigation Acts. To remedy this circumstance, parliament passed an additional act in 1696 to codify and clarify existing laws.[47]

At the same time it dealt with the Navigation Acts, parliament passed legislation to form a new agency to replace the Privy Council committee that had handled colonial affairs since 1675. The king rejected this bill but then created a Board of Trade and Plantations on 15 May 1696 to oversee domestic and foreign trade and colonial affairs. Whigs dominated the board's members.

John Locke (1632–1704). Locke, well known philosopher, was an associate of the earl of Shaftesbury and followed him into exile in 1684. A member of the Royal Society, one of Locke's best known philosophical works, *An Essay Concerning Humane Understanding and Treatises on Government,* was published in 1690. Portrait by Michael Dahl, courtesy of the National Portrait Gallery, London.

Of the eight members named to it, seven were Whigs, the exception being William Blathwayt. Included in the board's membership was the earl of Bridgewater, who served as president, and John Locke, former secretary to Charles II's *bete noire*, the earl of Shaftesbury. Locke was secretary of the Council of Trade and Plantations until its 1675 dissolution. He was a close friend of the lord chamberlain, Sir John Somers, who had represented the Massachusetts agents at Andros's 1690 hearing. Two of the most ardent Whigs in England, Somers and Locke wanted to reduce the number of Tory governors, with Andros high on their list. Locke, on taking office with the newly created board, immediately antagonized William Blathwayt. The two usually managed to avoid open friction, as Blathwayt made it a point to be away from London in the summer while Locke fled the city during the winter. The absence of Blathwayt meant that there was no protection on the board in the summers for Tory appointees, such as Andros.[48] The ultimate intent of the Whigs on the new Board was to extend their version of administration to the colonies by decreasing the power of the governor and the council and by increasing that of the burgesses. In other words, in Virginia, the Whigs wanted to reverse Charles II's policy.[49]

Andros, not immediately realizing the political situation was again changing in England, continued the pattern in Virginia established by Charles II. He governed with the assistance of a council whose members were mostly loyal to him. Despite curbs on its power, the house of burgesses was willing to cooperate with the governor, raising enough money to defend the colony and to assist New York in its defense. Virginia was spared the trauma of either a foreign invasion or Indian attacks during Andros's tenure. While the Virginia years were hardly edenic, Sir Edmund Andros managed to provide for the province's defense, enforce trade regulations, and work effectively with the council and assembly. In spite of advancing age and chronic illness, Andros persevered.

13
Virginia, 1692–1698

Part 2

[Andros] chooses his friends and favorites only out of such as
are Enemies to the College, and that there is no certainer way
to loose his favor than by being a zealous friend to it.

—James Blair[1]

THE ESTABLISHMENT OF THE COLLEGE OF WILLIAM AND MARY PRO-
vided the means whereby Francis Nicholson and the Anglican
priest, James Blair, could put Andros in an unfavorable light
before the Whig dominated Board of Trade. Following the lead of
member, John Locke, the Board was only too willing to listen to
complaints about Andros, a Tory. Also willing to listen to complaints about Andros were high ranking prelates in England.
Andros was in effect tried *in absentia*, the third time he had faced
charges stemming from his conduct as a governor. The end
desired by Nicholson and Blair was achieved when Andros, tired
of resisting, tendered his resignation.

By training and personality, Sir Edmund Andros was ill
equipped to tolerate opposition. Increasingly during his six year
tenure as governor of Virginia, opposition came from an unlikely
source—ministers in the Church of England. As an Anglican governor and as the personal representative of the head of the
Church of England, Andros might reasonably have expected that
the Church's ministers in the province would offer him their
wholehearted support, as had the Church of England ministers
in New York and New England. In theory at least, and with an
established church, there should not have been any tension
between church and state. Such was not the case, with James
Blair heading the opposition to Andros. Convinced that Andros

did not support either the church or the proposed college, Blair worked with Francis Nicholson to secure Andros's recall.

Nicholson eagerly joined in the attack on Andros because he was angry at having been passed over for the Virginia governorship. He believed "his behaviour had earned him the government if it fell vacant, and especially [resented] Sir Edmund Andros, against whom he has a particular pique on account of some earlier dealings with him." Nicholson never diminished his "pique" and worked for six years to achieve Andros's recall and his own appointment to the Virginia post.[2] Andros fully reciprocated Nicholson's dislike. Blair commented that Andros "hates every thing that looks like an imitation of Governor Nicholson." Indeed, Andros had been annoyed with Nicholson even before the Glorious Revolution. His annoyance escalated to loathing when Nicholson failed to assist him during the New England phase of the Glorious Revolution. Andros undoubtedly took pains to show his displeasure both by words and actions.

Nicholson was named as lieutenant governor of Maryland in February 1692 to serve the first royal governor of that province, Lionel Copley, named in 1690. Copley had missed a convoy to America in early 1692, finally arriving there in April 1692 only to collide with surveyor general of customs, Edward Randolph.[3] Randolph suspected that the king's tobacco duty was being directed to the pockets of Copley and his customs collector at St. Mary's, Nehemiah Blakiston. The latter, with his brother-in-law, John Coode, had led the rebellion against Lord Baltimore's proprietary government. Randolph brought charges against Blakiston, but the jury refused to convict despite overwhelming evidence.[4] In December 1692, Copley told his council that in looking over correspondence from Randolph to Andros, just recently installed as governor of Virginia, he found "reflections made [by Randolph] upon the govr and Governmt of Maryland." On 6 April 1693, an order was issued by Copley to apprehend Randolph, who was charged with "offering & divulging severall false malicious & seditious speeches and reports scandalously reflecting" on Maryland's government, as well as accepting a bribe to clear a ship.[5]

Randolph was arrested in Virginia on 20 April 1693 by Maryland's Somerset County sheriff, Stephen Luff. The sheriff transported Randolph back to Maryland with the permission, or perhaps the assistance, of Accomac County, Virginia justice of the peace, William Anderson, who permitted Luff "to take and Carie away Edward Randolph Esqr." Andros was furious when he heard that a Virginia justice of the peace had permitted a Maryland sheriff to arrest Randolph on Virginia soil. He promptly summoned the luckless Anderson to Jamestown and suspended him as justice of the peace "and from all other Offices and places whatsoever Civill or Military."[6]

Andros wrote to Copley to demand that Randolph be "returned to this Government from whence he hath been so Carried contrary to all Rules of Government." Copley did not have to bother finding excuses as to why he would not release Randolph because Randolph had escaped. Copley suspected that Andros had something to do with the escape since he ordered Sheriff Luff to give him an account of "what has passed between him & the governor of Virginia." Randolph returned to Virginia, and on 29 April 1693, was in the hands of an "honest constable" who gave him lodging in his house. Randolph planned to stay there until he heard from Andros, who he was rightly convinced "will not abandon me to the fury of my enemies." Andros ordered him released from custody on 26 May 1693. An irate Copley wrote to Andros, demanding that Randolph be returned to Maryland. Not surprisingly, Andros ignored him.[7]

In revenge, Copley instigated attacks on both Andros and Randolph that arose out of their close relationship with the deposed king, James II. Copley accused Randolph of consorting with papists in Maryland and accused Andros of advocating the restoration of James II to the English throne. The accusations hit close to home. Prior to Andros's departure for Virginia, John Churchill, earl of Marlborough, also known for his past close association with James II, had in January 1692 been thrown into the Tower and deprived of profitable posts worth £12,000 a year. Later that same year, Marlborough was "suspected by the King to have made his peace with France." Copley hoped for a similar outcome from his charges of Jacobitism aimed at Andros. The accusations were made by several people, including Maryland residents, Gilbert Turbevile and innkeeper Garret van Sweeringen, the latter a business associate of the now deceased Jacob Leisler and Jacob Milborne. Andros, in a letter to Copley, urged him to take action against the two men who he was convinced were the "Abbettors if not Contrivers of what alledgeth to have been said falsly Reflecting on my self & their Majestys Council."[8]

Copley's enmity to Andros ended with his death on 9 September 1693. Maryland's lieutenant governor Nicholson was still in England at the time Copley died, shoring up his alliances with influential church officials. The colony that had so recently suffered a revolution and a dramatic change in leadership was now at risk of further rebellion. Richard Lee made a dire report to Andros and the Virginia council concerning conditions in Maryland following Copley's death, outlining a struggle for control between two factions. Fearing the outbreak of civil war in Maryland, Andros acted, citing a clause in his commission that required him to take over as commander-in-chief of Maryland in the event of Copley's absence and/or Nicholson's death. The reverse situation existed now, but the threat to Maryland's security was very real. The Virginia council, "not knowing how far the destractions amongst them, might Concerne soe near Neighbours as this Countrey," urged Andros to go to Maryland.[9]

The governor, arriving at St. Mary's City on September 25, found the council and assembly quite willing to accept his authority. In fact, it was almost with a sense of relief that the council decided "that the Governmt of this Province doth from henceforth divolve upon his Exncie the said Sr Edmond Andros." Andros ordered all civil and military officers to continue in their posts and had a proclamation issued the next day announcing he was in charge. That same day, Andros sent a messenger to the Maryland burgesses summoning them to the council chamber. On their arrival, Andros dissolved the assembly.[10]

After naming councilor Nicolas Greenberry as acting governor, Andros returned to Virginia in early October. As Andros reported, he had "put everything in order as well as I could in so short a time." Back in Virginia, he urged the home government to appoint a governor for Maryland. He did not, however, urge that Nicholson receive the appointment even though he was well aware that Nicholson was already lieutenant governor. Andros simply reminded the ministry that the volatile situation in Maryland made it "very necessary that a Governor or Lieutenant-Governor be sent to Maryland."[11]

Andros returned to Maryland in May 1694 to attend the provincial court. After concluding the court's business, he went back to Virginia, but before leaving, he requested the Maryland council to compensate him for his time and trouble in governing Maryland. The council authorized receiver general George Plater to "pay Unto his Exncy Sr Edmond Andros . . . the Sume of ffive hundred Pounds sterling."[12] The Maryland situation was finally resolved when Francis Nicholson was named governor, with Andros commissioned to take over as commander-in-chief in the event of Nicholson's absence and Nicholson commissioned to take a similar role in Virginia in case of Andros's absence. The appointment of Nicholson to the governorship of an adjacent colony drew Andros into a bitter conflict.[13] Nicholson, sailing from England, arrived in Virginia in July 1694 on his way to Maryland to assume his governorship. As Andros reported, Nicholson "has stayed some dayes with me att Jamestown." Much to Andros's relief, Nicholson left for Maryland on 19 July 1694.[14]

While in England, Nicholson heard that Andros had assumed control of Maryland. Andros's actions could rightly be interpreted as a criticism of Nicholson for his absence from the colony. Nicholson had also heard rumors that Maryland "would in all probability have been in as great confusion and distraction as it was in the time of the Revolution if in case his Excncy Sr Edmond Andros Governour of Virginia had not come over to appease and settle the same in quiet." Virginians speculated that if Andros had not returned to Maryland in the spring, that colony's courts "must have fallen for want of sufficient number of Justices to hold the same whereby a totall failure of Justice must consequently have followed."[15]

Nicholson could not bear the thought that Andros would gain the credit for stepping in and saving his colony. He was further irritated when he reached St. Mary's to find "an Empty Treasury & a Militia without arms & Ammunition." Short of money, he focused on "the 500 £ Sr. Edmd. Andros had from the Go[vern]m[en]t."[16]

Nicholson, seeking evidence of Andros' mismanagement during the latter's brief term as commander-in-chief of the colony, was determined to invent what he could not find. What particularly rankled Nicholson was the money paid to Andros. Nicholson wasted no time in telling Receiver General Plater that he would not approve the colony's expenses until that money was repaid. If Andros did not return it, then Nicholson would hold Plater responsible. Plater wrote to Andros on 16 August 1694 and told the governor that he found "a difficulty and obstruction in passing that Article of ffive hundred pounds Sterr paid Yor Excency . . . His Excenncy the Governor [Nicholson] being dessirous of a further Satisfaction from Yor Self . . . the Money being Wanted here for Supply of Armes and Ammunition. . . . I must presume to press upon Yor Excency for a full and a Satisfactorey Answer being my self lyable to pay that Money Unless Yor Exacency pleases to Honor me with a Lyne intimateing your right thereto." Plater, who had only obeyed the orders of the council in paying Andros the money, was clearly on the horns of a dilemma. Andros answered Plater's letter, but he was so infuriated with the demand that his sputtering reply was scarcely coherent. He told

Plater that "I would not have thought from you I presume as soone as thought you were Satisfyed was Effectually Answered at first in Yor Owne hands."[17]

Andros soon heard from the English attorney general that Nicholson had complained to the bishop of London, a member of the Privy Council committee of trade, about his taking over the government after Copley's death and receiving £500 in salary for his efforts. On 20 March 1695, Andros noted to Blathwayt that "Govr Nicholson in Mary Land has been very bussey in faulting and condemning His Majties Comission to me and to find out Imputations agt me for my going to Maryland on the Death of Coll. Copley and made Complaints home of my receiving five hundred pounds I had by Advice and Consent of the Councill there on Account of Salary as Comandr in Cheife all acknoledging my Service for the peace and quiet of that place, off wch I gave an account to the Lords of the Committee and Treasury." Andros was faced with pressure from authorities in England. They decided that Andros acted "by ill-grounded use of his commission," and instructed him in October 1696 to return £300 of the £500 to George Plater in Maryland. In his defense, he explained to the Lords of Trade that he had taken the money only after securing the advice and consent of the Maryland council.[18]

The two governors also fought over Maryland's Piscataway Indians, or at least over the remnants of the tribe who remained in that colony. Most of the tribe had fled north to the Susquehanna Valley after 1677, where they fell under Iroquois control. In 1693, the Maryland Indians were again on the move because of pressure from encroaching white settlement, a small number of Indians being seen crossing the Potomac into Virginia. Any Indian threat to English colonists had considerably lessened by the end of the seventeenth century. Virginia's Indians had been on reservations and disarmed since the 1640s. Further demoralized and their ranks depleted by Bacon's Rebellion, Andros estimated that there were no more than 362 warriors in Virginia. If this figure was accurate, then there could not have been more than a thousand Indians in all of Virginia. Nevertheless, the sighting of the Piscataways alarmed the Virginians. A message was immediately sent to the "Emperor of said Indians," demanding they stay on the other side of the Potomac River. When more strange Indians were spotted on the James and Potomac Rivers, Andros ordered additional rangers sent there.[19]

The Maryland Indians wanted to move to Virginia for several reasons. Marylanders had cheated the Indians in land deals, the

Indians' cornfields had been destroyed, and they were being denied justice in Maryland courts. They were also accused of sheltering the murderer of a slave. In June 1697, Nicholson appointed ten agents to visit the straying Indians. The sachems denied harboring the murderer but, to preserve peace, agreed to pay a fine of sixty buckskins and agreed "to Return into Maryland again," but delayed their return.[20]

In June 1697, Andros ordered militia officer Captain George Mason in Stafford County, Virginia, to send word to the chiefs "that their settling there is not advisable or safe for them." In July, Andros learned that Senecas were among the nomadic Maryland Indians. The Senecas and the other four Iroquois tribes had concluded a peace treaty with Effingham in 1684 whereby they promised not to attack Virginia colonists or Indians.[21] Some of the Senecas may have moved south or were perhaps continuing their decades long practice of sending war and hunting parties down through the Susquehanna Valley to the Chesapeake, hundreds of miles away from Iroquoia. Many Maryland Indians, in addition to the Piscataways, had accepted tributary status with the Iroquois in exchange for protection. The Senecas may have been trying to ensure a safe relocation for the Piscataways in Virginia under a governor they knew they could trust.[22] As was true in upper Ohio, where many Senecas sent out as part of hunting parties elected to stay, the Senecas sent to Virginia also chose to stay there and asked Andros for permission to do so.[23] Andros, having enjoyed a long and sympathetic relationship with the Iroquois, welcomed the Senecas to Virginia but insisted the Piscataways return to Maryland.

Andros, as he had in New York, tried to keep officials from other colonies from coming into his territory to negotiate with the Indians. He was determined to keep Indian affairs under his personal control to prevent the outbreak of another full scale Indian war. He had seen from personal experience in New England how quickly any misunderstanding could lead to retaliation and escalation. He was, of course, annoyed when Nicholson sent his agents to talk to the Piscataways in Virginia. On 11 August 1697, the Virginia council met and complained that Maryland agents had traveled through Virginia without Andros's knowledge or permission, much "to the disturbance of the Government." The councilors requested Andros "to Acquaint the Governr of Maryland that before any treaty with any Indians in this Government be permitted his Exncy be made timely acquainted therewith." The only people permitted to negotiate with Indians in Virginia were to be those approved by Andros.[24]

On 16 October 1697, Nicholson demanded that Andros arrest Esquire Tom, an Indian charged with a murder in Maryland, and ordered Virginians not to sell ammunition to the Indians. The Virginia council refused to order the arrest or to take any other action, considering Nicholson's demand "neither advisable nor available," and further labeled Nicholson's charges that Virginians had armed Indians as "Groundless."[25]

John Coode provided the occasion for continuing the quarrel between Andros and Nicholson. A perennial rebel and critic of government, Coode accused Nicholson of being a papist, an inept administrator, and a womanizer. Nicholson, having no patience with the revolutionaries of 1689, called Coode and his associates "Rebells," threatening "to hang them with Magna Charta about their necks." The Maryland governor had already hit Coode with his cane for drunken brawling during church services.[26] Not satisfied with this informal punishment, Nicholson ordered his arrest and that of several other people on charges of seditious behavior, seditious language, and blasphemy. Coode evaded capture and fled to Virginia. Nicholson, on 15 December 1696, sent Andros an outstanding warrant for Coode, dated 3 May 1696. Andros, on 3 January 1697, issued a warrant for Coode, but made no effort to enforce it. Coode remained at large, despite Nicholson's persistent demands. Andros and his council took no further action. Coode continued to live quietly in Virginia's Westmoreland Country throughout Andros's governorship.[27]

Andros's support of Coode, a rebel who toppled a legitimate government in 1689, might be surprising, but Andros despised Nicholson to such a degree that he was willing to support any one who annoyed the latter. Coode had ousted Lord Baltimore's government, and Andros did not like Baltimore, who had criticized his attempts to retain Delaware for the duke of York. Andros was also a friend of Pennsylvania proprietor, William Penn, another enemy of Baltimore's. Also, Baltimore was Catholic and Coode was Protestant. In 1689, Coode had acted in Maryland to destroy the power of a Catholic proprietor, an act that was condoned and considered politically correct in the post revolutionary world of the 1690s.

In addition to petty harassment, religion was the main weapon used by Nicholson to achieve his goal of being named Virginia governor. He sought the assistance of high ranking Church of England officials, his ally in Virginia being the commissary and

priest, James Blair. The latter was only too willing to help Nicholson because he believed that Andros was determined to destroy
his pet project in Virginia—the establishment of William and
Mary College. Sir Edmund Andros initially fought off Nicholson's
attacks and launched successful counter attacks of his own. He
was ultimately to fail because of the Whig ascendancy in English
government that caused a change in colonial administration.
Andros was too closely associated with Charles II and James II,
now identified by Whigs as despotic tyrants, to survive an administration dominated by Whigs.

Blair, almost as stubborn and dedicated as Andros was, conveniently ignored facts or altered them to suit his own purposes. He
believed that he was doing God's work, so that any who opposed
him were thoroughly evil. Permanently mounted on a moral high
horse, Blair found willing ears in England to believe his increasingly strident and vicious criticisms of Andros. Blair broke with
Andros primarily over the college issue. Blair had returned to
England during Nicholson's term as lieutenant governor to
secure a charter and government financial backing for a college
in Virginia. Planned to serve as a seminary for the Church of
England, the college would, in addition to divinity, teach Latin,
Greek, philosophy, and mathematics. It also had the backing of
Nicholson, who, as lieutenant governor, successfully proposed the
establishment of a college to the Virginia council in 1691. When
the assembly gave Nicholson a present of £300, he asked the king
for permission to keep the money, promising to donate half of it
to the college. Nicholson backed the college because of the "interest it might create him with the bishops in England."[28]

By supporting Blair's project, Nicholson made the right choice.
The king and queen, after whom it was named, also favored the
college. The monarchs gave almost £2,000 toward its building,
the money to be taken out of Virginia's quit rents. The king and
queen also awarded the college 20,000 acres of land, 10,000 on the
south side of Black Water swamp and 10,000 on Pamunkey Neck
in Bruton Parish, Middle Plantation (Williamsburg).[29] Blair
brought to Virginia the college charter, which named Blair president for life. He presented "their Majts Graciouse Charter for the
Erecting & building of a Colledge in Virginia" to Sir Edmund
Andros and his council on 1 September 1693. The foundation
stone for "the Coledge of William & Mary in Virginia" was laid
on 8 August 1695 with Andros and his council in attendance.[30]

While Andros's lukewarm support of the college was the main
source of contention between the minister and the governor,

James Blair (1656–1743). Virginia commissary of the Bishop of London, Blair was a constant thorn in the side of Virginia's governors until his death. Zealous in protecting the interests of the Church of England in Virginia, Blair was largely responsible for obtaining the charter of the College of William and Mary, established February 8, 1693. Courtesy of the Virginia Historical Society, Richmond, Virginia.

Blair was also annoyed that the governor refused to support the establishment of ecclesiastical courts in Virginia "to try incestuous marriages and all other spiritual causes." Blair's presiding over such a court would bring him an income of £200 a year. Nicholson and other high church Anglicans had supported the idea, and Nicholson had established a similar court in Maryland. Andros, on his arrival in Virginia, had refused to do so because he realized "the impracticableness of that scheme, by reason of the corruption of the Clergy and the irreconciliable aversion of the Laity" to ecclesiastical courts. Andros, therefore, "forbore to prosecute this affair so zealously." Blair was "offended," further charging that Andros did not appoint enough ministers, there being only twenty-two ministers for fifty parishes, thereby permitting the vestries to save the cost of salaries. Despite his charge against Andros, Blair himself admitted "that several of these parishes are so small or ill peopled that they are not able to keep a minister."[31]

Nicholson claimed to be as convinced as Blair that Andros was opposed to the college. Henry Coursey visited Andros during the latter's tenure as commander-in-chief in Maryland. Andros had closely supervised and drastically circumscribed Coursey's diplomatic errand when he had come to New York to negotiate with the Iroquois in 1677. Coursey reported to Nicholson that he told Andros "that there was no sort of provision made in this Countrey for the Education of Youth, but that he hoped when the Colledge of Virginia was built it would be of great benefit & Service to all these parts, to which Sr Edmond made answer, pish, it will come to nothing."[32]

Nicholson and Blair took Coursey's report as indicative of Andros's lack of support for the college. In fact, any statement of Andros's that in any way touched on the college was given the same interpretation. Nicholson also made note of a conversation Andros had with Philip Clarke, who reported Andros had said, "I will go and shew you the Colledge," then being built in Middle Plantation at the end of Duke of Gloucester Street, "but you'l expect I should show you the ffree schole first, but I suppose this Colledge is to teach children their A: B: C:." Andros was, of course, commenting on the lack of primary schools in Virginia. The absence of planning on the part of the college directors was apparent since they made no effort to ensure that potential students were prepared for college level work. Clarke went on to observe "that the Reason why Sr Edmond was angry with Mr Blaire was for his preaching a Sermon wherein he did say, that they who withdraw back & did not put forward their helping hand towards the Building of the Colledge would be Damned."[33]

Blair was convinced that Andros was one of those who would be damned. The governor was so opposed to the college, Blair said, that he "chooses his friends and favorites only out of such as are Enemies to the College, and that there is no certainer way to lose his favor than by being a Zealous friend to it." Supporters of the college were excluded from the assembly, Blair charged, although he did not detail how Andros managed to control elections. If supporters of the college were elected to the House of Burgesses, Blair continued, they were not chosen speaker, conveniently ignoring the fact that his ally, Philip Ludwell, Sr., had served in that position. Blair claimed he was at a loss to understand Andros's opposition but noted that the governor "shows a stiffness and obstinacy in opposing" the college and had not contributed a farthing to its construction, nor had his friends who had reneged on paying their subscriptions. Andros was not opposed to the college; he was opposed to Blair. Despite his dislike of the minister, Andros had urged the assembly in October 1693 to pass an act that would bring £100 a year to the college. In 1696, Andros had personally placed an order with auditor William Byrd to supply at his expense bricks for a college chapel. The governor also accepted an offer to join the society of college governors in 1694 and donated £56.7s.6d. for its windows.[34]

Nor was the governor anti-clerical or anti-religious. In fact, Andros as governor was entitled to the support of the Church of England and its leading minister in Virginia. Shortly after his arrival, Andros had indicated his willingness to establish a rapport with the church of which he was titular head by donating a large silver plate to the Bruton Parish Church. He periodically urged the assembly to make adequate provisions for the clergy.[35] Despite such support, Blair remained convinced Andros was an enemy to the church. Blair was a presence Andros could not avoid. In 1694, Andros was ordered by the king to admit him and Blair's friend, Henry Hartwell, to the council. Both Blair and Hartwell were nominated for the council by the bishop of London. Hartwell, an English-born attorney who had long been active in Virginia politics, was a trustee of the college. Andros could count on both men creating tension.[36] Once a councilor, Blair charged that Andros and his friends on that body contrived to keep information from him. He also said that Andros hindered surveys of the land awarded to the college by the king. Andros had, in fact, issued patents to his favorites for large tracts of land in the territory granted to the college. As Blair charged, Andros "opened those tracts to all mankind" and gave very generous patents "to several of his creatures," even though the college "charter says we should have first choice." Some of the land had already been occupied, either by legal residents or by squatters. Among these people, resentment against the college was high, with some doing all they could to thwart the surveyors, even by stealing their instruments.[37]

It was probably Blair's irritating attitude and contentious personality that dissuaded not only Andros from more fully supporting the college, but also those planters who refused to honor their subscriptions, the economic depression having left them short of cash. Blair was correct in stating that subscriptions were slow since, by 1697, only £500 of the £3,000 pledged had been paid. Particularly irritating to backers was the fact that Blair, as president of the college, well before the first brick for the college was laid, paid himself a salary of £100 for 1693 and £150 a year thereafter. Subscribers complained "they won't give their Money to make a Salary for the President." Donors believed the money should have been used for construction costs.[38]

What also bothered Andros about the college was Nicholson's involvement. Nicholson kept coming back to Virginia, ostensibly for college board meetings but in reality to plot with Blair against Andros, or so Andros suspected. Blair noted that at first Andros "tried to make him [Nicholson] weary by dryness, and frowns, and asking uncivil questions—demanding the reason how he came to leave his Government, or what he had to do in Virginia to amuse the people?" The college meetings were frequent and lasted "for several Weeks together." Blair and Nicholson were "in great Privacy together without going near the Governor [Andros] or so much as giving any notice of his arrival." Andros met Nicholson on the street during one such visit and told "him that twas not Customary for any Governor to come into the Goverment of another without letting him know something of it." Nicholson became "very cholerick and told Sir Edmund, that he did not understand there was any reason for such civility, and that truly he could hardly think himself out of his own goverment when he was in Virginia." Andros responded, "You must pardon me Sir . . . I have the honour to have the Kings Commission here, and if you claim from any other, you ought to be securd by the Sheriff."[39]

Blair described quite a different arrest incident that centered around Daniel Parke, who Blair believed to be a "sparkish Gentleman." Blair claimed Parke easily took offense at "the least thing that looks like an affront or Injury." Parke had a colorful, as well as a successful, public life and one that he played out in Europe and the West Indies, as well as in Virginia. One of the wealthiest planters in Virginia, Parke was related through his mother to John Evelyn, the English diarist and public official who had recommended Parke for the Virginia council. He was equally well connected in Virginia, having married Jane Ludwell, whose uncle was Philip Ludwell. Parke, in 1693, was elected to the House of Burgesses, was a member of the board for the new college, and was a vestryman at Bruton Parish Church. Andros befriended Parke on his arrival, showering him with favors. As the feud between Andros and Nicholson escalated, Parke shifted his allegiance completely to the former.[40]

Parke, an ally of Andros by 1695, assumed the role of harassing Nicholson. An expert fencer, in September, Parke confronted Nicholson at Blair's house in Middle Plantation, having just come from Andros's house. The men were at breakfast, and Parke waited until they had left the table before he told them why he had come. He was offended because Nicholson had allowed a letter from Parke to be sent by the "common post to be read by every body in Virginia." Parke was so put off by Nicholson's lack of tact that he challenged him to a duel.[41]

Parke came to Blair's house prepared to fight, carrying a sword much longer than he usually wore and having had it "ground sharp in the point that morning." Nicholson refused, explaining that he could not fight Parke in Virginia or Maryland, but would be pleased to meet him anywhere else. Parke continued to goad Nicholson, reminding him of "how he used to huff & hector when he was Lord Govr of Virginia but now he had met with his match he had nothing to say."[42] Despite his notoriously hot temper, Nicholson refused to meet Parke's challenge.

Blair claimed that Nicholson visited Andros at his house that same afternoon to complain about Parke. The sheriff of James City was present, and when a quarrel broke out between the governors, Andros ordered the sheriff to take Nicholson into custody. After half an hour, Andros, "being afraid of the consequence of imprisoning and detaining one of the King's Governors, ordered that he [Nicholson] should have his liberty."[43]

Nicholson returned to Maryland but soon was back in Virginia. Parke did not relent in his pursuit of Nicholson, sending letters to friends in New York and New England telling his correspondents that the Maryland governor was a coward. The standoff

continued for over a year until a college board meeting in Jamestown on Saturday, 26 February 1697, with both Parke and Nicholson in attendance. Parke informed Nicholson that he was to go
to England so he could duel with him. Nicholson said he would
not go to England and called Parke a liar. Parke had a horsewhip
in his hand and ran at "the Govr of Maryland, who was sitting
bareheaded, & gave him a slash with the horsewhip over the
head." Nicholson did not have a sword, but "flew to Col. Park
with his naked fist," only to be separated by the other men in the
room.[44]

Andros heard of the incident at a council meeting on 1 March
1697. Andros was visibly upset and "imediately restrained the
said Coll. Park," ordering the sheriff to take him into custody.
Andros then sent Christopher Wormeley "to wait upon the Governr of Maryland at Green Spring where it is said he is, to prevent
further ill consequences." It was an embarrassing situation for
Andros, and one that could only reflect badly on him. The next
day, when Nicholson came to Jamestown with Blair, Andros
ordered Ralph Wormeley, William Byrd, and Edward Hill to see
about "composing ye Quarrell."[45]

Parke did not confine his defense of Andros to attacks on Nicholson. Parke was a Ludwell relative and, as such, was entitled to
sit in the Ludwell pew at the Middle Plantation church. Blair and
his wife, Sarah, daughter of Benjamin Harrison, were former
Jamestown residents who had moved to Middle Plantation, renting a house from the Ludwells. The Blairs did not have a pew of
their own, so their landlords invited them to sit in their pew.
There was room in the pew because Daniel Parke had stopped
going to church after the minister, Samuel Eburne, had preached
"a little too [close to] home against adultery, in several sermons
wherein he [Parke] took himself to be reflected on." Parke still
had living with him "a Gentleman's Lady, one Mistress Berry,
whom he had conveyed away from her husband in London in the
year 1692, and carried to Virginia along with him, calling her by
the name of his cousin Brown." Parke stayed away from the
church until January 1696, at which time Mrs. Blair had been
occupying the pew for about two years. On a Sunday morning in
January, just as the minister Eburne had started the service,
Parke rushed into the church and "with a mighty violence with
which he frightened the poor Gentlewomen who were in the pew
(without any man to defend them as fearing no attacks in such a
sanctuary), he seized Mistress Blair by the wrist, and with great
fury and violence pulled her out of the Pew in the presence of the

Minister and Congregation."[46] The shaken minister Eburne promptly resigned, "declaring his Intentions of leaving the Country," undoubtedly yearning for a safer post in England. Blair's father-in-law, Benjamin Harrison, indignant at his daughter's treatment, later charged that Eburn had been forced out by Parke. Blair, outraged at the insult to his wife, complained in vain to Andros and the council.[47]

Blair blamed Andros for everything that went wrong in Virginia, including Parke's ill considered actions. He also blamed Andros for keeping clergy salaries low. King William had promised Blair that if the Virginia revenue proved adequate for expenses, quit rents could be used to supplement ministers' salaries. With war and decreased trade, there was no surplus because the money was spent on defense. Blair complained that Andros had "contrived such strange and unusual ways partly to lessen and partly to consume the Revenue." Andros spent the money, Blair charged, on such frivolous expenses as "raising an old fort at Jamestown, & in building a powder house," both measures paid for out of quit rents. Blair also criticized Andros for sending money to aid New York's governor Fletcher. Blair had no comprehension of the need for defense, never considering the consequences to all the English colonies if New York fell to the French or the effect such an invasion would have on the Indian tribes in other English territories. Blair saw Andros's efforts to defend Virginia as part of a deliberate plan to divert money away from Virginia's clergy. Blair criticized Andros for hiring a sloop to protect Virginia's coast, even though the governor had acted on the instructions of the home government. The commissary saw this, too, as evidence that Andros deliberately squandered the quit rents to keep them from the college. Despite the fact that many of Blair's complaints were downright frivolous, ecclesiastical and civil authorities in England apparently chose to take them seriously.[48]

Blair did not understand that with tobacco prices down and no London fleets able to sail to Virginia to buy the crop, there was a serious shortage of money in Virginia. Many planters were unable to pay their taxes, much less honor their pledges to the college. The shortage of money meant that revenue was uncollected, placing the government, like the people, short of funds. The assembly was reluctant to vote more money for ministers simply because they were already hard pressed to find funds to pay existing government expenses.

The governor and the commissary also disagreed about the

issue of ministers' tenure. In each local church, clergymen in Virginia served at the pleasure of the vestry. Blair complained that ministers were treated like "hired servants" and were "dismissed if they please at the expiration of such agreement." Lifelong tenure was assured only if the vestrymen requested the governor, as the king's ordinary, to induct the minister. If the minister was not recommended for induction, then he continued to serve as long, and only as long, as he pleased the vestrymen. To Andros, this seemed a fair arrangement since so many of the ministers sent to Virginia by the Church of England were poorly qualified, noted for their lack of morality, "and the irregularity of their Lives and Conversations." Blair, of course, disagreed that this was the case, arguing that Andros should have initiated inductions.[49]

The feud between the minister and the governor escalated when Andros read to the council for their approval his proposed speech to the assembly that was to meet on 19 April 1695. The councilors approved of Andros's speech, except for James Blair, who was outraged that Andros did not strongly recommend to the assembly that they increase clergy salaries. In fact, Blair "reflected very indecently upon Sir Edmund Andros; nay so injurious were the Termes he used towards Him that He himself thought proper to deny them." After this outburst, the councilors were further disturbed to hear that when church wardens asked him to appoint a qualified minister for the Jamestown church during a period when Blair was ill, Andros did so, "promissing to gratifie the said Minister out of his own purse." Blair protested that the governor did not have the authority to appoint a minister and neither did the king, "also that the Ministers need not produce to the Govr their Orders, being Sufficient they shewed them to him the said Mr. Blair." Facing a challenge to the royal authority he represented, Andros approved the council's decision to suspend Blair "from Sitting Voting, & Assisting as one of their Majties Councill of Virginia."[50]

The legislature refused to yield on the clergy salary issue, claiming that the ministers were already well paid and did not need a raise. While Blair left them unmoved, the burgesses paid more attention to the king who, on 25 February 1695, ordered Andros to have the assembly consider ministers' salaries and to see that acts passed to provide for the support of ministers were enforced. In May, the assembly raised salaries to 13,333 $\frac{1}{2}$ pounds of tobacco a year. When the more generous council increased the sum to 16,000 pounds, the burgesses reluctantly agreed.[51]

Andros sent to England a full account of Blair's ouster from the council, while Blair sent an equally full (and equally biased) account to Francis Nicholson and church authorities in England. Andros notified the Board of Trade that Blair had been suspended, "notwithstanding all endeavours, [he] was not to be satisfied . . . [and was] unfit to sit at that board." Blair appealed directly to the bishop of London, who complained to the king. William ordered Blair to be reinstated. Andros, receiving the letter on 12 August 1696, sent council clerk James Sherlock "to acquaint" Blair that the council was meeting. Blair was too ill to attend but finally rejoined the council on 25 September 1696. On 14 October 1696, the governor showed the council a letter he received from the bishop of London, reiterating Blair's complaints that the clergy was slighted and oppressed, but Blair denied writing about these matters to the bishop.[52] The council again justified its actions regarding clergy support, claiming the ministers had "been as well respected and taken care of as at any time since their remembrance . . . & his Excellcy always ready to espouse ye concerns of & help ye Clergy, And give all dispatch and assistance in what relates to the College." The councilors later pointed out that Virginia's clergy made out better financially than their counterparts in England because their perquisites were much higher.[53] The councilors, except for Blair, were unanimous in stating that clerical salaries were more than adequate.[54]

Blair refused to accept the council's position and in 1697, called a meeting of the clergy at Jamestown. They prepared an address complaining about low salaries that Blair was pleased to pass along to the governor. To Blair's complaint that many ministers lacked housing, the governor responded that he would see that such ministers were accommodated. To Blair's complaint that none were as yet inducted, Andros said he was willing to induct ministers but that none had been recommended by either the vestries or by individual patrons.[55]

By the spring of 1697, the building of the college had come to a halt for lack of funds, the trustees having already spent £170 more than they had received. They asked Blair to go again to England to raise enough money for the building to be completed. Blair was happy to oblige since the journey would also give him the opportunity to work directly for Andros's recall.[56] Andros tried to anticipate Blair's accusations against him by writing to the duke of Shrewsbury. He told the duke that he realized "that

I am reflected upon" by Blair "as an obstructor of the royal commands for the church and college," acknowledging that it was
"not possible for me to please Commissary Blair."[57] At a council
meeting on 20 April 1697, Blair raised the issue as to whether he,
as a Scot, could continue to serve as councilor in light of the
recently passed parliamentary act that barred Scots from certain
offices. The councilors were delighted to agree he should not
serve, particularly since he was sailing for England so soon. Blair
termed the incident his second dismissal from the council and
used it as further ammunition against Andros.[58]

Even before Blair's arrival in England, his complaints against
Andros had started to bear fruit with the Board of Trade. Blair
charged that the Virginia General Court was ineffectual because
Andros discriminated against those "Lawyers and parties which
he doth not favour." The council was also deemed ineffectual
because it members, knowing they held their posts at the governor's discretion, tried to please Andros. The result, according to
Blair, was an arbitrary government.[59]

Other people in addition to Blair had told the Board of Trade
that the reason Virginia's population remained low was because
of the practice of giving large land grants to councilors. This
meant the poorer people had either to become tenants or secure
land on the frontier, where they were "exposed to danger, & often
times proves the Occasion of Warr with the Indians."[60] Blair's
ally, Edward Chilton, also complained that Virginia councilors
enjoyed immunity from the law in the recovery of debts and that
councilors sat as judges in civil cases without taking an oath.[61]

The Whig dominated board in February 1697 questioned
Andros about these practices. Andros explained that councilors
were issued summons to appear in court instead of by common
writ. Failure on their part to appear automatically caused the
judgment to be made against them. Andros further explained
that the judges on the general court, being councilors, had
already taken the councilor's oath. Land, he said, was always
granted by patent and he could see no particular disadvantage to
the large tracts of land already granted. This last statement was
surprising, since Andros had formerly refused to approve large
land grants in either New York or New England. It may be that
his anger at Blair led him to defend a position he had long
abhorred only because it would annoy Blair. Much of the land in
question was land Blair wanted for the college. It may also be that
Andros wanted to keep council members, the chief beneficiaries
of large grants, content.[62]

In London, the Whig members of the Board were impatient with the casual attitude of Andros, who was now an old courtier seriously out of date with the practices of the newly created bureaucracy. Andros, as usual, was caught in the maelstrom of English politics.[63] The Board of Trade wrote another critical letter to Andros in September 1697, soon after Blair arrived in London in July 1697. The Board was outraged that Andros had neglected to send an account of Virginia's revenue as well as an inventory of the colony's arms and ammunition, as he had been instructed. Neither had Andros informed them if the duty imposed to raise the permanent revenue was sufficient. Nothing could be determined about Virginia's fiscal situation until Andros forwarded to them his accounts. With ill concealed annoyance, they told Andros they wanted precise answers to questions concerning the number of ships and seamen in Virginia, not merely to be told in general terms there were "many" or "few." They also wanted exact information as to whether it was feasible to manufacture naval stores in Virginia and, if so, needed an estimate as to the expected quality of the products. They further criticized Andros for the assembly's failure to complete the revision of the colony's laws, a revision begun by Andros's first assembly in 1693 and still underway. In addition, the reports Andros sent back to England were not uniformly presented with ample margins that were wide enough to hold notes summarizing the contents.[64]

Andros apologized to the board for his carelessness in answering queries, explaining he had been "much indisposed on my health" when he had sent the material to the Board. He now forwarded the auditor's accounts for 1695, 1696, and 1697 through to April 24. The revision of the colony's laws had still not been completed because, as Andros explained, so many councilors were absent from meetings, but he assured the board he had appointed a panel of councilors to oversee the revision. He said the reason the revenue was insufficient was because of the money Virginia had sent to New York. He cited the cost of maintaining a sloop to prevent violations of the Navigation Acts, extraordinary wartime expenses, and the fact that no London fleet had reached Virginia in two years. He included an account of the arms and ammunition in Virginia. In a later letter, he explained that although pitch and tar were already manufactured in Virginia, the quality of the tar was not good. Andros had determined the number of ships in Virginia, reporting there were four ships, two barques, four brigantines, and seventeen sloops.[65]

Andros's report temporarily mollified the board, at least until Blair presented his charges against Andros to them and to the bishop of London. Church authorities were concerned about conditions in Virginia, as was the Board of Trade. The board called before it James Blair and Henry Hartwell, along with former Virginia resident, Edward Chilton, to answer specific questions about Andros.[66] Blair and his associates gave the board ample ammunition to confirm their already negative attitude toward Andros. Blair had a willing assistant in his campaign to oust Andros in John Locke, leader of the "reform" party, and in lord chamberlain, Sir John Somers, Locke's patron and close friend.[67] Locke, taking a particular interest in Virginia and in Andros, had accumulated a large file on the colony. Blathwayt, the sole member determined to protect the Tories and Andros, had left London in the summer of 1697 and did not attend council meetings. In Blathwayt's absence, Locke, in late August or early September 1697, met with Blair and asked him to spell out his grievances against the Virginia government. Blair obliged and Locke used Blair's complaints to forward a list of questions concerning Virginia to the Board of Trade on 9 September 1697.[68]

With Locke's assistance, as well as that of the bishop of London (a former member of the Privy Council's Committee of Trade), and Thomas Tenison, archbishop of Canterbury, Blair pointed out that Andros was now too old, no longer "able to serve on horseback, partly by reason of his age, partly because of a fall he had from his horse, which they say has burst him. Hence it proceed that the militia is ill disciplined; the Rangers negligent; and an opportunity given to the Indian enemy to grow insolent." Blair reminded the board that Sir William Berkeley's "age and weaknes was the chief occasion of the beginning & growth of Bacons Rebellion in that Country." Blair claimed that Andros could not get along with the governors of the neighboring colonies of the Carolinas and Maryland, that he was secretive and despotic, and that he could not work well with the assembly. Nor could Andros control the Indians, Blair said. In what was obviously further distortions of the truth, considering Andros's past record of Indian diplomacy, Blair reported an incident that occurred in 1693. An Indian sachem who called on Andros at his house, "after a long conversation with him whereat the Indian appeared to be exceeding uneasy, he came into the Governour's kitchin, and finding a Case-knife upon the dresser, immediately cut his own throat therewith, and dyed." Blair claimed that Andros might be deserving of respect and consideration if he had an admirable record of "former Services," but this was not the case, clearly forgetting Andros's many accomplishments in Europe, the West Indies, New York, and New England. Blair said that Andros "never did any considerable Service to the King, nor the people. He was," Blair said, "a great instrument of Arbitrary power in the late Reigns, and is thought to have no kindnes for this." [69]

Following Blair's attack on Andros at the Board of Trade, an ecclesiastical hearing was held on Monday, 27 December 1697 at Lambeth Palace. In attendance was the archbishop of Canterbury, the bishop of London, James Blair and his brother-in-law Benjamin Harrison, Jr., William Byrd, II, representing Andros, and Andros's friend, Ralph Marshall. The Board of Trade sent clerk John Povey to observe the proceedings and to provide information. William Byrd II handled the bulk of Andros's defense. Son and heir of the Virginia auditor, the young Byrd, only twenty-three years old in 1697, was educated in England, returned briefly to Virginia where he was elected to the House of Burgesses in 1696, then went back to England in 1697. In 1698, he was appointed English agent for the Virginia council. Trained as an attorney at the Middle Temple and knowledgeable about Virginia affairs, Byrd, despite his youth, was a logical choice to defend the governor. Both young Byrd and his father realized that Blair's intent was not only to secure Andros's recall but to have Nicholson named as Andros's successor, a choice not appealing to the Byrds. Young William Byrd came to the meeting with a prepared statement, which he probably was not given the opportunity to read. [70]

From the transcript of the conference, it is obvious that Canterbury and London were predisposed in Blair's favor. Harrison confirmed Blair's charges against Andros. Povey, seemingly intimidated to be in the presence of an archbishop and a bishop, offered few comments, and these were couched in language of extreme diffidence. Marshall spoke only briefly to introduce Byrd, who was competent but inexperienced. It is doubtful that the course of the hearing would have been different even if Byrd had been bolder or had been permitted to read his statement. The clerics seemed convinced that Blair was more sinned against than sinning.

The lack of sympathy among the churchmen for Andros's position was made clear in the first few minutes of the proceedings. After Byrd commented that Blair had made accusations about Andros to the archbishop, Canterbury replied that Blair had not accused Andros, but that he "had heard that he [Andros] discouraged the College long before Mr. Blair came over."[71] Byrd tried in vain to take the offensive against Blair, insisting he answer the governor's charges against him that he had filled the church and the college with Scots and that he had misapplied money slated for the college. Scottish ministers, said Byrd, were all "discontented troublesome Men murmuring at the shortness of their salaries with which the Ministers were very well contented formerly." When Blair, himself a Scot, asked what harm the Scots had done, Povey volunteered the information that one "Mr. Greig that was guilty of Sodomy and one Mr. Doyley that his Parish complained of and one Mr. Munroe," at which point Blair interrupted him and said that both Greig and Doyley were English. Byrd interposed that Gordon was a Scot and a drunk. Blair agreed, but pointed out that Gordon had preceded him to Virginia. Povey weakly conceded that "it is a very hard thing to persuade good men to go over into the Plantations." Blair then defended his taking an initial salary of £100 the first year he served as college president and a subsequent salary of £150 a year, money that his critics charged should have been spent on construction costs. Blair countered that he had not disobeyed any instructions contained in the college charter and the archbishop pointed out that Blair was entitled to a salary.[72]

Blair now seized the offensive after claiming that it was "a pretty hard task for me who am a subject of Virginia to say anything that may look like an accusation of Sir Edmund Andros." He then proceeded to make those accusations in detail and at length. Andros, by example, prevented people from paying the money they had pledged to the college. Andros did not induct ministers even though he had the power to do so as ordinary, leaving ministers "in the nature of hired servants." Andros did not support the granting of a salary increase to ministers. He permitted ministers who expressed critical opinions of powerful people in their congregations to be turned out of office.

Byrd explained that it was not Andros's fault that it had taken the assembly so long to address the issue of ministerial salaries and that Andros had supported the college, even ordering bricks from the senior Byrd's brickyard for the building of a chapel. Byrd also cited Virginia council records to prove that Blair had continually undermined Andros. One example was a letter that the bishop of London wrote to Andros in which he repeated many of the charges that had obviously been made by Blair. When Andros read the letter in a council meeting, Blair denied he had reported the incidents to the bishop. Relating these events at the hearing did not help Andros's cause. Instead the bishop was indignant that Andros had never answered his letter and had read it to the Virginia council.[73]

Blair then launched into a lengthy monologue, detailing again the governor's lack of support for him and the college. He was bitter at what he termed his two dismissals from the council, which he considered as part of a plot by Andros to prevent him from examining the colony's accounts. Blair said his dismissals arose because of a decision by the queen that Virginia's quit rents be used to support the clergy for three years. This order had prompted immediate complaints from Andros, who said that if the quit rents were used for the clergy, the government would not be able to subsist. The king was finally "prevailed upon to recall that grant," said Blair, because the accounts sent by Andros to London showed the government needed the quit rents. The minister further accused Andros of cheating the king of tobacco revenue and of wastefully sending money to New York or spending it on fortifications "in a time of peace," ignoring the fact that the war with France had ended in 1697, and news of the signing of the Peace of Ryswick was not received in Virginia until 9 January 1698.[74] Povey pointed out that Virginia's accounts were simple and accurate and offered to let Blair examine the accounts at any time. Despite this concession, Blair remained convinced that he would "discover a great Mystery of inequity in them." The meeting was adjourned at the suggestion of the archbishop.[75]

No inequity was ever found in Virginia's accounts during Andros's administration, but the combined attack by Whig politicians and church officials was effective. Blair, on 20 January 1698, thanked Locke profusely for his assistance in discrediting Andros. Andros, in March 1698, aware of the situation in London, decided he had had enough and asked to be recalled from Virginia due to poor health.[76] Before Andros's letter was received, his friend Ralph Marshall, fearing that Andros would be discharged, asked that "a letter of revocation may be sent for Sir Edmund Andros, as has been usual in like cases, and particularly in that of governor Fletcher of New York no complaint of mismanagement having been brought against Sir Edmund in his Government of Virginia." There had been specific charges of mismanagement brought against Fletcher. In fact, it was only after his successor, Lord Bellomont, assumed office that the extent of Fletcher's dealings with pirates came to light. There were no such damaging charges against Andros. Blair's accusations were vague, inaccurate, and false, but, for political expediency, widely believed by the board members. The arrival of Andros's letter asking that he be permitted to resign must have come as a relief to Whig Board members who no longer had to seek whatever justification a recommendation for dismissal would require.[77]

The official announcement out of Whitehall on 31 May 1698 said that Andros had asked "leave of the King to resign his Government of Virginia, that he may return unto England about his own affairs." Appointed in his place as governor of Virginia because of Blair's lobbying efforts was Francis Nicholson, a Tory, who was a surprising choice for the Whig dominated board. Nicholson could thank Blair for the appointment but, in fact, did not.[78] Locke and Somers had achieved their desired end of reducing the power of council and governor. Nicholson's instructions required that all councilors had to take oaths to serve as judges and were to be prevented from monopolizing government offices. New land granting methods and tax reform were to go into effect.[79]

Andros endured a final summer's heat in Virginia to call his last assembly session in September. He dissolved that body when the assembly attempted to defy him by admitting a member not born in England, Ireland, or the colonies, as required by parliamentary law. On 20 October 1698, as he waited to transfer power to Nicholson, Andros faced a crisis in the form of a fire at the Jamestown State House and its arsenal. The records, which Andros had been concerned to organize and preserve, survived because they were thrown out of the windows. The next day, an order was issued to "all persons that have found or know of any persons that have found or taken up any bookes or papers," to "bring the Said Bookes & papers into the Secretaryes office," temporarily located at Mrs. Sherwood's house. There they were "sorted and listed" and then "put in good order." Mrs. Sherwood owned one of the few brick houses in Jamestown and permitted the colony's records to be stored there. She also gave permission for the general court and council to meet in her great hall. A few days later, on October 29, Andros presided over his last council meeting.[80]

On December 9, Nicholson was sworn in as governor, but Andros did not attend the ceremony, nor, in a final and spiteful gesture, did he turn over to Nicholson the records of his administration. The former governor, Sir Edmund Andros, remained five weeks in Virginia and then, with his wife, sailed to England, "mighty angry," according to Blair but more likely greatly relieved to be going home. His colonial career was over.[81]

Conclusion: Time's Winged Chariot, 1698–1714

But at my back I always hear
Time's winged chariot hurrying near;
And yonder all before us be
Deserts of vast eternity.
                         —Andrew Marvell, "To His Coy Mistress"[1]

As GOVERNOR-GENERAL OF NEW YORK, THE DOMINION OF NEW
England, and Virginia, Sir Edmund Andros represented the best
of the new professional army officers who were called to administer England's North American empire. The new officer class, promoted because of ability, not birth, provided the means by which
England achieved and maintained its far flung empire. These
men were the driving force that first challenged, then ultimately
eliminated the French presence in North America. Andros epitomized the governors-general who effected these ends. Such men
began the centralization of government authority that would be
the rule in the next century, thereby accelerating the reduction
in influence of local elites. Colonial elites disliked this process and
resisted it whenever they had the opportunity, until finally in
1776, the situation produced a split between colonies and mother
country. Nevertheless, after 1776, the centralization started by
Andros and other governors-general was incorporated into the
new American government that was balanced with representative government, as it had been under most of English rule.

Edmund Andros was a highly effective instrument in implementing centralization and in firmly establishing England's presence in North America. On his return to England in 1698, he
continued his service to crown and country on Guernsey, the
island of his childhood, where he resumed his post as bailiff. He
returned to Guernsey at a time when its economy, much like that
of New York's, was booming because of piracy and smuggling.
Contributing to growth and prosperity were advances in agriculture, principally in apple orchards that produced hard cider, and

266

in the establishment of sheep herds that fostered the production of wool. The booming economy stimulated land sales on the island, but Andros was faced with a threat to his income when local officials decided that the bailiff's signature was not necessary on contracts for the sale of land or on mortgages, thereby depriving Andros of the fees. Andros, intent on protecting his rank, privileges, and income from the attacks of local elites, knew how to exploit his royal connections. In 1703, he complained directly to the queen about the officials' decision. The Privy Council reasserted central authority by ruling that no one but the crown appointed bailiff had the power to sign such documents.

Andros divided his time between Guernsey and London, where he lived in a house on Denmark Hill. In 1703, his second wife, Elizabeth Crispe Clapham Andros, died and on August 18 was buried at St. Giles in the Fields, Middlesex. The next year, Queen Anne named Andros as lieutenant governor of Guernsey under Governor Lord Hatton. His appointment coincided with England's participation in another war against the French, the War of the Spanish Succession. The successful allied forces, led by Andros's old acquaintance, John Churchill, now duke of Marlborough, scored a series of victories, with the most dramatic at Blenheim in 1705. Andros's volatile Virginia friend and supporter, Daniel Parke, now aide-de-camp to the duke, carried news of the victory to the queen.

Old soldier that he was, Andros was concerned about protecting Guernsey from French invasion during the war. This fear was constant, and in late June 1708, Andros reported to the earl of Sunderland that such an invasion might be imminent. His report was based on information supplied by three Englishmen who had been held prisoner by the French. Andros immediately ordered the island's defenses prepared, but by mid July, it was apparent the French assault was aimed elsewhere.[2]

Queen Anne, daughter of his old patron, James II, who had died in September 1701, had succeeded Andros's childhood friend, William III, who had died in 1702. With Hatton's 1706 death, Andros returned to London and did not seek, nor was he offered, another government post. On 21 April 1707, he married Elizabeth Fitzherbert. Andros's last known official letter was written to Queen Anne in 1712, congratulating her on England's victories in the War of the Spanish Succession.[3]

Andros died in his seventy-seventh year, in London on 19 February 1714, preceding Queen Anne in death by only a few months. Thus, Andros died before the end of the Stuart monar-

chy he had served so well. The crown now passed to the Hanover-
ian line, as determined by Parliament in 1701 with the Act of
Succession. The new king, George of Hanover, was a descendent
of Sophia, Electress of Hanover, the youngest daughter of
Andros's royal Stuart patron, Elizabeth of Bohemia, the Winter
Queen.

Andros was buried on 27 February 1714 with the honors,
pomp, and ceremony that befitted an officer and the governor-
general of New York, the Dominion of New England, and Virginia. His funeral retinue consisted of sixty-six men, each carrying white wax branch lights. There were twenty coachmen and
horsemen with six mourning coaches, each pulled by six horses.
The cost of the funeral was £80.16s.6d. Elizabeth Andros died on
12 February 1717, the only one of Andros's three wives to be buried near him at St. Anne's Church in Soho. The original church
building of St. Anne's was destroyed in the World War II blitz,
as were the churchyard and tombs. No traces remain of Andros's
grave. A new, modern church, also called St. Anne's, now occu-
pies the site.

Andros did not get rich from his long years of service to the
Stuarts. He left a modest estate of only £2,300. By the terms of
his will, Andros's wife was left £100 and two small yearly annuities paid by Parliament of £50 each, but only "upon condition that
she shall not claim any interest right or title in or to any lands"
or other property. After his wife's death, the annuities were to be
paid to Christopher Clapham, his second wife's son from a previous marriage. Cash awards were left to nieces and nephews, but
the most generous bequests were to his nephews, George and
John. Andros left George (son of Andros's brother, George) his
"interest in the Island of Alderney," given to him by the king in
1684, as well as £500 and the income from two additional parliamentary annuities. Evidently displeased with his nephew John's
lifestyle (John being the son of his deceased brother, John),
Andros left him a generous bequest of £500 with the stipulation
that he "build a good suitable house on or at the Manor of Sac-
mores in Guernsey." If John failed to build the house, he was to
pay the £500 to his cousin George.[4]

The payments of these bequests marked the end of Sir Edmund
Andros's worldly concerns. Before the end of Andros's life, he witnessed, but probably did not fully understand, the decline of
divine right monarchy and the beginning of the rise of parliament
that followed the 1688 Glorious Revolution. It was parliament in
1689 that made the decision to bestow the crown jointly on Wil-

liam and Mary. The rise of parliament was assured when William in 1694 approved the Triennial Bill after rejecting it on two previous occasions. No future monarch could rule without calling parliament but, in fact, persistent warfare and the accompanying need for money meant that parliament was rarely out of session during the next century. Parliament's rise and the concomitant decline of royal power occurred slowly over the course of the century following the Revolution. William came to the throne with virtually as much power as any of his predecessors. The king supported, but did not particularly favor, parliamentary rule, accepting it because he had little choice. In addition, his frequent absences, because of war or his trips back to the Netherlands, made it a bit easier for parliament to assert a growing authority. Whether or not he approved of the changes brought on by the Glorious Revolution, Andros, like the king and most Englishmen, accepted them.

Throughout the next century, even though the military imperialism of the late Stuart era gave way to the commercial imperialism of the Walpole era, government in the provinces remained, for the most part, in the hands of soldier-administrators such as Edmund Andros. The appointment of such men reflected the belief among the Stuart and Hanoverian monarchs and many members of England's elite that military experience was a necessary prerequisite to colonial service. The need for such gentlemen officers was predicated not only by concerns for defense, with both Indians and other European nations posing continual threats to the safety of England's colonies, but also because officers could usually be relied upon to implement imperial policy. Provincials did not like the end result of that policy any more in the eighteenth century than they had in the seventeenth century.

Neither did provincials during the reigns of the later Stuarts like the concentration on colonial administration among English bureaucrats. As administrations changed and Whigs succeeded Tories, policies were occasionally ignored or reversed, but the intent was always clear. Monarchs and administrators were determined to centralize government authority and draw the provinces closer into the imperial orbit. That this policy was often ineffective does not mean it did not exist. It simply means that implementation of that policy was often beyond the capabilities of English administrators, or that these administrators were distracted by more important European concerns. Nevertheless, the intent of the British ministry remained constant. When imperial and provincial interests collided, the former prevailed. Provincials did have rights, but those rights remained distinctly inferior to those of Englishmen at home.

Edmund Andros shared this view of provincials. His attitude earned him the unremitting animosity of some colonists, but many others recognized his considerable ability and effectiveness. Andros faced dissension and strife throughout his American public career, as did all royal governors, but he also enjoyed notable successes. In all three governorships, he had preserved English territory, maintained good relations with Indians, and ensured internal order until events in England had superseded his efforts. In each post, he had implemented ducal or royal policy to the best of his ability. Colonists may not have always liked that policy, but the English monarchs he served were pleased with Andros's performance.

Andros's career spanned half a century of service to England. His standards for colonial administration were high. A skilled diplomat who negotiated a lasting treaty with the Five Nations of the Iroquois, he believed in fair and equitable treatment of Native Americans, reflecting imperial attitudes toward Indians. While the end result desired by imperialists such as Andros and by settlers remained the same in that both wanted to obtain land held by Indians, the means used to secure that land were distinctly at odds. Indian relations could have been conducted in a fairer and more ethical manner if Andros's example had been followed. That they were not is still a cause for regret.

Andros, a proponent of a united military defense, insisted that both the colonial military establishment and the government be supported through a fair system of taxation. He implemented a united government in New England, New York, and New Jersey, thereby anticipating the union of the thirteen colonies that would follow almost a century later. In New York and New England, he refused to favor large landowners who were only interested in exploiting the land and other colonists. Instead, he encouraged settlement by small planters in the colonies he governed. Above all, he insisted the colonies were subordinate to central authority as represented by the proprietor or the king. To repeat the words of William Penn, Andros was a man "not without objection," but he most "certainly did great things."

Schooled in court, a confidante of princes, aware of the importance of diplomacy, and an accomplished diplomat, Andros was the epitome of the seventeenth century soldier-administrator-courtier. He had an encompassing perspective that led him to take a broader view of what was best for the empire, not necessarily what was best for any individual colony at any particular time. Cognizant of imperial needs, Andros was not hampered by narrow provincial concerns. As such, he was an asset to the English crown. Edmund Andros's life contributed to the shaping of the English empire and the future American empire. In fact, there would not have been a United States if there had not first been an English empire. Edmund Andros and others like him defined the nature of that empire and ensured its existence.

Notes

Introduction

1. *The Selected Poetry of Marvell*, ed. Frank Kermode (New York and Toronto, 1967).

2. Viola Florence Barnes, *The Dominion of New England: A Study in British Colonial Policy* (New Haven, 1923 and New York, 1960), 46.

3. Edith F. Carey, *Essays on Guernsey History* (Guernsey, 1936), 78.

4. *The Andros Tracts*, ed. W. H. Whitmore, 3 vols., (Boston, 1868, 1869), 1:xxvii, xxxvii, hereafter cited as *Andros Tracts*.

5. Cadwallader Colden to Alexander Colden (25 June 1759), in William Smith, *History of the Province of New-York*, ed. Michael Kammen, 2 vols. (Cambridge, Mass., 1972), 1:291–93.

6. Stephen Saunders Webb, *1676: The End of American Independence* (Syracuse, 1984, 1995), 303.

7. Thomas Hutchinson, *The History of the Colony and Province of Massachusetts-Bay,* ed., Lawrence Shaw-Mayo, 3 vols. (Cambridge, Mass., 1935 and New York, 1970), 1:301, 353, hereafter cited as Hutchinson, *History.*

8. John Gorham Palfrey, *History of New England*, 4 vols. (Boston, 1882–1885), 3:517; also quoted in *Andros Tracts*, 1:xxiii.

9. Jack P. Greene, "The Role of the Lower Houses," in *Negotiated Authorities: Essays in Colonial, Political, and Constitution History*, (Charlottesville and London, 1994), 172.

10. See Winifred B. Rothenberg's review of John Frederick Martin, *Profits in the Wilderness: Entrepreneurship and the Founding of New England Towns in the Seventeenth Century* (Chapel Hill, 1991) in *Journal of Economic History*, 52 (1992): 957–59.

11. Jeanne Gould Bloom, "Sir Edmund Andros: A Study in Seventeenth Century Colonial Administration" (Ph.D. diss., Yale University, 1962).

12. Edward Randolph to William Blathwayt (21 May 1687), in Edward Randolph, *His Letters and Official Papers, 1676–1703*, ed. Robert Noxon Toppan (Boston, 1898 and New York, 1967), 6:224, hereafter cited as Randolph, *Papers.*

13. See, for instance, Francis Jennings, *The Ambiguous Iroquois Empire* (New York and London, 1984).

14. On metropolitan attitudes toward Indian relations, see Michael Leroy Oberg, *Dominion and Civility: English Imperialism and Native America, 1585–1685* (Ithaca and London, 1999); on Indian removal, see Anthony F. C. Wallace, *Jefferson and the Indians: The Tragic Fate of the First Americans* (Cambridge, Mass. and London, 1999), particularly chapters 7 and 8, "President Jefferson's Indian Policy" and "The Louisiana Territory," 106–75.

15. On Knox's Indian policy, see Michael Darryl Carter, "Nationbuilding and the Military: The Life and Career of Secretary of War Henry Knox, 1750–1806"

(Ph.D. diss., West Virginia University, 1997), particularly chapters 13 and 14, "Knox and the Southern Tribes" and "Paved with Good Intentions," 274–320.

16. Penn quoted in Webb, *1676*, 303, 403.

17. Wesley Frank Craven, *The Colonies in Transition* (New York, Evanston, and London, 1968), 217.

18. T. H. Breen, "Transfer of Culture: Chance and Design in the Shaping of Massachusetts Bay, 1630–1660," in *Puritans and Adventurers: Change and Persistance in Early America* (New York and Oxford, 1980), 70.

19. Barnes, *Dominion of New England*, vii.

20. K. G. Davies, "The Revolutions in America," in *The Revolution of 1688*, ed. Robert Bedford (Oxford, 1991), 264–65, 268–69.

CHAPTER 1. CIVIL WARS AND RESTORATION

1. *The Selected Poems of Marvell*, ed. Frank Kermode.

2. Webb, *1676*, 305; Bloom, "Sir Edmund Andros," iv.

3. *Documents Relative to the Colonial History of the State of New York*, ed. Edmund B. O'Callaghan and Berthold Fernow, 15 vols. (Albany, 1856–87), 3:740n., hereafter cited as *DRNY*; *Andros Tracts*, 1:vi–vii, viii. For brief biographical sketches of members of the Andros family and histories of Guernsey, see Jonathan Duncan, *History of Guernsey* (London, 1841); Carey, *Essays on Guernsey History*; Ferdinand Brock Tupper, *The History of Guernsey and Its Bailiwick* (London, 1876); Bloom, "Sir Edmund Andros," iv.

4. *Andros Tracts*, 1:xlviii; Tupper, *Guernsey*, 291; Webb, *1676*, 311.

5. *Andros Tracts*, 1:xlvii; Ronald Hutton, *Charles II, King of England, Scotland, and Ireland* (Oxford, 1989), 43; Webb, *1676*, 309–10.

6. Quoted in C. V. Wedgwood, *The Trial of Charles I* (London, 1964), 138.

7. Petition of John Riggs, Read in Council (28 July 1689), CO 5/855, PRO; Hutton, *Charles II*, 71, 86; Suzette Van Zuylen Van Nyevelt, *Court Life in the Dutch Republic, 1638–1689* (London and New York, 1906), 178–79.

8. *Andros Tracts*, 1:x; Webb, *1676*, 311.

9. William, earl of Craven (1606–97) had a long career of service to the Stuart monarchs and their kin. After serving both Maurice of Orange and Frederick Henry, Craven was knighted by Charles I in 1627. His service to Elizabeth began in 1631, when she and her husband were refugees at The Hague. Craven assisted Frederick in his vain attempts to regain his Bohemian throne. When Charles I was unable to pay the yearly pension of £10,000 to Elizabeth because of his involvement in England's Civil Wars, Craven personally paid the sum and gave money to Charles as well. His estates were confiscated by Cromwell, and Craven petitioned in vain for their return. His property was returned to him after the Restoration. A soldier throughout his life, in 1664 he was named Viscount Craven and Earl of Craven. He was a member of the privy council, colonel of the Grenadier and Coldstream Guards, lieutenant general of the kingdom, and, like Andros's father, master of ceremonies to the king. See *Dictionary of National Biography*, ed. Leslie Stephen and Sidney Lee, 22 vols. (New York, 1908).

10. Webb, *1676*, 311.

11. Samuel Pepys, *The Diary of Samuel Pepys,* ed. R. C. Latham and William Matthews, 11 vols. (Berkeley and Los Angeles, 1970–83), 1:133–34, 136–37, 137n.; Van Nyevelt, *Court Life*, 210.

12. Pepys, *Diary*, 1:130, 137, 137n., 141, 143, 154.

13. Pepys, *Diary*, 2:156; *Andros Tracts*, 1:vi–vii; Tupper, *History of Guernsey*, 357; Van Nyevelt, *Court Life*, 217–18.

14. Stephen Saunders Webb, *Lord Churchill's Coup: The Anglo-American Empire and the Glorious Revolution Reconsidered* (New York, 1995), 15; *English Army Lists and Commissions Registers, 1661–1714*, ed. Charles Dalton (London, 1960), 1:28.

15. Maurice Ashley, *James II* (London, Toronto, and Melbourne, 1977), 78–79; John Childs, *The Army, James II and the Glorious Revolution* (New York, 1980), 1.

16. Ashley, *James II*, 75.

17. Robert C. Ritchie, *The Duke's Province: A Study of New York Politics and Society, 1664–1691* (Chapel Hill, 1977), 15.

18. A. P. Thornton, *West-India Policy Under the Restoration* (Oxford, 1956), 124, 128.

19. Sir Richard Worsley, *The History of the Isle of Wight*, intro. R. M. Robbins (London, 1781, 1975), 136–38.

20. Culpepper eventually found greener (or more golden) pastures in Virginia. See Stephen Saunders Webb, *Governors-General: The English Army and the Definition of the Empire, 1569–1681* (Chapel Hill, 1979), 103–6; Webb, *1676*, 313.

21. Webb, *1676*, 313, 315.

22. Ibid., 314.

23. Dalton, *Army Lists*, 1:75; Vincent T. Harlow, *A History of Barbados, 1625–1685* (New York, 1926, 1969), 180.

24. C. S. S. Higham, *The Development of the Leeward Islands Under the Restoration, 1660–1688* (Cambridge, Eng., 1921), 49, 50.

25. Harlow, *History of Barbados*, 168–69; Higham, *Leeward Islands*, 51; Thornton, *West-India Policy*, 129.

26. Thornton, *West-India Policy*, 130; Higham, *Leeward Islands*, 52–53, 88.

27. Cyril Hamshere, *The British in the Caribbean* (Cambridge, Mass., 1972), 57; Allan Burns, *History of the British West Indies* (London, 1954), 301; Harlow, *History of Barbados*, 144, 153.

28. Willoughby hated the Dutch, to whom he referred as "Brewers and Cheese mongers." See Harlow, *History of Barbados*, 187; Higham, *Leeward Islands*, 55.

29. Tobias Bridge to His Majesty (27 May 1668), CO 1/22, PRO; Webb, *1676*, 315–16, 317.

30. Harlow, *History of Barbados*, 192; Webb, *1676*, 321.

31. Harlow, *History of Barbados*, 189; Webb, *1676*, 319.

32. Tobias Bridge to His Majesty (27 May 1668), CO 1/22, folio 190, PRO.

33. Tobias Bridge to Lord Arlington (17 May 1668), Warrant to Pay Major Andros . . . for clothes (19 Jan. 1671), to pay Major Andros (May 1671), and Tobias Bridge to Andros (15 June 1671), in *Calendar of State Papers Colonial Series, America and West Indies, 1574–1736*, ed. W. Noel Sainsbury, et al., 42 vols. (London, 1860–1953), 157, 221–22, 227, 572–73, hereafter cited as *CSPC*; Tobias Bridge to His Majesty (27 May 1668), CO 1/22, PRO; Harlow, *History of Barbados*, 206; Thornton, *West-India Policy*, 246.

34. Add. Mss. 28076, folio 3, British Library; Webb, *1676*, 322–23.

35. Add. Mss. 19553, 307, British Library; Webb, *1676*, 323, 324; Dalton, *Army Lists*, 1:168–69.

36. Meriol Trevor, *The Shadow of a Crown: The Life Story of James II of England and VII of Scotland*, (London, 1988), 67, 69–70.

37. Webb, *1676*, 324.

38. Hutton, *Charles II*, 272, 282, 284.

39. Trevor, *Shadow of a Crown*, 66.

40. John Evelyn, *Diary of John Evelyn*, ed. E. S. DeBeer, 6 vols. (Oxford, 1955), 4:7. For James's marriage, see 4:27.

41. Trevor, *Shadow of a Crown*, 66; Webb, *1676*, 179.

42. "List of Landgraves . . . in Carolina, 1671–1686," *CSPC*, 312; Webb, *1676*, 326; Stephen Saunders Webb, "The Trials of Sir Edmund Andros," in *The Human Dimensions of Nation Making*, ed. James Kirby Martin (Madison, 1976), 23–53.

43. Webb, *Lord Churchill's Coup*, 82.

44. Memorial of Commissions for Barbados Regiment (30 March 1672), Conditions for Officers of Barbados Regiment (30 March 1672), *CSPC*, 344; *Catalog 150, Sir Edmund Andros, 1637–1714* (New York, 1978), 18–19; Webb, *1676*, 325, 498.

45. Ritchie, *The Duke's Province*, 88.

46. Sir John Knight to earl of Shaftesbury (29 Aug. 1673), *DRNY*, 3:209.

47. "Petition to King and Council" (3 June 1674), *CSPC*, 590.

48. Grant of New Yorke to His Royal Highness (29 June 1674), CO 5/111, PRO; Webb, *1676*, 328.

49. For an acknowledgement by colonials of Andros's linguistic expertise in Dutch and French, see Reverend Rudolphus Varick to the Classis of Amsterdam (30 Sept. 1688) and Reverend Henry Selyus to the Classis of Amsterdam (10 Oct. 1688). Varick mistakenly believed Andros "was a member of the Dutch Reformed Church. *Ecclesiastical Records of the State of New York*, 6 vols., ed. E. G. Corwin (Albany, 1905), 2:956, 958. My thanks to Thomas Carney for calling this correspondence to my attention. See also Bloom, "Sir Edmund Andros," 230.

50. On the necessity for metropolitan authorities to maintain order on the frontier and the ultimate failure of that policy, see Oberg, *Dominion and Civility,* particularly chapters 4 and 5, 113–216, and Conclusion, 217–27.

51. Tupper, *History of Guernsey*, 377.

52. Webb, "The Trials of Sir Edmund Andros," in *The Human Dimension of Nation Making*, ed. Martin, 23–53; Webb, *1676*, 329.

53. Tupper, *History of Guernsey*, 377; Webb, *1676*, 328–29, 330, 331; Webb, "The Trials of Sir Edmund Andros," in *The Human Dimensions of Nation Making*, ed. Martin, 23–53.

54. Commission of Major Edmund Andros (1 July 1674) and Commission of Major Andros to be Captain of a Company of Foot (1 July 1674), *DRNY*, 3:215, 219.

55. *CSPC*, 590, 594, 595, 603; *DRNY*, 2:733; *The Documentary History of the State of New York*, 4 vols., ed. Edmund B. O'Callaghan (Albany, 1850–51), 3: 67, 68, hereafter cited as *DHNY*; Childs, *James II*, 104; Webb, *1676*, 333; Dalton, *Army Lists*, 1:174.

56. Commission Major Edmund Andros (1 July 1674) and Order to Put the Duke's Laws in Force (6 Aug. 1674), *DRNY*, 3:215, 226; Sir John Werden to Edmund Andros (28 Jan. 1676), CO 5/1112, 21, PRO.

57. Webb, *1676*, 338.

58. *CSPC*, 152, 603; Warrant . . . seize Colonel Lovelace's Estate (6 Aug. 1674), *DRNY*, 3:221; Warrant (8 Aug. 1674), CO 5/1112, folio 15, PRO.

59. Knapton was married to Andros's sister, Carterette. Andros's sister was named for her ancestor Elizabeth Carteret, married to grandfather Thomas Andros in 1606. Edmund Andros's younger brother John (born 1642) married Anne Knapton, probably Caesar's sister. His brother George, who later commanded a Maine fort while Edmund was governor-general of the Dominion of New England, married Anne Blondel in 1671. *Andros Tracts*, 1:vi–vii; Carey, *Essays on Guernsey History*, 17; Webb, *1676*, 334; Bloom, "Sir Edmund Andros," 21.

60. Webb, *1676*, 334; Bloom, "Sir Edmund Andros," 240n.; *DHNY*, 3:67–68; Commissions of Anthony Brockholes, Christopher Billop, Caesar Knapton (2 July 1674) and Commission of William Dyre (22 July 1674), *DRNY*, 3:220, 221; John Gourdon Appointed (19 July 1674), CO 5/1112, f. 16, PRO; Instructions for William Dyre (19 July 1674), CO 5/1112, f. 11–13; Bloom, "Sir Edmund Andros," 240n.; Manning was found guilty, publicly humiliated, and stripped of his rank. See Dennis Joseph Maika, "Commerce and Community: Manhattan Merchants in the Seventeenth Century" (Ph.D. diss., New York University, 1995), 430–31n.

CHAPTER 2: NEW YORK: SECURING THE DUKE'S PROVINCE

1. *The Selected Poetry of Marvell*, ed. Frank Kermode.

2. Jasper Dankers and Peter Sluyter, *Journal of a Voyage to New York*, trans. Henry C. Murphy (Brooklyn, 1867 and Ann Arbor, 1966), 100.

3. Edmund Andros to Anthony Colve (22, 23, and 24 Oct. 1674), *DHNY*, 3:68–69; Webb, *1676*, 335.

4. Committee Appointed to Welcome Edmund Andros (3 Nov. 1674), Edmund Andros to Anthony Colve (28 Oct. 1674), proposals sent by Colve (27 Oct. 1674), and Andros to Colve (7 Nov. 1674), *DHNY*, 3:73–76.

5. Colve Absolves Dutch from Allegiance (9 Nov. 1674), Ibid., 3:77.

6. Edmund Andros to Anthony Colve (2 Nov. 1674), Ibid., 3:72.

7. Answers to Inquiries . . . by Sir Edmund Andros, PRO, CO/1111; Ritchie, *The Duke's Province*, 27.

8. Ibid., 20, 23.

9. Ibid., 23.

10. Grant to His Royal Highness of Lands in New England (29 Feb. 1664), CO 5/111, PRO.

11. *DHNY*, 1:68–69, 81, 149–50; *Minutes of the Common Council of the City of New York, 1675–1776*, ed. Herbert L. Osgood (New York, 1905), 1:50–62; Bloom, "Sir Edmund Andros," 241n.

12. Answers to Inquiries . . . by Sir Edmund Andros, CO 5/1111, PRO. See also *DRNY*, 3:311–12; *Calendar of Council Minutes, 1668–1783*, New York State Library *Bulletin*, 58 (Albany, 1902); Dankers and Sluyter, *Journal*, 112; Webb, *1676*, 336.

13. *DHNY*, 1:89.

14. Webb, *1676*, 337; Mary L. Booth, *History of the City of New York* (New York, 1859), 199.

15. Ritchie, *The Duke's Province*, 102.

16. Order to Attach Governor Lovelace's Estate (12 Nov. 1674), *DRNY*, 13:481.

17. Sir John Werden to Andros (13 Feb. 1675), Ibid., 3:229.

18. Ritchie, *Duke's Province*, 104–106, 108; James to Andros (24 May 1680) and Instructions for Willliam Dyre (19 July 1674), CO 5/1112, CO 5/1111, PRO; List of Duties, *Andros Papers*, 3 vols., ed. Peter R. Christoph and Florence A. Christoph (Syracuse, 1989–91), 1:287, hereafter cited as *Andros Papers*; *DHNY*, 1:92; Werden to Andros (28 Jan. 1676), *DRNY*, 3:236.

19. *DRNY*, 3:237.

20. Answers to Inquiries by Andros, CO 5/1111, PRO; Answers to Inquiries (16 Apr. 1678), *DRNY*, 3:262; Ritchie, *The Duke's Province*, 108; Bloom, "Sir Edmund Andros," 23. On New York's formerly active overseas trade with the Netherlands, see Maika, "Commerce and Community," 137–50.

21. On the Navigation Acts, see Oliver M. Dickerson, *The Navigation Acts and the American Revolution* (Philadelphia, 1951), particularly chapters 1 and 2.

22. Charles M. Andrews, *The Colonial Period in American History*, 4 vols. (New Haven, 1937), 3:105–6.

23. Sir John Werden to Andros (13 Feb. 1674), *DRNY*, 3:229.

24. Sir John Werden to Andros (28 Jan. 1676), CO 5/1112, PRO.

25. The instruction was worded as follows: "Lastly, and in regard it may soe happen yt there may be some things omitted wch cannot be soe well foreseen here, as observed by my Leiut Goverr when he shalbe upon ye place; you are therefore to observe and follow such further rules and direccons as you shall from time to time receave from him for ye manageing and collecting of my said Customes." See *DRNY*, 3:222–23. My thanks to Dennis Maika for pointing out the significance of Dyre's instructions. See Maika, "Commerce and Community," 384–85.

26. Sir John Werden to Andros (7 May 1677), *DRNY*, 3:247; Firth Haring Fabend, *A Dutch Family in the Middle Colonies, 1660–1800* (New Brunswick and London, 1991), 20–21. The influence of Andros's Dutch friends was particularly resented by English colonists on Long Island. See Ritchie, *The Duke's Province*, 108. On Andros's favoritism to a select group of Dutch merchants, see Webb, "The Trials of Sir Edmund Andros," in *The Human Dimensions of Nation Making*, ed. Martin, 23–53; Dankers and Sluyter, *Journal*, 353. On the successful business careers of many Dutch women, see K. H. D. Haley, *The British and the Dutch* (London, 1988), 111–12.

27. Cathy Matson, *Merchants and Empire: Trading in Colonial New York* (Baltimore and London, 1998), 79.

28. Dankers and Sluyter, *Journal*, 353.

29. Webb, *1676*, 337; Ritchie, *The Duke's Province*, 108, 122; Maika, "Commerce and Community," 401.

30. Maika, "Commerce and Community," 457.

31. J. M. Sosin, *English America and the Restoration Monarchy of Charles II* (Lincoln, Nebraska, 1980), 148–49.

32. Ritchie, *The Duke's Province*, 116–17; Bloom, "Sir Edmund Andros," 108; Maika, "Commerce and Community," 460.

33. Ritchie, *The Duke's Province*, 114; Sosin, *English America and the Restoration Monarchy*, 146; Maika, "Commerce and Community," 472.

34. Proclamation (14 Mar. 1677), Extracts Edward Randolph's Report (1676) and Sir John Werden to Andros (31 Jan. 1676), *DRNY*, 13:504, 3:241–42, 3:238; Werden to Andros (28 Jan. 1676), CO 5/1112, PRO.

35. Ritchie, *The Duke's Province*, 112; Werden to Andros (31 Jan. 1676), *DRNY*, 3:238.

36. Andros Answers (1678), *DHNY*, 1:91.

37. Werden to Andros (31 Jan. 1676) and Proceedings (11 July 1677), *DRNY*, 3:238, 13:509; Webb, *1676*, 339; Ritchie, *The Duke's Province*, 112; Sosin, *English America and the Restoration Monarchy*, 247.

38. Duke of York to Andros (6 Apr. 1675), *DRNY*, 3:231; Council Minutes, *DHNY*, 1:22.

39. Sir John Werden to Andros (28 Jan. 1676), CO 5/1112; "Prospectus for a Joint Stock Company in the Cod-Fishing Industry" (8 Jan. 1675), in *Andros Papers*, 1:101–102; Matson, *Merchants and Empire*, 50; Sung Bok Kim, *Landlord and Tenant in Colonial New York: Manorial Society, 1664–1775* (Chapel Hill, 1978), 14–15, 19, 20–21.

40. Warrant to Andros (18 May 1678) and Commission to Andros (20 May 1678), *DRNY*, 3:268; Webb, *1676*, 339.

41. Andros's Answer to Mr. Lewin's Report (31 Dec. 1681), *DRNY*, 3:313; Webb, *1676*, 338–39.

42. Webb, *1676*, 337; Ritchie, *The Duke's Province*, 98; Bloom, "Sir Edmund Andros," 242n.; Maika, "Commerce and Community," 379.

43. Answers of Andros (16 Apr. 1678), *DRNY*, 3:260.

44. Petition of Inhabitants of Jamaica to Andros (received 1 Dec. 1674), *Andros Papers*, 1:37.

45. *DRNY*, 13:482.

46. Childs, *James II*, 104; Ritchie, *The Duke's Province*, 101.

47. Duke of York to Andros (6 Apr 1675 and 28 Jan. 1676), *DRNY*, 3:231, 235.

48. Webb, *1676*, 341. On the selection process for the Mayor's Court, see Maika, "Commerce and Community," 461–62.

49. See, for instance, Petition John and Susannah Scudamore to Andros (22 July 1675), Petition Samuel Barker to Andros (1676), John Pell to the Constable of Mamaroneck (3 Nov. 1675), and Bond of Sarah Mintall, (8 Nov. 1675), *Andros Papers*, 1:194, 229, 252, 257.

50. Duke of York to Andros (28 Jan. 1676), *DRNY*, 3:235.

51. Francis Jennings, *The Invasion of America: Indians, Colonialism, and the Cant of Conquest* (New York, 1975), 301.

52. Dixon Ryan Fox, *Yankees and Yorkers* (New York, 1940), 122.

53. Ritchie, *The Duke's Province*, 97–98; Richard S. Dunn, *Puritans and Yankees: The Winthrop Dynasty of New England, 1630–1717* (Princeton, 1962), 181.

54. Duke of York to Andros (6 Apr. 1675), *DRNY*, 3:231; Webb, *1676*, 342–43; Jennings, *Invasion of America*, 301.

55. Andros Proclamation (9 Nov. 1674), *DHNY*, 3:79. On Dutch technical, economic, and social achievements, see Haley, *The British and the Dutch*, 109–10.

56. Andros refused to confirm the patent for Rensselaerswyck, despite the fact that it had been approved by the duke. The title was finally confirmed by Thomas Dongan in 1685 and included about a million acres. Kim, *Landlord and Tenant*, 10–11, 19–20, 36. On the manor, see S. G. Nissenson, *The Patroon's Domain* (New York, 1937).

57. Duke of York to Andros (23 July 1674), *DRNY*, 3:225.

58. Complaint of Nicholas van Rensselaer (17 Aug. 1676), Attestation of 12 Members (17 Aug. 1676); From the Albany Court (22 Aug. 1676), van Rensselaer vs. Jacob Leisler (23 Aug. 1676), Albany Court Minutes (29 Aug. 1676), and Declaration Albany Church Elders (29 Aug. 1676), Leisler Papers Project, ed. David William Voorhees, New York University. Dr. Voorhees supplied me with

all material concerning the trial. His assistance is greatly appreciated. For an account of van Rensselaer's turbulent career, see Lawrence H. Leder, "The Unorthodox Domine: Nicholas van Rensselaer," *New York History* 35 (1954): 166–76; Donna Merwick, "The Writing Man: The Shrinking World of the 'Note Republic' in Dutch Albany"; *de Halve Maen,* 69 (1996): 57–66. For Andros's relations with the Dutch, see Mary Lou Lustig, "Edmund Andros and the Dutch in New York, 1674–1681," *de Halve Maen,* 69 (1996): 67–75. For Cadwallader Colden's view of Andros's role in this dispute, see his 25 June 1759 letter to Alexander Colden in Smith, Jr., *History of the Province of New York,* 1:291–92. See also Sosin, *English America and the Restoration Monarchy,* 246.

59. Edmund Andros to Albany Magistrates (16 Sept. 1676), Proclamation by Governor (18 Sept. 1676), Governor in Council (23 Sept. and 23 Oct. 1676), Leisler Papers Project, ed. David William Voorhees. New York University.

60. *DRNY,* 3:300–301, 680; Andros to Albany Officials (16 Sept. 1676), *Andros Papers,* 1:436.

61. *DRNY,* 3:300–301.

62. Webb, *1676,* 337. On the precedent for the officials' refusal to take the oath, see Maika, "Commerce and Community," 431.

63. Petition of the Dutch Burghers n.d., *DRNY,* 2:740–43; Sosin, *English America and the Restoration Monarchy,* 245; Webb, *1676,* 337.

64. Werden to Andros (28 Jan. 1676), *DRNY,* 3:237.

65. See Warrant to Seize the Property of Nicolas Bayard (13 Oct. 1675), *Andros Papers,* 3:165; Maika, "Commerce and Community," 433.

66. Council Minutes (1 and 2 Nov. 1675), *Andros Papers,* 1:243, 245; Maika, "Commerce and Community," 435.

67. Petition of Cornelius Steenwyck, et al. to Andros (2 Nov. 1675) and Council Meeting (3 Nov. 1676), *Andros Papers,* 1:248–50, 251; Maika, "Commerce and Community," 434–45.

68. Craven, *The Colonies in Transition,* 106, 202.

69. Sosin, *English America and the Restoration Monarchy,* 146–47.

70. Andrews, *Colonial Period,* 3:292–93.

71. Commissions to Cantwell and Tom (Nov. 1674), *DRNY,* 12:515.

72. Andros to Governors of Maryland and Virginia (Nov. 1674), *DRNY,* 12:513–14.

73. Andros to Edmund Cantwell (27 Mar. 1675), *Documents Relative to the Colonial History of the State of New Jersey,* ed. William A. Whitehead, 43 vols. (Newark, N. J., 1880–1949), 1:179–80, hereafter cited as *DRNJ*; Maryland had long disputed the duke's claim to Delaware, arguing that Baltimore's patent extended north of New Castle. See Council to Col. Francis Lovelace, *Archives of Maryland, Proceedings of the Council of Maryland,* 69 vols. ed. William Hand Browne (Baltimore, 1887), 5:58, hereafter cited as *Maryland Archives.*

74. Andros to Cantwell (23 Apr. 1675) and Conference of Andros with Magistrates, 1675, *DRNJ,* 1:181, 183; *DRNY,* 12:530; Webb, *1676,* 346.

75. Andros to Lord Baltimore (15 May 1675), *Andros Papers,* 1:144–45; Council's Opinion (1675), *DRNY,* 13:487.

76. J. M. Sosin, *English America and the Revolution of 1688* (Lincoln and London, 1982), 232–33.

77. Webb, *1676,* 350; Andros's Warrant (25 Sept. 1676) and Council Meeting (5 Dec. 1676), *DRNJ,* 1:187–88, 189. On the Quakers' reluctance to pay duties to New York, see Sosin, *English America and the Restoration Monarchy,* 234.

78. Andros to Commander at Newcastle (8 Nov. 1676), Meeting Commander

and Justices at Newcastle (8 Dec. 1676 and 9 May 1678), Council Meeting (22 May 1678), Council Order (22 May 1678), C. Billop, et al. to J. Fenwicke (3 June 1678), Fenwick's Answer (4 June 1678), Court to New York Council, Meeting Commander at Newcastle (17 and 24 July 1678), Andros' Warrant (28 Oct. 1678), and Council Order to Fenwick (22 May 1678), *DRNJ,* 1:189, 190–91, 191–92, 196–97, 198, 199, 201, 202–3, 204, 279; John E. Pomfret, *Colonial New Jersey: A History* (New York, 1973), 39.

79. Robert G. Johnson, *An Historical Account of the First Settlement of Salem . . . by John Fenwick* (Philadelphia, 1839), 38; Webb, *1676,* 350.

80. *DRNJ,* l:215; Pomfret, *Colonial New Jersey,* 39.

81. Ritchie, *The Duke's Province,* 119.

82. Werden to Andros (31 Aug. 1676), *DRNY,* 3:239; Ritchie, *The Duke's Province,* 119. Fenwick's wife apparently followed Andros to England in 1678 in an attempt to secure her husband's release. Andros was adamant that the decision to release Fenwick had to come from the court of assizes. In discouragement, Mrs. Fenwick warned her husband that Andros "has great power and friendship, as I hear, more than ever," indicating it would be unwise to alienate him further. See Johnson, *An Historical Account of the First Settlement of Salem,* 46–50; also quoted in Bloom, "Sir Edmund Andros," 262n.

83. *DRNJ,* 1:292.

84. Webb, *1676,* 344; Jennings, *Invasion of America,* 300–301; Fox, *Yankees and Yorkers,* 123–26.

85. Duke of York to Andros (6 Apr. 1675), *DRNY,* 3:230; Andros, "Heads of an Inquiry," CO 5/111, PRO.

CHAPTER 3. THE IROQUIS AND THE GOVERNOR, PART 1

1. Governor Dongan's Report on the State of the Province (1684), *DRNY,* 3:393.

2. Daniel K. Richter, "War and Culture: The Iroquois Experience," *William and Mary Quarterly,* 3d ser., 40 (1983): 528–59, hereafter cited as *W&MQ.*

3. Wraxall, *DRNY,* 3:393.

4. Cadwallader Colden, *The History of the Five Indian Nations Depending on the Province of New-York in America,* 2 vols. (1727, 1747, Ithaca, 1958), xxi.

5. Paul A. W. Wallace, *Indians in Pennsylvania,* rev. ed. (Harrisburg, 1961, 1981), 93, 95; Anthony F. C. Wallace, *Death and Rebirth of the Seneca* (New York, 1969, 1972), 21; Dean R. Snow, *The Iroquois* (Oxford and Cambridge, Mass., 1994), 110; "Adriaen Cornelissen van der Donck, Description of New Netherland, 1653," trans. Diederik Goedhuys, in *In Mohawk Country: Early Narratives About a Native People,* ed. Dean R. Snow, Charles T. Gehring, and William A. Starna (Syracuse, 1996), 104–30.

6. Thomas Elliot Norton, *The Fur Trade in Colonial New York, 1686-1776* (Madison, 1974), 12; *Peter Wraxall's An Abridgment of the Indian Affairs in the Colony of New York, 1678-1751,* ed. Charles H. McIlwaine (Cambridge, Mass., 1915), lvi.

7. James Axtell, "The First Consumer Revolution," in *Beyond 1492: Encounters in Colonial North America* (New York and Oxford, 1992), 132, 135–36, 138; Norton, *Fur Trade,* 43.

8. Bruce G. Trigger, *The Huron: Farmers of the North* (New York, 1969), 1; Norton, *Fur Trade,* 10; Webb, *1676,* 292; Snow, *The Iroquois,* 114–17.

9. Wallace, *Indians in Pennsylvania*, 21.

10. Letter from New London to Andros (29 June 1675) and John Winthrop to [Andros?] (29 June 1675), *Andros Papers*, 1:180, 181; Webb, *1676*, 351–52; Jennings, *Invasion of America*, 302.

11. *Narratives of the Indian Wars,* ed. Charles H. Lincoln (New York, 1913, 1941, 1966), 5, 9; Sydney V. James, *Colonial Rhode Island, A History* (New York, 1975), 65; Douglas Edward Leach, *Flintlock and Tomahawk: New England in King Philip's War* (New York, 1958, 1966), 34.

12. Andros to Winthrop, Andros to Various Other Governors, Andros to Carteret (4 July 1675), *Andros Papers*, 1:182–83; Jennings, *Invasion of America,* 302–4.

13. As Bernard Bailyn points out, the Restoration was doubly troublesome for New England Puritans. Not only did it establish the authority and pre-eminence of Anglicanism, it also further defined all who refused the authority of the Church of England as Nonconformists. The colonies' growing trade also caused English officials to attempt to achieve a better control over that trade through its administrative apparatus. See *New England Merchants in the Seventeenth Century* (Boston, 1955 and New York, 1964), 112–14.

14. George Cartwright to Sir Henry Bennet (7 Feb. 1665) *DRNY*, 3:89; Ritchie, *The Duke's Province,* 19–20.

15. Andros to John Winthrop (4 July 1675) and Andros to Philip Carteret (4 July 1675), *Andros Papers*, 1:183; Jennings, *Invasion of America*, 307.

16. Meeting Governor and Council (8 July 1675) and Letter to Robert Chapman and Capt. Thomas Bull, 8 July 1675, *Public Records of the Colony of Connecticut from 1665–1678,* ed. J. Hammond Trumbull, 15 vols., (Hartford, 1852 and New York, 1968), 3:334, hereafter cited as *Public Records Connecticut.*

17. Governor Dongan's Report of the State of the Province (1684), *DRNY*, 3:393; Robert Chapman to John Winthrop (8 July 1675), *Public Records Connecticut*, 2:580, 582n.; *DHNY*, 1:117; Webb, *1676*, 351; Jennings, *Invasion of America*, 307–8; Dunn, *Puritans and Yankees*, 183–84.

18. *Public Records Connecticut*, 2:583–84, 262. Before returning to New York, Andros sent one sloop to New London to inquire about the health of Fitz-John Winthrop, who was ill since late June. Dunn, *Puritans and Yankees*, 206; Webb, *1676*, 352.

19. Andros to Magistrates of Connecticut (8 July 1675) and Andros to Governor of Boston (8 July 1675), *Andros Papers*, 1:184; Governor and Council of Connecticut (22 July 1675), *Public Records Connecticut*, 3:342–43; Jennings, *Invasion of America*, 307.

20. Knight, *Orthodoxies in Massachusetts*, 14–16, 22.

21. Robert Chapman to Capt. Thomas Bull (13 July 1675), *Public Records Connecticut*, 2:583–84; Webb, *1676*, 353.

22. Andros Instructions (30 Aug. 1676), *DRNY*, 12:486; Webb, *1676*, 361, 363; Norton, *Fur Trade*, 45.

23. Ritchie, *The Duke's Province,* 113; Norton, *The Fur Trade*, 43, 46–47; Andros to Magistrates (31 Oct. 1678), *Andros Papers*, 3:38; Andros's Instructions to Commissaries at Schenectady (30 Aug. 1675), *DRNY*, 13:486; Lawrence H. Leder, *Robert Livingston and the Politics of Colonial New York, 1654–1728,* (Chapel Hill, 1961), 15, 19.

24. Council Minutes (24 Oct. 1675), *DRNY*, 13:491; Leder, *Robert Livingston*, 15.

25. Short Account of General Concerns in New York (1678) and Proclamation (16 Sept. 1675), *DRNY*, 3:254, 13:484–85.

26. Edward Randolph Report, *DRNY*, 3:243; Oberg, *Dominion and Civility*, 166.

27. Roger F. Duncan, *Coastal Maine: A Maritime History* (New York, 1992), 127–30.

28. Andros Proclamation (16 Sept. 1675), *DRNY*, 13:484–85.

29. Minutes Meeting with Unchechaug Indians (23 May 1676), *Andros Papers*, 1:373, 374.

30. Minutes Meeting Tackpousha and Sequetauk Indians (13 and 27 Mar. 1677) and Order to Hempstead by Andros (13 Mar. 1677), *Andros Papers,* 2:33–34, 52.

31. Deputy Governor and Council to Andros (6 Oct. 1675), *Collections*, Connecticut Historical Society, 31 vols. (Hartford, 1924), 21:226; Reading of "Heads of Inquiry," by Sir Edmund Andros (9 April 1678), Answer of William Stoughton and Peter Buckley (24 April 1678), and Order in Council (24 April 1678), CO 5/111, CO 5/1111, PRO.

32. Massachusetts Puritans were also accused by Edward Randolph of conducting "a private trade with the French and Indians" from Nova Scotia. See Extracts Edward Randolph's Report to the Council of Trade (1676), *DRNY*; Webb, *1676*, 365–66. For New York sales of weapons to the French, see Mary Lou Lustig, *Privilege and Prerogative: New York's Provincial Elite, 1710–1776* (Madison, Teaneck, London, and Toronto, 1995), 62.

33. Council Minutes (24 Oct. 1675), *DRNY*, 13:491; Andros Order (11 Mar. 1676), *Andros Papers,* 1:345; Webb, *1676*, 365–66.

34. Andros to William Leete (6 Jan. 1676), *Public Records Connecticut*, 2:397; Webb, *1676*, 367.

35. Andros to Magistrates at Esopus (6 Jan. 1676), *DRNY*, 13:493.

36. Leete to Andros (13 Jan. 1676), *Public Records Connecticut*, 2:398; Jennings, *Invasion of America*, 314.

37. Leete to Andros (13 Jan. 1676), *Public Records Connecticut*, 2:398.

38. Andros to Council (20 Jan. 1676), *Public Records Connecticut*, 2:404.

39. *DRNY*, 3:255, 13:493–94; *Narratives Indian Wars*, 89; Jennings, *Invasion of America*, 313. Governor Winthrop died in Boston on 6 April 1676. Andros to Leete (4 Feb. 1676), Council to Andros (10 Feb. 1676), Council to Andros (7 Mar. 1676), and Council to Andros (19 Mar. 1676), *Public Records Connecticut*, 2:406, 407, 414, 420.

40. Short Account of the General Concerns of New York (1678), *DRNY*, 3:255; Webb, *1676*, 368.

41. *DRNY*, 3:265; Jennings, *Invasion of America*, 315.

42. Council Meeting (26 Feb. 1676), *DRNY*, 13:493–94.

43. Andros to Lt. Gerrit Teunise (4 March 1676, *DRNY*, 13:495; Webb, *1676*, 369, 370; Jennings, *Invasion of America*, 314.

44. Andros to Lt. Gerrit Teunise (4 March 1676), Short Account (Mar. 1678), Minutes Meeting with Two Sachems (14 Apr. 1676), Meeting with Sachems (27 Apr. 1676), and Council Meeting (29 May 1676), *DRNY*, 13:495–96, 497, 3:255; Andros to Teunise (4 March 1676), can also be found in *Andros Papers*, 1:337; Webb, *1676*, 369–70; Jennings, *Invasion of America*, 317.

45. Council to Andros (19 Mar. 1676), *Public Records Connecticut*, 2:420.

46. William Coddington to Governor and Council of Massachusetts (9 Jan. 1676), *Andros Papers*, 1:315; James, *Colonial Rhode Island*, 25–26, 93; William G. McLoughlin, *Rhode Island, A Bicentennial History* (New York, 1970), 21, 36–37; *Narratives Indian Wars*, 6; Leach, *Flintlock and Tomahawk*, 177.

47. Andros to Governor of Massachusetts (22 May 1676), *Andros Papers*, 1:371.

48. Council Minutes (29 May 1676), *DRNY*, 13:496–97; Jennings, *Invasion of America*, 317–18.

49. Duke of York to Andros (28 Jan. 1676), Short Account (Mar. 1678), *DRNY*, 3:235, 255; Andros to Connecticut Council (n.d.), *Public Records Connecticut*, 2:437.

50. Andros to Council (5 July 1676), Council to Andros (8 July 1676), and Council to Andros (19 Mar. 1676) and 4 Sept. 1677, *Public Records Connecticut*, 2:461, 462, 466–67, 419–20; Webb, *1676*, 372–73; Jennings, *Invasion of America*, 321.

51. Council to Andros (19 Aug. 1676), *Public Records Connecticut*, 2:469–70; Jennings, *Invasion of America*, 317–18, 321.

52. Council to Andros (19 March 1676 and 4 Sept. 1677), *Public Records Connecticut*, 2:419–20, 21:268; Webb, *1676*, 372–73; Jennings, *Invasion of America*, 321.

53. *Narratives of the Indian Wars*, 105; Edward Randolph's Report to the Council of Trade and Plantations, 1676, *DRNY*, 3:243–44. Jill Lepore notes that minister Cotton Mather went to Plymouth several years after the war to see Philip's head. While viewing it, he stole the jaw. See Lepore, *The Name of War: King Philip's War and the Origins of American Identity* (New York, 1998), 175.

54. Council Minutes (8 Sept. 1676 and 11 Oct. 1676), *DRNY*, 13:501–2.

55. Duncan, *Coastal Maine*, 130.

56. Colin G. Calloway, *The Western Abenakis of Vermont, 1600–1800: War, Migration and the Survival of an Indian People* (Norman, Okla. and London, 1990), 79, 82–83.

57. Council Minutes (12 Mar. 1677), *DRNY*, 13:503. Colin Calloway notes that during the first year well over two hundred Sokokis, Pocumtucks, Nonotucks, Woronokes, Agawans, Pennacooks, Narragansetts, Nipmucks, and Wampanoags settled at Schaghticoke where they gradually lost their tribal identities. See *The Western Abenakis of Vermont, 83.*

58. Andros to Leete (3 Apr. 1677) and Council Meeting (10 Apr. 1677), *Public Records Connecticut*, 2:492, 493; Snow, *The Iroquois*, 125.

59. Pynchon and Richards to Andros (Apr. 1677), *Public Records Connecticut*, 2:494.

60. *DRNY*, 13:529.

61. Jennings, *The Ambiguous Iroquois Empire*, 149; Wraxall, *Indian Affairs*, 8; Colden, *History of the Five Indian Nations,* 21; Lawrence H. Leder, ed., *Livingston Indian Records* (Gettysburg, 1956), 46; Short Account (March 1678), *DRNY*, 3:246.

62. *Collections*, Connecticut Historical Society, 21:268–69.

63. Short Account (Mar. 1678), *DRNY*, 3:255–56, 260; Jennings, *Invasion of America*, 325; Duncan, *Coastal Maine,* 130.

64. *Narratives of the Indian Wars*, 184–85.

65. Calloway, *The Western Abenakis*, 83.

66. Andros to Blathwayt (16 Sept. 1678), *DRNY*, 3:271–72.

67. T. H. Breen, "War, Taxes, and Political Brokers: The Ordeal of Massachusetts Bay," in *Puritans and Adventurers: Change and Persistence in Early America* (New York and Oxford, 1980), 87.

68. Michael Garibaldi Hall, *Edward Randolph and the American Colonies, 1676–1703* (Chapel Hill, 1960), 32–35.

CHAPTER 4. THE IROQUOIS AND THE GOVERNOR, PART 2

1. Mohawk Answers (6 Aug. 1677), *Livingston Indian Records*, ed. Leder, 43–46.

2. On the effects of Iroquois expansion on England's colonies, see Webb, *1676*, xvii, 3–4.

3. *Livingston Indian Records*, ed. Leder, 22; Webb, *1676*, 71–72, 290–91; Jennings, *Invasion of America*, 26; Jennings, *Ambiguous Iroquois Empire*, 127.

4. Jennings, *Ambiguous Iroquois Empire*, 136, 139.

5. Andros to Albany Commissioners (19 Apr. 1675), *DRNY*, 13:483, Snow claims the Susquehannas were thoroughly defeated by the Iroquois by 1672. *The Iroquois*, 121. Norton places the year at 1675. *The Fur Trade*, 16.

6. Andros to Edmund Cantwell (n.d. and 27 Mar. 1675), *DRNY*, 12:516, 518.

7. Andros to Cantwell (23 Apr. 1675), *DRNY*, 12:519.

8. Matthias Nicolls to Captain Chambers and George Hall (24 Apr. 1675), *DRNY*, 13:484.

9. Andros to Edmund Cantwell (30 Apr. 1675), *DRNY*, 12:520.

10. For conflicting land use patterns of the English and the Indians, see Oberg, *Dominion and Civility*, 227.

11. Conference (13 May 1675), *DRNY*, 12:523–24

12. Andros to Cantwell (10 Dec. 1675), *DRNY*, 12:542.

13. Edmund Cantwell to Andros (11 May 1676), *DRNY*, 12:546.

14. Special Court (13 May 1675), *DRNY*, 12:524.

15. Court at Peter Rambo's (17 May 1675), *DRNY*, 12:527; Webb, *1676*, 348–49.

16. *Narratives of the Insurrections, 1675–1690*, ed. Charles M. Andrews (New York, 1915, 1967), 16–17, 19–20, 105–6; Letter to King (1676); *Maryland Archives*, 5:134; Jennings, *Ambiguous Iroquois Empire*, 145.

17. Council Minutes (22 Sept. 1675), *DRNY*, 12:541.

18. Andros to Thomas Notley (21 Oct. 1675), *DRNY*, 13:491.

19. Andros to Thomas Notley (10 Dec. 1675), *DRNY*, 12:543.

20. Webb, *1676*, 57–65, 84.

21. Werden to Andros (30 Nov. 1676), *DRNY*, 3:245; Webb, *1676*, 85–86, 99, 128–39, 159, 163.

22. Letter to King (1676), *Maryland Archives*, 5:148.

23. Minutes Meeting Susquehanna Indians (2 June 1676)and Indians' Reply (3 June 1676), *Andros Papers*, 1:378–79; Jennings, *Ambiguous Iroquois Empire*, 149.

24. Indians' Reply (3 June 1676), *Andros Papers*, 1:379.

25. Minutes Meeting (2 and 3 June 1676), *DRNY*, 13:498; Webb *1676*, 293.

26. Notley to Berkeley (6 Aug. 1676), *Maryland Archives*, 15:122; Jennings, *Ambiguous Iroquois Empire*, 151.

27. Andros Commission and Instructions to John Collier (23 Sept. 1676), *DRNY*, 12:556–57; Jennings, *Ambiguous Iroquois Empire*, 152.

28. Notley to Baltimore (22 Jan. 1677), *Maryland Archives*, 5:153; Webb, *1676*, 295.

29. Resolution (6 April 1677), *DRNY*, 12:572.

30. Commission to Henry Coursey (30 Apr. 1677), *Maryland Archives*, 5:244. Typical Indian presents included duffels, shirts, pants, socks, hats, kettles, knives, lead, and powder. See "Indian Present" (1676), *DRNY*, 13:502.

31. Notley to Coursey (2 June 1677), *Maryland Archives*, 5:247–49.

32. Instructions to Coursey (30 Apr. 1677), *Maryland Archives*, 5:245–46.

33. Instructions to Coursey (30 April 1677) and Maryland Council Meeting (24 June 1677), *Maryland Archives*, 5:246, 15:154; Helmer Wiltbank to Andros, 26 Feb. 1677 and 11 June 1677, *DRNY*, 12:571, 576; Andrews, *Colonial Period American History*, 3:293.

34. Propositions made by Col. Henry Coursey from . . . Maryland (22 June 1677), *Maryland Archives*, 5:251–52.

35. Notley to Virginia Governor (22 June 1677), *Maryland Archives*, 5:250–51; Webb, *1676*, 384–85.

36. Andros to Albany Magistrates (12 July 1677), *DRNY*, 13:509.

37. Council Minutes (6 June 1677), *DRNY*, 13:507, 12:576–77; *Maryland Archives*, 5:243–46; Webb, *1676*, 295.

38. Propositions of Col. Henry Coursey (30 June 1677), *Livingston Indian Records*, ed. Leder, 42.

39. Ibid., 42; Propositions made to the Maques and Sinnequo Indians (19 July 1677), *Maryland Archives*, 5:254.

40. Onondaga and Oneida Answers to Propositions of Coursey (20 and 21 July 1677) and Mohawk Answers (6 Aug. 1677), *Livingston Indian Records*, ed. Leder, 43–46; *Maryland Archives*, 5:254–57; *DRNY*, 13:510.

41. Seneca and Caiuga Answers (22 Aug. 1677), *Maryland Archives*, 5:258–60.

42. Webb, *1676*, 298.

43. Morgan quoted in Wraxall, *Indian Affairs*, xxxvii.

44. Jennings, *Ambiguous Iroquois Empire*, 374–75; Wallace, *Jefferson and the Indians*, 338.

45. Wallace, *Jefferson and the Indians*, 214–15; Wallace, *Indians in Pennsylvania*, 108–9.

46. Mohawk Answers (6 Aug. 1677), Proclamation (5 Oct. 1677), and Lord Baltimore to the Governor of New York (4 Mar. 1682), *Maryland Archives*, 5:256–58, 15:157; Leder, *Livingston Indian Records*, 42, 43, 45.

47. Lord Baltimore to William Blathwayt (11 Mar. 1682), *Maryland Archives*, 5:348–49. On Blathwayt's long and successful career, see Stephen Saunders Webb, "William Blathwayt, Imperial Fixer: From Popish Plot to Glorious Revolution" and "William Blathwayt, Imperial Fixer: Muddling Through to Empire, 1689–1717" *W&MQ*, 3d ser., 25 (1968): 3–21 and 26 (1969): 373–415.

48. Duke of York to Andros (7 May 1677), *DRNY*, 3:246.

49. Werden to Andros (7 May 1677), *DRNY*, 3:247.

50. A Short Account of the General Concerns of New York, *DRNY*, 3:257.

51. Power of Attorney, Andros to Marie Andros (16 Nov. 1677), *Andros Papers*, 2:162, 234; Short Account (Mar. 1678), *DRNY*, 3:247, 257.

Chapter 5. Andros and Imperial Machinations

1. *Dryden, Poems and Prose*, comp. Douglas Grant (New York, 1955).

2. John Evelyn, *The Diary of John Evelyn*, ed. E. S. DeBeer, 6 vols. (Oxford, 1955), 4:122, 124; Trevor, *Shadow of a Crown*, 76; Haley, *Shaftesbury*, 434–45.

3. On Shaftesbury's role in the formation of the Whig party see Haley, *Shaftesbury*, particularly chapter 17, "The 'Country Party,' 1674–1675," 348–71. On Shaftesbury's relationship with Monmouth, see 465–66.

4. Jones, *The First Whigs*, 5.

5. A Short Account of the General Concerns of New York from Edmund Andros (March 1678), *DRNY*, 3:254–57.

6. *CSPC*, Lords of Trade (8 Apr. 1678), 236.

7. Order in Council Calling for Information about New York and New England (8 Apr. 1678), Andros Answers Questions about New England, (9 Apr. 1678), and Andros' Short Account of Assistance, (18 Apr. 1678), *DRNY*, 3:260–65.

8. Sosin, *English America and the Restoration Monarchy*, 248.

9. Ritchie, *The Duke's Province*, 115.

10. Andros to Blathwayt (10 Sept. 1678), CO 5/1111, PRO; Salisbury to Brockholes (27 June 1678 and 11 July 1678), *DRNY*, 13:520–21.

11. Orders and Instructions for S. Ely and B. Waite (11 July 1678), Salisbury to Brockholes (15 July 1678, 23 July 1678, and 25 July 1678), and Mohawk Answers (July 1678), *DRNY*, 13:522, 525, 527, 528.

12. Brockholes to Salisbury (2 Aug. 1678), *DRNY*, 13:529–30.

13. Commissioners to Andros (6 Sept. 1678), Andros to Commissioners (10 Sept. 1678), Commissioners to Andros (14 Sept. 1678), William Leete to Andros (18 Sept. 1678), and Andros to Commissioners (25 Sept. 1678 and 27 Sept. 1678), *DRNY*, 3:273, 274, 275, 276. See also William Leete and John Allyn to Andros (29 Oct. 1678) and Andros to Leete and Allyn (18 Nov. 1678), *Public Records Connecticut*, 3:263, 264.

14. Andros to William Blathwayt (16 Sept. 1678 and 12 Oct. 1678), *DRNY*, 3:271–73; Andros to Blathwayt (10 Sept. 1678), CO5/1111, PRO.

15. Andros to Blathwayt (16 Sept. 1678) CO5/1111, PRO; *DRNY*, 3:217–73.

16. Andros to Blathwayt (25 Mar. 1679); CO5/1111, PRO, 3:277; *CSPC*, 10:344–45.

17. Colden, *History of the Five Indian Nations*, 25.

18. Ibid., 26.

19. Ibid., 27; Wraxall, *Indian Affairs*, 9.

20. Council Minutes (31 July 1679 and 2 Aug. 1679), *Andros Papers*, 3:135, 136; Andros to Salisbury (8 Aug. 1679), *DRNY*, 13:536–37.

21. Evelyn, *Diary*, 4:153–54; Trevor, *Shadow of a Crown*, 87, 91; Ashley, *James II*, 119. On the Popish Plot, see Haley, *Shaftesbury*, chapters 21 and 22, "The Popish Plot" and "The End of the Cavalier Parliament," 453–67, 468–97.

22. Trevor, *Shadow of a Crown*, 93; John Miller, *Popery and Politics, 1660–1688* (Cambridge, Eng. 1973), 155–56.

23. Jones, *First Whigs*, 6, 34, 35, 69.

24. Quoted in Ashley, *James II*, 121.

25. Jones, *Charles II*, 153–54; Trevor, *Shadow of a Crown*, 105–6, 107; Ashley, *James II*, 122, 127–29.

26. Trevor, *Shadow of a Crown*, 107; Ashley, *James II*, 128–29.

27. Proposition of William Kendall to Mohawks (26 Sept. 1679), Colden, *History of the Five Indian Nations*, 30; Council Minutes (28 Sept. 1679), *Andros Papers*, 3:143; Proposition by William Kendall (25 Sept. 1679), and Sachems' Reply (6 Oct. 1679), *Livingston Indian Records*, ed. Leder, 49, 52.

28. Kendall Replies (6 Oct. 1679) and Proposition of Kendall to Oneidas (30 Oct. 1679), *Livingston Indian Records*, ed. Leder, 52–54.

29. Oneidas' Answer (31 Oct. 1679), *Livingston Indian Records*, ed. Leder, 55–56.

30. Hall, *Edward Randolph*, 53–54, 80–83.

31. Craven, *Colonies in Transition*, 203.

32. Dankers and Sluyter, *Journal*, 347, 352n.

33. Andros to Carteret (8 Mar. 1680), *Andros Papers*, 3:238.

34. Andros to Carteret (8 Mar. 1680), *DRNY*, 13:539. See also *Andros Papers*, 3:238; Carteret to Andros (8 Mar. 1680), *DRNJ*, 1:294–95.

35. Declaration (13 Mar. 1680), *DRNY*, 13:539 and *Andros Papers*, 3:244; Carteret to Andros (29 Mar. 1680), *DRNJ*, 1:299.

36. Matthias Nicolls's Account (5 Apr. 1680), *Andros Papers*, 3:256–59.

37. Andros to Blathwayt (18 May 1680), Blathwayt Papers, Colonial Williamsburg.

38. Carteret to Mr. Coustrier, 9 July 1680 *DRNJ*, 1:316.

39. Dankers and Sluyter, *Journal*, 348, 352n.

40. Ibid., 349.

41. Ibid., 350.

42. Ibid., 351.

43. Ibid., 346, 351, 352, 352n. Minutes Special Court of Assizes (27 and 28 May 1680), and Carteret to Capt. Bollen (9 July 1680), *DRNJ*, 1:303–4, 316–17. Andros was apparently disturbed by the proceedings. Dankers and Sluyter reported that when they visited the governor-general on June 7, Andros kept them "waiting a long time." When the men were finally called before the governor, he addressed them "not with his accustomed kindness, but a little peevishly, as if he were tired of us and we annoyed him." See *Journal*, 345. Philip Carteret resumed his post in New Jersey in March 1681, after Andros left for England. See John E. Pomfret, "Philip Carteret," in *The Governors of New Jersey, 1664–1974*, ed. Paul A. Stellhorn and Michael J. Birkner (Trenton, 1982), 15–17.

44. Deposition Richard Mann (9 June 1680) and Warrant to New York Sheriff (9 and 11 June 1680), *Andros Papers*, 3:290, 291, 294.

45. Council Minutes 13 Aug. 1680, *DRNJ*, 1:322.

46. Matthias Nicolls, Journal (1–7 June, 1680) and Answers New Jersey Assembly (2 June 1680). *Andros Papers*, 3:287, 288, 300–302; New Jersey Assembly (2 June 1680) and Address New Jersey Assembly 2 June 1680, *DRNJ*, 1:311.

47. Isaac Whitehead to Andros (10 June 1680), Council Meeting (2–12 June 1680), and Council Minutes (4 June 1680), *Andros Papers*, 3:293, 296–99, 303; New York Council Meeting (12 June 1680), *DRNJ*, 1:311.

48. Protest of Woodbridge Residents (14 July 1680), Justices of Woodbridge and Piscattaway to Andros (16 July 1680), and Order to Constables (25 Aug. 1680), *Andros Papers*, 3:331, 367.

49. Warrant (4 Aug. 1680) and Council Minutes (13 Aug. 1680), *DRNJ*, 1:322.

50. Brockholes to Andros (14 May 1681), *DRNY*, 13:550; Andrews, *Colonial Period American History*, 3:154, 169–70.

51. Werden to Penn (16 July 1681), *DRNY*, 3:290; Maryland Council Minutes (13 Apr. 1683); *Maryland Archives*, 5:392–93; Andrews, *Colonial Period American History*, 3:293–94; Vincent Buranelli, *The King and the Quaker: A Study of William Penn and James II (Philadelphia, 1962)*, 60.

Chapter 6. The Trial of Sir Edmund Andros

1. Andros's Answers (31 Dec. 1681), *DRNY*, 3:303 and CO 1/47, PRO.

2. Trevor, *Shadow of a Crown*, 110–11, 115; Ashley, *James II*, 133.

3. Philip Carteret to Sir George Carteret (9 July 1680), *DRNJ*, 1:314–15; Sosin, *English America and the Restoration Monarchy*, 240.

4. Sir John Werden to Andros (10 Mar. 1679), *DRNY*, 3:276; Bloom, "Sir Edmund Andros," 258n.

5. Ritchie, *The Duke's Province*, 119.

6. Duke of York to Andros (24 May 1680) and Sir John Werden to Andros (24 May 1680), *DRNY*, 3:283, 284; CO 5/1112, PRO.

7. Stephen Saunders Webb, "William Blathwayt, Imperial Fixer: From Popish Plot to Glorious Revolution," *W&MQ*, 3d ser., 25 (1968): 3–21. See also Sosin, *English America and the Restoration Monarchy*, 174–75.

8. Werden to Andros (24 May 1680) and (1 July 1680), *DRNY*, 283–84 and CO 5/1112, PRO.

9. Governor Andros's Answer (24 Dec. 1681), *DRNY*, 3:308. On Culpepper's brief but profitable Virginia career, see Webb, "The Reluctant Dragon: Thomas Culpepper and the Constitution of the Empire," chap. 8 in *Governors-General*, 373–425. See also Webb, "The Trials of Sir Edmund Andros," in *Human Dimensions of Nation Making*, ed. Martin, 23–53.

10. Duke's Commission to John Lewen (24 May 1680) and Instructions for John Lewen (24 May 1680), *DRNY*, 3:279–82; Council Meeting (29 and 30 Oct. 1680), *Andros Papers*, 3:439, 440.

11. Quoted in Ritchie, *The Duke's Province,* 123.

12. Ibid., 124.

13. Evelyn, *Diary*, 4:225, 226, 233.

14. Trevor, *Shadow of a Crown*, 120–22; Jones, *Charles II*, 8, 161, 165, 167. The king's order to Craven is quoted in J. R. Jones, *Charles II, Royal Politician* (London, Boston, and Sydney, 1987), 167.

15. Haley, *Shaftesbury*, 121, 636.

16. Jones, *Charles II*, 167; Trevor, *Shadow of a Crown*, 131; Ashley, *James II*, 131; Haley, *Shaftesbury*, 637–38.

17. Court of Assizes, New York, to Secretary of State (1681) and Proceedings Against Mr. Dyre (29 June 1681), *DRNY*, 3:287, 288–89, and CO 1/47, PRO; Webb, "The Trials of Sir Edmund Andros," in *Human Dimensions of Nation Making*," ed. Martin, 23–53; Sosin, *English America and the Restoration Monarchy*, 249.

18. Haley, *Shaftesbury*, 709.

19. Ibid., 639.

20. J. R. Jones, *The First Whigs: The Politics of the Exclusion Crises, 1678–1683* (London, 1961), 182, 189–90, 193–94; Jones, *Charles II*, 173; Haley, *Shaftesbury*, 654, 680, 732.

21. Mr. Lewen's Report (1681), *DRNY*, 3:303–7 and CO 1/47, PRO; Webb, "The Trials of Sir Edmund Andros," in *Human Dimensions of Nation Making*," ed. Martin, 23–53.

22. Andros's Answers (31 Dec. 1681), *DRNY*, 3:308–9 and CO 1/47, PRO.

23. *DRNY,* 3:310–12 and CO 1/47, PRO.

24. *DRNY,* 3:313 and CO 1/47, PRO.

25. Webb, "The Trials of Sir Edmund Andros," in *The Human Dimensions of Nation Making,* ed. Martin, 23–53.

26. *DRNY,* 3:313.

27. Ibid., 3:314.

28. Ibid., 3:316.

29. Case of Milborne against Andros (1681), *DRNY* 3:300–301; Webb, "The

Trials of Sir Edmund Andros," in *The Human Dimensions of Nation Making,* ed. Martin, 23–53.

30. Werden to Andros (12 May 1681), *DRNY,* 3:286; Petition of Edward Griffeth (22 Dec. 1682) and Answer of Sir Edmund Andros to Complaint (1 Feb. 1683), Leisler Papers Project, ed. David William Voorhees.

31. Penn quoted in Webb, *1676,* 403.

32. *Andros Tracts,* 1:xlix; Carey, *Essays on Guernsey History,* 77; Haley, *Shaftesbury,* 708.

33. Werden to Brockholes (11 Feb. 1682) and Duke of York to Brockholes (28 Mar. 1682), *DRNY,* 3:317–18; Sosin, *English America and the Restoration Monarchy,* 250; Lustig, *Privilege and Prerogative,* 5–6.

34. Petition of Dyre to King (1682), Order In Council (21 July 1682), and Report Dismissing Charges (30 Sept. 1682), *DRNY,* 3:318–19, 320, 321; Lords of His Majesty's Honoble Privy Council (14 Sept. 1681), CO 1/47, PRO.

35. Evelyn, *Diary,* 4:321, 323, 352; Jones, *Charles II,* 182; Webb, *Lord Churchill's Coup,* 5, 77, 80; Haley, *Shaftesbury,* 709–10, 717–18.

36. Evelyn, *Diary,* 4:353; Jones, *Charles II,* 10.

37. Evelyn, *Diary,* 4:323, 353; Haley, *Shaftesbury,* 708.

38. Evelyn, *Diary,* 4:320, 342–43, 342–43n.; Jones, *Charles II,* 9.

39. Lord Culpepper to Lords of Trade (9 Aug. 1681), CO 1/47, PRO.

40. *The Glorious Revolution in America,* ed. Michael G. Hall, Lawrence H. Leder, and Michael G. Kammen (Chapel Hill, 1964), 28.

41. Abstract Proceedings Against Massachusetts and Account of Proceedings by Edward Randolph (12 Sept. 1681), Proclamation, Charles II (21 Oct. 1681), and Approval of Privy Council and Copy of Letter, CO 5/856, CO 1/47, PRO.

42. Abstract Proceedings Against Massachusetts, Simon Bradstreet to Edward Randolph (8 Dec. 1684), CO 5/856, CO 1/56, PRO.

43. Penn quoted in Buranelli, *The King and the Quaker,* 65.

44. Evelyn, *Diary,* 4:361–63; Carey, *Essays on Guernsey History,* 3–4.

45. Evelyn, *Diary,* 4:405–7, 406n., 408, 409–10, 415; Webb, *Lord Churchill's Coup,* 83; Webb, "The Trials of Sir Edmund Andros," in *The Human Dimensions of Nation Making,* ed. Martin 23–53.

46. Evelyn, *Diary,* 4:413.

47. Proclamation (1685) and Lords of Trade to Dongan (5 Mar. 1685), CO 1/57, PRO.

48. Evelyn, *Diary,* 4:440–41.

49. Ibid., 449n.

50. Peter Earle, *Monmouth's Rebels: The Road to Sedgmoor, 1685* (New York, 1977), 141.

51. *Andros Tracts,* 1:xlix; Evelyn, *Diary,* 449; Webb, *Lord Churchill's Coup,* 85.

52. Evelyn, *Diary,* 4:451–52; Ashley, *James II,* 173–74; Earle, *Monmouth's Rebels,* 91; Webb, *Lord Churchill's Coup,* 90–91.

53. Evelyn, *Diary,* 4:455–56; Earle, *Monmouth's Rebels,* 164.

54. Shaftesbury quoted in Christopher Hill, *Some Intellectual Consequences of the English Revolution* (Madison, 1980), 12; Childs, *The Army, James II, and the Glorious Revolution,* 1–2.

55. Earle, *Monmouth's Rebels,* 138–39, 161; James II quoted in Earle, *Monmouth's Rebels,* 136; Ashley, *James II,* 177; Webb, "The Trials of Sir Edmund Andros," in *The Human Dimensions of Nation Making,* ed. Martin, 23–53; Webb, *Lord Churchill's Coup,* 96, 97, 99–100.

56. *Andros Tracts*, 1:xlix; Webb, *Lord Churchill's Coup*, 101, 187.
57. Childs, *The Army, James II, and the Glorious Revolution*, 49, 84–85.
58. Webb, *Lord Churchill's Coup*, 98; Sosin, *English America and the Restoration Monarchy*, 307.

CHAPTER 7: THE DOMINION OF NEW ENGLAND

1. Hutchinson, *History*, 1:308.
2. Randolph to Blathwayt (21 May 1687), Randolph, *Papers*, 6:224.
3. J. M. Sosin, *English America and the Revolution of 1688* (Lincoln and London, 1982), 10–12.
4. On the decline of New England's "brokers" during this period, see T. H. Breen, "War, Taxes and Political Brokers: The Ordeal of Massachusetts Bay, 1675–1692," in *Puritans and Adventurers*, 81–105.
5. For the threat posed by the Dominion of New England to towns and local officials, see Martin, *Profits in the Wilderness*, 5, 259, 262–65, 266.
6. Gilbert Burnet, *History of His Own Time*, 6 vols. (Oxford, 1833), 3:75, 80; Evelyn, *Diary*, 4:485.
7. Abstracts of Proceedings of Charles I against Massachusetts, Powers desired by Agents of New England, and Heads of a Charter for the Colony of Massachusetts Bay, CO 5/856, PRO; Dunn, *Puritans and Yankees*, 183.
8. Abstract of some of the Printed Laws of New England, *Andros Tracts*, 1:14–16.
9. Peter Lake, *Anglicans and Puritans?: Presbyterianism and English Conformist Thought from Whitgift to Hooker* (London, 1988), 2, 5–7. On early discord in New England, see David S. Lovejoy, *Religious Enthusiasm in the New World: Heresy to Revolution* (Cambridge, Mass. and London), 1985; Janice Knight, *Orthodoxies in Massachusetts: Rereading American Puritanism* (Cambridge, Mass. and London, 1994); Andrew Delbanco, *The Puritan Ordeal* (Cambridge, Mass. and London, 1989); John Frederick Martin, *Profits in the Wilderness: Entrepreneurship and the Founding of New England Towns in the Seventeenth Century* (Chapel Hill and London, 1991).
10. Hall, *Edward Randolph*, 90; Hutchinson, *History*, 1:302; T. J. Wertenbaker, *The Puritan Oligrachy: The Founding of American Civilization* (New York, 1947), 247.
11. Wertenbaker, *Puritan Oligarchy*, 226–27, 242–44; Stephen Foster, *The Long Argument: English Puritanism and the Shaping of New England Culture, 1570–1700* (Chapel Hill and London, 1991), 199.
12. Joseph Dudley's sister, the poet Anne, was married to Simon Bradstreet. Joseph was educated for the ministry at Harvard but found politics more appealing. See Kenneth Silverman, *The Life and Times of Cotton Mather* (New York, 1985), 202–3.
13. Bailyn, *New England Merchants*, 40, 134. Massachusetts since its earliest days had seen opposition to its orthodox leadership, most noticeably during the 1637–38 Antinomian Controversy when Thomas Dudley, Sr. was pitted against founder, John Winthrop. So were the younger Dudley and his advocates pitted against the orthodox leaders, who in the 1680s sought to retain control of Massachusetts. See Knight, *Orthodoxies in Massachusetts*, 2–5, 16, 19, 22–23 and David S. Lovejoy, *Religious Enthusiasm in the New World: Heresy to Revolution* (Cambridge, Mass. and London, 1985), 67, 77, 87; Bailyn, *New England Mer-*

chants, 40. As Andrew Delbanco points out, colonists were drawn from all parts of England and, once in New England, were torn by internal strife. See Delbanco, *The Puritan Ordeal*, 17. Some historians, such as Perry Miller and Sacvan Bercovitch, see unity in the first generation.

14. Simon Bradstreet to Edward Randolph (8 Dec. 1684), CO 1/56, PRO; Larzer Ziff, *Puritanism in America: New Culture in a New World* (New York, 1973), 208–9; Stephen Foster, *The Long Argument*, 182.

15. Mather quoted in Foster, *The Long Argument*, 233. See also Theodore Dwight Bozeman, *To Live Ancient Lives: The Primitive Dimension in Puritanism* (Chapel Hill and London, 1988), 316–17.

16. Bailyn, *New England Merchants*, 156, 159; Ziff, *Puritanism in America*, 208–9; Knight, *Orthodoxies in Massachusetts*, 2–3, 5.

17. Massachusetts General Court to Joseph Dudley (20 May 1686), *Records of the Colony of Rhode Island and Providence Plantations in New England*, ed. John Russell Bartlett, 10 vols. (Providence, 1857 and New York, 1968), 3:203, hereafter cited as *Rhode Island Records*; Hall, *Edward Randolph*, 99–100.

18. Hall, *Edward Randolph*, 58; Bailyn, *New England Merchants*, 169.

19. Foster, *The Long Argument*, 248. Former governor, Simon Bradstreet, and his son Dudley declined to serve. See Lovejoy, *Glorious Revolution in America*, 180.

20. Theodore B. Lewis, "Land Speculation and the Dudley Council of 1686," *W&MQ*, 3d ser., 31 (1974): 255–72.

21. For Andros's commission, see *Rhode Island Records*, 3:212–17. See also *Andros Tracts*, 1:xxv; K. G. Davies, "The Revolutions in America," in *The Revolutions of 1688*, ed. Robert Beddard (Oxford, 1991), 258; Hall, *Edward Randolph*, 111.

22. Hutchinson, *History*, 1:308.

23. For Nicholson's early career see Stephen Saunders Webb, "The Strange Career of Francis Nicholson," *W&MQ*, 3d ser., 23 (1966): 513–48; Bruce T. McCully, "From North Riding to Morocco: The Early Years of Governor Francis Nicholson, 1655–1686," *W&MQ*, 3d ser., 19 (1962): 534–56. As Wesley Frank Craven suggests, what was remarkable was "the peaceful submission of the people" to the Dominion government. See *Colonies in Transition*, 217–18.

24. Earl of Clarendon quoted in Sosin, *English America and the Revolution of 1688*, 64.

25. The Revolution in New England Justified (1691), *Andros Tracts,* 1:1.

26. Samuel Sewall, 23 Aug. 1686, *The Diary of Samuel Sewall,* ed. Harvey Wish (New York, 1967), 46; Edward Randolph to John Winthrop, Randolph, *Papers,* 4:120; William Penn to William Blathwayt (21 Nov. 1682), Blathwayt Papers, Colonial Williamsburg, v–vii; Penn also quoted in David Lovejoy, *The Glorious Revolution in America* (Middletown, Conn., 1972, 1987), 257.

27. Warrant from George, Lord Dartmouth (13 Sept. 1686), *CSPC*, 242.

28. Randolph, *Papers*, 2:5.

29. Randolph to William Blathwayt (22 Dec. 1686), Ibid., 6:207. Andros's mother died on 25 Dec. 1686, shortly after his arrival in Boston. See *Andros Tracts,* 1:x.

30. Andros to Blathwayt (23 Dec. 1686), Blathwayt Papers, Colonial Williamsburg; Hutchinson, *History*, 1:300.

31. Hutchinson, *History,* 1:300; Hall, *Edward Randolph*, 58–59.

32. Sewall, *Diary,* 21 Dec. 1686, 47; Barnes, *Dominion of New England*, 127–28; Sosin, *English America and the Revolution of 1688*, 71.

33. Palfrey, *History of New England*, 3:534, 536; Hall, *Edward Randolph*, 54; Lovejoy, *Glorious Revolution in America*, 196–97.

34. *Public Records Connecticut*, 3:222n.; Instructions to Andros (13 Sept. 1686), Andros to Rhode Island Officials (22 Dec. 1686) and Andros to Walter Clarke (22 Dec. 1686), *Rhode Island Public Records*, 3:218, 219; Randolph, *Papers*, 4:135; Palfrey, *History of New England*, 3:518n. *Quo warranto* proceedings were again instituted against Maryland's charter. See Order King in Council (28 May 1687), *CSPC*, 377; Lovejoy, *Glorious Revolution in America*, 198–99.

35. Connecticut Governor and Council to Andros (26 Jan. 1686), *CSPC*, 351.

36. Randolph to Robert Treat (23 Dec. 1686) and Andros to Robert Treat (22 Dec. 1686), *Public Records Connecticut*, 3:222n., 375, 377, 377n.; Andros to Robert Treat (22 Dec. 1686), Randolph, *Letters*, 4:136–37; Lovejoy, *Glorious Revolution in America*, 205.

37. General Court to earl of Sunderland (26 Jan. 1687), Andros to Robert Treat (25 Feb. 1687, 28 Feb. 1687, and 13 June 1687) and Council to Andros (30 Mar. 1687 and 18 June 1687), *Public Records Connecticut*, 3:378, 379, 380, 381, 383.

38. Dongan to Board of Trade (Mar. 1687) and King James to Andros (27 June 1687), *CSPC*, 334, 387; Andros to earl of Sunderland (30 Mar. 1687), *Rhode Island Records*, 3:224; Dongan to General Court (4 Oct. 1687), *Public Records Connecticut*, 3:387.

39. William Whiting to John Allyn (21 Sept. 1687) and Andros to Robert Treat (22 Oct. 1687), *Public Records Connecticut*, 3:386, 387.

40. Dunn, *Puritans and Yankees*, 241–42; Randolph to Blathwayt (30 Sept. 1687), Randolph, *Papers*, 6:232; Richard S. Dunn, "The Dominion of New England," in *Interpreting Colonial America*, ed. Martin, 214–32.

41. Connecticut Annexation, 31 Oct. 1687, *Public Records Connecticut*, 3:389; Randolph to Blathwayt (23 Nov. 1687) and Andros to Board of Trade, *CSPC*, 472; Lovejoy, *Glorious Revolution in America*, 207. For a recounting of the story about the disappearing charter and the oak tree, see Dunn, *Puritans and Yankees*, 242 and Bloom, "Sir Edmund Andros," 283n.

42. Andros to Blathwayt (28 Nov. 1687), Blathwayt Papers, Colonial Williamsburg; Connecticut Annexation, *Public Records Connecticut*, 3:390–91; Andros to Board of Trade (28 Nov. 1687), CO 1/63, PRO; Edward Randolph to King (9 Aug. 1687), CO 1/22, f. 105, PRO.

43. Veto of Act entitled Charter of Liberties and Privileges (3 Mar. 1684), *DRNY*, 3:357; Barnes, *Dominion of New England*, 41–42, 71; Sosin, *English Americann and the Revolution of 1688*, 16.

44. Randolph to Board of Trade (23 Aug. 1686), *Rhode Island Records*, 3:206; B. Katherine Brown, "The Controversy over the Franchise in Puritan Massachusetts, 1954 to 1974," *W&MQ*, 3d ser., 33 (1976): 212–41.

45. William Speck, *Reluctant Revolutionaries: Englishmen and the Revolution of 1688* (Oxford, 1988), 66–67.

46. Lewis, "Land Speculation and the Dudley Council of 1686," *W&MQ*, 3d ser., 31 (1974): 255–72.

47. Andros to Board of Trade (30 Mar. 1687) and Instructions to Andros (16 Apr. 1688), *CSPC*, 351, 528; Andros to Lord Sunderland (30 Mar. 1687), *Rhode Island Public Records*, 3:224; Barnes, *Dominion of New England*, 82–88; Dunn, "The Dominion of New England," in *Interpreting Colonial America*, ed. Martin, 214–32; Bailyn, *New England Merchants*, 175–76. See also Richard R. Johnson, *John Nelson, Merchant Adventurer: A Life Between Empires* (New York and

Oxford, 1991), 42; Philip S. Haffenden, "The Crown and the Colonial Charters, 1675–1688: Part II," *W&MQ*, 3d ser., 15 (1958): 452–66; Lewis, "Land Speculation and the Dudley Council of 1686," *W&MQ*, 3d ser., 31 (1974): 255–72.

48. Randolph to Blathwayt (3 Feb. 1686), Randolph, *Papers*, 6:211.

49. Order (21 Dec. 1686), Randolph, *Papers*, 4:133; Sewall 30 Dec. 1686, in *Diary*, 47; Andros to Earl Sunderland (30 Mar. 1687), *Rhode Island Records*, 3:224; State of the King's Revenue (3 Aug. 1687), *CSPC*, 422; Bailyn, *New England Merchants*, 175, 176; Herbert L. Osgood, *American Colonies in the Seventeenth Century*, 3 vols. (New York, 1957), 3:403; Barnes, *Dominion of New England*, 82–83, 91–92; Hall, *Edward Randolph*, 112.

50. Andros to Blathwayt (3 Mar. 1687) Blathwayt Papers, Colonial Williamsburg; Answer to John Palmer, *Andros Tracts*, 1691, 1:81; Andros to Lord Sunderland (30 Mar. 1687), *Rhode Island Public Records*, 3:224; State of King's Revenue (3 Aug. 1687), Andros to Lords of Trade (31 Aug. 1687), and King James to Andros (7 Nov. 1687), *CSPC*, 422, 464; Barnes, *Dominion of New England*, 84–85, 93; Hall, *Edward Randolph*, 112. Martin points out that the tax burden was more fairly distributed under Andros than under the charter government, which favored elite interests. Under the Dominion, large landowners had to pay their fair share of taxes. Martin says this, rather than the issue of taxation without a representative assembly, was the basis of New England complaints. *Profits in the Wilderness*, 41.

51. Grievances Against Governor Andros, 1687–1689, in *Glorious Revolution*, ed. Hall, Leder, and Kammen; Hutchinson, *History*, 1:307; Barnes, *Dominion of New England*, 78–79.

52. *Andros Tracts*, 1:138, 140–41; Narratives of the Proceedings of Andros, in *Narratives of the Insurrections*, ed. Andrews, 241; Declaration (18 Apr. 1689), *Andros Tracts*, 1:17.

53. Hutchinson, *History*, 1:301; Richard R. Johnson, *Adjustment to Empire: The New England Colonies, 1675–1715* (New Brunswick, 1981), 82–83.

54. Declaration (18 Apr. 1689), *Andros Tracts*, 1:13–14.

55. Lease Secretary's Office (3 May 1687), Randolph, *Letters*, 4:155–58.

56. Declaration (18 Apr. 1689), *Andros Tracts*, 1:13–14; Randolph to John Povey, 24 Jan. 1687, Randolph, *Letters*, 4:198. See also Viola F. Barnes, "The Refusal of Massachusetts to Become a Part of the British Colonial System," in *Interpreting Colonial America*, ed. Martin, 204–13.

57. Randolph to Povey (21 June 1688), Randolph, *Papers*, 4:226–28; Palfrey, *History of New England*, 3:533.

58. Andros to Blathwayt (23 May 1687), Blathwayt Papers, Colonial Williamsburg; Hutchinson, *History*, 1:301n.; *Narratives of the Insurrections*, ed. Andrews, 174 n.; Hall, *Edward Randolph*, 109, 110.

59. Declaration (18 Apr. 1689), *Andros Tracts*, 1:13.

60. Randolph to Thomas Povey (21 June 1688), Randolph, *Papers*, 4:227.

61. Hutchinson, *History*, 1:299, 304; Lovejoy, *Glorious Revolution in America*, 180; Declaration (18 Apr. 1689), *Andros Tracts*, 1:15; Palfrey, *History of New England*, 3:522.

62. Andros to Blathwayt (28 Sept. 1687), Blathwayt Papers, Colonial Williamsburg; Charges Against Andros, et al. (1689–90), John Palmer, An . . . Account of the State of New England (1690), and Revolution in New England Justified (1691), *Andros Tracts*, 1:153, 45–46, 85–86; Barnes, *Dominion of New England*, 87; K. G. Davies, "The Revolutions in America," in *The Revolutions of 1688*, ed. Beddard, 259.

63. John Palmer, An Impartial Account, *Andros Tracts,* 1:45–46.

64. Andros to Blathwayt (28 Sept. 1687), Blathwayt Papers, Colonial Williamsburg; Andros to Board of Trade (28 Nov. 1687), *CSPC,* 472; Answer to John Palmer, 1691, *Andros Tracts,* 1:81–82; Francis J. Bremer, *The Puritan Experiment: New England Society from Bradford to Edwards* (New York, 1976), 160.

65. *Andros Tracts,* 1:85.

66. Ibid., 85–86; Andros to Blathwayt, 28 Sept. 1687, Blathwayt Papers, Colonial Williamsburg; Barnes, *Dominion of New England,* 87–90.

67. John Palmer, An Impartial Account, 1690, *Andros Tracts,* 1:38–39; Barnes, *Dominion of New England,* 117.

68. Declaration (18 Apr. 1689), *Andros Tracts,* 1:14.

69. *Andros Tracts,* 1:88–90. On the economic success of the Puritan "errand into the wilderness" and the threat posed by Andros in putting land titles in doubt, see Stephen Innes, *Creating the Commonwealth: The Economic Culture of Puritan New England* (New York and London, 1995), 24–25, 28, 43.

70. Declaration (18 Apr. 1689), *Andros Tracts,* 1:16.

71. Randolph to Blathwayt (2 Apr. 1688), Randolph, *Papers,* 6:251; *Andros Tracts,* 1:113.

72. Declaration (18 Apr. 1689) and Answer to John Palmer, *Andros Tracts,* 1:16, 98; Hall, *The Last American Puritan,* 207; Barnes, *Dominion of New England,* 84.

73. Answer to John Palmer, 1691, *Andros Tracts,* 1:92; Palfrey, *History of New England,* 3:552; Barnes, *Dominion of New England,* 201.

74. Answer to John Palmer, 1691, *Andros Tracts,* 1:99, 100–101; Hall, *Edward Randolph,* 113.

75. Hall, *Glorious Revolution,* 199–200. The struggle among Massachusetts, Connecticut, and Rhode Island over ownership of the Narragansett territory was not settled until a boundary line was drawn in 1728, dividing the area between Connecticut and Rhode Island. See Douglas Edward Leach, *Flintlock and Tomahawk, New England in King Philip's War* (New York, 1958, 1966), 248.

76. Administration of Sir Edmund Andros, *Rhode Island Records,* 3:210–11; Lovejoy, *Glorious Revolution in America,* 199; Bailyn, *New England Merchants,* 171; Theodore Lewis, "Land Speculation and the Dudley Council," *W&MQ,* 3d ser., 31 (1974): 255–72.

77. Randolph to Blathwayt (21 May 1687), Randolph, *Papers,* 6:222.

78. Order of King in Council (13 Jan. 1688), Petition of Thomas, Lord Culpepper, et al. to King, Lords of Trade to King (10 Apr. 1688), *CSPC,* 486, 487, 527; Bailyn, *New England Merchants,* 172; Craven, *Colonies in Transition,* 221.

79. Andros's Report on Claims to Narragansett Country (1687), *CSPC,* 423 and CO 1/22, f. 113–18, PRO; Bailyn, *New England Merchants,* 173; Hall, *Edward Randolph,* 102; Sosin, *English America and the Revolution of 1688,* 72–73; Martin, *Profits in the Wilderness,* 108–9, 261. Andros visited the Pojebscot tract in Maine in the spring of 1688. See Randolph to John Povey (21 June 1688), Hutchinson, *History,* 2:304.

80. Bailyn, *New England Merchants,* 175, 191; Craven, *Colonies in Transition,* 222; Sosin, *English America and the Revolution of 1688,* 72–73; Martin, *Profits in the Wilderness,* 261.

81. Martin, *Profits in the Wilderness,* 262, 264–65, 299.

82. Sewall, *Diary,* 1 July 1687, 12 July 1688, 14 July 1688, and 24 July 1688,

51, 55, 56; Sewall to Increase Mather (24 July 1688), in *Glorious Revolution in America,* ed. Hall, Leder, Kammen, 29; Ola Winslow, *Samuel Sewall of Boston* (New York, 1964), 94–95; Hall, *Edward Randolph,* 112–13; Dunn, *Puritans and Yankees,* 250; Barnes, *Dominion of New England,* 199, 201.

83. Dunn, *Puritans and Yankees,* 250; Sosin, *English America and the Revolution of 1688,* 74; Innes, *Creating the Commonwealth,* 25. See also Dunn, "The Dominion of New England," in *Interpreting Colonial America,* ed. Martin, 214–32.

84. Andros to Blathwayt (4 June 1688), Blathwayt Papers, Colonial Williamsburg; Randolph to Blathwayt (21 May 1687), Randolph, *Papers,* 6:224.

CHAPTER 8. THE DOMINION OF NEW ENGLAND, PART 2

1. Mather quoted in Palfrey, *History of New England,* 3:517n.

2. On Andros's introduction of bayonets to America, see John K. Mahon, "Anglo-American Methods of Indian Warfare, 1676–1794," *The Mississippi Valley Historical Review,* 45 (1958): 254–75.

3. Sewall, 24 Dec. 1686 *Diary,* 47; Declaration (18 Apr. 1689), *Andros Tracts,* 1:13; Winslow, *Samuel Sewall,* 79; Childs, *The Army, James II, and the Glorious Revolution,* 2; Wesley Frank Craven comments that the full complement of one hundred troops were "hardly more than a bodyguard" and not sufficient to be a threat to colonists. They were, however, a threat to the people of Boston, and all New Englanders were aware that more regulars could be sent to reinforce the Boston garrison. *Colonies in Transition,* 217.

4. Andros Commission, 3 June 1686, *Rhode Island Records,* 3:212–17; Childs, *The Army, James II, and the Glorious Revolution,* 104; Barnes, *Dominion of New England,* 218; Sosin, *English America and the Revolution of 1688,* 14. On the social disruption caused by Andros's arrival, see Timothy H. Breen and Stephen Foster, "The Puritans' Greatest Achievement: A Study of Social Cohesion in Seventeenth-Century Massachusetts," *The Journal of American History,* 60 (1973): 5–22.

5. Palfrey, *History of New England,* 3:517n.

6. For the unpopularity of James's standing army in England, see Childs, *The Army, James II, and the Glorious Revolution,* particularly chapter 4, "Popularity and Politics," 83–118.

7. *Andros Tracts,* 3:195.

8. Dunn, *Puritans and Yankees,* 243–44.

9. CO 5/855, PRO; Andros to earl of Sunderland (30 Mar. 1687), *Rhode Island Records,* 3:224. Despite the military backgrounds of Andros and many other governors during this era, Ian Steele argues the governors themselves saw their rule as more civil than military. See "Governors or Generals?: A Note on Martial Law and the Revolution of 1689 in English America," *W&MQ,* 3d ser., 46 (1989): 304–14.

10. Andros to Lord President (30 Aug. 1687) and Andros to Secretary of the Admiralty (5 Sept. 1687), *Andros Tracts,* 1:73, 75.

11. On the use of troops to control cities in England, see Webb, *Governors-General,* particularly chapter 1, "Garrison Government," 3–56; Dunn, *Puritans and Yankees,* 240.

12. Andros to William Blathwayt (28 Sept. 1687, 28 Nov. 1687, and 4 Apr. 1688), Blathwayt Papers, Colonial Williamsburg; Andros to Board of Trade (31

Aug. 1687), CO 1/63, PRO; Andros to Lord President (31 Aug. 1687) and Andros to Secretary of the Admiralty (5 Sept. 1687), *Andros Tracts*, 3:73, 75; Andros to Lord Dartmouth (28 Nov. 1687), Representations of Flag, *CSPC*, 474, 526; Barnes, *Dominion of New England*, 217–18; Palfrey, *History of New England*, 3:517n.

13. Andros to Blathwayt (28 Nov. 1687), Blathwayt Papers, Colonial Williamsburg.

14. Edward Randolph to William Blathwayt (16 Jan. 1688 and 2 Apr. 1688), Randolph, *Papers*, 6:238, 252; Sewall, 22 Jan. 1688, in *Diary*, 52; Winslow, *Samuel Sewall*, 91; Palfrey, *History of New England*, 3:549n.

15. Sewall, *Diary*, 25 Dec. 1686, 47.

16. Ibid., 31 Jan. 1687 and 23 Apr. 1687, 48–49; Trevor, *Shadow of a Crown*, 143, 146.

17. Randolph to Hinkley (22 June 1686 and 5 Mar. 1687), quoted in Hutchinson, *History*, 1:303–4n.

18. Sosin, *English America and the Revolution of 1688*, 69; Barnes, *Dominion of New England*, 125.

19. Randolph to Blathwayt (5 Aug. 1687), Randolph, *Papers*, 6:225.

20. Webb, *Lord Churchill's Coup*, 127.

21. Silverman, *Cotton Mather*, 64.

22. W. H. Speck, *Reluctant Revolutionaries: Englishmen and the Revolution of 1688* (Oxford, 1988), 65–66.

23. Andros to Board of Trade (31 Aug. 1687), CO 1/63, PRO. For information on the Declaration of Indulgence, 4 Apr. 1687, see *Public Records Connecticut*, 3:393n.

24. Miller, *Popery and Politics in England*, 210.

25. Hutchinson, *History*, 1:304; Hall, *The Last American Puritan*, 207; Miller, *Popery and Politics*, 210; Craven, *Colonies in Transition*, 221.

26. Warrant for Arrest Increase Mather (24 Dec. 1687), Randolph, *Papers*, 4:193; Silverman, *Cotton Mather*, 64–65, 68–69; Hall, *The Last American Puritan*, 210–11.

27. Andros to William Blathwayt (3 Mar. 1687), Blathwayt Papers, Colonial Williamsburg; Sir Edmund Andros's Report of his Administration, 30 May 1690, *Andros Tracts*, 3:21; Barnes, *Dominion of New England*, 129–30; Silverman, *Cotton Mather*, 63.

28. Miller, *Popery and Politics*, 258; Duncan, *The History of Guernsey*, 121.

29. Miller, *Popery and Politics*, 258.

30. Sewall, *Diary*, 12 June 1687, 50.

31. Ibid., 22 June 1688, 54–55; Sosin, *English America and the Revolution of 1688*, 71.

32. Sewall, *Diary*, 16 Oct. 1688, 58; Sir Edmund Andros's Report on his Administration, 30 May 1690, *Andros Tracts*, 3:21.

33. Silverman, *Cotton Mather*, 63.

34. *Andros Tracts* 3:21, 1:212, 1:54.

35. Ibid., 1:80; Hutchinson, *History*, 1:302, 308; Osgood, *American Colonies in the Seventeenth Century*, 3:409; Barnes, *Dominion of New England*, 95.

36. J. A. Doyle, *English Colonies in America*, 2 vols. (New York, 1889), 2:243.

37. Revolution in New England Justified, 1689, *Andros Tracts*, 1:103, 107–8.

38. Randolph to Blathwayt (21 May 1687), Randolph, *Papers*, 6:223.

39. Andros to Sunderland (30 Mar. 1687), *Rhode Island Records*, 3:224; Randolph to Povey (24 Jan. 1688), Randolph, *Papers*, 4:199.

40. On piracy, see Robert C. Ritchie, *Captain Kidd and the War Against the Pirates* (Cambridge, Mass. and London, 1986).

41. Stephen Saunders Webb has shown that a portrait owned by Edmund Andros and believed by his heirs to be that of the pirate Sir Henry Morgan was actually painted around 1649 by Pieter Verelst and is either of Amias Andros or of his son, Edmund. See photo essay in *1676*, 288–89. Carey, *Amias Andros*, 47–48; Bloom, "Sir Edmund Andros," 290n.

42. Francis Nicholson to [Thomas Povey?] (31 Aug. 1688), *DRNY*, 3:552.

43. Randolph to Blathwayt (14 Mar. 1687), Randolph, *Papers*, 6:216.

44. Order to Andros from King James (12 Oct. 1686), *Catalog 150: Sir Edmund Andros, 1637–1714* (New York, 1978), 50.

45. Richard R. Johnson, "The Revolution of 1688–1689 in the American Colonies," in *Essays on the Glorious Revolution and Its World Impact*, ed. Jonathan Israel (Cambridge, N.Y. and Melbourne, 1997), 222.

46. Dunn, *Puritans and Yankees,* 238. See also Richard S. Dunn, "The Dominion of New England," in *Interpreting Colonial America*, ed. Martin, 214–32.

CHAPTER 9. ANDROS, THE FRENCH, AND THE INDIANS

1. Denonville to Seignilay (12 July 1684), *DRNY*, 9:297. See also Jennings, *Ambiguous Iroquois Empire*, 194.

2. Project of Chevalier de Callieres (Jan. 1689), *DHNY*, 1:285–86.

3. Webb, *Lord Churchill's Coup*, 4, 115–17; Sosin, *English America and the Revolution of 1688,* 14.

4. Marquis de Denonville's Answer to Mr. Dongan's letter of 22 Aug. 1687, n.d. *DRNY*, 3:469.

5. Thomas Dongan to M. De La Barre (24 June 1684 and July 1684), *DHNY*, 1:101, 102.

6. Iroquois Meeting (Aug. 1682) and Dongan's Proposals (25 April 1687), *Livingston Indian Records*, ed. Leder, 70, 112.

7. Denonville to Seignilay (12 July 1684), *DRNY*, 9:297.

8. Extract from King's Instruction to the Marquis de Denonville (10 Mar. 1685), *DHNY*, 1:193. French aggression and the lack of assistance from the English during King William's War led the Iroquois in 1701 to sign a treaty of neutrality with both powers. See Anthony F. C. Wallace, "Origins of Iroquois Neutrality: The Grand Settlement of 1701," *Pennsylvania History*, 34 (1957): 223–35.

9. Extract from King's Instruction to the Marquis de Denonville (10 Mar. 1685), M. de Denonville's Memoir (8 Sept. 1686), Memoir for the Marquis of Seignelay (Jan. 1687), and M. de Denonville to Minister (25 Aug. 1687), *DHNY*, 1:193, 213–24, 231, 237–40; Rev. Fr. Bechefer to M. Cabort de Villermont (19 Sept. 1687), *The Jesuit Relations and Allied Documents*, ed. Reuben Gold Thwaites, 73 vols. (Cleveland, 1900), 63:271–73.

10. Dongan to earl of Sunderland (25 Oct. 1687), *CSPC*, 457–58; Rev. Fr. Bechefer to M. Cabort de Villermont (19 Sept. 1687), *Jesuit Relations*, ed. Thwaites, 63:279.

11. Andros to Blathwayt (17 Aug. 1687), Blathwayt Papers, Colonial Williamsburg; His Excellency's Answer (Oct. 1687), *Andros Tracts*, 3:76–78. W. H. Whitmore, editor of the *Andros Tracts,* attributes this letter to Andros, but it

was almost certainly written by Dongan. Andros had no authority to deal with the Iroquois in 1687 and was in Boston preparing to travel to Connecticut at the time of Dongan's initial meeting with the Iroquois. See also Paul A. W. Wallace, *Indians in Pennsylvania*, rev. ed. (Harrisburg, 1961, 1981), 105; Webb, *Lord Churchill's Coup*, 121.

12. *Andros Tracts*, 1:201, 3:20.

13. James to Andros (11 Nov. 1687), *CSPC*, 465.

14. Andros to Blathwayt (4 Apr. 1688), Blathwayt Papers, Colonial Williamsburg; Andros to Board of Trade (2 Dec. 1687), CO 1/63, PRO; Dongan to Andros (18 Nov. 1687), Andros to Dongan (2 Dec. 1687), and Andros to Board of Trade (4 April 1688), *CSPC*, 476, 524.

15. Barnes, *Dominion of New England*, 222.

16. Edward Randolph to William Penn (9 Nov. 1688), Hutchinson, *History*, 1:309.

17. Andros to Board of Trade (7 July 1688) and Andros to James (9 July 1688), *CSPC*, 567; Randolph to Povey (21 June 1688), Randolph, *Papers*, 4:224–25; Hutchinson, *History*, 1:309; Duncan, *Coastal Maine*, 134–35.

18. Andros to Blathwayt (4 June 1688), Blathwayt Papers, Colonial Williamsburg; Andros to Board of Trade (7 July 1688), CO 1/65, PRO; Randolph to Board of Trade (8 Oct. 1688), Randolph, *Papers*, 4:239–40; *Andros Tracts*, 1:118, 155.

19. *Narratives of the Indian Wars*, 186–87.

20. Barnes, *Dominion of New England*, 216, 219.

21. Francis Nicholson to [Thomas Povey?] (31 Aug. 1688), *DRNY*, 3:554; Andros to Lords Trade and Plantation (7 July 1688), CO 1/65, PRO; Lovejoy, *Glorious Revolution*, 208–9. See also Philip S. Haffenden, "The Crown and the Colonial Charters, 1675–1688," *W&MQ*, 3d ser., 15 (1958): 452–66; Johnson, *Adjustment to Empire*, 83.

22. Randolph to William Blathwayt (2 Oct. 1688), Randolph, *Papers*, 6:262.

23. Randolph to Board of Trade (8 Oct. 1688), Randolph, *Papers*, 4:240; Nicholson to Lords Trade and Plantations (31 Aug. 1688), CO 1/57, PRO; Dunn, *Puritans and Yankees*, 247.

24. Andros to Blathwayt (18 Aug. 1688), Blathwayt Papers, Colonial Williamsburg.

25. Randolph to William Blathwayt, 2 Oct. 1688, Randolph, *Papers*, 6:263–64; K. G. Davies, "The Revolution in America," in *The Revolutions of 1688*, ed. Robert Beddard (Oxford, 1991), 250; Lovejoy, *Glorious Revolution*, 210.

26. Speck, *Reluctant Revolutionaries*, 69.

27. Randolph to Board of Trade (8 Oct. 1688), Randolph, *Papers*, 4:241–43.

28. Monsieur de Denonville to Dongan (20 Aug. 1688), *DRNY*, 3:556.

29. Proceedings Between Andros and the Five Nations (19–21 Sept. 1688), *DRNY*, 3:558–59.

30. *Andros Tracts*, 1:201; Johnson, *Adjustment to Empire*, 87.

31. Andros to Denonville (19 Sept. 1688), *DRNY*, 3:557.

32. Randolph to Board of Trade (8 Oct. 1688), *DRNY*, 3:568; Andros to Blathwayt (4 Oct. 1688), Blathwayt Papers, Colonial Williamsburg; Barnes, *Dominion of New England*, 227.

33. Andros to Denonville (1 Oct. 1688) and Denonville to Andros (23 Oct. 1688), *DRNY*, 3:566, 571; Osgood, *American Colonies in the Seventeenth Century*, 3:412.

34. Francis Nicholson to William Blathwayt (31 Aug. 1688), *CSPC*, 588.

35. Sir Edmund Andros's Account" (27 May 1690), *CSPC*, 270; Sir Edmund Andros's Report, *Andros Tracts*, 3:21–22; Randolph to Board of Trade (8 Oct. 1688), Randolph, *Papers*, 4:242–43.

36. Andros to Col. Tyng, *Andros Tracts*, 20 Sept. 1688, 3:87–88; A Proclamation (Oct. 1688), and An Account of the Late Revolution (6 June 1689), CO 1/57, CO 5/855, PRO; Barnes, *Dominion of New England*, 225. On Tyng's career, see Martin, *Profits in the Wilderness*, 21.

37. *Narratives of the Indian Wars*, ed. Lincoln, 188; *Andros Tracts*, 2:207–8.

38. Dunn, "The Dominion of New England," in *Interpreting Colonial America*, ed. Martin, 214–32; Hall, *Edward Randolph*, 122; Lovejoy, *Glorious Revolution*, 218; Johnson, *Adjustment to Empire*, 86; Barnes, *Dominion of New England*, 227; Webb, *Lord Churchill's Coup*, 183; Dunn, *Puritans and Yankees*, 251.

39. Andros to Blathwayt (10 Nov. 1688), Blathwayt Papers, Colonial Williamsburg.

40. *Andros Tracts*, 3:33–34; Andros to Randolph (26 Jan. 1689), Randolph, *Papers*, 4:259; Lovejoy, *Glorious Revolution in America*, 218, 219; Dunn, *Puritans and Yankees*, 251; Webb, *Lord Churchill's Coup*, 183; Barnes, *Dominion of New England*, 227.

41. *Narratives of the Insurrections*, ed. Andrews, 198, 231–32; Duncan, *Coastal Maine*, 135; Dunn, *Puritans and Yankees*, 252.

42. *Narratives of the Insurrections*, ed. Andrews, 209, 263; *Andros Tracts*, 2:182, 3:22, 231, 232; Petition Andros to Lords of Trade (28 Sept. 1691), *CSPC*, 548; Barnes, *Dominion of New England*, 228–29.

43. Barnes, *Dominion of New England*, 229.

44. Andros's Petition (4 June 1689), Blathwayt Papers, Colonial Williamsburg. For the generally poor relations between British officers and colonial troops, see Douglas Edward Leach, *Roots of Conflict: British Armed Forces and Colonial Americans, 1677–1763* (Chapel Hill and London, 1986). For military events in the late 1680s, see 13–19.

45. Quoted in Webb, *Lord Churchill's Coup*, 183–84.

46. *Narratives of the Insurrections*, ed. Andrews, 197; Agents' Answer to Andros's Account (30 May 1690), *Andros* Tracts, 3:36; Hutchinson, *History*, 1:314.

47. Ashley, *James II*, 241; Breen, *Puritans and Adventurers*, 93; Charges Against Andros and Others, 1690, *Andros Tracts*, 1:151–55.

48. *Andros Tracts*, 1691, 1:76n.; Sosin, *English America and the Revolution of 1688*, 90; Webb, *Lord Churchill's Coup*, 182.

49. *Andros Tracts*, 3:232; A Short Account of the Loss of Pemaquid Fort (3 Aug. 1689), CSPC, 114–15; Hutchinson, *History*, 1:316.

CHAPTER 10. THE GLORIOUS REVOLUTION, PART 1

1. *Poets of the Seventeenth Century*, ed. John Broadbent, 2 vols. (New York, 1974).

2. Webb, *Lord Churchill's Coup*, x–xi. See also Childs, *The Army, James II, and the Glorious Revolution*, 103. For the many similarities between conditions in old and New England, see Dunn, "The Dominion of New England," in *Interpreting Colonial America*, ed. Martin, 214–32.

3. See Webb, *Lord Churchill's Coup*, particularly chapter 3, "Rebellion and Empire: 1683–1687," 77–123.

4. Miller, *Popery and Politics*, 215.

5. Humble Petition of Increase Mather (1688) and Humble Memorial of the present Condition of the Dissenters (1688), CO 1/57, PRO.

6. A Narrative of the Miseries of New England, probably written by Increase Mather, *Andros Tracts*, 2:5–7; Barnes, *Dominion of New England*, 231–32; Sosin, *English America and the Revolution of 1688*, 27, 75–77; Hall, *The Last American Puritan*, 214, 217, 224.

7. His Majesty gives New England (1688), CO 1/57, PRO; Robert Beddard, "The Protestant Succession," in *The Revolutions of 1688*, ed. Robert Beddard (Oxford, 1991) 2, 8–9; Trevor, *Shadow of a Crown*, 202–3, 203–5.

8. On Dartmouth's actions see Webb, "Inglorious Revolution: The Channel Fleet in 1688," app. in *Lord Churchill's Coup*, 271–86.

9. Beddard, "The Unexpected Whig Revolution of 1688," in *The Revolutions of 1688*, ed. Beddard, 11.

10. Childs, *The Army, James II, and the Glorious Revolution*, 5, 21, 23, 27–28, 95.

11. Ibid., 50, 85, 101, 113.

12. Burnet, *History of His Own Time*, 3:334–36.

13. James II quoted in John R. Western, *Monarchy and Revolution: The English State in the 1680s* (London, 1972), 35. On Anne's flight, see Mary Lou Lustig, *Robert Hunter, 1666–1734: New York's Augustan Statesman* (Syracuse, 1983), 14–16.

14. Beddard, "The Unexpected Whig Revolution of 1688," in *The Revolutions of 1688*, ed. Beddard, 13–14; Ashley, *James II*, 253, 255; Childs, *The Army, James II, and the Glorious Revolution*, 50, 85. Several of the officers who deserted James would in later years be active in colonial affairs. Churchill, as duke of Marlborough, handled colonial appointments under Queen Anne. Lovelace and Cornbury both served as governors of New York, as would Robert Hunter, a young dragoon officer in 1688 who rode with the bishop of London as part of Anne's bodyguard.

15. Miller, *Popery and Politics*, 259; Beddard, "The Unexpected Whig Revolution of 1688," in *The Revolutions of 1688*, ed. Beddard, 13–14.

16. Webb, *Lord Churchill's Coup*, 158; Trevor, *Shadow of a Crown*, 249–50. Craven died in 1697 at the age of 91.

17. Ashley, *James II*, 263.

18. Evelyn, *Diary*, 4:616, 616n., 621, 624; Trevor, *Shadow of a Crown*, 252.

19. *Andros Tracts*, 2:276, 277, 279; Hall, *The Last American Puritan*, 221–22; Sosin, *English America and the Revolution of 1688*, 83–84.

20. *Acts of the Privy Council of England, Colonial Series, 1680–1720*, ed. W. L. Grant and James Munro (London, 1910 and Liechtenstein, 1966), 2:124–26.

21. Journal Lords Trade and Plantations (22 Feb. 1689) and Order King in Council (26 Feb. 1689), *CSPC*, 8, 11; *Andros Tracts*, 2:280.

22. Capt. George to Secretary of the Admiralty (12 June 1689), *CSPC*, 67.

23. *Andros Tracts*, 3:3–5; John George to Secretary of the Admiralty (12 June 1689), *CSPC*, 66; Nicholson to J. Allen (4 Dec. 1688), *Public Records Connecticut*, 3:454–55 and Randolph, *Papers*, 4:256.

24. Webb, *Lord Churchill's Coup*, 143–44.

25. Act Against Immigration (15 Apr. 1689), *Andros Tracts*, 3:92; Hutchin-

son, *History*, 1:316–17; Johnson, *Adjustment to Empire*, 90; Barnes, *Dominion of New England*, 240n.

26. Silverman, *Cotton Mather*, 69.

27. Randolph to bishop of London (25 Oct. 1689), *CSPC*, 165.

28. Webb, *Lord Churchill's Coup*, 185–87; Silverman, *Cotton Mather*, 69.

29. *Narratives of the Insurrections*, ed. Andrews, 200; Randolph to Board of Trade (29 May 1689), Randolph, *Papers*, 4:280; Webb, *Lord Churchill's Coup*, 187–88; Silverman, *Cotton Mather*, 69.

30. *Andros Tracts*, 1:4, 8; John George to Secretary of the Admiralty (12 June 1689) and Narratives of the Proceedings (16 July 1689), *CSPC*, 66–68, 92; Abstract of a Letter from Bristoll (29 Apr. 1689), CO 5/855, PRO; Johnson, *John Nelson: Merchant Adventurer*, 45; Johnson, *Adjustment to Empire*, 90; Webb, *Lord Churchill's Coup*, 188–89.

31. *Narratives of the Insurrections*, ed. Andrews, 187; Johnson, *Adjustment to Empire*, 89.

32. Hutchinson, *History*, 1:318.

33. *Narratives of the Insurrections*, ed. Andrews, 188; Hutchinson, *History*, 1:319; Barnes, *Dominion of New England*, 242. My thanks to Lieutenant Colonel Robert Leonhard for supplying information on seventeenth-century weaponry.

34. *Narratives of the Insurrections*, 188–89; Randolph to the Governor of Barbados (16 May 1689), Randolph, *Papers*, 4:266; Johnson, *Adjustment to Empire*, 91; Webb, *Lord Churchill's Coup*, 191, 193. On Andros's non-military response to a civilian uprising, see Ian Steele, "Governors or Generals?: A Note on Martial Law and the Revolution of 1689 in English America," *W&MQ*, 3d ser., 46 (1989): 304–14.

35. A Narrative of the Proceedings (n.d.), CO 5/855, PRO; Randolph to Lords of Trade (29 May 1689), Randolph, *Papers*, 4:280–81. The ministers were Joshua Moody, James Allen, Samuel Willard, Cotton Mather, and William Milborne. See also *DRNY*, 3:582, 582n.; T. H. Breen, "War, Taxes and Political Brokers: The Ordeal of Massachusetts Bay, 1675–1692," in *Puritans and Adventurers: Change and Persistence in Early* America (New York and Oxford, 1980), 81–105; Lovejoy, *Glorious Revolution*, 302; Barnes, *Dominion of New England*, 241, 243.

36. *Andros Tracts*, 1:20.

37. Ibid., 1:5, 20, 3:59; Narrative of the Proceedings (16 July 1689), CO 5/855, PRO and *CSPC*, 92; Webb, *Lord Churchill's Coup*, 192.

38. Randolph to Blathwayt (20 July 1689), Randolph, *Papers*, 6:289–92.

39. Mark Goldie, "The Political Thought of the Anglican Revolution," in *The Revolutions of 1688*, ed. Beddard, 104; Account of the Late Revolution, 1689, *Andros Tracts*, 2:196.

40. Randolph to Lords of Trade (29 May 1685), Randolph, *Papers*, 4:280.

41. Randolph to My Lord Privy Seal (23 July 1689), Randolph, *Papers*, 4:285.

42. *Andros Tracts*, 2:196; Randolph to Blathwayt (20 July 1689) and Randolph to the Governor of Barbados (16 May 1689), Randolph, *Papers*, 4:265, 6:291.

43. Gershom Bulkeley, "Will and Doom," in *Public Records Connecticut*, 3:455; Barnes, *Dominion of New England*, 237; Mather quoted by Barnes, 238n.

44. Randolph to Council Trade & Planations (5 Sept. 1689), Randolph, *Papers*, 4:297; Randolph to the Bishop of London (25 Oct. 1689), *CSPC*, 165.

45. Account of the Late Revolution in New England, *Andros Tracts*, 1689, 2:196.

46. John Palmer, An Impartial Account (1690), *Andros Tracts*, 1:29–30; Dunn, *Puritans and Yankees*, 254.

47. Declaration, 18 Apr. 1689, *Andros Tracts,* 1:15–17.

48. Ibid., 1:13–17.

49. Ibid., 3:23.

50. Ibid., 1:6, 7, 153; *Narratives of the Insurrections*, ed. Andrews, 202; Randolph to Council Trade & Plantations, Randolph, *Papers*, 4:280–81; Silverman, *Cotton Mather*, 71; K. G. Davies, "The Revolutions in America," in *The Revolutions of 1688*, ed. Beddard, 246–69; Webb, *Lord Churchill's Coup*, 192; Barnes, *Dominion of New England*, 260.

51. *Narratives of the Insurrections*, ed. Andrews, 203; Narrative of the Proceedings (16 July 1689), *CSPC*, 93; Webb, *Lord Churchill's Coup*, 193.

52. *Andros Tracts*, 1:7; *Narratives of the Insurrections*, 202–4. For a complete list of those imprisoned, see *Narratives of the Insurrections,* ed. Andrews, 172–74, 172n., 174n.

53. *Andros Tracts*, 3:25; Lovejoy, *Glorious Revolution*, 241, 245; Barnes, *Dominion of New England*, 244; Dunn, *Puritans and Yankees*, 87.

54. Gershom Bulkeley, "Will and Doom," in *Connecticut Public Records*, 3:456; *Rhode Island Records*, 3:257; Extract Letter (10 June 1689) and Deputy Governor Rhode Island to King (30 Jan. 1690), *CSPC*, 82, 214; *Andros Tracts*, 3:25–26.

55. Bradstreet to King (20 May 1689), *CSPC*, 42; Hall, *The Last American Puritan*, 225.

56. Barnes, *Dominion of New England*, 247.

57. Voorhees, "The 'fervent zeale' of Jacob Leisler," *W&MQ*, 3d ser., 51 (1994): 447–72.

58. Minutes Council New York (18 May 1689), *CSPC*, 757; Nicholson to Randolph, Randolph, *Papers*, 4:253; Webb, *Lord Churchill's Coup*, 195.

59. Abstract Nicholas Bayard's Journal (28 June 1689) and Stephen van Cortlandt to Andros (9 July 1689), *CSPC*, 75, 80–81.

60. Adrian Howe, "The Bayard Treason Trial: Dramatizing Anglo-Dutch Politics in Early Eighteenth-Century New York City," *W&MQ*, 3d ser., 47 (1990): 57–89.

61. For the domino effect of the Glorious Revolution on events in the Delaware River Valley, see David William Voorhees, " 'To assert our Right before it be quite lost': The Leisler Rebellion in the Delaware River Valley," *Pennsylvania History* 64 (1997): 5–27.

62. [?] to Lord Baltimore (Oct. 1687), Blathwayt Papers, Colonial Williamsburg; also quoted in Lovejoy, *Glorious Revolution in America*, 258. See also Lovejoy, 264–68; Hall, Leder, Kammen, ed., *Glorious Revolution*, 144–45, 167–68.

63. *Narratives of the Insurrections*, ed. Andrews, 205.

64. Ibid., 171–72; *Andros Tracts*, 1:7–8; Johnson, *John Nelson*, 54.

65. Randolph to Lords of Trade (29 May 1681), Randolph, *Papers*, 4:281.

66. *Narratives of the Insurrections*, ed. Andrews, 208; Account of the Late Reverend Nathaniel Byfield, 29 Apr. 1689, *Andros Tracts*, 1:8.

67. Randolph to Lords of Trade (29 May 1689) and Order to Remove Andros to Castle (6 June 1689), *CSPC*, 47, 62; *Narratives of the Insurrections*, 187.

68. *Andros Tracts*, 2:211–12; Bailyn, *New England Merchants*, 176; Sosin, *English America and the Revolution of 1688*, 93.

69. Resolution of the Convention Concerning Sir Edmund Andros, Joseph Dudley, and Edward Randolph (n.d.), CO 5/855, PRO.

70. An Account of the Late Revolutions in New-England (6 June 1689), CO 5/855, PRO; *Andros Tracts*, 1:175; *Narratives of the Insurrections*, ed. Andrews, 172, 172n., 173, 173n., 174, 174n., 189; Hutchinson, *History*, 1:328; Randolph to Lord Privy Seal (23 July 1689) and Randolph to Bishop of London (25 Oct. 1689), Randolph, *Papers*, 4:284, 307.

71. Randolph to Bishop of London (25 Oct. 1689)and Randolph to Robert Chaplin (28 Oct. 1689), *CSPC*, 165, 169–70; *Andros Tracts*, 1:175, 3:23.

72. Hutchinson, *History*, 1:392; Bradstreet to Robert Treat (3 Aug. 1689), *Connecticut Public Records*, 3:468–69; *Andros Tracts*, 3:95–96, 100; John Tudor to Nicholson (Aug. 1689), Elizabeth Usher to John Usher (16 Oct. 1689), and Deputy Governor Rhode Island to King (30 Jan. 1690), *CSPC*, 132, 158, 214; Barnes, *Dominion of New England*, 261.

73. *Andros Tracts*, 3:97–98, 100–02, 235; Randolph, *Papers*, 2:111n.

74. *Andros Tracts*, 3:104, 106; Randolph to Dr. Cooke (25 Nov. 1689), and Randolph to William Blathwayt (20 July 1689), Randolph, *Papers*, 5:22, 6:289; Barnes, *Dominion of New England*; 255n.

75. *Narratives of the Insurrections*, ed. Andrews, 205; *Andros Tracts*, 3:23, 39n.; Short Account Loss of Pemaquid Fort (3 Aug. 1689), *CSPC*, 114–15; Randolph to Lords of Trade (29 May 1689), Randolph, *Papers*, 4:277–78.

76. Extract Letter (10 June 1689) and Lords of Trade to King (12 June 1690), *CSPC*, 82, 282; Barnes, *Dominion of New England*, 257.

77. *Andros Tracts*, 3:26; A Short Account of the Loss of Pemaquid Fort (2 Aug. 1689) and Copy of a Letter from Boston, (24 Oct. 1689), *CSPC*, 114–15, 206.

78. Copy Letter from Boston (24 Oct. 1689), *CSPC*, 206; *Andros Tracts*, 3:26.

79. Short Account Loss of Pemaquid Fort (3 Aug. 1689), Randolph to Lords of Trade (5 Sept. 1689), same to same (15 Oct. 1689), Charles Redford to Andros (7 March 1690), Present State of Great Island, N.H., and Report of Captain Holmes (July 1690), *CSPC*, 114–15, 140, 263, 156–57, 222–23, 30; *Andros Tracts*, 2:182, 3:24–25; Robert Livingston to Andros (14 Apr. 1690), *DRNY*, 3:708; Randolph to William Blathwayt (20 July 1689), Randolph, *Papers*, 6:291. The frustrated soldier is also quoted by Barnes, *Dominion of New England*, 260.

80. See Breen, "War, Taxes and Political Brokers: The Ordeal of Massachusetts Bay, 1675–1692," in *Puritans and Adventurers*, ed. Breen, 81–105. Theodore Dwight Bozeman is another of many historians who sees King Philip's War as a turning point in New England history. See *To Live Ancient Lives: The Primitivist Dimension in Puritanism* (Chapel Hill and London, 1988), 312.

CHAPTER 11. THE GLORIOUS REVOLUTION, PART 2

1. *The Oxford Book of Light Verse*, comp. W. H. Auden (London, Oxford, and New York, 1938, 1973).

2. Christopher Hill, *The Century of Revolution, 1603–1714* (New York and London, 1961, 1980), 265. On the worsening conditions for the lower orders of English society following the Glorious Revolution, see Angus McInnes, "The Revolution and the People," in *Britain After the Glorious Revolution, 1689–1714*, ed. Geoffrey Holmes (London, 1969), 80–95. For an opposing view on the effects of the Glorious Revolution on American colonists, see Jack P. Green, "The Glorious Revolution and the British Empire, 1688–1783," in *Negotiated Authorities: Essays in Colonial Political and Constitutional History*, ed. Jack P.

Greene (Charlottesville and London, 1994), 78–92. On the positive effects of the Glorious Revolution on England's government and the influence of the Netherlands on England's political, cultural, and social development following William's accession and the rejection of French influence, see William Speck, "Britain and the Dutch Republic," in *A Miracle Mirrored: The Dutch Republic in European Perspective*, ed. Karel Davids and Jan Lucassen (Cambridge, UK, 1995), 173–95.

3. Address Charlestown Inhabitants (Jan. 1690]) and Address Church of England Members (25 Jan. 1690), *CSPC*, 212, 213.

4. Boston Merchant to London Merchant (16 May 1689), Narrative of the Present State of Great Island, N. H. (15 May 1690) and Report of Capt. Holmes (July 1690), *CSPC*, 40, 263, 301.

5. *Andros Tracts*, 1:17–18, 2:178; Order King in Council, (25 July 1689) and King to Revolutionary Government (30 July 1689), *CSPC*, 105, 111; CO 5/855, PRO; Bloom, "Sir Edmund Andros," 148–49.

6. Hall, *The Last American Puritan*, 229; Barnes, *Dominion of New England*, 254.

7. Randolph to archbishop of Canterbury (28 May 1689) and Petition of Andros, Randolph presented at Council of Trade Meeting (29 July 1689), Randolph, *Papers*, 4:268–71, 289; Sosin, *English America and the Revolution of 1688*, 94.

8. Randolph to Dr. William Sancroft, archbishop of Canterbury (28 May 1689), Randolph, *Papers*, 4:270–71; Petition John Riggs (22 July 1689), CO 5/855, PRO and *CSPC*, 100. See also *CSPC*, 263, 282, 301; Petition Andros, Randolph, presented at Council of Trade Meeting (29 July 1689), Randolph, *Papers*, 4:289.

9. Council of Trade Meeting (29 July 1689), Randolph, *Papers*, 4:289–90; Order King in Council (25 July 1689) and King to Revolutionary Government (30 July 1689), *CSPC*, 105, 111.

10. *Andros Tracts*, 2:276, 3:3–5.

11. Nicholas Bayard to Francis Nicholson (10 Dec. 1689) and Randolph to Lords of Trade (10 Jan. 1690), *CSPC*, 190, 205–6.

12. Randolph to Governor of Barbados (16 May 1689), Randolph, *Papers*, 4:266; Andros and others to Governor and Council (26 Dec. 1689), CO 5/855, PRO.

13. Case of Massachusetts Colonists (18 May 1689), *CSPC*, 40; Brief in the Case of Sir Edmund Andros and others, CO 5/855, PRO.

14. *DRNY*, 3:659; *Andros Tracts*, 1:30, 105, 106, 118, 150, 155.

15. Nicholas Bayard to John West (14 Jan. 1690), *CSPC*, 208.

16. *Andros Tracts*, 1:153.

17. Ibid., 1:150, 151, 152.

18. Order to Captain John Fairweather (12 Dec. 1689), Instructions Massachusetts Government (24 Jan. 1690), and Warrant to Gilbert Bant (5 Feb. 1690), *CSPC*, 206, 212, 251; *Andros Tracts*, 1:25, 3:113; Order to Gilbert Bant, commander of Mahitabell (n.d.), CO 5/855, PRO; Hall, *Edward Randolph*, 129; Hall, Leder, and Kammen, ed., *Glorious Revolution in America*, 69; Sosin, *English America and the Revolution of 1688*, 130.

19. Webb, "The Trials of Sir Edmund Andros," in *The Human Dimensions of Nation Making*, ed. Martin, 23–53; Theodore B. Lewis, ed., "Sir Edmund Andros's Hearing before the Lords of Trade and Plantations, 17 April 1690," American Antiquarian Society, *Proceedings* (1973): 241–50.

20. Lewis, ed., "Sir Edmund Andros's Hearing," 241–50.

21. *Andros Tracts*, 2:176–77; Charges Against Andros, CO 5/855, PRO.

22. *Andros Tracts*, 2:173; Johnson, *Adjustment to Empire*, 171; Sosin, *English America and the Revolution of 1688*, 131; Webb, "The Trials of Sir Edmund Andros," in *The Human Dimensions of Nation Making*, ed. Martin, 23–53. On the Massachusetts charter, see Minutes of the Order of Council (30 Apr. 1691), CO 5/856, PRO.

23. Report of the Proceedings Against Andros and others (Apr. 1690), *Andros Tracts*, 1:173; Barnes, *Dominion of New England*, 265; Hall, Leder, and Kammen, ed., *Glorious Revolution in America*, 70–71; Johnson, *Adjustment to Empire*, 173.

24. Lewis, ed., "Sir Edmund Andros's Hearing," 241–50; Webb, "The Trials of Sir Edmund Andros," in *The Human Dimensions of Nation Making*, ed. Martin, 23–53.

25. *Andros Tracts*, 173n.

26. Richard R. Johnson, "The Revolution of 1688–1689 in the American Colonies," in *The Anglo-Dutch Moment: Essays on the Glorious Revolution and Its World Impact*, ed. Jonathan I. Israel (Cambridge, New York, and Melbourne, 1991), 231.

27. *Andros Tracts*, 1:173–74n., 175–76, 3:41–43; Order King in Council 24 Apr. 1690), *CSPC*, 252; Hall, Leder, and Kammen, ed. *Glorious Revolution in America*, 71–72.

28. Mather quoted in Hall, *The Last American Puritan*, 233; Webb, "The Trials of Sir Edmund Andros," in *The Human Dimensions of Nation Making*, ed. Martin, 23–53.

29. *Andros Tracts*, 2:179–82.

30. Ibid

31. Answers of Sir Edmund Andros, CO 5/855, PRO; *Andros Tracts*, 2:179–82, 3:26; Answers of the late Governor (24 Apr. 1690), *CSPC*, 251.

32. Answers of the late Governor, (24 Apr. 1690), *CSPC*, 251.

33. *Andros Tracts*, 3:20–27, 34–36; Andros's Report, *CSPC*, 270–71.

34. Andros's Report, *CSPC*, 273–74; Hall, Leder, and Kammen, ed. *Glorious Revolution in America*, 73; Webb, "The Trials of Sir Edmund Andros," in *Human Dimensions of Nation Making*, ed. Martin, 23–53.

35. Cooke and Oakes Report, *CSPC*, 274–75.

36. Massachusetts Agents Describe Events (16 Oct. 1690), in *Glorious Revolution in America*, ed. Hall, Leder, and Kammen, ed., 72–73.

37. *Andros Tracts*, 1:35–36, 38, 40. See also Lovejoy, *The Glorious Revolution*, 331–32.

38. *Andros Tracts*, 1:40.

39. Ibid., 2:76.

40. Henry Sloughter to William Blathwayt (7 May 1691), *CSPC*, 429–30.

41. Ibid.

42. Commission Benjamin Fletcher Governor New York and Pennsylvania (21 Oct. 1692), *CSPC*, 725; Report Board of Trade on Penn's Petition (1 and 3, Aug. 1694) and Queen to Fletcher (21 Aug. 1694), *DRNY*, 3:108–9.

43. Lustig, *Privilege and Prerogative*, 6–8.

44. Hall, *The Last American Puritan*, 237–38; Johnson, *Adjustment to Empire*, 183.

45. Hall, *The Last American Puritan*, 249–50; Barnes, *Dominion of New England*, 269–70.

46. Minutes and Abstract of Proceedings (30 Apr. 1691), and Powers desired by Agents, Heads of a Charter, CO 5/856, PRO; *Andros Tracts*, 2:280–84.

47. Hall, *The Last American Puritan*, 251; *Narratives of the Insurrections*, ed. Andrews, 284–85, 296; Lovejoy, *The Glorious Revolution*, 347–49.

48. Lewis, ed., "Sir Edmund Andros's Hearing," 241–50; *Andros Tracts*, 2:280.

49. Bloom, "Sir Edmund Andros," vi.

50. *Andros Tracts*, xxxvi.

51. Minutes Virginia Council (3 June 1690), King to Effingham (10 June 1688), Lord Nottingham to Lords of Trade (4 Feb. 1692), and Order King in Council (11 Feb. 1692), *CSPC*, 277, 560, 597, 598.

CHAPTER 12: VIRGINIA, PART 1

1. *The Oxford Book of English Verse, 1250–1918*, ed. Sir Anthony Quiller-Couch (New York and Toronto, 1939).

2. *Executive Journals of the Council of Colonial Virginia*, ed. H. R. McIlwaine (Richmond, 1925), 1:269, hereafter cited as *Journal Virginia Council*.

3. Richard L. Morton, *Colonial Virginia*, 2 vols. (Chapel Hill, 1960), 1:332–33.

4. Webb, *Lord Churchill's Coup*, 233, 240.

5. Randolph to William Blathwayt (Jan. 1692), Randolph, *Papers*, 7:423–44; Benjamin Fletcher to William Blathwayt (10 Sept. 1692) and Andros to Committee of Trade (3 Nov. 1692), *CSPC*, 698, 734.

6. Minutes Virginia Council (20 Sept. 1692), *CSPC*, 713; Webb, "The Strange Career of Francis Nicholson," *W&MQ*, 3d ser., 23 (1966): 513–48.

7. Morton, *Colonial Virginia*, 1:335.

8. Bloom, "Sir Edmund Andros," 192; Carl Bridenbaugh, *Jamestown, 1544–1699* (New York and Oxford, 1980), 118, 142. The present day entrance to the largely rebuilt church at Jamestown is believed to date from the seventeenth century and is constructed of brick.

9. On European reactions to American climate, see Karen Ordahl Kupperman, "The Puzzle of the American Climate in the Early Colonial Period," *American Historical Review* 87 (1982): 162–89; Helen C. Rountree, *The Powhatan Indians of Virginia* (Norman, Okla. and London, 1989), 17.

10. Andros to Council of Trade (22 July 1693), Journal Council of Trade (16 Mar. 1694), King William to Andros (29 Mar. 1694), Effingham to earl of Sunderland (29 June 1687), and Effingham to King James (29 June 1689), *CSPC*, 132, 265, 276, 388; Norton, *Fur Trade*, 41, 46; Richard L. Morton, *Struggle Against Tyranny and the Beginning of a New Era, Virginia, 1677–1699* (Williamsburg, Va., 1957), 41, 46.

11. On the construction and appearance of housing in Virginia, see "A Frenchman's Description of Housing in Virginia, 1687," in *A Huguenot Exile in Virginia, or Voyages of a Frenchmen Exiled for His Religion*, ed. Gilbert Chinard (New York, 1934), 119–20; quoted in *The Old Dominion in the Seventeenth Century, A Documentary History of Virginia, 1606–1689*, ed. Warren M. Billings (Chapel Hill, 1975), 306. On life, economic pursuits, society, agriculture, and slavery in Virginia, see Darrett B. Rutman and Anita H. Rutman, *A Place in Time: Middlesex County, Virginia, 1650–1750* (New York and London, 1984).

12. Andros to William Blathwayt, 23 Oct. 1693 Blathwayt Papers, Colonial Williamsburg; Bridenbaugh, *Jamestown*, 124.

13. Robert Beverley, *The History and Present State of Virginia* (Indianapolis and New York, 1971), 56.

14. On tobacco cultivation in Virginia, see T. H. Breen, *Tobacco Culture: The Mentality of the Great Tidewater Planters on the Eve of the Revolution* (Princeton, 1985).

15. Andros's Answers to Queries (22 Apr. 1697), *CSPC*, 456.

16. On slavery in seventeenth-century Virginia, see T. H. Breen and Stephen Innes, *"Myne Owne Ground:" Race and Freedom on Virginia's Eastern Shore, 1640–1676* (New York and Oxford, 1980); Alan Kulikoff, *Tobacco and Slaves: The Development of Southern Cultures in the Chesapeake, 1680–1800* (Chapel Hill and London, 1986); Edmund S. Morgan, *American Slavery, American Freedom: The Ordeal of Colonial Virginia* (New York and London, 1975).

17. T. H. Breen, "A Changing Labor Force and Race Relations," in *Puritans and Adventurers,* ed. Breen, 127–47. For the effects of Bacon's Rebellion on the institution of slavery, see Morgan, "Toward Slavery," chap. 15 in *American Slavery, American Freedom*, 295–315.

18. *Journal Virginia Council,* 1:317; Philip Alexander Bruce, *Economic History of Virginia in the Seventeenth Century*, 2 vols. (New York, 1895, 1935), 2:118.

19. On the effect of the war on trade, see Andros to Board of Trade (22 July 1693), CO 5/1308, PRO.

20. Randolph to Board of Trade (26 Apr. 1698), Randolph, *Papers*, 5:172.

21. Andros to William Blathwayt (22 July 1693), Blathwayt Papers, Colonial Williamsburg; Bruce, *Economic History*, 2:346n.

22. Board of Trade Minutes (7 Apr. 1697), CO 391/91, PRO.

23. Memorial of Sir Thomas Lawrence (25 June 1695), *CSPC*, 518.

24. *Journal Virginia Council,* 1:294; Proclamation (25 May 1693), and Andros to Council of Trade (22 July 1693), CO 5/1308, PRO; Morton, *Colonial Virginia,* 1:343.

25. Randolph to William Blathwayt (14 Mar. 1693), Randolph, *Papers,* 7:431.

26. Board of Ordnance to Board of Trade (9 June 1694), CO 5/1308, PRO.

27. Andros to William Blathwayt (16 Jan. 1693), Blathwayt Papers; *Journal Virginia Council,* 1:278, 322; *The Correspondence of the Three William Byrds of Westover, Virginia,* ed. Marion Tinling (Charlottesville, Va., 1977) 1:177; Andros to Council of Trade (22 July 1693), Andros to earl of Nottingham (22 July 1693), and John Povey to Lieutenant General of Ordnance (1 June 1694), *CSPC,* 132, 292.

28. *Journal Virginia Council,* 1:280; Henry Hartwell, James Blair, and Edward Chilton, *The Present State of Virginia and the College*, ed. Hunter Dickinson Farish (Williamsburg, 1940), 22.

29. For the emergence of a ruling elite in Virginia, see Bernard Bailyn, "Politics and Social Structure in Virginia," in *Interpreting Colonial America*, ed. Martin, 186–204.

30. Memorandum (Apr. 1692) and Andros to Board of Trade (5 June 1698), *CSPC,* 265, 619; Morton, *Struggle Against Tyranny*, 14–15; Bloom, "Sir Edmund Andros," 186.

31. On the Virginia legal system, see Oliver Perry Chitwood, *Justice in Colonial Virginia* (Baltimore, 1905), 19–27; Lovejoy, *The Glorious Revolution*, 54, 64.

32. Jan Kukla, *Speakers and Clerks of the Virginia House of Burgesses, 1643–1776* (Richmond, 1981), 86, 92–93, 96.

33. *Journal Virginia Council*, 1:270.

34. Lord Effingham to Board of Trade (10 Feb. 1686), Memorandum Board of Trade (10 May 1686), King James to Effingham (1 Aug. 1686), and Effingham to Lord President Board of Trade (22 Feb. 1687), CO 5/1357, PRO; Morton, *Struggle Against Tyranny*, 36–37; Morton, *Colonial Virginia*, 1:330; Osgood, *American Colonies in the Seventeenth Century*, 3:303.

35. Andros to Secretary of State (31 Oct. 1698), CO 5/1307, PRO; *Journal Virginia Council*, 1:275, 277; Andros to Blathwayt (16 Jan. 1693), Blathwayt Papers, Colonial Williamsburg; Andros to James Vernon (31 Oct. 1698), *CSPC*, 516.

36. The question of bulk tobacco had long been a concern of the ministry. See "Reasons why the exportation of bulk tobacco from Maryland and Virginia should be prohibited" (13 Aug. 1687), Minutes Virginia Assembly (9 May 1688), and Andros Speech to Assembly (12 Oct. 1693), *CSPC*, 182, 418, 544; Abstract Proceedings General Assembly (10 Oct. 1693), CO 5/1308, PRO.

37. Andros to William Blathwayt (22 July 1693 and 5 Jan. 1694), Blathwayt Papers, Colonial Willamsburg; Kukla, *Speakers and Clerks of the Virginia House of Burgesses*, 86; Bloom, "Sir Edmund Andros," 169–70.

38. Andros to duke of Shrewsbury (4 June 1695), CSPC, 497; *Journal Virginia Council*, 1:296; Morton, *Colonial Virginia*, 1:343; Morton, *Struggle Against Tyranny*, 58–59; Bloom, "Sir Edmund Andros," 201–2.

39. *Journal Virginia Council*, 281, 296.

40. William to Andros (1 Mar. 1693), Andros to Board of Trade (22 July 1693), Benjamin Fletcher to Board of Trade (9 Oct. 1693), and Andros to Board of Trade (4 May 1694), *CSPC*, 36, 132, 171, 285; Jennings, *Ambiguous Iroquois Empire*, 202, 205, 206; Norton, *Fur Trade*, 18. On Iroquois population, see Snow, *The Iroquois*, 110.

41. Randolph to William Blathwayt (18 May 1694 and 3 July 1694), Randolph, *Papers*, 7:461, 464.

42. Kukla, *Speakers and Clerks of the Virginia House of Burgesses*, 92–93.

43. *Journal Virginia Council*, 1:303, 311; Andros to Board of Trade (14 May 1694) and William to Andros (1 May 1695), *CSPC*, 286, 469; *Correspondence of the Three William Byrds*, ed. Tinling, 1:175.

44. Queen Mary to Andros (21 Aug. 1694), Andros to Sir John Trenchard (20 Mar. 1695), Andros to Board of Trade (4 June 1695), Andros to duke of Shrewsbury (4 June 1695), and Minutes Council of New York (15 Aug. 1695), *CSPC*, 335, 442, 495–96, 497; *Journal Virginia Council*, 1:321, 343, 344; Andros to Board of Trade (27 June 1696) and Council to Board of Trade (24 Apr. 1697), CO 5/1309, CO 5/1359, PRO; Bloom, "Sir Edmund Andros," 174–75.

45. Ritchie, *Captain Kidd and the War Against the Pirates*, 43–44, 46; Stephen B. Baxter, *William III and the Defense of European Liberty, 1650–1702* (New York, 1966), 309.

46. Herbert L. Osgood, *The American Colonies in the Eighteenth Century*, 4 vols. (Gloucester, Mass., 1958), 1:128.

47. Michael G. Hall, "The House of Lords: Edward Randolph and the Navigation Act of 1696," *W&MQ*, 3d ser., 14 (1957): 494–515.

48. *Acts of the Privy Council* (21 June 1694), 2:272; Osgood, *The American Colonies in the Eighteenth Century*, 1:132–33, 135, 138; Jennifer Carter, "The Revolution and the Constitution," in *Britain After the Glorious Revolution,*

1689–1714," ed. Geoffrey Holmes (London, 1969), 39–58; Ian Steele, *The Politics of Colonial Policy: The Board of Trade in Colonial Administration, 1696–1720* (Oxford, 1968), 20, 23–24; Peter Laslett, "John Locke, the Great Recoinage, and the Origins of the Board of Trade, 1695–1698," *W&MQ*, 3d ser., 14 (1957): 370–402.

49. Board of Trade Minutes (15 Jan. 1697), CO 5/1359, PRO.

CHAPTER 13. VIRGINIA, PART 2

1. *Papers Relating to the History of the Church in Virginia, 1650–1776,* ed. William Stevens Perry (1870), 6, hereafter cited as *Virginia Church.*

2. *Acts of the Privy Council* (11 Feb. 1692), 2:206; James Blair Named Commissioner (15 Dec. 1689) and James Blair to [earl of Nottingham?] (29 March 1693), *CSPC,* 69, 192.

3. Lionel Copley to Board of Trade (29 July 1692), Randolph, *Papers,* 5:77–80.

4. Copley to Board of Trade (29 July 1692) and Randolph to Blathwayt (28 July 1692), Randolph, *Papers,* 5:80, 7:397; Osgood, *American Colonies in the Eighteenth Century,* 1:166–67, 171.

5. Order to Search the Lodging of... (7 April 1693), Randolph, *Papers,* 5:92; Copley to Council of Trade (11 Apr. 1693) and Council of Trade Journal (15 Sept. 1693), *CSPC,* 80, 81, 159.

6. *Journal Virginia Council,* 1:284, 287; Maryland Council Meeting (21 Dec. 1692), Order to Arrest Randolph (6 Apr. 1693), and Andros to Copley (27 Apr. 1693), Randolph, *Papers,* 5:82, 91, 99, 100; Randolph Letters to Council of Trade (Apr. 1693), *CSPC,* 82.

7. Andros to Copley (27 Apr. 1693), Randolph, *Papers,* 5:99; Randolph to [?] (29 Apr. 1695), *CSPC,* 382; *Journal Virginia Council,* 1:287.

8. *Virginia Church,* 9; Webb, *Lord Churchill's Coup,* 248–49.

9. Andros to earl of Nottingham (23 Oct. 1693), CO 5/1307, PRO.

10. Maryland Council Minutes (25 Sept. 1693), *Maryland Archives,* 20:6; Journal Assembly Maryland (23 Sept. 1693 and 26 Sept. 1693), *CSPC,* 166.

11. Andros to Council of Trade (23 Oct. 1693), *CSPC,* 189.

12. Andros to Blathwayt (23 Oct. 1693, 4 May 1694, and 9 May 1694), Blathwayt Papers, Colonial Williamsburg; Randolph to Blathwayt (3 Dec. 1693), Randolph, *Papers,* 7:455; Andros to Board of Trade (4 May 1694), *CSPC,* 285; Maryland Council Minutes (5 May 1694 and 7 May 1694), *Maryland Archives,* 20:57, 59.

13. Council Minutes (26 July 1693), *Maryland Archives,* 20:120; Journal Board of Trade (12 Jan. 1694), *CSPC,* 231.

14. Andros to Blathwayt (20 July 1694), Blathwayt Papers, Colonial Williamsburg; Maryland Council Minutes (27 July 1694), *Maryland Archives,* 20:120–21; Maryland Council Minutes (27 Sept. 1694), *CSPC,* 359.

15. Maryland Council Minutes (27 July 1692), *Maryland Archives,* 20:122.

16. Randolph to Blathwayt (22 Aug. 1694), Randolph, *Papers,* 7:466–67; Maryland Council Minutes (27 July 1692 and 24 Sept. 1694), *Maryland Archives,* 20:122, 140–41; Maryland Council Minutes (27 July 1694), *CSPC,* 314.

17. Plater to Blathwayt (18 Dec. 1694), Randolph, *Papers,* 7:469; Maryland

Council Minutes (29 Sept. 1694), *Maryland Archives*, 20:147–48; Osgood, *American Colonies in the Eighteenth Century*, 1:171, 185.

18. Andros to Blathwayt (20 Mar. 1695), Blathwayt Papers, Colonial Williamsburg; Maryland Council Minutes (11 Dec. 1696 and 18 Mar. 1697), *Maryland Archives*, 20:553, 23:72.

19. Andros to Blathwayt (20 July 1694), Blathwayt Papers, Colonial Williamsburg; Maryland Council Minutes (14 Mar. 1698), *Maryland Archives*, 22:12–13; Andros to Sir John Trenchard (21 July 1694) and Andros to Board of Trade (4 June 1695), *CSPC*, 312, 496; Paul A. W. Wallace, *Indians in Pennsylvania*, 111–12; Osgood, *American Colonies in the Seventeenth Century*, 3:289; Bloom, "Sir Edmund Andros," 180–81. On Virginia's indigenous Indians, see Rountree, *The Powhattan Indians of Virginia*, and Stephen R. Potter, *Commoners, Tribute, and Chiefs: The Development of Algonquian Culture in the Potomac Valley* (Charlottesville and London, 1993).

20. Minutes Virginia Council, *Journal Virginia Council*, 1:368, 369, 370; Maryland Agents' Journal (8–10 June 1697), Agents to Andros (9 June 1697 and 12 June 1697), and Maryland Council Meeting (23 Mar. 1698), *Maryland Archives*, 23:143–45, 23:146, 22:28.

21. Morton, *Struggle Against Tyranny*, 31.

22. Wallace, *Indians in Pennsylvania*, 112–13; Jennings, *Ambiguous Iroquois Empire*, 249; Wesley Frank Craven, *White, Red, and Black* (Charlottesville, 1971), 63–64.

23. Wallace, *Indians in Pennsylvania*, 109.

24. *Journal Virginia Council*, 1:371; Andros to Nicholson (12 June 1697), Nicholson to Andros (24 June 1697), and Virginia Council Minutes (11 Aug. 1697), *Maryland Archives*, 23:142, 301.

25. Nicholson to Andros (16 Oct. 1697), Maryland Council Minutes (25 Mar. 1698), *Maryland Archives*, 22:38, 23:143, 301; Virginia Council Minutes, 10 Nov. 1697, *Journal Virginia Council*, 1:376.

26. Hall, Leder, and Kammen, ed., *Glorious Revolution in America*, 194.

27. Copies of Proceedings John Coode (1 July 1698) and Minutes Maryland Council (10 Aug. 1698), *CSPC*, 299, 373, 517; Maryland Council Minutes (19 Feb. 1697, 11 Jan. 1698, 30 June 1698, and 1 July 1698), *Maryland Archives*, 23:35, 374–75, 438–39, 445; Abstract of Gerald Slye's Letter, Fulham Palace Papers, Misc., no. 49; also quoted in Webb, "Strange Career of Francis Nicholson," *W&MQ*, 3d ser., 23 (1966): 513–48; Bloom, "Sir Edmund Andros," 182.

28. Beverley, *The History and Present State of Virginia*, 53.

29. *Journal Virginia Council*, 1:294; *Correspondence of the Three William Byrds*, ed. Tinling, 168.

30. *Journal Virginia Council*, 1:294, 301, 324.

31. For a biography of Blair, see Parke Rouse, Jr., *James Blair of Virginia* (Chapel Hill, 1971); "Memorial concerning Sir Edmund Andros by Dr. Blair," in *Virginia Church*, ed. Perry, 11–12, 15, 16.

32. Maryland Council Minutes (18 May 1695), *Maryland Archives*, 20:235.

33. Maryland Council Minutes (17 May 1695), *Maryland Archives*, 20:237.

34. *Journal Virginia Council*, 1:319; Bruce T. McCully, "Governor Francis Nicholson: Patron 'Par Excellence' of Religion and Learning in Colonial America," *W&MQ*, 3d ser., 39 (1982): 310–33; "Documents Relating to the Early History of the College of William and Mary and to the History of the Church in Virginia," contributed by Herbert L. Ganter, *W&MQ*, 2d ser., 19 (1939): 348–54.

35. Philip Alexander Bruce, *Institutional History of Virginia in the Seventeenth Century*, 2 vols. (New York and London), 1:111.

36. Andros to Sir John Trenchard (21 July 1694), *CSPC*, 312; Hartwell, Blair, and Chilton, *The Present State of Virginia*, xxix.

37. Perry, *Virginia Church*, 19–20, 44–45.

38. Ibid., 20.

39. "Sir Edmund Andros's Conduct," in *Virginia Church*, ed. Perry, 23.

40. *Journal Virginia Council*, 1:332, 337; Helen Hill Miller, *Colonel Parke of Virginia: The Greatest Hector in Town* (Chapel Hill, 1989), 80.

41. Perry, ed., *Virginia Church*, 24–28; Miller, *Colonel Parke*, 84–85.

42. In an 15 Oct. 1759 letter to his son, Alexander, Cadwallader Colden noted of Nicholson that "he was subject to excessive fits of passion so far as to lose the use of his reason. After he had been in one of these fits while he had the command of the army, an Indian said to one of the officers, 'The general is drunk.' 'No,' answered the officer, 'he never drinks any strong liquor.' The Indian replied, 'I do not mean that he is drunk with rum. He was born drunk.' " See Smith, *History of the Province of New York*, 1:305.

43. Perry, ed., *Virginia Church*, 25.

44. Ibid., 27–28.

45. Andros to duke of Shrewsbury (27 Apr. 1697), CO 5/1359, PRO; Louis B. Wright, "William Byrd's Defense of Sir Edmund Andros," *W&MQ*, 3d ser., 2 (1945): 47–62; Miller, *Colonel Parke*, xvii.

46. Sarah Harrison Blair, a member of one of Virginia's wealthiest and most powerful families, was apparently not a woman to be trifled with. At her 1687 marriage ceremony to Blair, the presiding minister asked her several times to take the customary vow to obey, to which she steadfastly answered, "No obey." The frustrated minister had no choice but to continue the ceremony. Kathleen Brown, *Good Wives, Nasty Wenches, and Anxious Patriarchs: Gender, Race, and Power in Colonial Virginia* (Chapel Hill and London, 1996), 339.

47. Perry, ed., *Virginia Church*, 26–27. Parke's personal life was as colorful as his public life. He did indeed bring his pregnant mistress, widow of a sea captain, to Virginia in 1692 and installed her in the house with his wife and two legitimate daughters, Frances and Lucy. When he returned to England in 1697, he took his mistress with him but left their son, Julius Caesar, with his wife to raise. See Miller, *Colonel Parke of Virginia*, xv–xvi, 69, 71.

48. Perry, ed., *Virginia Church*, 13–14, 32–33.

49. Ibid., 15–16, 47–48. On the issue of untenured clergy, see William H. Seiler, "The Anglican Parish Vestry in Colonial Virginia," *The Journal of Southern History* 22 (1956): 310–37.

50. *Journal Virginia Council*, 1:317, 323, 324–25; Perry, ed., *Virginia Church*, 12; Andros to Board of Trade (4 June 1695) and Andros to duke of Shrewsbury (4 June 1695), *CSPC*, 496, 497; Osgood, *Eighteenth Century*, 1:348.

51. William III to Andros (25 Feb. 1695), *CSPC*, 32.

52. Minutes Virginia Council (14 Oct. 1696), *CSPC*, 178; Andros to duke of Shrewsbury (27 Apr. 1697), CO 5/1359, PRO.

53. Council of Virginia to Board of Trade and Address of Burgesses to Andros (24 Apr. 1697), *CSPC*, 462, 463–64.

54. *Journal Virginia Council*, 1:350, 352, 356.

55. Andros to duke of Shrewsbury (27 June 1697), *CSPC*, 27. See also Petition of Clergy to Edmund Andros (25 June 1696), *CSPC*, 24–25.

56. Trustees of the College to Andros (24 March 1697), *CSPC*, 457.

57. Andros to duke of Shrewsbury (27 Apr. 1697), *CSPC*, 466–67.

58. *Journal Virginia Council*, 1:356, 363, 364.

59. James Blair to Archbishop of Canterbury (21 Jan. [1696/7?], in "Documents Relating to the Early History of the College of William and Mary," *W& MQ*, 2d ser., 19 (1939): 348–54.

60. Randolph Report (31 Aug. 1696), Randolph, *Papers*, 7:487, 490; Randolph to Board of Trade (6 Oct. 1696), CO 5/1359, PRO.

61. Minutes Board of Trade (15 July 1696 and 19 Aug. 1696), CO 391/9, PRO.

62. Board of Trade to Andros (1 Feb. 1697) and Andros to Board of Trade (1 July 1697), *CSPC*, 344, 528–29; Webb, "William Blathwayt, Imperial Fixer: Muddling Through to Empire, 1689–1717," *W&MQ*, 3d ser., 26 (1969): 373–415.

63. Benjamin Fletcher in New York was another Tory who was unacceptable to the board. Fletcher was severely criticized for granting large tracts of land, interfering with elections, and aiding pirates. Fletcher was replaced by the Whig Bellomont in 1697. See John D. Runcie, "The Problem of Anglo-American Politics in Bellomont's New York," *W&MQ*, 3d ser., 25 (1969): 191–217; Rex Maurice Naylor, "The Royal Prerogative in New York, 1691–1775," *New York History* 5 (1924): 221–53.

64. Board of Trade to Andros (22 Sept. 1697), *CSPC*, 594–56 and CO 5/1359, PRO; Board of Trade to Andros (2 Sept. 1697), CO 5/1359, PRO.

65. Andros to Board of Trade (14 Mar. 1698, 5 June 1698, and 8 July 1698), *CSPC*, 132–33, 265, 327.

66. Minutes Board of Trade (18 Aug. 1697, 23 Aug. 1697, 25 Aug. 1697, 20 Sept. 1697, 8 Oct. 1697, 20 Oct. 1697, 22 Oct. 1697, and 29 Oct. 1697 CO 391/91, PRO; William Popple to Henry Hartwell (9 Sept. 1697), Hartwell to Popple, (14 Sept. 1697), and Hartwell, Blair, and Chilton to Board of Trade (20 Oct. 1697), CO 5/1359, PRO.

67. J. P. Kenyon, *Revolution Principles: The Politics of Party, 1689–1720* (Cambridge, London, New York, and Melbourne, 1977), 1.

68. Peter Laslett, "John Locke, the Great Recoinage, and the Origins of the Board of Trade: 1695–1698," *W&MQ*, 3d ser., 14 (1957): 370–402; Webb, "Strange Career of Francis Nicholson," *W&MQ*, 3d ser., 23 (1966): 513–48. See also Morgan, *American Slavery, American Freedom*, 350.

69. James Blair to John Locke (20 Jan. 20 1698), Bodleian Library, Oxford, Class MS Locke c.4; Blair to Canterbury (21 Jan. [1696/7?]), in "Documents Relating to the Early History of the College of William and Mary," *W&MQ*, 2d ser. 19 (1939): 348–54; Webb, "Strange Career of Francis Nicholson," *W&MQ*, 3d ser., 23 (1966): 512–48; Morton, *Colonial Virginia*, 1:352; Morton, *Struggle Against Tyranny*, 67–68.

70. Blathwayt to Bishop of London (1697), Blathwayt Papers, Gloucestershire Records Office, Class D 1799/x5; Andros to Board of Trade (31 Oct. 1698), *CSPC*, 516; Louis B. Wright, "William Byrd's Defense of Sir Edmund Andros," *W&MQ*, 3d ser., 2 (1945): 47–62. For a biography of Byrd, see Richard Croom Beatty, *William Byrd of Westover* (Boston and New York, 1932); Louis B. Wright, "William Byrd's Opposition to Governor Francis Nicholson," *The Journal of Southern History* 11 (1945): 68–79.

71. Perry, ed., *Virginia Church*, 37.

72. Ibid., 37–38, 40, 42.

73. Ibid., 43, 54. On Virginia's churches and ministers, see William H. Seiler, "The Anglican Parish Vestry in Colonial Virginia," *The Journal of Southern History* 22 (1956): 310–37.

74. Morton, *Colonial Virginia*, 1:352; Bloom, "Sir Edmund Andros," 188.
75. Perry, ed., *Virginia Church*, 64–65.
76. In March 1698, Andros was so ill that he could not send assembly acts to the Board of Trade. He remained ill in October. See Edmund Jennings to Board of Trade (15 Mar. 1698) and Andros to Secretary Vernon (31 Oct. 1698), *CSPC*, 137, 516; Blair to Locke (20 Jan. 1698), Bodleian Library, Oxford, Class MS Locke, c.4; Webb, "William Blathwayt, Imperial Fixer: Muddling Through to Empire, 1689–1717," *W&MQ*, 3d ser., 26 (1969): 373–415; Laslett, "John Locke, the Great Recoinage, and the Origins of the Board of Trade, 1695–1698," *W&MQ*, 3d ser., 14 (1957): 370–402.
77. Marshall to Board of Trade (15 June 1698), *CSPC*, 273; John D. Runcie, "Bellomont's New York," *W&MQ*, 3d ser., 25 (1969): 191–217; Rex Maurice Naylor, "The Royal Prerogative In New York," *New York History* 5 (1924): 221–53.
78. In supporting Nicholson to succeed Andros, Blair backed the wrong horse. At the end of the Lambeth Palace hearing, Byrd observed that Blair expected "to lead that worthy Gentleman [Nicholson] by the nose as much as he pleases. But if he should prove restiff, I expect he will blacken him as much as he has done Sir Edmund Andros." Both predictions proved accurate. After Nicholson achieved the Virginia post, he rejected Blair. The latter then worked to secure Nicholson's recall, using the same techniques of slander, innuendo, and outright lies he had so successfully used against Andros. See Louis B. Wright, "William Byrd's Opposition to Governor Francis Nicholson," *The Journal of Southern History* 11 (1945): 68–79. On the use of slander to achieve political ends, see Patricia U. Bonomi, *The Lord Cornbury Scandal: The Politics of Reputation in British America* (Chapel Hill and London, 1998).
79. Andros to Board of Trade (14 Mar. 1698), Edmund Jennings to Board of Trade (15 Mar. 1698), Mr. Secretary Vernon to Board of Trade (31 May 1698), Andros to Secretary Vernon (31 Oct. 1698), *CSPC*, 138, 137, 259, 516; Peter Laslett, "John Locke, the Great Recoinage, and the Origins of the Board of Trade, 1695–1698," *W&MQ*, 3d ser., 14 (1957): 370–402.
80. Andros to James Vernon (31 Oct. 1698) and Andros to Board of Trade (31 Oct. 1698), *CSPC*, 516; Beverley, *History and Present State of Virginia*, 56; Bruce, *Institutional History of Virginia*, 1:549n.
81. *Journal Virginia Council*, 1:392–93, 397, 398–99; Nicholson to Board of Trade (4 Feb. 1699), CO 5/1359, PRO. Andros was owed £1,487.6s.3d. for salary and house rent from the Virginia assembly. He was still not paid on 28 March 1700. See William Lowndes to Blathwayt, 28 Mar. 1700, T27/16, PRO; William Byrd to William Blathwayt (6 Mar. 1699), *Correspondence of the Three William Byrds*, ed. Tinling, 181.

CONCLUSION

1. *Selected Poetry*, ed. Frank Kermode (New York, 1967).
2. Andros to earl of Sunderland (22 June 1708), same to same (15 July 1708), and Thomas Hopkins to Prince's Council (29 June 1708), Add. Mss. 61128, 61546, 61653, British Library. My thanks to Stephen Saunders Webb, whose notes are herein used. For Guernsey history, see also Duncan, *The History of Guernsey*, 128–29.
3. Bloom, "Sir Edmund Andros," 238n.
4. Will of Sir Edmund Andros, *Andros Tracts*, 1:xl.

Bibliography

PRIMARY SOURCES

Public Records: England

Bodleian Library, Oxford
  Class MS Locke
British Library
  Add. Ms. 19553, 28076, 29533, 29554, 61128, 61546, 61653
Gloucestershire Record Office
  Blathwayt Papers
Public Record Office, Kew Gardens
  Colonial Office, 5, 21, 22, 47, 56, 57, 63, 64, 67, 73, 391
  Treasury 27

Public Records: USA

Colonial Williamsburg
  Blathwayt Papers
New York State Library
  New York Colonial Manuscripts
New York University
  Leisler Papers Project, David William Voorhees, ed.

Published Primary Sources

Andrews, Charles M., ed. *Narratives of the Insurrections, 1675–1690.* New York, 1915, 1969.

Bartlett, John Russell, ed. *Records of the Colonies of Rhode Island and Providence Plantations in New England.* 10 vols. Providence, 1857.

Beverley, Robert. *The History and Present State of Virginia.* Indianapolis and New York, 1705, 1971.

Billings, Warren M., ed. *The Old Dominion in the Seventeenth Century: A Documentary History of Virginia, 1606–1689.* Chapel Hill, 1975.

Browne, William Hand, ed. *Archives of Maryland, Proceedings of the Council of Maryland, 1693–1697.* 69 vols. Baltimore, 1887–1903.

Burnet, Gilbert. *History of His Own Time.* 6 vols. Oxford, 1833.

Catalog 150. Sir Edmund Andros, 1637–1714. New York, 1978.

Christoph, Peter R. and Florence A. Christoph, ed. *The Andros Papers.* 3 vols. Syracuse, 1989–91.

Colden, Cadwallader. *The History of the Five Indian Nations Depending on the Province of New-York in America.* 1727, 1747, Ithaca, 1958.

Connecticut Historical Society. *Collections.* 31 vols. Hartford, 1924.

Corwin, E. G., ed. *Ecclesiastical Records of the State of New York.* 6 vols. Albany, 1905.

Dalton, Charles, ed. *English Army Lists and Commission Registers, 1661–1714.* 6 vols. London, 1892–1960.

Dankers, Jasper and Peter Sluyter. *Journal of a Voyage to New York.* Translated by Henry C. Murphy. Brooklyn, 1867 and Ann Arbor, 1966.

DeBeer, E. S., ed. *The Diary of John Evelyn.* 6 vols. Oxford, 1955.

Ganter, Herbert L., contributor. "Documents Relating to the Early History of the College of William and Mary and to the History of the Church in Virginia." *William and Mary Quarterly,* 2d ser., 19 (1939): 348–54

Grant, W. L. and James Munro, ed. *Acts of the Privy Council of England, Colonial Series.* Leichtenstein, 1966.

Hall, Michael, Lawrence H. Leder, and Michael G. Kammen, ed. *The Glorious Revolution in America.* Chapel Hill, 1964.

Hartwell, Henry, James Blair, and Edward Chilton. *The Present State of Virginia and the College.* Edited by Hunter Dickinson Farish. Williamsburg, 1940.

Henning, W. W., ed. *The Statues at Large, Being A Collection of all Laws of Virginia.* 13 vols. Richmond, 1805–23.

Hutchinson, Thomas. *Hutchinson Papers.* Prince Society. 2 vols. Boston, 1865 and New York, 1967.

Johnson, R. G. *A Historical Account of the First Settlement of Salem.* Philadelphia, 1839.

Latham, R. C. and W. Matthews, ed. *The Diary of Samuel Pepys.* 11 vols. Berkeley and Los Angeles, 1970–83.

Leder, Lawrence H., ed. *The Livingston Indian Records, 1666–1723.* Gettysburg, 1956.

Lewis, Theodore B., ed. "Sir Edmund Andros's Hearing Before the Lords of Trade and Plantations, 17 April 1690: Two Unpublished Accounts." American Antiquarian Society. *Proceedings* (1913): 241–50.

Lincoln, Charles H., ed. *Narratives of the Indian Wars, 1675–1699.* New York, 1913, 1941, 1966.

McIlwaine, H. R., ed. *Executive Journals of the Council of Colonial Virginia.* 3 vols. Richmond, 1925.

————. *Peter Wraxall's an Abridgment of the Indian Affairs in the Colony of New York, 1678–1751.* Cambridge, Mass., 1915.

McIlwaine, H. R. and J. P. Kennedy, ed. *Journals of the House of Burgesses of Virginia.* 13 vols. Richmond, 1905–15.

O'Callaghan, Edmund B., ed. *The Documentary History of the State of New York.* 4 vols. Albany, 1850–51.

O'Callaghan, Edmund B. and Berthold Fernow, ed. and John R. Brodhead, compiler. *Documents Relative to the Colonial History of the State of New York.* 15 vols. Albany, 1856–87.

Osgood, Herbert L., ed. *Minutes of the Common Council of the City of New York, 1675–1776.* New York, 1905.

Perry, William Stevens, ed. *Historical Collections Relating to the American Colonial Church.* 2 vols. Hartford, 1870 and New York, 1969.

———. *Papers Relating to the History of the Church in Virginia, 1650–1776.* 1870.

Sainsbury, W. Noel, et al., ed. *Calendar of State Papers, Colonial Series, America and the West Indies.* 42 vols. London, 1860–1953.

Snow, Dean R., Charles T. Gehring, and William A. Starna, ed. *In Mohawk Country: Early Narratives About a Native People.* Syracuse, 1996.

Thwaites, Reuben Gold, ed. *The Jesuit Relations and Allied Documents.* 73 vols. Cleveland, 1900.

Tinling, Marion, ed. *The Correspondence of the Three William Byrds of Westover, Virginia.* Charlottesville, 1977.

Toppan, Robert Noxon, ed. *Edward Randolph: His Letters and Official Papers, 1676–1703.* Boston, 1898 and New York, 1967.

Trumbull, J. Hammond, ed. *Public Records of the Colony of Connecticut from 1665–1678.* 15 vols. Hartford, 1852 and New York, 1968.

Whitehead, William A., ed. *Documents Relative to the Colonial History of the State of New Jersey,* 1st ser. 43 vols. Newark, 1880–1949.

Whitmore, W. N., ed. *The Andros Tracts.* 3 vols. Boston, 1868, 1869.

Wish, Harvey, ed. *The Diary of Samuel Sewall.* New York, 1967.

Wright, Louis B. "William Byrd's Defense of Sir Edmund Andros." *William and Mary Quarterly,* 3d ser., 2 (1945): 47–62.

Secondary Sources

Books

Andrews, Charles M. *The Colonial Period of American History.* 4 vols. New Haven, 1937.

Ashley, Maurice. *James II.* London, Toronto, and Melbourne, 1977.

Axtell, James. "The First Consumer Revolution." In *Beyond 1492: Encounters in Colonial America,* ed. James Axtell. New York and Oxford, 1992.

Bailyn, Bernard. *New England Merchants in the Seventeenth Century.* Boston, 1955 and New York, 1964.

———. "Politics and Social Structure in Virginia." In *Interpreting Colonial America,* 2d ed., ed. James Kirby Martin. New York, 1978.

Barnes, Viola Florence. *The Dominion of New England: A Study in British Colonial Policy.* New Haven, 1923 and New York, 1960.

———. "The Refusal of Massachusetts to Become a Part of the British Colonial System." In *Interpreting Colonial America,* 2d ed., ed. James Kirby Martin. New York, 1978.

Baxter, Stephen B. *William III and the Defense of European Liberty, 1650–1702*. New York, 1966.

Beatty, Richard Croom. *William Byrd of Westover*. Boston and New York, 1932.

Beddard, Robert. "The Protestant Succession," In *The Revolutions of 1688: The Andrew Browning Lectures, 1988*, ed. Robert Beddard. Oxford, 1991.

——. "The Unexpected Whig Revolution of 1688." In *The Revolutions of 1688: The Andrew Browning Lectures, 1998*, ed. Robert Beddard. Oxford, 1991.

Bonomi, Patricia U. *The Lord Cornbury Scandal: The Politics of Reputation in British America*. Chapel Hill and London, 1998.

Bourne, Russell. *The Red King's Rebellion: Racial Politics in New England, 1675–1678*. New York and Oxford, 1990.

Bozeman, Theodore Dwight. *To Live Ancient Lives: The Primitivist Dimension in Puritanism*. Chapel Hill and London, 1988.

Breen, T. H. and Stephen Innes. *"Myne Owne Grounde:" Race and Freedom on Virginia's Eastern Shore, 1640–1676*. New York and Oxford, 1980.

Breen, T. H. *Tobacco Culture: The Mentality of the Great Tidewater Planters on the Eve of the Revolution*. Princeton, 1985.

——. "Transfer of Culture: Chance and Design in the Shaping of Massachusetts Bay, 1630–1660." In *Puritans and Adventurers: Change and Persistence in Early America*, ed. T. H. Breen. New York and Oxford, 1980.

Bremer, Francis J. *The Puritan Experiment: New England Society from Bradford to Edwards*. New York, 1976.

Bridenbaugh, Carl. *Jamestown, 1544–1699*. New York and Oxford, 1980.

Brown, Kathleen M. *Good Wives, Nasty Wenches, and Anxious Patriarchs: Gender, Race, and Power in Colonial Virginia*. Chapel Hill and London, 1996.

Bruce, Philip Alexander. *Economic History of Virginia in the Seventeenth Century*, 2 vols. New York, 1895, 1935.

Buranelli, Vincent. *The King and the Quaker: A Study of William Penn and James II*. Philadelphia, 1962.

Burns, Allan. *History of the British West Indies*. London, 1954.

Bushman, Richard L. *King and People in Provincial Massachusetts*. Chapel Hill and London, 1985.

Calloway, Colin G. *New Worlds for All: Indians, Europeans, and the Remaking of Early America*. Baltimore and London, 1997.

——. *The Western Abenakis of Vermont, 1600–1800: War, Migration, and the Survival of an Indian People*. Norman, Okla. and London, 1990.

Carey, Edith F. *Essays on Guernsey History*. Guernsey, 1936.

Carroll, Peter N. *Puritanism and the Wilderness: The Intellectual Significance of the New England Frontier, 1629–1700*. New York, 1969.

Carter, Jennifer. "The Revolution and the Constitution." In *Britain After the Glorious Revolution, 1689–1714*, ed. Geoffrey Holmes. London, 1969.

Childs, John. *The Army, James II, and the Glorious Revolution*. New York, 1980.

Chitwood, Oliver Perry. *Justice in Colonial Virginia*. Baltimore, 1905.

Davis, K. G. "The Revolutions in America." In *The Revolutions of 1688: The Andrew Browning Lectures, 1988*, ed. Robert Beddard. Oxford, 1991.

Delbanco, Andrew. *The Puritan Ordeal*. Cambridge, Mass. and London, 1989.

Dickerson, Oliver M. *The Navigation Acts and the American Revolution.* Philadelphia, 1951.

Doyle, J. A. *The English Colonies in America.* 2 vols. New York, 1889.

Duncan, Jonathan. *The History of Guernsey.* London, 1841.

Duncan, Roger F. *Coastal Maine: A Maritime History.* New York, 1992.

Dunn, Richard S. "The Dominion of New England." In *Interpreting Colonial America*, 2d ed., ed. James Kirby Martin. New York, 1978.

———. *Puritans and Yankees: The Winthrop Dynasty of New England, 1630–1717.* Princeton, 1962.

Earle, Peter. *Monmouth's Rebels: The Road to Sedgemoor, 1685.* New York, 1977.

Fabend, Firth Haring. *A Dutch Family in the Middle Colonies, 1660–1800.* New Brunswick and London, 1991.

Foster, Stephen. *The Long Argument: English Puritanism and the Shaping of New England Culture, 1570–1700.* Chapel Hill and London, 1991.

Fox, Dixon Ryan. *Yankees and Yorkers.* New York, 1940.

Goldie, Mark. "The Political Thought of the Anglican Revolution." In *The Revolutions of 1688: The Andrew Browning Lectures, 1988*, ed. Robert Beddard. Oxford, 1991.

Greene, Jack P. *Negotiated Authorities: Essays in Colonial, Political, and Constitutional History*, ed. Jack P. Greene. Charlottesville and London, 1994.

———. *Peripheries and Center: Constitutional Development in the Extended Polities of the British Empire and the United States, 1607–1788.* Athens, Ga., 1986, New York and London, 1990.

Haley, K. H. D. *The British and the Dutch.* London, 1988.

———. *The First Earl of Shaftesbury.* Oxford, 1968.

Hall, Michael Garibaldi. *Edward Randolph and the American Colonies, 1676–1703.* Chapel Hill, 1960.

———. *The Last American Puritan: The Life of Increase Mather, 1639–1723.* Middletown, Conn., 1980.

Hamshere, Cyril. *The British in the Caribbean.* Cambridge, Mass., 1972.

Harlow, Vincent T. *A History of Barbados, 1625–1685.* New York, 1926, 1969.

Higham, C. S. S. *The Development of the Leeward Islands Under the Restoration, 1660–1688.* Cambridge, Mass., 1921.

Hill, Christopher. *Some Intellectual Consequences of the English Revolution.* Madison, 1980.

———. *The Century of Revolution, 1603–1714.* New York and London, 1961, 1980.

Horwitz, Henry. "The Role Played by Parties in the Revolution." In *The Revolutions of 1688: The Andrew Browning Lectures, 1988*, ed. Robert Beddard. Oxford, 1991.

Hutchinson, Thomas. *The History of the Colony and Province of Massachusetts-Bay.* Edited by Lawrence Shaw-Mayo. 3 vols. Cambridge, Mass, 1936 and New York, 1970.

Hutton, Ronald. *Charles the Second, King of England, Scotland, and Ireland.* Oxford, 1989.

Innes, Stephen. *Creating the Commonwealth: The Economic Culture of Puritan New England.* New York and London, 1995.

James, Sydney. *Colonial Rhode Island: A History.* New York, 1975.

Jennings, Francis. *The Ambiguous Iroquois Empire.* New York and London, 1984.

————. *The Invasion of America: Colonialism and the Cant of Conquest.* New York, 1975.

Johnson, Richard R. *Adjustment to Empire: The English Colonies, 1675–1715.* New Brunswick, 1981.

————. "The Revolution of 1688–1689 in the American Colonies." In *The Anglo-Dutch Moment: Essays on the Glorious Revolution and Its World Impact,* ed. Jonathan I. Israel. Cambridge, New York, and Melbourne, 1991.

————. *John Nelson, Merchant Adventurer: A Life Between Empires.* New York and Oxford, 1991.

Jones, J. R. *Charles II: Royal Politician.* London, Boston, and Sydney, 1987.

————. *The First Whigs: The Politics of the Exclusion Crisis, 1678–1683.* London, 1961.

Kenyon, J. P. *Revolution Principles: The Politics of Party, 1689–1720.* Cambridge, London, New York, and Melbourne, 1977.

Kim, Sung Bok. *Landlord and Tenant in Colonial New York: Manorial Society, 1664–1775.* Chapel Hill, 1978.

Knight, Janice. *Orthodoxies in Massachusetts: Rereading American Puritanism.* Cambridge, Mass. and London, 1994.

Kukla, Jan. *Speakers and Clerks of the Virginia House of Burgesses, 1643–1776.* Richmond, 1981.

Kulikoff, Allan. *Tobacco and Slaves: The Development of Southern Cultures in the Chesapeake, 1680–1800.* Chapel Hill and London, 1986.

Lake, Peter. *Anglican and Puritans: Presbyterianism and English Conformist Thought from Whitgift to Hooker.* London, 1988.

Leach, Douglas Edward. *Flintlock and Tomahawk: New England in King Philip's War.* New York, 1958, 1966.

————. *Roots of Conflict: British Armed Forces and Colonial Americans, 1677–1763.* Chapel Hill and London, 1986.

Leder, Lawrence H. *Robert Livingston and the Politics of Colonial New York, 1654–1728.* Chapel Hill, 1961.

Lepore, Jill. *The Name of War: King Philip's War and the Origins of American Identity.* New York, 1998.

Lovejoy, David. *The Glorious Revolution in America.* Middletown, Conn., 1972, 1987.

————. *Religious Enthusiasm in the New World: Heresy to Revolution.* Cambridge, Mass. and London, 1985.

Lustig, Mary Lou. *Privilege and Prerogative: New York's Provincial Elite, 1710–1776.* Madison, Teaneck, London, and Toronto, 1995.

————. *Robert Hunter, 1666–1734: New York's Augustan Statesman.* Syracuse, 1983.

Martin, John Frederick. *Profits in the Wilderness: Entrepreneurship and the*

Founding of New England Towns in the Seventeenth Century. Chapel Hill, 1991.

Matson, Cathy. *Merchants and Empire: Trading in Colonial New York*. Baltimore and London, 1998.

McInnes, Angus. "The Revolution and the People." In *Britain After the Glorious Revolution, 1689–1714*, ed. Geoffrey Holmes. London, 1969.

McLoughlin, William G. *Rhode Island: A Bicentennial History*. New York, 1970.

Miller, Helen Hill. *Colonel Parke of Virginia: "The Greatest Hector in the Town."* Chapel Hill, 1989.

Miller, John. *Popery and Politics in England, 1660–1688*. Cambridge, 1973.

Morgan, Edmund S. *American Slavery, American Freedom: The Ordeal of Colonial Virginia*. New York and London, 1975.

Morton, Richard L. *Colonial Virginia*. 2 vols. Chapel Hill, 1960.

———. *Struggle Against Tyranny and the Beginning of a New Era: Virginia, 1677–1690*. Williamsburg, 1957.

Nissenson, S. G. *The Patroon's Domain*. New York, 1937.

Norton, Thomas Elliot. *The Fur Trade in Colonial New York, 1686–1776*. Madison, 1974.

Oberg, Michael Leroy. *Dominion and Civility: English Imperialism and Native America, 1585–1685*. Ithaca and London, 1999.

Osgood, Herbert L. *The American Colonies in the Eighteenth Century*. 4 vols. New York, 1958.

———. *The American Colonies in the Seventeenth Century*. 3 vols. New York, 1957.

Palfrey, John Gorham. *History of New England*. 4 vols. Boston, 1882–85.

Pomfret, John E. *Colonial New Jersey: A History*. New York, 1973.

Potter, Stephen R. *Commoners, Tribute, and Chiefs: The Development of Algonquian Culture in the Potomac Valley*. Charlottesville and London, 1993.

Ritchie, Robert C. *Captain Kidd and the War Against the Pirates*. Cambridge, Mass. and London, 1986.

———. *The Duke's Province: A Study of New York Politics and Society, 1664–1691*. Chapel Hill, 1977.

Rountree, Helen C. *The Powhatan Indians of Virginia*. Norman, Okla. and London, 1989.

Rouse, Parke, Jr. *James Blair of Virginia*. Chapel Hill, 1971.

Rutman, Darrett B. and Anita H. Rutman. *A Place in Time: Middlesex County, Virginia, 1650–1750*. New York and London, 1984.

Silverman, Kenneth. *The Life and Times of Cotton Mather*. New York, 1985.

Smith, William. *History of the Province of New York*, ed. by Michael Kammen. 2 vols. Cambridge, Mass., 1972.

Snow, Dean R. *The Iroquois*. Oxford and Cambridge, Mass., 1994.

Sosin, J. M. *English America and the Restoration Monarchy of Charles II*. Lincoln, 1980.

———. *English America and the Revolution of 1688*. Lincoln and London, 1982.

Speck, W. A. "Britain and the Dutch Republic." In *A Miracle Mirrored: The*

Dutch Republic in European Perspective, ed. Karel Davids and Jan Lucassen. Cambridge, 1995.

―――. *Reluctant Revolutionaries: Englishmen and the Revolution of 1688.* Oxford, 1988.

―――. "The International and Imperial Context." In *Colonial British America,* ed. Jack P. Greene and J. R. Pole. Baltimore, 1984.

Steele, Ian. *Politics of Colonial Policy: The Board of Trade in Colonial Administration, 1696–1720.* Oxford, 1968.

Stellhorn, Paul A. and Michael J. Birkner, ed. *The Governors of New Jersey, 1664–1974.* Trenton, 1982.

Thornton, A. P. *West-India Policy Under the Restoration.* Oxford, 1956.

Trevor, Meriol. *Shadow of a Crown: The Life Story of James II of England and VII of Scotland.* London, 1988.

Trigger, Bruce G. *The Huron: Farmers of the North.* New York, 1969.

Tupper, Ferdinand Brock. *The History of Guernsey and its Bailiwick.* London, 1876.

Van Nyevelt, Suzette van Zuylen. *Court Life in the Dutch Republic, 1638–1689.* London and New York, n.d.

Wallace, Anthony F. C. *Death and Rebirth of the Seneca.* New York, 1969, 1972.

―――. *Jefferson and the Indians: The Tragic Fate of the First Americans.* Cambridge, Mass. and London, 1999.

Wallace, Paul A. W. *Indians in Pennsylvania.* Rev. ed. Harrisburg, 1961, 1981.

Webb, Stephen Saunders. *The Governors-General: The English Army and the Definition of the Empire, 1569–1681.* Chapel Hill, 1979.

―――. *1676: The End of American Independence.* Chapel Hill, 1984 and Syracuse, 1994.

―――. *Lord Churchill's Coup: The Anglo-American Empire and the Glorious Revolution Reconsidered.* New York, 1995.

―――. "The Trials of Sir Edmund Andros," In *The Human Dimensions of Nation Making,* ed. James Kirby Martin. Madison, 1976.

Wedgwood, C. V. *The Trial of Charles I.* London, 1964.

Wertenbaker, T. J. *The Puritan Oligarchy: The Founding of American Civilization.* New York, 1947.

Western, John R. *Monarchy and Revolution: The English State in the 1680s.* London, 1972.

Winslow, Ola Elizabeth. *Samuel Sewall of Boston.* New York, 1964.

Worsley, Sir Richard. *The History of the Isle of Wight.* London, 1781, 1975.

Ziff, Larzer. *Puritanism in America: New Culture in a New World.* New York, 1973.

Journal Articles

Breene, Timothy H. and Stephen Foster. "The Puritans' Greatest Achievement: A Study of Social Cohesion in the Seventeenth Century." *The Journal of American History* 60 (1973): 5–22.

Brown, Katherine B. "The Controversy over the Franchise in Puritan Massachusetts. *William and Mary Quarterly,* 3d ser., 33 (1976): 212–41.

George, Christopher T. "The Feuding Governors: Andros and Nicholson at Odds in Colonial Maryland." *Maryland Historical Magazine* 90 (1995): 334–48.

Haffenden, Philip S. "The Crown and the Colonial Charters, 1675–1688: Part 2." *William and Mary Quarterly*, 3d ser., 15 (1958): 452–66.

Hall, Michael Garibaldi. "The House of Lords, Edward Randolph, and the Navigation Act of 1696." *William and Mary Quarterly*, 3d ser., 14 (1957): 494–515.

Howe, Adrian. "The Bayard Treason Trial: Dramatizing Anglo-Dutch Politics in Early Eighteenth Century New York City." *William and Mary Quarterly*, 3d ser., 47 (1990): 57–89.

Kupperman, Karen Ordahl. "The Puzzle of the American Climate in the Early Colonial Period." *American Historical Review* 87 (1982): 162–89.

Laslett, Peter. "John Locke, the Great Recoinage, and the Origins of the Board of Trade, 1695–1698." *William and Mary Quarterly,* 3d ser., 14 (1957): 370–402.

Leder, Lawrence H. "The Unorthodox Domine: Nicholas van Rensselaer." *New York History* 35 (1954): 166–76.

Lewis, Theodore B. "Land Speculation and the Dudley Council of 1686." *William and Mary Quarterly,* 3d ser., 31 (1974): 255–72.

Lustig, Mary Lou. "Edmund Andros and the Dutch in New York, 1674–1681." *de Halve Maen* 69 (1996): 67–75.

Mahon, John K. "Anglo-American Methods of Indian Warfare, 1676–1794." *The Mississippi Valley Historical Review* 45 (1958): 254–75.

McCully, Bruce T. "From the North Riding to Morocco: The Early Years of Governor Francis Nicholson, 1655–1686." *William and Mary Quarterly*, 3d ser., 19 (1962): 534–56.

Merwick, Donna. "The Writing Man: The Shrinking World of the 'Note Republic' in Dutch Albany." *de Halve Maen* 69 (1996): 57–66.

Naylor, Rex Maurice. "The Royal Prerogative in New York, 1691–1775." *New York History* 5 (1924): 221–53.

Richter, Daniel K. "War and Culture: The Iroquois Experience." *William and Mary Quarterly*, 3d ser., 40 (1983): 528–59.

Runcie, John D. "The Problem of Anglo-American Politics in Bellomont's New York." *William and Mary Quarterly,* 3d. ser., 25 (1969): 191–217.

Seiler, William H. "The Anglican Parish Vestry in Colonial Virginia." *The Journal of Southern History* 22 (1956): 310–37.

Steele, Ian. "Governors or Generals? A Note on Martial Law and the Revolution of 1689 in English America." *William and Mary Quarterly*, 3d ser., 46 (1989): 304–14.

Voorhees, David William. "The 'fervent Zeale' of Jacob Leisler." *William and Mary Quarterly*, 3d ser., 51 (1994): 447–72.

———. "'To assert our Right before it be quite lost:' The Leisler Rebellion in the Delaware River Valley." *Pennsylvania History* 64 (1997): 5–27.

Webb, Stephen Saunders. "William Blathwayt, Imperial Fixer: From Popish Plot to Glorious Revolution." *William and Mary Quarterly*, 3d ser., 25 (1968): 3–21.

———. "William Blathwayt, Imperial Fixer: Muddling Through to Empire, 1689–1717." *William and Mary Quarterly*, 3d ser., 26 (1969): 373–415.

———. "The Strange Career of Francis Nicholson." *William and Mary Quarterly*, 3d ser., 23 (1966): 513–48.

Wright, Louis B. "William Byrd's Defense of Sir Edmund Andros." *William and Mary Quarterly*, 3d ser., 2 (1945): 47–62.

———. "William Byrd's Opposition to Governor Francis Nicholson." *The Journal of Southern History*, 11 (1945): 68–79.

Unpublished Ph.D. Dissertations

Bloom, Jeanne Gould. "Sir Edmund Andros: A Study in Seventeenth–Century Colonial Administration." Ph.D. diss., Yale University, 1962.

Carter, Michael Darryl, "Nationbuilding and the Military: The Life and Career of Secretary of War Henry Knox, 1750–1806." Ph.D. diss., West Virginia University, 1997.

Maika, Dennis Joseph. "Commerce and Community: Manhattan Merchants in the Seventeenth Century." Ph.D. diss., New York University, 1995.

Index